New Musical Figurations

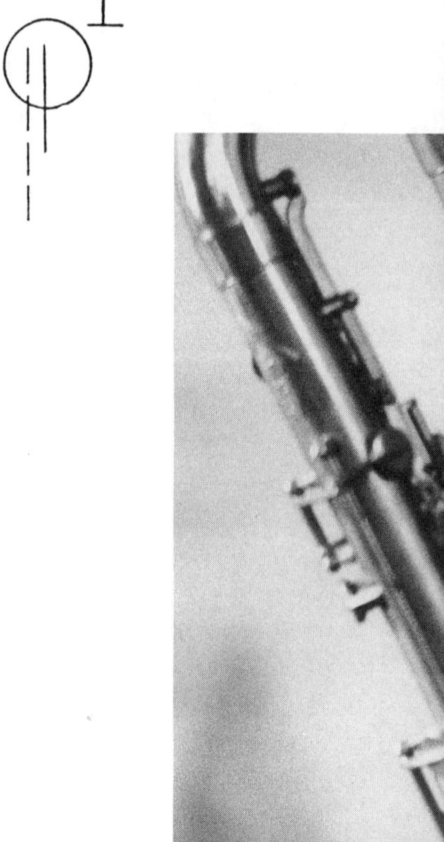

New Musical Figurations

Anthony Braxton's Cultural Critique

Ronald M. Radano

The University of Chicago Press • Chicago and London

Ronald M. Radano is assistant professor of Afro-American studies and music, University of Wisconsin, Madison.

Title page photo: Anthony Braxton playing a contrabass clarinet.
Photo courtesy Bill Smith.

The University of Chicago Press, Chicago 60637
The University of Chicago Press, Ltd., London

Printed in the United States of America

02 01 00 99 98 97 96 95 94 93 1 2 3 4 5

ISBN: 0-226-70195-6 (cloth)
0-226-70196-4 (paper)

Radano, Ronald Michael.
New musical figurations : Anthony Braxton's cultural critique / Ronald M. Radano.
p. cm.
Includes index.
Discography: p.
1. Braxton, Anthony. 2. Jazz—History and criticism. 3. Jazz musicians—United States—Biography. I. Title.
ML419.B735R3 1993
788.7′165′092—dc20 93-1878
CIP
MN

∞ The paper used in this publication meets the minimum requirements of the American National Standard for Information Sciences—Permanence of Paper for Printed Library Materials, ANSI Z39.48-1984.

For my mother,
Anna Derkacs Radano,

and

In memory of my father,
Robert Nicholas Radano

Contents

List of Illustrations ix

Acknowledgments xi

A Note on Sources and Methods xv

1 Introduction: A New Musical Balance 1

2 Chicago as Aesthetic Center 28

3 Musical Assertions of Black Identity 77

4 New Musical Convergences: Paris and New York 140

5 Defining a Black Vanguard Aesthetic 180

6 Black Experimentalism as Spectacle 238

Epilogue: Jazz Recast 269

Appendix A
Picture Titles of Compositions Cited 277

Appendix B
Recordings Cited/Anthony Braxton on Record 285

Music Index 297

General Index 301

Illustrations

Figures

3.1 First page of *Piano Piece No. 1* 121
3.2 A page from the score of *Composition 10* 123
3.3 "Line notations" for *Composition 77A* 134
3.4 Picture title for *Composition 8K* (ca. 1968) 137
4.1 Braxton's manuscript of *Composition 6I* 175
5.1 Framework guiding three versions of *Composition 26B* 193
5.2 Author's transcription of *Composition 23B*, phrases I and II 199
5.3 Author's transcription of the gravallic basic in *Composition 23G* 202
5.4 Braxton's manuscript of *Composition 40G* 207
5.5 Schematic outline of *Composition 37* 213
5.6 Cell structures in Zone C and performance-score instructions, *Composition 37* 214
5.7 A double-page spread from the score of *Composition 76* 215
5.8 Author's transcription of the opening brass/woodwind cluster in *Composition 51* 217
5.9 Outline of ensemble activity in *Composition 25* 220
5.10 Reduction of formal sequences in *Composition 25* 221
5.11 Braxton's schematic of *Performance 9/1/1979* 224
5.12 Relationship between superimposed line notations and the form of picture title *(Composition 69E)* 227
5.13 Schematic diagram from Braxton, *The Tri-Axium Writings* 233

Photographs

Anthony Braxton directing the recording session for the album *Creative Orchestra Music 1976* 2

Muhal Richard Abrams (ca. 1967) 76

Anthony Braxton with Joseph Jarman in Chicago's Hyde Park (ca. 1968) 113

Anthony Braxton in a studio rehearsal at Delmark Records, Chicago (ca. 1967) 119

Cover page of the French magazine *Jazz Hot,* April 1972 187

Anthony Braxton playing contra alto clarinet in a concert rehearsal during the mid-1970s 195

Anthony Braxton at a New York studio rehearsal for the album *Creative Orchestra Music 1976* 204

Anthony Braxton performing on alto saxophone at the Rising Sun, Montreal, in the mid- to late 1970s 241

Front cover of the album *Five Pieces 1975* 253

Photographic portrait of Anthony Braxton (1988) 271

Acknowledgments

The qualities of dialogue and interaction that give life to jazz also describe the process by which this book has developed. Accordingly, it is with gratitude and a profound sense of pleasure that I thank the eclectic mix of mentors, friends, relatives, colleagues, informants, and advisers who have contributed to the evolution of my thinking about culture and music. At the University of Michigan, I received a rigorous training in music history, music analysis, and ethnomusicological theory, which culminated in a first attempt at making sense of Anthony Braxton's music in American life. The openmindedness of that faculty enabled me to pursue my special interests as it encouraged me to challenge conventional modes of interpretation. In particular, I thank Judith Becker, Alton L. Becker, James Dapogny, William P. Malm, Piotr Michalowski, Glenn Watkins, and particularly Richard Crawford, who, in various ways, helped to guide my learning.

At the Smithsonian's National Museum of American History, I greatly benefited from the intellectual dynamism of its seminars and discussion groups, through which I was introduced to the discipline of American studies and to many of the critical theories that inform this book. Of special importance were the members of the reading group with whom I explored literature in cultural studies: Wayne Durrill, Karen Linn, Charlie McGovern, Mary Panzer, Kathy Peiss, and Rebecca Zurier. Also helpful were several colleagues, notably John Hasse and Barbara Clark Smith, with whom I enjoyed a regular exchange of ideas, and Pete Daniel and Grace Palladino, special Washington friends who kept things going on our Tuesday-night roundups. The late Martin Williams was yet another Washington friend and colleague who encouraged me—despite a profoundly different view of jazz, the arts, and culture—to take a critical path. I regret not having had the opportunity to debate with him the arguments presented herewith.

The support I received from the University of Wisconsin ultimately made the difference to this study. Without it, *New Musical Figurations* might not have been realized and most certainly would not have taken the form it has. An honorary fellowship in the School of Music initially brought me to Madison, while the vital initiatives of the Department of Afro-American Studies and its former chair, Carl Grant, led me to stay. With affiliations in both, I proceeded to shape a curriculum that helped to flesh out many of the matters addressed in these pages. The responses of students and colleagues have enabled me to strengthen my positions and to clarify some of my murkier speculations. I am especially grateful in a very tangible way to Wisconsin's Graduate School for its faculty grant and research support, and to Afro-American Studies, which, with funding from the Ford Foundation, granted leave time and the resourceful assistance of Eric Rasmussen, Chris DeSantis, and David Hancock. Also significant has been the guidance and encouragement I have received from my Wisconsin colleagues. In particular, I would like to thank Craig Werner, who read and commented on drafts of this book and related manuscripts. Our regular exchanges have been highly valued.

Outside of my immediate circle of culture I have received advice and help from a host of women and men far too numerous to identify here. At the least, I note those who have contributed in some particularly meaningful and direct ways. David N. Baker, Scott DeVeaux, Krin Gabbard, Lawrence Grossberg, and Bernice Johnson Reagon took the time to read and comment on all or part of the manuscript. John Szwed, Chris Waterman, and John Litweiler reviewed the manuscript for the press and offered many valuable suggestions. Houston A. Baker, Jr., and the Center for the Study of Black Literature and Culture at the University of Pennsylvania, granted a Rockefeller Fellowship for a new project that also enabled smooth completion of the production stage of this one. Gordon Massman, Dan Morgenstern, Chuck Nessa, Terry Martin, Joseph Jarman, Roscoe Mitchell, Leon Paparella, Geri Laudati, Guido Podestá, Cornel West, and Dismas Masolo offered help and guidance at various points; Doug Mitchell provided the insights and good-natured encouragement that only a fine editor can offer. Guy Klucevsek was an important inspiration when I was a composer in training, as were Manny Albam and the late Harry Leahey when I first explored the language of jazz.

A special expression of thanks goes to Anthony Braxton, whose contributions to this study are quite obvious. Yet beyond the wealth of provisions in the form of books, manuscripts, recordings, musical scores, and comments, he has provided something much more. Agreeing to be a party to the peculiar relationship between scholar and subject, he graciously put up with my formalities, my idiosyncrasies, and my struggles with racial understanding, as he helped to attune my thinking to the complexities of categorizing musical expression. The fact that my interpretations at times greatly differed from his own inspired no effort to control, no attempt to sidestep issues. Anthony has challenged me on several points and on more than one occasion. But he has also recognized the value of critical opinion, one that at least attempts, in good faith, to consider all the angles. As such, our collaborations have produced a complex, enduring relationship—and ultimately, a friendship—that will remain an important part of my life.

In the deepest and most personal way, I express my heartfelt thanks to the family and longtime friends who have provided such vital, continuous support. My mother, my late father, my brothers and their own families, my relatives to the north, and three very special friends, Greg Viglianti, Roger Horne, and Larry Weil, have been there along the way. Last, there is Colleen A. Dunlavy, my companion, who, on first encounter—in an unsuitably inauthentic space, a Smithsonian copy room—charmed me with her very *real* presence. Life hasn't been the same since. Memory serves.

Portions of this text have appeared previously as "Jazzin' the Classics" in *Black Music Research Journal,* vol. 12, no. 1, Spring 1992, published by the Center for Black Music Research, Columbia College, Chicago; and as "Braxton's Reputation" in *Musical Quarterly,* no. 4, © 1986 Oxford University Press.

A Note on Sources and Methods

This book relies on an unusual variety of sources, including commercial recordings, music manuscripts, and published literature (both scholarly and journalistic), together with twelve formal interviews conducted with Anthony Braxton from 1982 to 1984, and again from 1989 to 1990. The dates of the interviews are specified in the citations to quoted material. At times, a particular quotation may cite more than one interview, as indicated. Discussions also draw on several informal conversations that took place over the years, particularly in the past eighteen months (1991–1992). Additional interviews and conversations with Roscoe Mitchell (1988), and materials from a prior study involving David Liebman and Richard Beirarch (1980), provide complementary oral historical information. Performance scores were supplied by Braxton, while the diagrams and transcription of commercial recordings were prepared by the author.

The reader will note that in order to encourage dialogue across critical disciplines—and as a response to the inadequacy of static images in representing a dynamic music—I have kept transcriptions to a minimum. Similarly, the musical commentary itself reflects as much a desire to reach a multidisciplinary readership as it seeks to go beyond the formal, scientistic conventions of jazz scholarship, offering speculative interpretations of Braxton's creative expression. Such a mode of inquiry seems imperative for an appreciation of Braxton's musical artistry, particularly in places where he seems to be eluding literal-minded readings. Musicians may find the detailed analyses in chapters 3 and 4, and particularly in chapter 5, most specific to their interests, though nonmusicians should also be able to apprehend these discussions with little difficulty.

1 Introduction: A New Musical Balance

For a stretch of time in the mid-1970s, composer-saxophonist Anthony Braxton stood at the center of a controversy that laid bare the inadequacies of conventional jazz criticism. Demonstrating inimitable improvising skills, while simultaneously transgressing traditional aesthetic and social boundaries, Braxton challenged critics to come to terms with a creative world that called into question accepted definitions of jazz and the jazz musician. Their failure to meet that challenge led to a period of confusion, contradiction, and myth-making as writers praised Braxton's undeniably original jazz work while obfuscating the meaning of his rarefied artistic concepts. The curious, ironic tension between accolade and mocking condescension exposed the limitations of traditional jazz categories, categories that could not make sense of an artist who responded to the new aesthetic licenses of the postmodern epoch.

Braxton initially occupied a premier position in the jazz ranks. Indeed, for a time, he seemed to be just what writers and record producers were looking for: an imaginative, spirited artist who could rival the appeal of rock and fusion and set jazz on a new course of development. Critically acclaimed in the early 1970s for his contributions to free jazz, Braxton appeared by mid-decade to be turning away from his prior radicalism, toward a more accessible synthesis of free and "mainstream" practices. On his European and Japanese releases from 1973 and on his first albums with a major American label, Arista Records, from 1975,[1] he openly embraced the mainstream style that had developed out of bop. The recordings suggested that here finally was a truly original innovator, arguably the best saxophonist since John Coltrane, who could make sense of free jazz while maintaining the integrity of the tradition. Braxton, it seemed, would lead the way toward a

1. *Four Compositions 1973; In the Tradition,* volumes 1 and 2 (1974): *Quartet Live at Moers New Jazz Festival* (1974). Both Arista albums, *New York Fall 1974* and *Five Pieces 1975,* were released in 1975. During this time, Braxton also recorded an album with Dave Brubeck and Lee Konitz (two of his teenage musical idols), released under Brubeck's name as *All the Things You Are* (1974). For more complete discographical information, see Appendix B.

Anthony Braxton directing the recording session for the album *Creative Orchestra Music 1976*. Photo courtesy Bill Smith.

new jazz, as he turned radical experiments into fodder for mainstream stylistic advancement. For many critics and a growing sector of the listening audience, then, Braxton was the man to watch.

Yet a closer look at Braxton and his music revealed artistic dimensions unfamiliar in the jazz world. Despite formidable skills as a jazz composer and improviser, Braxton clearly had other creative ambitions, ambitions that he made public repeatedly in album notes and to the press. While interviewers spoke of Charlie Parker and John Coltrane, for example, Braxton, as much as he admired those innovators, seemed to prefer discussing the complexities of modernist concert music.[2] He often went on at length about European modernists such as

2. Modernism has commonly served as a synonym for avant-garde. In this study, however, I have attempted to distinguish between the terms according to the model presented by Peter Bürger in his book *The Theory of the Avant-Garde* (Minneapolis: University of Minnesota Press, 1984). Bürger argues that modernism originally identified the turn-of-the-century movement in which artists moved toward abstraction while perpetuating social and aesthetic hierarchies associated with high culture/low culture. The pre–World War II "historical avant-garde," on the other hand (represented in the movements of dada, surrealism, and constructivism), sought to overthrow traditional aesthetic and institutional paradigms and thus to initiate the collapse of the hierarchical,

Schoenberg, Webern, Boulez, and Stockhausen, figures most jazz listeners had never even heard of, but whose works provided a model for Braxton's own jazz/concert-music hybrids. Or else Braxton would address his other favored subjects, aesthetics and mysticism. In these discussions, he would invariably employ, perhaps in part to poke fun at some of his more literal-minded interviewers, a difficult and idiosyncratic technical language that suggested exposure to analytical philosophy as much as a familiarity with world religions and the occult. Braxton surely lacked the aesthetic centeredness writers and listeners had come to expect from a true jazz trendsetter. While his departure from free jazz fit the critical speculation of the vanguard gone mainstream, he frequently contradicted that speculation by circling back to perform and record highly esoteric, abstract music. At one moment he might appear to be an unrivaled saxophonist, playing straight-ahead jazz; yet with a blink of the eye he could become a cerebral modernist, whose arcane musical deviations confounded the efforts of the critical community.

Journalists' difficulties in locating Braxton in their worldview generated frequent reports of controversy and broad visibility. Ironically, the controversy had, in the end, only a marginal relationship to Braxton's music;[3] more often than not, it merely reflected the selective way in which writers themselves chose to report on his art and ideas. When Arista began vigorously to market his mainstream-oriented albums from 1975 onward, jazz journals and popular magazines latched on to aspects of Braxton's interests that would make effective selling points in their coverage about him. In profiles and record reviews, critics called attention less to what he was playing than to what they deemed to be the artist's "eccentricities": his commentary on concert-music modernists; his unusual diagrams that served as compositional

socioartistic framework of Western culture. Sharing similarities in style (if not in aesthetics) and contempt toward the bourgeoisie, the movements of modernism and avant-garde ultimately became confused. After World War II, moreover, modernism, as "high modernism," had assumed a posture of conventionality as it became associated with middle-class, dominant culture. Taking into account both Bürger's clarification and contemporary usage, I will employ "modernism" in two ways: as a stylistic category to refer to artistic abstraction in twentieth-century music; as a social category ("high modernism"), identifying the institutions that perpetuate elitist categories of art.

3. Out of over 130 articles, profiles, and record reviews, only a handful spoke negatively about Braxton's music. An actual controversy therefore seems unlikely, since most critics were in general agreement. Furthermore, American listeners typically heard only Braxton's well-marketed records, which were released on the Arista label. The more esoteric European releases were hard to come by, usually sought out only by Braxton's most avid followers. See chapter 6.

titles; his esoteric philosophical proclamations informed by Afrocentric theories of Western culture.[4] And while writers repeated the claim that Braxton's "highly difficult" music had prompted the uproar, the critically generated "controversy" soon became the formula of choice for identifying the artist, even as Braxton continued to deliver to the American public an accessible form of jazz. Finally, by the end of the decade, as Braxton became increasingly conspicuous in his modernist ventures, the journalistic formula broke down and the critics abandoned their efforts to assimilate his music. By 1982, Braxton had lost his contract with Arista and his decline as a popular figure turned into a free-fall that, for all practical purposes, had effectively eliminated him from the jazz picture.

The inability of popular jazz writers to come to grips with Braxton's creative world reflected the inadequacy of the musical paradigm with which they worked. Their narrow vision of proper jazz practice and behavior could not accommodate the broad, transformative changes that were taking place in culture and the arts. For the Braxton controversy, like the community's unsettled response to free jazz in the 1960s, signified a profound and dramatic shift in the character of jazz and, indeed, of American artistic life as a whole. Free jazz represented not an aberration, but a fracture in the continuum of a tentative, constructed mainstream. In this way, the movement shared resemblances with other artistic challenges to institutional authority at a time when the entire terrain of cultural expression was being reconfigured. Braxton, moreover, personified a new phase in the development. His work widened the fracture into a rift as he forged an art and sensibility that transcended conventional categories of jazz. The subsequent efforts to restore the fiction of continuity, understandable though they may be, have generated at best new constructs of past musical practice, constructs that rest precariously within the utterly confused and perplexing context of postmodern culture.

A study of Braxton, then, must take into account the complex of culture to which his creative world relates. It should also, in its breadth, match the expanses of his intellectual interests and artistic imagination. Braxton's affinity for modernist music, together with his philosophical attachment to vanguardist artistic principles, calls to mind a particular realm, the world of experimentalism, which, under

4. Originally visual symbols of serious artistic intent, the titles later served as both diagrams of compositional structure and metaphorical codes of mystical meaning. The theories, moreover, not only argue that ancient Egyptian civilizations were black and African, but that an African essence has informed black perspectives ever since. See Molefi Kete Asante, *Afrocentricity,* rev. ed. (Trenton: African World Press, 1980/1988).

the aesthetic leadership of John Cage, became this half-century's musical emblem of intellectual crisis and uncertainty. But unlike previous experimentalists who tended to refer to musical experiences in a white world, Braxton, in a multitude of ways, has drawn from the African-American legacy. His articulation of a vital, dynamic art that referred to the modernist legacy but in a distinctly African-American creative voice signaled the appearance of a dramatically new kind of musician: the *black experimentalist.* As a piece of the cultural puzzle, moreover, Braxton's experimentalism was symptomatic of an overarching pattern commonly associated with the postmodern condition. His creative reality expressed, in its fusion of disparate artistic realms, the convolution of dominant hierarchies relating to class, race, and social identity. Perhaps more so than any other "jazz" artist at the time, Braxton responded to the crisis of confluence that has identified the character of Western art since the rise of the culture industry in the 1920s and 1930s and that initiated a massive fracture in style and genre during the post–World War II era. As such, he embodied, as a multivoiced African-American artist, the ambiguities and contradictions inherent in postmodern musical life, contradictions that posed a challenge to traditional definitions of jazz and the jazz musician.

I

In his provocative analysis of the creative-intellectual climate in the 1960s, Leonard Meyer presented a bold outline for a new musical epoch whose contours would be patterned on the ideological fluxus of the postwar era. According to Meyer, "the history of the arts in our time has been characterized by change,"[5] a statement of the obvious, perhaps, were it not for the peculiar character of change that he had identified. Central to Meyer's interpretation was the concept of a radically "dynamic stasis" of coexisting forms and styles undergoing transformation at differing rates of speed. "Cultural growth" had become a complex and multilayered process that had supplanted former patterns of unilinear progression. Uniform artistic change, Meyer predicted, had finally come to an end at a moment when social motivations for stylistic progression no longer existed, when equations of artistic "health" and cultural progress no longer seemed tenable. Significantly, Meyer's characterization of confluence could be easily

5. Meyer, *Music, the Arts and Ideas* (Chicago: University of Chicago Press, 1967), 87. See part 2, "As It Is and Perhaps Will Be," and especially chapter 8, "The Probability of Stasis."

transposed to the seemingly halcyon decades of the 1970s and 1980s, when the pattern of stylistic change and the integrity of genre grew increasingly difficult to discern. A similarly dynamic stasis challenged stability in virtually all areas of culture, eroding previously distinct artistic categories and undermining a once stable aesthetic order. In music, moreover, the new visibility of expressions that had circumvented traditional hierarchical divisions helped to pull the rug out from under a tidier musical world in which styles and genres were once more clearly distinguished. Already in the 1950s, ten years prior to Meyer's analysis—and to some extent even before, with the initial rise of modernism—the certainties that had officiated between styles and their corresponding social categories seemed to be breaking down. By the 1970s, a cultural sensibility reflecting the dynamic range of artistic interface had taken shape, inspiring a new literature that sought to map out its elusive boundaries.[6] Today, we have reached a point where diversity and confluence occupy central positions in our musical life, even as the representation of its character so often takes on a reductionist scheme that celebrates the ordered vision of an official consensus.

As the popular press has typically described it, diversity and confluence—for that matter, the whole of stylistic change and interaction—constitute "pluralism." An epithet drawn from mainstream political theory, pluralism has become the watchword of the contemporary critic who frequently celebrates the rich variety of styles that coexist in the framework of urban culture. Musicological studies beyond Meyer's notable efforts have rarely analyzed the condition of stylistic multiplicity and confluence, preferring, in the main, to focus on the formal features of a genre or composition. Of the few publications that have addressed the interactive complex of culture, most reinforce mainstream journalistic and music-historical perceptions, developing social theory from the analysis of patterns of stylistic exchange ("histories of music"). Interpreting the nature of musical culture from the inside out, they tend to bypass the complex of social, ideological, and racial factors to which creative expressions are inextricably linked. When social factors are considered, they appear as contexts distinguishable from a reified category of "art," thus preserving formalist notions of absolute value.[7] Pluralism, as an American musical concept,

6. For historical background on the idea of postmodernism, see Andreas Huyssen, *After the Great Divide: Modernism, Mass Culture, Postmodernism* (Bloomington: Indiana University Press, 1986), esp. "The Search for Tradition" and "Mapping the Postmodern."

7. See Steven Lukes's *Power: A Radical View* (London: Macmillan Press, 1974) for

calls to mind the mythology of a glorious sonic melting pot. It is, in the end, a fictional world of social and stylistic equivalence, a place where musical interaction resembles, as one writer has put it, a "happy babble of overlapping dialogues."[8]

Since the popular notion of pluralism proves inadequate, one must look elsewhere for analytical guidance in interpreting the dynamic of postwar musical culture. Particularly noteworthy are studies of cultural criticism that observe the arts as literal embodiments of the pastiche that constitutes our sociocultural environment. Shifting critical focus from the art object to the complex relationship between cultural expressions and the forces that mediate change and perception, these studies have provided new insights into the nature of American cultural experience in the second half of the twentieth century.[9] Significantly, some of the most notable commentaries, in the spirit of Meyer, identify a process by which contradictory expressions appear and recede according to the unstable fluctuations of hierarchy and power. Increases in institutional control and cultural commodification exacerbate through public spectacle the empowerment of previously marginalized expressions; an irreverent white youth culture embodying a conservative American dream of freedom doubles the irony by building musical identity on the appropriation of black creativity.[10] Playing a principal, causal role in this process, moreover, have been mass media, which, as the overarching mechanisms of representation, re-create as symbolic pastiche a grand matrix of disparate and often oppositional imagery. Through the institutions of record corporations, radio stations, popular magazines, and, most recently, music television, mass media have generated contradictory impulses that both vi-

---

a compelling analysis of the pluralist perspective in sociology and political science. See also Hal Foster, "Against Pluralism," in *Recodings: Art, Spectacle, and Cultural Politics* (Seattle: Bay Press, 1985), 13–32.

8. John Rockwell, *All American Music* (New York: A. A. Knopf, 1983), 4.

9. The Frankfurt School's legacy continues to inform American and British critical perspectives, while studies specific to the mass media are typically indebted to French semiological and poststructuralist theory since Barthes. A good source that encompasses many of these themes is Dick Hebdige, *Subculture: The Meaning of Style* (New York: Methuen, 1979/1985).

10. Lawrence Grossberg, "You [Still] Have to Fight for Your Right to Party: Music Television as Billboards of Post-modern Difference," *Popular Music* 7:3 (1988): 315–22. Grossberg argues that after its World War–time successes, America came to believe the "dream" had been realized and embodied in postwar youth. As a result, youth culture lived within a frame of contradiction, representing an elusive, and now conservative, national identity ("the dream") as it recast that identity into a voice of resistance.

talize and subvert expressions against a similarly constructed idea of "consensus." By the 1970s, the flux of images once outlining a dialectical tug-of-war between dominant culture and the periphery had given way to a vast system of unresolved cultural symbols, to what Lawrence Grossberg has called "the changing space of a proliferation of difference."[11]

From this perspective, contemporary musical life seems best understood not in terms of the peaceful coexistence that pluralism denotes, but rather as a complex, contradictory, and nearly schizophrenic world fraught with differences often leading to conflict. Institutional and aesthetic challenges to the prevailing patterns of ideological and aesthetic authority have upset an earlier stability, producing an environment in which styles and their subcultures not only converge but clash as factions perpetuate old rivalries between the categories to which they relate. Such a perspective may not, in the end, identify the precise mechanisms initiating change. It does, however, convey a sense of the social web in which contemporary music-making has operated and of the conditions that have shaped creativity in the postwar environment.

In the new musical balance, styles no longer fit neatly into well-defined categories; at best they scatter along lines vaguely defined by the fractured vestiges of a prior order. What remains is a hazy opposition of conflicting aesthetic postures that collapse into a decentered, fluctuating matrix. The traditional hierarchy of high art/low art, for example, has been revised into a calamity of artistic values, from institionally enforced aesthetics originating in elite culture—expressions "imposed upon the present by the past"[12]—to vigorous aesthetic challenges to the high cultural tradition.[13] The conditions of stasis and

11. Ibid., 319.

12. Hayden White, "The Burden of History," *History and Theory 5:2 (1966); reprinted in The Tropics of Discourse: Essays in Cultural Criticism* (Baltimore: Johns Hopkins University Press, 1978), 39.

13. After introducing his concept of the culture industry in *Dialectic of Enlightenment* (1947), Theodor Adorno elaborated on the term, making specific reference to its effect on the hierarchy of high and low: "The culture industry intentionally integrates its consumers from above. To the detriment of both, it forces together the spheres of high and low art, separated for thousands of years. The seriousness of high art is destroyed in speculation about its efficacy; the seriousness of the lower perishes with the civilizational constraints imposed on the rebellious resistance inherent within it as long as social control was not yet total." Adorno, "The Culture Industry Reconsidered," published originally in *Ohne Leitbild* (Frankfurt am Main, 1967), English translation in Stephen Eric Bronner and Douglas MacKay Kellner, eds., *Critical Theory and Society: A Reader* (New York: Routledge, 1989), 128. An early expression of this view

flux endemic to the new balance relate to the antiteleological character of a culture in which vanguardism has lost its potency, in which notions of authenticity, originality, and essence have been confounded—ironically, in a climate of radical Otherness—by an eroding sense of difference. In the postmodern era, cultural projections appear "flat," divorced from history and traditional mystifications, as mechanical reproduction, electronic communication, and standardized packaging have turned art into a technological mix of hierarchically confused, commodified symbols. At the same time, the power of mass mediation has also given new voice to commonplace expressions as it has sought to transform creativity into an all-encompassing consensus of commodity capitalism.[14]

Popular culture, for example, has for decades overwhelmingly dominated public information about the arts, its sheer conspicuousness—through the "Learning from Las Vegas"—effectively blurring distinctions between value and visibility. Already a transformational force prior to World War II, it most dramatically revised musical taste and perception thereafter, as style and meaning became intertwined with the institutional framework of the music industry. In the song genre, stars such as Frank Sinatra challenged prior distinctions between high culture and entertainment as they came to embody an everyday image of the romantic artist, a larger-than-life figure who helped to transform "American popular song [into] a kind of classical art form."[15] Changes in the institutional configuration of the culture industry, moreover, encouraged conspicuous presentation of formerly obscure, local styles and expressions, paving the way for the rise of country and western, black gospel, urban blues, and, most notably, rock 'n' roll.[16] The success of a new interracial corps of working-class

---

appears in "The Social Situation of Music" (1932). An English translation by Wes Blomster was published in *Telos* 35 (Spring 1988): 128–64.

14. Frederic Jameson, "Postmodernism and Consumer Society," *The Anti-Aesthetic;* Jameson, "Postmodernism, or the Cultural Logic of Late Capitalism," *New Left Review* 146 (1984): 53–92. See also Jackson Lears, "A Matter of Taste: Corporate Cultural Hegemony in a Mass-Consumption Society," in *Recasting America: Culture and Politics in the Age of Cold War,* ed. Lary May (Chicago: University of Chicago Press, 1988), 38–60.

15. Jim Miller, "All-American Music," *Newsweek* (September 8, 1986), 62. Miller was referring, in particular, to Sinatra's album *Songs for Young Lovers* (1954). Related and noteworthy are Jon Stratton, "Capitalism and Romantic Ideology in the Record Business," *Popular Music* 3 (1984): 143–56; David Buxton, "Rock Music, the Star System, and the Rise of Consumerism," in *On Record, Rock, Pop and the Written Word,* ed. Simon Frith and Andrew Goodwin (New York: Pantheon, 1990), 427–40.

16. According to Richard A. Peterson and David G. Berger, "The degree of diversity

southern musicians not only challenged previous conceptions of value, artistry, and genre but called into question hardened binary oppositions relating to class, race, and gender. The ensuing dialogic character of postwar popular music, as a matter of course, would not only erode the distinction between "what is art" and "what is not," but also the epistemological certainties that had gone hand-in-hand with it.[17]

In concert music, meanwhile, traditional music lovers fought a rearguard action, seeking to impose upon the present an old-world vision of high culture and to perpetuate the canon of "great music" that still, in good measure, represented Western society's notions of artistic truth. In the playhouse of mass culture, however, proclamations of the canon's absolute greatness had become anachronistic, apparitions from the past that attempted to reverse its declining prestige and rank. For example, a once towering figure such as Arturo Toscanini would be transformed through the power of the culture industry into a pop icon, embodied in the puerile hit song *Music, Maestro Please*.[18] In the 1960s, moreover, efforts to accommodate concert music's new middle-class populist audience exacerbated an appropriative process that brought "the classics" into the everyday.[19] Demystified and defrocked, the common-practice repertory soon lost much of its meaning as a cherished art form, as the centerpiece of concert ritual. Reproduction and electronic media had successfully separated the rep-

---

in musical forms is inversely related to the degree of market concentration"; the period of rock 'n' roll's appearance marked an era of inordinate competition. See "Cycles in Symbol Production: The Case of Popular Music," *American Sociological Review* 40 (1975); reprinted in Frith and Goodwin, *On Record,* 156. Furthermore, Peterson shows how the constraints of legal regulation, technology, industrial structure, and market helped to determine the appearance of rock 'n' roll in "Why 1955? Explaining the Advent of Rock Music," *Popular Music* 9:1 (1990): 97–116.

17. George Lipsitz, "'Ain't Nobody Here But Us Chickens': The Class Origins of Rock 'n' Roll," in *Class and Culture in Cold War America: A Rainbow at Midnight* (New York: Praeger, 1981; Bergin and Garvey, 1982); Bruce Tucker, "'Tell Tchaikovsky the News': Post-modernism, Popular Culture, and the Emergence of Rock 'n' Roll," *Black Music Research Journal* 9:2 (Fall 1989): 271–95.

18. Adorno, "On the Fetish Character of Music and Regression of Listening," *The Essential Frankfurt School Reader,* ed. Andrew Arato and Eike Gebhardt (New York: Urizen, 1978; Continuum, 1982), 276.

19. This process was, in turn, motivated by increases in democratic representation in education, politics, and corporate funding, as outlined in Paul DiMaggio's lectures, "Institutional Change in the Arts," Havens Center, Department of Sociology, University of Wisconsin, February 1988. For background on the institutional formation of an elite musical culture and its canons, see DiMaggio, "Cultural Entrepreneurship in Nineteenth-Century Boston: The Creation of an Organizational Base for High Culture in America," *Media, Culture, and Society* 4 (1982): 33–50.

ertory from the performance experience, transforming it into a sonic atmosphere accessible at the touch of a button. Populist efforts to revive concert music through pops concerts and commercial spectacles helped to broaden its appeal somewhat, but only at greater expense to the social and aesthetic distance that had previously defined its position at the pinnacle of American culture.[20] Similarly, the challenge of serialism and atonality, which promised to turn music into a form of scholarly inquiry, was met—particularly in the 1950s and 1960s—with scorn and rejection from much of the concert-going public. From a populist perspective, and despite its obvious value to insiders, it appears to have been a last-ditch effort to revive art music's predominance, and one that succeeded only in casting it into a marginalized fringe group set off in academe.[21]

Today, the nebulous categories of popular and art blur into a complex and encompassing web of subverted binaries, perpetuating Marshall McLuhan's vision of an "all-inclusive nowness," a world in which "fragmentation is the essence."[22] The previously stratified categories of culture, existing on opposite sides of what Andreas Huyssen calls the "Great Divide," have begun to look like outmoded constructs.[23] Urban music in the postwar United States has come to resemble an extended series of fusions and oppositions existing in the

20. Michael Sahl describes more recent concertgoers as a "technical class" whose inclinations often seem more oriented to the spectacle than to the particularities of the music's rich and complex past. See "Thoughts on the State of Classical Music in the United States," *Musical Quarterly,* no. 4 (1986): 523–28.

21. In an overview of the state of concert music from 1950, Virgil Thomson lamented that all of it, "written no matter by whom, is surprisingly non-committal. No shadow of willful charm lies over it; no plain or urgent communication peers through its complex surface." "Music in the 1950s," *Harper's* (November 1960), 59–63. Other writers cast direct blame on serialism and its frequent atonal applications. In *The Agony of Modern Music,* for example (New York: Simon and Schuster, 1955), Henry Pleasants argued that concert music had reached a state of stylistic exhaustion, a condition reflected in the excesses of serialist method. He believed that the music continued to survive only because of the zealous efforts of a small clique of self-serving concert composers. Interestingly, Pleasants identified the wave of the future not in concert music, but in "popular" music, most notably in jazz and tin pan alley. Milton Babbitt's infamous essay from 1958, titled by journal editors as "Who Cares If You Listen?" may well have been a reply to Pleasants's controversial book. *High Fidelity* (February 1958), reprinted in *Esthetics Contemporary,* ed. Richard Kostelanetz (Buffalo: Prometheus Books, 1978). Years later Samuel Lipman would write about concert music: "Like an empire shorn of everything but its history, it scratches out a living on the explosion of creativity which lasted from before Bach to World War I." *Music after Modernism* (New York: Basic Books, 1979), vii.

22. McLuhan, *Understanding Media* (New York: McGraw-Hill, 1964), 8, 335.

23. Huyssen, *After the Great Divide.*

matrix of mass culture. The patterns of interaction and conflict, too complex and intertwined to be sorted out systematically in this brief analysis, relate inextricably to former hierarchical divisions as well as to the new institutional formations that affect the contours of American life as a whole. These have not only encouraged stylistic intersection, but have challenged the effectiveness of the standard categories by which we define musical practice. Former classifications of musical genre, while perhaps still somewhat useful as means of distinguishing aspects of style, appear less and less helpful in providing an accurate appraisal of the complexities of contemporary artistic life.

II

In jazz, the ambiguities of value, genre, and hierarchy had a liberating effect, ultimately working to elevate the music's social rank. Here, the comparisons that critics drew in the 1950s between the history of jazz and the legacy of European concert music were symptomatic of efforts to reclassify its meaning in terms of art. Building on the classicizing efforts of musicians and publicists from before the war, many writers capitalized on the circumstances of the new balance, challenging prior trivializations and reinventing the music's past in the image of the European classical tradition.[24] Employing a recycled version of the doctrine of progress, they constructed an evolutionary account of jazz history in which simple folk strains grew inexorably into complex patterns of greatness.[25] Popular acceptance of bop, particularly after the

24. Prewar models include Paul Whiteman's symphonic jazz, Gershwin's concert-jazz combinations, and the jazz-concert movement, coalescing in John Hammond's "From Spirituals to Swing." The concertizing efforts of publicists are described in Scott DeVeaux, "The Emergence of the Jazz Concert, 1935–45," *American Music* 7:1 (Spring 1989): 6–29. Yet despite these developments, jazz could not adopt a truly "artistic" posture until after the war, when the dominant hierarchies were more effectively challenged. A description of the blanket dismissals of jazz published prior to World War II appears in Morroe Berger, "Jazz: Resistance to the Diffusion of a Culture Pattern," *Journal of Negro History* (October 1947), reprinted in Charles Nanry, ed., *American Music: From Storyville to Woodstock* (New Brunswick: Transaction Books, 1972), 11–43.

25. References to folk survivals in jazz appear throughout the literature. In his essay "Jazz Evolvement as Art Form" (*Down Beat* [January 27, 1950]: 12), for example, Dave Brubeck argues that jazz was "too dynamic, too all-consuming, too great a force in American life to remain in the relatively timeless, changeless state of folk material." As such, Brubeck not only dismisses all folk expressions, but perpetuates a biased ethnocentricism in which "simple," rural cultures lag behind sophisticated, "complex" urban environments. A perverse portrait of jazz evolution appears in Gavin T. Lyall's four-part

death and subsequent canonization of Charlie Parker, increased faith in historical continuity, thereby reinforcing the idea of a tangible jazz tradition.[26] Looking back at the jazz heritage, critics writing for popular literary magazines such as the *Saturday Review* betrayed their grounding in European-based, formalist aesthetics as they perpetuated a grand vision of stylistic continuity and order. For these writers, jazz had assumed a stable form that could be observed critically and "objectively," apart from time, place, and culture.[27] In France, moreover, André Hodeir reinforced such thinking in his landmark study, *Jazz: Its Evolution and Essence* (1954). In that work, the author conceptualized jazz according to a European musical framework, identifying "pre-classical" and "classical" phases in the seemingly inevitable development of swing. Hodeir's developmental model, built upon a questionable proposition that the stylistic evolution of jazz rep-

---

"Pictorial History of Jazz," *Jazz Journal* (July–October 1950): 19–20. The first frame, depicting dancing and drumming in tribal Africa, reads: "Jazz originated in the African jungle, in the chants and tom-toms of Negro Tribal Dances. Thus the essential jazz form of steady rhythm was evolved." The final frame identifies a direct line of evolution to musicians performing in New York clubs and concert halls.

26. This took place largely through the critical efforts of Leonard Feather, Ross Russell, and Barry Ulanov, and the record companies' efforts to assimilate bop, notably those of George Shearing and Parker's "Bird with Strings" recordings. Eventually bop or bop derivatives changed the character of commercial mainstream jazz, as lounges and clubs supported performances of "polite bop." Many musicians and critics objected to these efforts toward popularization. For the comments of one of the most vocal, see John S. Wilson, "Cliques Are Destroying Jazz: Lennie Tristano," *Down Beat* (October 6, 1950).

27. Such formalist methods of analysis suggest parallels with the "new criticism" of literary studies, with which these writers were familiar. Whitney Balliett refers to the contributors to Martin Williams's and Nat Hentoff's *Jazz Review* as representing jazz-music's circle of new criticism. Cited by Lawrence Gushee in his introductory comments to the panel, "The Institutionalization of Jazz Scholarship," Joint Conference of the Societies for Ethnomusicology, Musicology, and Music Theory, Oakland, Calif., November 8, 1990. The organic model of jazz evolution to which many writers ascribed appears to have developed out of conventional college-level surveys of the European musical tradition, which perpetuate an eighty-year-old theory of style—and before then, nineteenth-century views of history—outlined in Guido Adler's *Der Stil in der Musik* (1911). Carl Dahlhaus discusses the intellectual background of this notion in *Foundations of Music History,* trans. J. B. Robinson (New York: Cambridge University Press, 1983), 14–15. Moreover, my own reading of these curious constructions of jazz first appeared as a paper, "On Constructing a Jazz History," delivered at the Smithsonian conference, "Jazz in the Museum," at the National Museum of American History, Washington, D.C., in April 1990. Also related and noteworthy is Scott DeVeaux, "Constructing the Jazz Tradition: Jazz Historiography," *Black American Literature Forum* 25:3 (Fall 1991): 525–60.

licated, in compressed form, the five-hundred-year heritage of European concert music, proved to have as lasting an influence on critical thinking as his frequently brilliant formal analyses.[28]

Efforts to link jazz and concert music proved most apparent in the controversy about the definition and application of the critical term "mainstream." Whereas Stanley Dance and other English critics had first written of a mainstream oriented to small-group swing,[29] American writers subsequently redefined the center by broadening its meaning to include "progressive" and "modern" styles of bop, hard bop, and cool.[30] As mainstream grew into a familiar label for jazz

28. Hodeir, "The Evolution of Jazz and the Idea of Classicism," in *Jazz: Its Evolution and Essence* (Paris, 1954; New York: Grove Press, 1956), esp. p. 27. For Hodeir, "classical" defined the period 1935–1945, with "modern" beginning in 1945. Hodeir's "pre-classical" category for early swing (1927–1934) advanced a version of historical determinism held suspect in scholarly circles by that time.

29. The editors of *Jazz Journal* had spoken metaphorically of a main center of jazz in its first issues, though at this point it went by the name of swing. Dismissing all but swing's crucial musical essence, they wrote that "the road" centered between the "gutters" of bop and dixieland. "Lightly and Politely," *Jazz Journal* (May 1950), 4. The term *mainstream* itself appeared in Dance's essays "The Main-stream Jazz War," *Melody Maker* (April 16, 1955), 3, as well as in D. Stewart-Baxter's "Mainstream," *Jazz Journal* (January 1956), 7. Dance popularized its use in a series of "Lightly and Politely" columns: "Riparian Conversation," *Jazz Journal* (December 1958), 35; "No Checking Mainstream," *Jazz Journal* (August 1959), 7; "Far out in the Mainstream," *Jazz Journal* (October 1957), 24–25. In the latter essay, he acknowledged the British origins of the term, yet without mentioning its prior use by the early English critic of concert music, Sir Donald Tovey. Dance wrote: "When Basie was last here, he was asked how he felt about 'mainstream.' He had no feeling about it. He was baffled. He had never heard of it. Now he probably knows better, for America seems to be adopting the term in a biggish way." See also Dance's *Jazz Era: The 'Forties,* coedited with Albert McCarthy (London: MacGibbon and Kee, 1961), 13.

30. Leading the American way was Nat Hentoff, whose "Jazz Mainstream" was featured in the *Saturday Review* beginning on June 29, 1957. While Hentoff concentrated on swing artists, he also gave mention to bop and postbop artists. A brief examination of the concept of mainstream appears in his introduction to *Jazz Life* (New York: Dial Press, 1961; Da Capo, 1975). Dance discusses Martin Williams's challenge to the basis of mainstream in swing in "Mainstream Opposed," *Jazz Journal* (January 1960), 27. Williams himself offers his revision of the term in his review of John Coltrane's "Mainstream 1958," *Down Beat* (August 21, 1958), reprinted in *Jazz Masters in Transition, 1957–69* (New York: Da Capo, 1970), 20–21. By 1963, A. B. Spellman had identified Andrew Hill as part of a mainstream in his notes to *Black Fire.* By 1964, the term had become accepted to the point where Ralph Ellison called the music section of his *Shadow and Act,* "Sound and the Mainstream." It is noteworthy that McCarthy sought to reassert his idea of a mainstream in a journal by the same name, founded in 1974. Perhaps Joachim-Ernst Berendt expresses the term's transformation most succinctly in chapter 10 of his *Jazz: A Photo History* (Schirmer, 1979), which he titles "Bebop becomes Mainstream."

practice, the previous cultural and aesthetic distinctions between New Orleans and swing, black music and white, had, by the end of the decade, been glossed over. Bop, which writers had so easily dismissed in the 1940s, and indeed, which Parker himself had distanced from the massified "jazz tradition,"[31] was now woven into a seamless, organic continuum comprising the whole of the recorded legacy. By the 1960s, "mainstream" had evolved into a definer of historical inevitability, coordinating all that was considered meaningful after jazz had been institutionalized in the 1930s. Mainstream signified stylistic unity, an agreement on what jazz really was. As a category, it had become synonymous with a developing jazz canon and an effort to shape jazz into an analogue of the European musical heritage. By removing the music from the social and ideological categories that had previously given it meaning, the mainstream of jazz would stand or fall according to the measures of "all fine music," becoming, in the favored phrase, "America's classical art form."[32]

Outside of the subculture, institutional efforts to reformulate jazz according to classicist precepts helped to reinforce cold-war conceptions of a classless and raceless society. As an expression of "black genius," jazz music became a useful element in the State Department's campaign to project images of freedom, truth, and racial equality in the form of government-sponsored radio programming and tours of Africa, Latin America, and the Soviet Union.[33] At home, the deifying

31. Michael Levin and John S. Wilson, "No Bop Roots in Jazz: Parker," *Down Beat* (September 9, 1949), reprinted in the special issue, "Celebrating Bird," in *Down Beat* (December 1990), 60.

32. Grover Sales, *Jazz: America's Classical Music* (Englewood Cliffs: Prentice-Hall, 1984); Billy Taylor, "Jazz: America's Classical Music," *Black Perspective of Music* (Winter 1986), 21–25.

33. In his *Encyclopedia of Jazz,* rev. ed., Leonard Feather notes that the United States government "took official cognizance of jazz for the first time" in 1956 after recognizing that "global interest in America's foremost musical export might be turned to patriotic advantage." This led to State Department–sponsored tours led by Dizzy Gillespie, Woody Herman, Wilbur DeParis, Benny Goodman, and others (pp. 49–50). Feather himself had been hired by the State Department's Voice of America radio series as host of "Jazz Club U.S.A.," broadcoast behind the Iron Curtain. See "Name Feather to Beam Jazz at Iron Curtain," *Variety* (March 7, 1951), 43. A vast literature includes: "U.S. Jazz on Beam Round the World," *Variety* (April 11, 1956), 47; "Dizzy Gillespie a Hit with Middle East Cats on U.S. Goodwill Tour," *Variety* (April 25, 1956), 61; "Uncle Sam's a Cool Cat, Digs Jazz Beat," *Billboard* (November 24, 1956), 1; Edward L. Randal, "The Voice of American Jazz," *High Fidelity* (August 1958), 30–31, 86, 88; "Music News: The Reds and Dr. [Marshall] Stearns," *Down Beat* (July 9, 1959), 9–10; "Jazz as Diplomatic Tool Cries for Effective Use," *Billboard* (June 29, 1959), 22, 32. For an overview history of the Voice of America, see Robert

of the music's most notable (and often white) artists and the canonizing of their most memorable performances furthered the destabilization of jazz as a form of resistance. Through these actions, jazz on record would appear increasingly as an ahistorical and depoliticized abstraction, a collection of timeless masterpieces that, through an inversion of the modernist hierarchy, would assume a position at the top of the popular heap.[34] With the help of LP reissues of 78 RPM disks, jazz now assumed a new order, its recorded legacy presented as a seamless tradition existing parallel to the history of concert music. In the milieu of the home, the concert hall, and the college campus, mainstream jazz had become what *Good Housekeeping* called approvingly a "respectable" art, democratic, free, and defined by a fixed, absolute conception of the masterwork.[35] The music's close associations to concert music on levels aesthetic, social, moral, and pedagogical ulti-

---

William Pirsein, *The Voice of America: A History of the International Broadcasting Activities of the United States Government, 1940–1962* (New York: Arno Press, 1979); Holly Cowan Shulman, *The Voice of America: Propaganda and Democracy, 1941–45* (Madison: University of Wisconsin Press, 1990).

34. Soon after, jazz accordingly lost much of its appeal in hip culture. Writing in the 1960s, Tom Wolfe observed somewhat flippantly and hyperbolically that among creative intellectuals jazz had become "a hopelessly bourgeois taste . . . [the music of] Monk, Mingus, Ferguson—it has all been left to little executive trainees with their first apartment and a mahogany African mask from the free-port shop in Haiti." By "intellectuals," Wolfe meant "white intellectuals" who were mainly interested in rock 'n' roll. The situation in black circles was appreciably different. See *The Kandy-Kolored Tangerine-Flake Streamline Baby* (New York: Farrar, Strauss, and Giroux, 1965; Bantam, 1977), 40, 53.

35. Georg Marek, "From the Dive to the Dean, Jazz becomes Respectable," *Good Housekeeping* (June 1956), 120, 122–24. Formerly a music personified by someone who "behave[s] like a runaway idiot," jazz, according to Marek, had been transformed from the darker complected to something lighter, from the "boy with dirty hands" into another with "clean hands . . . found in the concert halls, the music conservatories, and by way of respectable and carefully produced LP records, in the nicest living rooms" (p. 120). The comment alludes to the red-scare image of "dirty hands," linking blackness and bop with communism. Moreover, John A. Kouwenhoven's essay "What's American about America," *Harper's* (January 14, 1956), 25–33, suggests that the Americanness of jazz related to a unified mainstream. "In our present context we need to focus upon what all the subspecies (Dixieland, Bebop, Swing, or Cool Jazz) have in common: in other words, we must neglect the by no means uninteresting qualities which differentiate one from another, since it is what they have in common which can tell us most about the civilization which produced them." Finally, the public image of jazz in the 1950s may be compared to the escalation of other forms of high modernism, notably abstract expressionism, which served similarly as an icon of American cultural dominance and freedom. See Serge Guilbault, *How New York Stole the Idea of Modern Art: Abstract Expressionism, Freedom, and the Cold War* (Chicago: University of Chicago Press, 1983).

mately inspired jazz innovators as well as concert composers to invent new ways of merging the two "classical" traditions, leading to the "thirdstream" experiments of John Lewis, Milton Babbitt, Spud Murphy, Gunther Schuller, and others.[36]

Yet the mainstream ultimately worked against itself, its visibility coming at a price: appropriated and depoliticized, this monumental recasting of jazz stood in direct conflict with values and perspectives grounded in the African-American vernacular. By revising the nature of black music to fit the tastes and attitudes of a white consensus, the construct denatured the "blues" character of an artistic heritage built upon the necessity of culturally affirmative, creative resistance. Further, by encouraging the growth of a routinized style as a basis for "serious" artistic progress, it went against the grain of a black ethos that had historically challenged codified common practice and the analytic frames of a European musical tradition. Of course, black musicians were not immune to institutional influence. As professionals immersed in mainstream American values and operating in the business of popular entertainment, they inculcated middle-class aesthetic sensibilities that had informed urban music-making since the nineteenth century.[37] At the same time, there were also important differences between black- and white-centered expressions that many

36. Throughout the 1950s, jazz magazines reported on efforts of musicians to lead jazz in a new direction, often with compositional techniques stemming from concert music. Stan Kenton's "progressive jazz," John Lewis's and the Modern Jazz Quartet's jazz fugues, Dave Brubeck's experiments with meter and form, Bill Evans's marginally functional, harmonic colorations, George Shearing's desire to "pen a fugue that swings" (*Down Beat* [August 25, 1954], 4), and Spud Murphy's hybrids of jazz and twelve-tone composition all reflected a turn toward practices first formulated in concert music. Conversely, Milton Babbitt, Lukas Foss, Harold Shapero, and above all, Gunther Schuller (the originator of the epithet "thirdstream") helped to promote serious appreciation of jazz among concert composers. As André Previn suggested in 1954, "Fairly soon I hope the integration of classical music and jazz will hit some kind of happy meeting ground, because more and more classical musicians are interested in jazz." Previn, "The Jazz Scene Today," *Down Beat* (January 23, 1954), 24. For a discussion of this latter direction, see Clarence J. Stuessy, "The Confluence of Jazz and Classical Music from 1950 to 1970" (Ph.D. diss., Eastman School of Music, 1977). For an insightful essay on thirdstream, see Martin Williams, "Third Stream Problems," *Evergreen Review* (May–June 1963); reprinted in *Jazz Masters in Transition, 1957–1969* (New York: Macmillan, 1970; Da Capo, 1980).

37. Dick Hebdige's comment about resistant subcultures is relevant here: "There is no reason to suppose that subcultures spontaneously affirm only those *blocked* 'readings' excluded from the airwaves and the newspapers (consciousness of subordinate status, a conflict model of society, etc.). They also articulate, to a greater or lesser extent, some of the *preferred* meanings and interpretations . . . favoured by and transmitted through the authorized channels of mass communication." Hebdige, *Subculture,* 86.

commentators on jazz have tended to minimize or overlook. For example, whereas a white-oriented mainstream had exalted European-based, canonical notions of art, the black vernacular historically defined musical value as a process relating to a socially oriented, often intimate public experience. Indeed, in the preindustrial South, musical "greatness" among African Americans seemed not to refer to objectified notions of value but to creative identifications of the self (the personal voice), associations with the community (call/response), and ultimately references to the sacred (soul). Similarly, repertories and songs were not the polished gems of a traditional legacy but extended from what Nelson George calls, somewhat romantically, the "create and move on" ethos of the African-American heritage. Speaking from experience as both a historian and performer of sacred-oriented music, moreover, Bernice Johnson Reagon stresses additional differences between the realms of the southern black and the northern white. She observes that songs and other artistic expressions in the vernacular were not ends in themselves, but rather creative tools that provided singers with "a way to get to singing." Art, Reagon continues, was not an authorized form of knowledge; it was, quite simply, "something that came with the territory."[38]

Advocating aesthetic distinctions according to race runs the risk of glorifying the black aesthetic, of turning "blackness" into a form of exotic romanticism—or even what Renato Rosaldo has called, in a related instance, "imperialist nostalgia."[39] The risk is a real one, for many early celebrations of black art advanced views that, with hindsight, now seem patronizing, and in certain cases, explicitly racist. Obviously, northward migrations introduced black musicians to sensibilities grounded in a Euro-American order, and the institutions of

38. Nelson George, *The Death of Rhythm & Blues* (New York: E. P. Dutton, 1988), 108; Bill Moyers interview with Bernice Johnson Reagon, PBS television broadcast, January 1991. For insight into traditional vernacular sensibilities, see Lawrence Levine, *Black Culture and Black Consciousness* (New York: Oxford University Press, 1977); Alan Dundes, ed., *Mother Wit from the Laughing Barrel* (Jackson: University Press of Mississippi, 1990); Roger Abrahams, *Talking Black* (Rowley, Mass.: Newbury House Publishers, 1976); Paul Oliver, *Songsters and Saints* (New York: Cambridge University Press, 1984). Recent studies in African-American literature have reshaped the polemics of 1960s cultural nationalism into a critical theory of black difference. Among the best known are Houston A. Baker, Jr., *Blues, Ideology, and Afro-American Literature* (Chicago: University of Chicago Press, 1984), and Henry Louis Gates, Jr., *The Signifying Monkey* (New York: Oxford University Press, 1988).

39. Rosaldo, "Imperialist Nostalgia," *Representations* 26 (Spring 1989): 107–22. Rosaldo defines imperialist nostalgia as a yearning on the part of the agents of colonialism "for the very forms of life they intentionally altered or destroyed" (107–8).

the popular dramatically revised attitudes about artistic practice as they did about life in general. Furthermore, overgeneralizations about the aesthetic difference between black southerners and white northerners can create a false image of hard-and-fast cultural totalities that may not stand up to scrutiny.[40] Yet given all of these factors, allowing complexity to preclude efforts in identifying aesthetic distinctions is to advocate another form of racism: one that denies the profound impact of race on American life. Complexity does not negate difference, any more than the ambiguities of racial distinctiveness erase the constructs of black and white. For despite the impact of urban institutions and media, there is considerable evidence to suggest that black musicians—and whites identifying with black sensibilities—have maintained an artistic insularity that goes beyond the obvious references to improvisation and swing. This insularity—and its "sounding" potential, as Houston A. Baker, Jr., has described it[41]—has reinforced differences in aesthetic meaning, as writers as diverse as Zora Neale Hurston, Ralph Ellison, Martin Williams, Albert Murray, and Imamu Amiri Baraka (LeRoi Jones) have demonstrated over the years.[42] And it is precisely the efforts to resist hegemonic co-optation in order to voice an affirmative celebration of black creative centricity that have profoundly influenced the larger patterns of stylistic change.

The formalization of the mainstream on a grand social scale ultimately fueled a spirit of opposition among musicians who had remained skeptical of outsiders' interpretations of a music that many believed no words could describe, no analysis could clarify.[43] Helping to shape this skepticism were the new contexts in postwar mass culture that encouraged questioning of traditional notions of historical

40. Consider, for example, the surprisingly high percentage of college-educated black musicians who received formal musical training. See John Chilton, *Who's Who of Jazz,* 4th ed. (London: Macmillan, 1985).

41. Baker, *Modernism and the Harlem Renaissance* (Chicago: University of Chicago Press, 1987), xvi, 65–68.

42. Hurston, *Mules and Men* (New York: Harper and Row, 1935, 1990); Ellison, *Shadow and Act* (New York: Vintage Books, 1964, 1972); Williams, *The Jazz Tradition,* 2d ed. (New York: Oxford University Press, 1983); Murray, *Stomping the Blues* (New York: McGraw-Hill, 1976; Da Capo, 1987); Baraka, *Blues People* (New York: William Morrow, 1963). Charles Keil views black-white stylistic interchanges as a dialectical process conforming to the appropriation/revitalization model of culture change advanced by Anthony Wallace. See Keil, *Urban Blues* (Chicago: University of Chicago Press, 1966), 43.

43. The expression "the music speaks for itself" typified this attitude, expressed perhaps most forcefully by Miles Davis, whose antipathy toward the jazz press was infamous. See, for example, Don DeMichael's profile of Davis in *Rolling Stone* (December 13, 1969), 23–26.

continuity, aesthetic absolutes, and the finality of artistic truth. For musicians responsive to such opinion, either intellectually or by sheer nature of a presentist popular sensibility, the world of the mainstream had become increasingly inhibiting and outmoded. And for those performers who took to heart black peoples' emerging political solidarity, who were witnessing through the actions of the civil rights movement, the church, and the courts a dramatic change in the position of blacks in the United States, who embraced progressive politics, formally or otherwise, and who saw black music as an important component in the new cultural epoch—a white-run, institutionally regulated jazz world must have seemed foreign and even antithetical to their creative concerns and perspectives.

Working against the background of the "new jazz art," many musicians began to assert their creative perspectives by moving aesthetically and stylistically away from the mainstream. Actualizing W. E. B. Du Bois's notion of "double consciousness," musicians embraced values originating in white-based institutions as they advanced art in response to their appropriative effects.[44] On one level, institutional efforts to transform bop into a jazz-based high modernism reinforced musicians' interests in creative progress as well as their views of themselves as certified artists. Yet these same frames of reference inspired forms of resistance in the spirit of bop, whose high-cultural pedigree may be construed, evoking the influence of Parker, as a kind of *Crazeology* that jazzed authorized notions of African-American classicism. In the 1950s, for example, the proponents of hard bop and funky jazz perpetuated a bop-based form of modernism while embracing a separatist aesthetic of "soul" rooted in the cultural background of the black vernacular.[45] In the 1960s, moreover, the innovators of free jazz voiced a similarly soulful rejection of mainstream tastes and values by revising the "artistic" experiments of progressive jazz, twelve-tone jazz, and thirdstream.

Seeking to express through an abstraction of the jazz language their identities as serious artists, black free-jazz musicians and their white colleagues were particularly successful at applying an appropriated version of modernism to assert a "black art" founded on the rhythmic and timbral impulses identified with the African-American heri-

44. Du Bois, *The Souls of Black Folk* (1903; Greenwich, Conn.: Fawcett Premier, 1961), 16–17.

45. To play jazz, one must have soul, and to have soul, one must have grown up black. John Szwed, "Musical Style and Racial Conflict," *Phylon* 27:4 (Winter 1966): 358–66; Nat Hentoff, "Race Prejudice in Jazz: It Works Both Ways," *Harper's* (June 1959), 72–77.

tage.[46] Rejecting the constraints of harmony and song form, they made rhythm the chief organizing principle of a rarefied art that highlighted intricate, multilinear interplay of collectively improvised lines. The intensity of improvisation was heightened by the players' explorations of the coloristic potential of their instruments, a practice that—recalling traditional black vocal arts and the sounds of grassroots instruments—reflected an African-American tendency to enrich artistic expression with the sonic textures of everyday life. In this way, free jazz represented a tradition-centered art, which revitalized the historically distinctive qualities of African-American music. Free jazz made this assertion through the arcane language of modernist concert music, to which it bore similarities in its emphasis on rhythm and texture as well as in its traditional opposition to middle-class values and culture. Musical modernism became, in the form of free jazz, the new tool of resistance in black performative expression.

In short, free jazz had achieved a tenuous balance between black vernacularism and radical change. It was a true African-American modernism, an "anti-jazz," as it was first called,[47] that yielded to abstraction in celebration of black culture's increased authority in the emerging postmodern era. An art in conflict with the conception of an enduring mainstream, it produced the most dramatic aesthetic and social rupture since the jazz tradition was first conceptualized in swing. Yet as a movement mindful of its roots in the black tradition, early free jazz was equally an extension—or better, a culmination—of the jazz mainstream.[48] Its innovators, both black and white, paid tribute in dialogic fashion to the black heritage by rejecting, yet nonetheless perpetuating, aspects of the classic-jazz construct. Accordingly, early free jazz represented an unresolved conflict between the musicians' radical conceptions of art and the traditionalist paradigm of mainstream jazz. As a movement, it stood at the nexus between the worlds of the modern and postmodern, an analogue to other oppositional artistic movements that had responded to the challenges of the new balance.

46. Early on, the free-jazz community was an integrated one, as reflected in the membership of the New York Jazz Composers' Guild.

47. The anti-jazz epithet appeared first in John Tynan's "Take 5" review in *Down Beat* (November 23, 1961), 40. Leonard Feather repeated it in articles published in *Show* (January 1962) and *Down Beat* (February 15, 1962). Frank Kofsky compares the free-jazz language to soul and funk as a kindred ghetto rhetoric. *Black Nationalism and the Revolution in Music* (New York: Pathfinder, 1970), 13.

48. Only after the appearance of a jazz common practice and a classically oriented jazz mainstream could a vanguardist reaction emerge.

III

Similar oppositions to the dominant institutions of American culture had begun to show up in concert music by the 1950s. Identified as "experimental" or, borrowing from Henry Cowell, "new" music, these oppositions reflected an ongoing resistance to the institutional framework of the concert orchestra, which had, at the turn of the century, set in stone the canon of masterworks.[49] Experimentalists opposed, sometimes defiantly, what has been called the "historicist mainstream" of classicism, neoclassicism, and serialist-based high modernism, together with the common belief in the higher virtues of an exalted European tradition.[50] In this way, the "experimental" epithet seemed appropriate: it referred to musicians and composers who operated without fixed ideas about the act of music-making or about the elements and frames that identify the musical object. Their movement would gain strength in the late 1950s and 1960s after serialism had transposed concert music from the public concert hall to the academy and when the rise of a new, mass-mediated popular culture, which celebrated the commonplace, the vernacular, and the everyday, signaled the declining authority of the common-practice orchestra.

At the helm of the experimental movement stood composer John Cage, whose challenge to the norms traditionally associated with art music found a powerful resonance in the emerging context of the postmodern. Cage not only called into question prevailing notions of correct compositional practice, but also rejected outright existing conceptions of historical continuity, aesthetic absolutes, and the masterwork. He did not adhere to the conventional assumption that human-made sonic forms could elicit superior aesthetic experience. To the contrary, Cage, anticipating literary deconstruction, argued that one could witness multiple, competing structures by simply paying attention to everyday sounds: he found "form everywhere."[51] Thus, in

49. See Joan Peyser, ed., *The Orchestra: Origins and Transformations* (New York: Charles Scribner's Sons, 1986). See also Charles Wuorinen's informative review of the same book in *Musical Quarterly,* no. 4 (1986). A comprehensive study of the modern American orchestra may be found in Philip Hart's *Orpheus in the New World* (New York: W. W. Norton, 1973). Ritualistic mystification of concert music, moreover, has helped to enforce the exclusivity and power of the artistic elite. The development of this process is analyzed in Bruce A. McConachie's essay, "New York Operagoing, 1825–50: Creating an Elite Social Ritual," *American Music* 6:2 (Summer 1988). See also DiMaggio, "Cultural Entrepreneurship in Nineteenth-Century Boston," 33–50.

50. J. Peter Burkholder, "Museum Pieces: The Historicist Mainstream in Music of the Last Hundred Years," *Journal of Musicology* 2:2 (Spring 1983): 115–34.

51. Roger Reynolds, "Interview with John Cage," in *Contemporary Composers on Contemporary Music,* ed. Barney Childs and Elliott Schwartz (New York: Holt, Rinehart, and Winston, 1967), 344.

the early 1950s, Cage began to work with chance-based compositional methods that produced nonsyntactic works, independent from conventional methods of determining form. By 1958, his methods had grown even more radical, leaving the musicians themselves free to create "compositions indeterminate of their performances."[52] The disruptive nature of Cage's works served a vanguardist function in unsettling the complacent listener who took for granted the authority of the composer to effect a meaningful aesthetic experience. Cage developed to an extreme a line of thought that recalled John Dewey's pragmatic prescriptions in *Art as Experience,* for he argued that musical meaning was determined not by the work of art but by the work of the listener.[53] Accordingly, existing notions of canon, the masterwork, and the well-practiced musician now took second place to the foremost concern, experience.

Cage's experimentalism signaled a radical departure from the conventions of classical and high-modernist concert music. To be sure, his "anything goes" dictum was ultimately debased by musicians who, while sharing Cage's irreverence toward traditional high culture and aesthetics, lacked his sense of discipline and commitment to the anarchic philosophy that suffused his creative work. Yet the radicalism of Cage's message had a powerful, freeing effect: it gave license to artists to develop methods and expressions of great variety and idiosyncrasy, many of which grew out of patterns in everyday life or shared resemblances with folk practices of the Anglo- and African-American heritage. The infusion of folk culture into vanguardist music-making—manifested in the use of found objects as instruments, reliance on improvisation, and preference for informal performance settings—identified an important characteristic of the experimental movement that affirmed the legitimacy of the vernacular and working class. Yet unlike previous bohemian cultures and vanguard movements that cultivated the way of life of "the people," experimentalists expressed a workaday sensibility stemming from familiar backgrounds and experience. Their artistic world quite literally re-created the everyday American lives that many had been living all along.

By the 1960s, then, free jazz and experimentalism stood together as art forms distinguished from, and largely opposed to, the traditional

52. In *Variations I,* for example, Cage employs abstractions of traditional notation that permit broad interpretation by the performer. As William Brooks comments, Cage sought mainly to enforce a sense of performance discipline, leaving the musical results to chance. See "Choice and Change in Cage's Recent Music," *TriQuarterly* 54 (Spring 1982): 148–66.

53. Cage referred to this as a kind of experimental listening in *Silence* (Middletown: Wesleyan University Press, 1961/1973), 7.

institutions of mainstream jazz and concert music. Free jazz was a tradition-centered yet ultimately antihistorical music rooted in the black vernacular that had summoned strength from nationalist celebration in its rejection of mainstream practices through an appropriated modernist aesthetic. Experimentalism, in its turn, developed out of the faltering authority of high modernism. Its innovators ultimately rejected the absolute prescriptions of high art and looked toward the popular and vernacular, through which they shaped a vanguardist expression based on the homegrown and everyday. Together they represented two parts of a complex configuration resulting from the collision of prior certainties about art and culture. Free-jazz artists stood as a black musical vanguard that rejected the construct of a jazz classicism with all of its appropriated and reified notions of high art; experimentalists, trained in or at least familiar with the tradition of European musical composition, demonstrated their defiance of concert-music institutions through a range of equally unconventional creative means. Rejecting the sameness of mass-mediated culture, moreover, both free jazz and experimentalism nonetheless reflected its influence, for the emergence of each in its own way underscored the new alignments that characterized a nascent postmodernism. As the visibility of free jazz and experimentalism began to increase in the mid-1960s, they seemed more and more like stylistically and culturally distinct expressions of the same aesthetic ethos, directly challenging the dominance of the mainstream, whether it be in concert music or in jazz.

IV

In this context, Braxton becomes particularly interesting because he seemed to respond in a highly personal yet equally tradition-sensitive way to the flux and fracture of the emerging postmodern condition. His creative life embodied the erosion of artistic categorization that gave way to the ascendancy of black expression and to profound stylistic and cultural intersection. Braxton's art and, indeed, his entire artistic perspective grew out of the coalescence of the previously distinct bifurcations of black and white, art and entertainment, highbrow and lowbrow, and, more specifically, out of the aesthetic convergence of free jazz and experimentalism.

Braxton's experimentalism reflected an independent approach to musical and intellectual learning that took shape outside the formal institutions of American musical life. He appeared to be drawn to musical modernism principally because of the intellectual, ideological, and philosophical associations that it evoked. Yet like many other American autodidacts in the vanguard, he resisted the conventions that formal training in modernist composition would impose. Even though he embraced the sound worlds and techniques of many contemporary composers, Braxton failed to show the kind of reverence for the European musical tradition that concert composers, typically trained in formal institutions, tend to share. Nor did he relinquish his ties to the black vernacular, to his early musical life on Chicago's South Side, which proved to be a determining factor in his artistic development. Braxton's early life in Chicago grounded him sufficiently in the black world so that he could explore new styles without losing grip on his cultural and historical identity. That legacy would, in fact, prove to be the shaping force of his creative psychology and sensibility, even as he grew increasingly committed to procedures and styles that, on the surface, seemed antithetical to the African-American musical legacy.

Assuming an aesthetically and ideologically radical posture, Braxton took a stand early in his career against the social category of jazz, which, he felt, had inhibited his eclectic artistic interests. Initially he aligned himself with the elite of free jazz as an alternative to the value systems of the mainstream, and in the Chicago-based Association for the Advancement of Creative Musicians, a black-music organization, he found the institutional support and ideological license to realize his unconventional artistic goals. Yet whereas most of his AACM colleagues remained committed to free-jazz practice in the mid-1960s, Braxton had already begun to express the liberties of the postmodern, ranging across genres and exploring high-modernist concert music and experimentalism. Soon he would transcend the jazz category altogether, actively participating in experimental-music circles, most notably in New York, where he collaborated with the composer-performers Philip Glass, David Behrman, and Frederick Rzewski. This experience ultimately led to greater activity in composition, for which he drew from the experimental repertory as well as from jazz and postwar European modernism.

In virtually all of Braxton's music, one can identify a fusion of his two principal musical influences, linkages that reflect the erosion of binary opposites associated with the postmodern moment. Working with improvisation and in a style based in jazz, Braxton developed a repertory of ensemble music that rejected primary jazz impulses such as collective interaction and rhythmic propulsion. As an improvising soloist, he produced a large recorded repertory of unaccompanied saxophone music, a genre with no real precedent in jazz, and that had been conceived in the image of modern, "scientific" composition. In the early 1970s, moreover, Braxton began to exercise an increasingly analytic approach to composition, developing a comprehensive model of stylistic interrelations that paid tribute to similar constructions by other systematic composers. These compositional structures appeared not only in certified concert music but also in the context of "jazz" quartet works, whose styles frequently made allusions to the atonal repertories of Webern, Stockhausen, and Boulez. Through symbolic picture titles, Braxton presented the works' structural properties and interconnections, playfully recasting the "serious" language and diagrams of concert composers through a revision of high-culture discourse.

Braxton's experimentalism is especially important because it expresses qualities of blackness beneath the surface of esoteric references to modernism. In all of his work, there has remained a fundamental sensitivity to black-based principles that has informed the character of his stylistic expressions and the orientation of his artistic pursuits. Extending his commitment to modernism, he has widened the range of his musical voice to encompass both compositionally and instrumentally several dimensions and styles. For Braxton, modernism has had a liberating effect, serving as a means of expressing ideas and impulses central to the African-American tradition. He has affirmed what Henry Louis Gates, Jr., has called the "signifying trope" of African-American creative expression, moving in multiple dualities that subvert notions of closure, binariness, and determinacy as he creates a multiply referring, contradictory whole.[54] The center of Braxton's decentered art is the voice of indirection, an *elusiveness* through which he has maintained a sense of autonomy and spiritual freedom while for a time also existing within the commercial constraints of official American culture. Braxton's efforts to defend these idiosyncratic expressions in a three-volume work, *The Tri-Axium Writings,* offers, in itself, further evidence of a fundamentally black-centered resistance to conventional, European-oriented approaches, even as it reinforces ties to the experimental legacy of literary-minded composers.[55]

54. Gates, *The Signifying Monkey.*

55. Sterling Stuckey argues that this uniting of opposites grows out of the West African heritage. Stuckey, *Slave Culture* (New York: Oxford University Press, 1987), 24. Imamu Amiri Baraka (LeRoi Jones) borrows from Ernest Borneman's observations to advance an early interpretation of a resistant, black-centered voice in *Blues People* (New York: William Morrow, 1963), 31. Furthermore, Donald Levine shows that perspectives built on ambiguity have dominated world culture, and that the quest for certainty is specific to a particular historical epoch rooted in seventeenth-century European rationalism. See *The Flight from Ambiguity* (Chicago: University of Chicago Press, 1985).

Braxton, then, continues to bear a marked resemblance to experimentalists, while also expressing qualities that explain those similarities in terms of his cultural and racial background. The black experience has ultimately shaped his creativity, just as the artistry of John Cage, Harry Partch, and Pauline Oliveros reflected their experience in a white world. Braxton's art has been imbued with practices and sensibilities derived from jazz and the African-American heritage, whether expressed directly in stylistic allusions, abstractly in deep-structural patterns, or figuratively in impulses from the black cultural tradition. Similarly, the aesthetic position he has mapped out in the *Tri-Axium* articulates the depth of that influence, both in its arcane theories of pan-Africanism and in the traditional black association between sound and the sacred.

Thus, Braxton has managed to give unitary expression to the converging aesthetics of free jazz and experimentalism, drawing on an extended and multifaceted range of dualisms that has shaped and patterned the texture of his life and work. He represents a new kind of musician, a black experimentalist, whose union of concert music's modernism and jazz has established an archetypal relationship that casts its shadow over nearly every facet of his creativity. Braxton's experimentalism, when turned inside out, reflects the social and musical complexities of the postmodern world as it refers to the legacy of black artists who recast the language of the dominant culture into a rhetorical structure affirming identity, self. In Braxton's life one may observe a black artist struggling with and transcending the constraints of his socially imposed identity. Yet one also discerns reflections of the African-American tradition that, despite profound cultural conflict and disruption, have remained so fundamental to his composerly expressions.

2 Chicago as Aesthetic Center

Anthony Braxton was not simply born an experimentalist. He acquired the foundation for that identity during the course of his early life, coming of age in post–World War II America. Braxton's experimentalism emerged from the changing landscape of urban American life, from a new order that encouraged new ways of thinking about black art and the black artist. A musician ever proud of his African-American background, he benefited aesthetically from the hierarchical confusion and cultural rootlessness of the postwar era, which enabled previously trivialized and devalued black vernacular expressions to gain new value and visibility. Over time Braxton would take the side of the skeptics who, recognizing a situation of aesthetic and representational crisis, would question the authority of highbrow tradition-makers to the point where "tradition," together with its normative restrictions, would be turned on its head. Braxton's intellectual inclinations and radical viewpoints ultimately led him down a creative pathway where artistic activity existed in an open field, where the music-maker found conventions and common practice, recalling an absurdist Marxian image, "firmly planted in mid-air."[1] Braxton never shared with his peers in the jazz world their allegiance to the legacy and community of jazz, not even to free jazz, which rested on a precarious middle ground between tradition and change. For him, the overarching hierarchies and categories defining American music never carried legitimate meaning. Musical life seemed rather like a mixed bag of conflicting stylistic and cultural oppositions caught in a continuous struggle for power. Braxton's perception of a Weberian world of diversity and conflict helped to liberate him from traditional categories and conceptions. At the same time, it created personal turmoil as his pursuits clashed with the reality of institutions supporting conventional notions of genre, style, and value.

1. Braxton's metaphor recalls the phrase, "All that is solid melts into air." Interview with Anthony Braxton (September 15, 1983).

I

From his birth on June 4, 1945, until he joined the army in 1963, Braxton rarely ventured outside of his Chicago neighborhood, the insular world of "Bronzeville," now identified nationally, with forbidding sentiment, as the black belt or South Side. At the end of World War II, the South Side was a kind of city within a city, a six-mile strip defined as much by racism as by urban geography, and housing most of Chicago's blacks.[2] During the next decade, the South Side would suffer from the same conditions that had plagued it since the black metropolis had become a reality after the first large-scale southern migrations earlier in the century. To most outsiders it seemed like a strange, hapless place, shouldering high levels of poverty, illegitimacy, infant mortality, street crime, and juvenile delinquency—conditions that grew progressively worse over the years. Particularly troubling was the acute problem of overcrowding, which would intensify as an incessant flood of new arrivals swelled its population from around 277,000 in 1940—when the area already seemed filled to the brim—to over 812,000 in 1960.[3] Fears of intrusion by what seemed to many like a strange, exotic, and even primitive cast of people led to an enduring condition of unrest as racist whites (and even some African-American politicians and store owners) sought to restrict influxes into segregated white neighborhoods.[4] The frequent, violent responses to racial integration inspired what Arnold Hirsch has called "an era of hidden violence," as the threat, harassment, and assault of blacks by whites went for a time unacknowledged by the local, white-controlled press.[5] As some families doubled up to cover the exorbitant rents, oth-

2. A vivid characterization of the neighborhood, circa 1945, appears in "Bronzeville," a chapter in St. Clair Drake and Horace R. Cayton's *Black Metropolis: Study of Negro Life in a Northern City,* 2 vols. rev. (New York: Harcourt, Brace, 1945; Harper and Row, 1962), 2:379–97.

3. Arnold Hirsch, *Making of the Second Ghetto* (Cambridge: Cambridge University Press, 1983), 17. Hirsch maps the expansion from 1940 to 1960 in an analysis of census reports (pp. 6–8). According to David Wallace, the black population of Chicago on the eve of World War II was "very close to being as concentrated as it could get." Wallace, "Residential Concentration of Negroes in Chicago" (Ph.D. diss., Harvard University, 1953), cited in Hirsch, 4.

4. Images of the black as Other were perpetuated in sensationalistic national reports, such as *Newsweek*'s story of a nine-month-old infant being chewed to death by rats. "War on Slums," *Newsweek* (November 16, 1953), 90–91. Gregory D. Squires et al. report that such restrictions on integration were until 1950 built into the National Real Estate's Code of Ethics. *Chicago: Race, Class and the Response to Urban Decline* (Philadelphia: Temple University Press, 1987), 9.

5. Hirsch, "An Era of Hidden Violence," *The Making of the Second Ghetto.* Hirsch

ers ultimately challenged white resistance, pushing the black belt into previously segregated neighborhoods. By 1960, the South Side had extended west at points to Ashland Avenue, east through the Oakland, Kenwood, Woodlawn, and Hyde Park areas to Lake Michigan, and four miles south into Park Manor and Englewood.[6] While its character varied according to class and surrounding, the South Side had come to be characterized by then as an expansive "Negro Ghetto" seemingly out of control and posing a serious threat to those who tried to remain beyond its margins.[7]

Braxton's firsthand accounts of life on the South Side affirm many of the reports from outsiders looking in. He recalls mass influxes of blacks in and around his neighborhood of Washington Park, which had become by the early 1950s a veritable holding ground for recent arrivals.[8] As newcomers swarmed in, Chicago's businesses began to move out, leading to a decline in jobs in some urban sectors and a general worsening of racial and ethnic ghettoization. Braxton also remembers half-hearted efforts on the part of the city to grapple with the problem by replacing makeshift single-family homes with segregated public structures or "projects" that, when available to blacks, ultimately reduced living space rather than increasing it. Over time, the projects built on the model of the Ida B. Wells Houses paid ironic tribute to the early advocate of black rights as they came to resemble the dilapidated homes they were meant to replace.[9] Rounding out

---

notes that a racially motivated bombing or arson occurred every twenty days in the late 1940s (p. 41). However, reports of Chicago's racial violence did appear in progressive publications, such as William Peters, "Race War in Chicago," *New Republic* (January 9, 1950), 10–12; "Mob Rule in Chicago," *New Republic* (April 10, 1950), 12–13. The silence ended after the riot in suburban Cicero in 1951, which received television coverage.

6. According to a contemporary report, the spread of population had reached two and one half blocks per week. "When Negroes Move North," *U.S. News and World Report* (April 13, 1956), 31. For a map of the population movement, see Alan B. Anderson and George W. Pickering, *Confronting the Color Line: The Broken Promise of the Civil Rights Movement in Chicago* (Athens: University of Georgia Press, 1986), 74–75. Expansion also took place to a lesser degree on the West Side.

7. The "race problem" became the subject of choice in national journalistic features, such as "Top Chicago Law Officer Talks on Race Problems" [Joseph D. Lohman], *U.S. News and World Report* (November 29, 1957), 72–78. For a contemporary account, see Nicholas Lemann, "The Origins of the Underclass," *Atlantic Monthly* (June 1986), 31–55, and his book *The Promised Land: The Great Black Migration and How It Changed America* (New York: A. A. Knopf, 1991).

8. Glen E. Holt and Dominic A. Pacyga, *Chicago: A Historical Guide to the Neighborhoods; the Loop and South Side* (Chicago: Chicago Historical Society, 1979), 99; Squires, *Chicago,* 97.

9. Squires, *Chicago,* 107, notes that funds earmarked for black projects were some-

Braxton's recollections were references to the sheer difficulties of life on the South Side, the street crime, gang fighting, presence of a mob-run policy racket, and hostile police action. His memories convey a sense of the continual frustration its inhabitants endured, living in a world where improprieties and injustice were a part of everyday life, where "machine" politics extended to the particulars of daily living, where racism frequently denied better jobs to even the hardest workers and despite a sense of loyalty to Mayor Daley's early administration.[10] Braxton's portrait of the South Side offers a poignant response to the image of a simple, carefree decade, to the nostalgic and self-congratulatory depiction of postwar American successes. From Braxton's vantage, and indeed from the perspective of most black Chicagoans, "American life" looked much different from that presented according to the perspective of a white middle class.

Braxton's reminiscences grow even more vivid when acknowledging documented reports of racial conflict that reach back to the riot of 1919 and postwar protests at the White City Roller Rink nearby on 63rd Street (1946).[11] He recalls contemporary reports of white mobs attacking black residents in suburban Cicero (1951) and Trumbull Park (1953–55), incidents that struck fear in the hearts of children and adults alike.[12] Postwar efforts to sustain a segregationist legacy were, according to Braxton, commonly discussed in adult conversation, as they were in the black press, which detailed oppositions to what would become a full-fledged civil rights movement. A review of coverage in the *Chicago Defender,* for example, reveals frequent references to racial antagonisms, from local conflicts to NAACP activity, from the Little Rock crisis to black riots in Africa.[13] One particularly

---

times diverted to build white housing. According to Hirsch, the Wells project was initially welcomed by the black community as a possible solution to a burgeoning housing problem in the 1930s; *Making of the Second Ghetto,* 10–12. A contemporary article in the *Defender* indicates that the city named the project after Wells through pressure from Chicago's women's clubs; Meredith Jones, "'City in City' Honors Ida B. Wells," *Defender* (January 9, 1954), 9.

10. Squires, *Chicago,* 76, 79, 84, 129; Hirsch, *Making of the Second Ghetto,* 15; Martin Meyerson and Edward C. Banfield, *Politics, Planning, and the Public Interest: The Case of Public Housing in Chicago* (Glencoe, Illinois: Free Press, 1955).

11. Allan H. Spear, "The Impact of the Migration: White Response," in *Black Chicago: The Making of a Negro Ghetto, 1890–1920* (Chicago: University of Chicago Press, 1967, 201–22.

12. Hirsch, *Making of the Second Ghetto,* 40, 53–54, 97–99, 177.

13. For example, "17 Die in Labor Riot in Africa" (March 5, 1955), 4; George McCray, "In New Africa, McCray Finds Surprise in Ghana: Just Like Home" (December 28, 1957), 1; "Little Rock Crisis—Closeup" (October 5, 1957), 21; Roy Wilkins, "South's Integration Crisis a Top Problem" (October 26, 1957), n.p. All articles ap-

frightening racial incident stands out in Braxton's recollections. In 1955 Emmett Till, a fifteen-year-old Chicago youth, was kidnapped while visiting his uncle in Money, Mississippi, and lynched by a group of whites. Reports of the Till incident, and the subsequent trials that made a mockery of the American judicial system, taught Braxton to fear whites. Braxton has said:

> Episodes like Emmett Till were the kinds of stories I was hearing when I was growing up. . . . And, like most young men on the South Side with vague notions about what was happening on the planet, I found myself wondering if white people were either devils or something else just as evil. There was a big separation between my experience and *Ozzie and Harriet*. "White people" was just a concept.[14]

Yet the single-sided portraits of "ghetto life," images of an ever-present cloud of white oppression on the minds of African Americans—images reaching back to Gunnar Myrdal's *American Dilemma* and Richard Wright's *Native Son*—seem inconsistent with most of Braxton's reminiscences. While acknowledging the difficulties and inequities of life on the South Side, Braxton balances such portraits with vivid recollections of a rich, wondrous childhood, a world where people created value and meaning with what they had. Braxton's South Side bristled with life and intensity. It was a place where people gathered on streets, street corners, front steps, and porches, talking, passing time. The South Side was a world in which urban density generated diversity and complexity, fostering the growth of a vast physical environment of wide boulevards and a busy network of stores, shops, libraries, theaters, churches, dance halls, and bars. As a center of black

---

peared in the *Defender*'s national edition. Coverage in the mainstream press included "The Race Issue Explodes" [relating to political fallout before the presidential election], *Time* (February 20, 1956), 18–19; "Segregation: Long Live the King" [King's conviction after helping to lead the Montgomery bus boycott], *Newsweek* (April 2, 1956), 26; "Races: Integration under Fire" [blacks' testing the Supreme Court ruling against segregated busing beyond Montgomery], *Newsweek* (January 7, 1959), 18–19.

14. This quotation combines comments from two interviews with Braxton: August 21, 1983, and July 12, 1984. References to the Till lynching appeared widely and on a regular basis in the *New York Times, Time,* the *Nation,* and countless other publications. Examples in volume 46 of *Newsweek* include "A Boy Goes Home" (September 12, 1955), 32; "The Accused" (September 19, 1955), 38; "No True Bill" (November 21, 1955), 34. Passing reference would appear subsequently, such as Carl Rowan, "Who Gets the Negro Vote?" *Look* (November 13, 1956), n.p. In the *Defender,* the Till lynching remained the principal story from September 10 through November 12, 1955, for which the newspaper took the unusual step of sending its own reporters to cover the case. For background, see Stephen J. Whitfield, *A Death in the Delta: The Story of Emmett Till* (New York: Free Press, 1989).

media, the South Side supported four black radio stations (including a gospel show hosted by Mahalia Jackson) and several black publications, including the *Defender* and John H. Johnson's magazines, *Ebony* and *Jet*. As a cultural showcase, it hosted countless revues, concerts, spectacles, and club performances; as a center of political activity, it fostered grassroots activism, national campaigns, and the nationalist prophecies of Elijah Muhammad, whose message appeared on community radio and in the newspaper *Muhammad Speaks*. The "black belt," with its poor housing, racism, vice, and crime, symbolized something beyond the statistics that measure humanity against the character of an American mainstream. For its inhabitants, it was a home with a history, a place that stood as a symbol of contemporary black culture, of a people whose lives were every bit as meaningful as the lives of those who enjoyed the comforts of greater material wealth. "Ghetto life," the pejorative label of liberal paternalism, provided Braxton with the basis of a rich experience and perspective, where he learned to be black, to take pride in a culture that did not always fit the prescription of conventional values and behavior.

From the perspective of working-class black Chicagoans, the America of Braxton's youth might well have seemed full of hope and promise. Economically, the benefits of postwar industrial expansion had dramatically improved employment opportunities for all Americans regardless of race, while progressive efforts on the part of black unions and political committees helped to secure positions in places previously off limits to people of color. Reports of job improvements throughout the decade paled only in comparison to advances in education, which, after the watershed decision of *Brown vs. Board of Education,* set the stage for what the *Negro History Bulletin* called "the new voice of America . . . the educated negro" who fought a winning battle against racism and intolerance "in this era of enlightenment."[15] Integrationist efforts in the wake of *Brown* soon extended beyond the realm of education and jobs, as activists, building on efforts of earlier generations, spearheaded campaigns to reverse segregation in housing, transportation, and places of worship. The new

15. "Voice of the New Negro," *Negro History Bulletin* 23 (April 1960): back page, 167. For reports on improvements in black employment during the late 1940s and early 1950s, see "Negroes Getting Better Jobs," *U.S. News and World Report* (December 5, 1948), 94–95; Drake and Cayton, *Black Metropolis,* vol. 1, xlii; Reynolds Farley, *Blacks and Whites: Narrowing the Gap?* (Cambridge: Harvard University Press, 1984), 39. Contemporary references to black successes in the workforce appeared frequently in *Ebony,* which promoted a positive, optimistic image of "Negro advancement." See, for one of many examples, "Speaking for the People," *Ebony* (February 1955), 4–5.

black urban presence, what Thomas C. Holt has called "the greatest political mobilization of blacks since the Reconstruction,"[16] empowered a generation of activists and national political leaders, notably Harlem's Adam Clayton Powell and Chicago's William Dawson, whose constituencies posed a serious threat to the survival of white politicians. On levels economic, educational, political, and social, blacks could point to numerous expressions of what *Ebony* called, in its series of the same name, "Negro Progress"—evidence that racial discrimination would ultimately be overturned.[17] While the enthusiastic expressions appearing in the press may now, with hindsight, seem remarkably naive, the advances of the time provided enough evidence for optimism about the possibility of massive social change, of a future when color distinctions would vanish, when perhaps the very notion of blackness would disappear.

Yet in the day-to-day reality of the South Side it is doubtful that many yearned for the erasure of racial distinctions. Such concerns as voiced in the press were perhaps more common among a small, upwardly mobile middle class whose notions of "respectability" sometimes conflicted with the downhome culture of the South. Most black Chicagoans, however, like earlier migrants, sought above all opportunities to secure better jobs and a higher standard of living while tenaciously holding on to traditions rooted in southern folk culture. While the black working class sought material gain and adapted readily to the strictures of an urban industrial culture, it also maintained the rural patterns and folkways that identified a sense of history and collective self. In fact, the reality of ghettoization may have even contributed to the endurance of the southern past. Encountering a perhaps more subtle yet equally real brand of racism, black newcomers avoided a hostile outer world by carving out of the urban context a version of downhome. Around the South Side images of the South appeared frequently in the names of restaurants, candy stores, and barbershops, as well as in the wholesale reconstruction of communities and social networks.[18] The recasting of the symbols of a southern

16. Holt, "African-American History," *The New American History,* ed. Eric Foner (Philadelphia: Temple University Press, 1990), 225.

17. The "Negro Progress" essays, which summarized black achievements during the prior year, appeared in *Ebony*'s January issues.

18. Such retentions were common among black Chicagoans during the first phase of migrations, prior to World War II. For a masterful analysis, see James Grossman, *Land of Hope: Chicago, Black Southerners, and the Great Migration* (Chicago: University of Chicago Press, 1989). During the 1950s, moreover, the *Defender* documented similar southern extensions in ads for chicken and "Pit Bar B Que" (at Tony's Famous

past helped to secure ties to a cultural and geographic home as it strengthened relations among the new urbanites themselves. As such, tensions between a southern rootedness embodied in the incessant stream of new arrivals and a community of "old settlers" now familiar with the ways of the urban North identified the contours of social interaction operating within the overarching constraints of racism and race consciousness.

Particularly powerful in asserting traditional values and identity was the institution of the black church, which remained a principal fixture in the lives of community members. Scattered along the streets of the South Side and numbering around 500 at one count in the late 1930s,[19] these organizations provided an anchor in traditional beliefs and culture for recent immigrants as they bridged the gap from farm and town to factory and city. If its strength seemed to falter somewhat during the shift, the church nonetheless supplied, as the oldest and wealthiest institution created by blacks themselves, a traditional and perhaps moral foundation for a new, "modern" (urban) way of life. Anchored securely in the traditions of the African-American experience, the church helped the southern-born black "to utilize his religious heritage in order to come to terms with changes in his own institutions as well as the problems of the world."[20] As a forum for musical expression, moreover, the church created a nexus of sacred/sonic linkages, fostering extensions of rural religious musics in the form of black gospel, a style and repertory that resonated with the moral certitudes of traditional African-American religion. When these sacred codes were transferred into the popular realm by Mahalia Jack-

---

Rendezvous; January 8, 1955, 13); merchants selling 'possum, bear, and "fancy coons" (January 15, 1955, 21); and conjurers marketing black cat bones (May 5, 1955, 41). Accompanying the ads were announcements for southern holidays, such as the annual Mississippi Day at Tabernacle Baptist Church (June 11, 1955, 6), and the Louisiana gumbo parties at Thelma's (November 2, 1957, 17). The newspaper also printed news (weddings, obituaries, etc.) about the southern towns from which many black Chicagoans originated. These appeared interspersed with ads for performances by Muddy Waters, Otis Rush, T Bone Walker, and other southern-born blues musicians. In its fiftieth anniversary issue (August 6, 1955, 20), the newspaper published a full-page graphic depiction of the Great Migration.

19. Drake and Cayton, *Black Metropolis* (1962), 2:381.

20. E. Franklin Frazier, "The Negro Church and Assimilation," in *The Black Church in America,* ed. Hart M. Nelsen, Raytha L. Yokley, and Anne K. Nelsen (New York: Basic Books, 1971), 136–37; *The Negro Church in America* (New York: Schocken, 1964). See also C. Eric Lincoln and Lawrence H. Mamiya, *The Black Church in the African American Experience* (Durham, N.C.: Duke University Press, 1990); Cornel West, *Prophetic Fragments* (Trenton, N.J.: Africa World Press, 1988), 4.

son and other Chicago-based performers, they "project[ed] a sincerity of purpose . . . [of] profound religious conviction" that blurred spiritual/secular dichotomies and underscored traditional associations between the sacred world and musical practice.[21] Gospel may have also been instructive as a voice of defiance, especially when civil rights leaders such as Reverend Martin Luther King, Jr., reaffirmed traditional black associations between protest and the church, thus actualizing black music as a moral center of African-American existence.

Also contributing to the sense of solidarity on the South Side was blacks' new identification with Africa, instigated by the liberation of Africans from colonial rule. Reversing a previous disdain for Africans and African influence, many black Americans took new interest in the political developments of the newly emerging states at a time when the world sought answers from America's white leadership about how the victors over fascism would handle racism at home. Interest in Africa was further propelled by the impact of new scholarly speculation about the African basis of African-American cultural distinctiveness and indeed about the very origins of Western civilization as a whole.[22] Soon black publications would begin publishing features on African figures such as Kwame Nkrumah and Haile Selassie, which served to contradict stereotypes of a primitive and debased heritage. By 1960, African culture would be transformed into an image of self-respect and self-determination, reflected in the teachings of Tom Mboya, chairman of the All-African People's Conference, in linkages between soul fashions and ethnic roots, and in the recasting of ancient Africa according to the models of classicism.[23]

21. Ralph Ellison, "As the Spirit Moves Mahalia," *Shadow and Act* (New York: Random House, 1964), 215.

22. Charles H. Wesley, "Resurgence in Africa's Historical Tradition and the American Reaction," *Negro History Bulletin* 24 (January 1961): 81–89; Phaon Goldman, "The Significance of African Freedom for the Negro American," *Negro History Bulletin* 25:1 (October 1960): 2, 6. Providing the scholarly background for this commentary was Melville Herskovits's landmark study, *The Myth of Negro Past* (New York: Harper and Row, 1941; Beacon, 1958). John Szwed contends that, beyond intellectual circles, there had been previously little interest in Africa among American blacks. "Musical Style and Racial Conflict," *Phylon* 27:4 (Winter 1966): 364. E. Franklin Frazier has argued further that "while there is some outward profession of pride in African independence and identification with Africa, the middle class rejects identification with Africa and wants above all to be accepted as 'just Americans.'" Frazier, "The Negro Church and Assimilation," 139.

23. In *Ebony,* see "Birth of an African Nation" (March 1957), 17–24; "Ten Biggest Lies about Africa" (May 1957); "Dark Leaders of the World" (March 1959), 23–30; Lerone Bennett, Jr., "Message from Mboya" (August 1959), 34–43; Bennett, "The African Past" (July 1961), 34–40.

II

Much of Braxton's early South Side experience was formed in the eleven-block neighborhood of Washington Park, which housed over 58,000 of the city's blacks.[24] Located in the southwest quadrant of the black belt, Washington Park bordered the west-side corner of the four-mile park giving it its name. To the west of the neighborhood were the train tracks servicing the Penn Central and Rock Island railroads, and to the north, 51st Street, which also defined the upper border of the park. To the south was 63rd Street, where light industry separated the Washington Park area from the Englewood and Greater Grand Center sections.[25] On a stroll around his neighborhood on South Michigan Avenue, Braxton might see children playing, a friend, a relative, street preachers and blues musicians, teenagers singing doo-wop. Turning the corner, he would pass by his school, the Betsy Ross Elementary School, the "clean-sweep" construction site of the Robert Taylor homes between 51st Street and 54th Place, or perhaps one of the four neighborhood stops of the "El" (Chicago's elevated rail system) running between Prairie and Calumet avenues, on which South Siders could travel the length of the city. On his paper route, delivering the *Chicago Defender,* he would encounter the intimidating presence of storefront pentecostal churches, whose message, Braxton recalls, "could make you beg forgiveness for sins you didn't even commit."[26] Heading toward the South Side's central business district, which by the mid-1950s had moved south from 47th Street to 63rd Street, he would pass by not only an assemblage of black- and white-owned businesses, but bars and clubs such as the Stage Door, the Crown Propellor Lounge, and the 520 and 620 clubs, which showcased major jazz acts and Chicago's urban blues artists. In Washington Park, the South Side's central outdoor recreational area, Braxton might see people playing softball, picnicking, or relaxing, and, on occasion, witness the preaching of evangelists and activists.[27] On the other side of the park, particularly around Cottage Grove Avenue and 63rd Street,

24. Holt and Pacyga, *Chicago: A Historical Guide to the Neighborhoods,* 99.

25. A map of the Chicago neighborhoods appears in L. Wirth and E. H. Bernert, *Local Community Fact Book of Chicago* (Chicago: University of Chicago Press, 1949/1963), unnumbered first page.

26. Conversation with Anthony Braxton (June 1990).

27. Drake and Cayton, *Black Metropolis,* 603. Dempsey J. Travis notes that communists held daily mass meetings in the park during the 1930s. See Dempsey J. Travis, *An Autobiography of Black Chicago,* with an introduction by Studs Terkel (Chicago: Urban Research Institute, 1981), 49. A map of blues clubs in the 1950s appears in Mike Rowe, *Chicago Breakdown* (New York: Drake Publishers, 1975), 216.

he could stroll past many of the area's best-known nightspots, including the Grove Circle Lounge, the Circle Inn, McKie's Disc Jockey Lounge, the Pershing Ballroom—a regular forum for Ahmad Jamal—and its El Grotto Supper Club (the bar tended by future radio personality Holmes "Daddy-o" Daylie), the Granada Ballroom, the Blue Heaven, and the exclusive (and at one time, exclusively white) Trianon Ballroom.[28] And sometimes Braxton might travel even farther east, toward Hyde Park, where Elijah Muhammad established his mosque on South Greenwood Avenue near the grounds of the University of Chicago.

When recalling his childhood, Braxton typically paints a vague and somewhat nostalgic picture, relying on the formulaic retellings that have appeared in numerous interviews. The difficulties that his family would ultimately face—including the tragic deaths of his brother and stepbrother—suggest that it too bore the burden of inner-city living, and that his portrait is as much one of preferred memories as a thorough account of life as it was lived. No doubt Braxton had, early in life, encountered the dark side of the South Side, had "finger[ed] its jagged grain," to uncover, in Ellison's phrase, the depth and pathos of the blues impulse.[29] Yet if these memories look beyond the true character of an early life, they can still, despite their selective focus, help us to understand something about the early perspective of an artist whose social and personal struggles affected the nature of his later creative work.

Common to Braxton's recollections are references to his mother, Julia Samuels Braxton (later Fouché), a newcomer from Tulsa, Oklahoma, and his stepfather, Lawrence Fouché, a worker at the Ford Motor Company, whom his mother married in the late 1940s. Together they provided Braxton, his brother, Clarence, Jr. ("Juno"), and two stepbrothers, Donald and Gregory, with the qualities of tolerance, perseverance, and spiritual acceptance of fate, qualities to which he attributes his decision ultimately to follow his interests and passions. Julia Fouché, Braxton recalls, was particularly careful about keeping a watchful eye over his studies and religious instruction, becoming active in both school and Baptist church functions as a means toward that end. At the same time, he fondly remembers his father, Clarence Dunbar Braxton, Sr., a native of Greeneville, Mississippi, who worked for the Burlington and Quincy Railroad and came by regularly to

28. Travis, *An Autobiography of Black Chicago,* 263–74. The Trianon closed in 1954.

29. Ralph Ellison, "Richard Wright's Blues," *Shadow and Act,* 78.

bring Anthony to parades and shows, and, when he was older, to shoot pool at a local hall.[30] Braxton has also referred to gatherings of relatives, notably with his mother's sister, a fine blues singer, and her brother, "Uncle Willie," whose stories of nights in jazz clubs captured the young boy's imagination.

Yet figuring most prominently in Braxton's boyhood memories are images of friends and play. With his brother, Juno, and neighborhood playmates Howard Freeman and Michael Carter, Braxton created an imaginary world based on the space-age icons of popular culture at a time when the United States had assumed a position of technological, economic, and military leadership. Together they built car models, collected hot-rod magazines, drew pictures of rocketships, imagined science-fictional beings, and created play cameras, a "mirror TV," and other toys modeled after the latest technological inventions and gadgetry. By reading comic books, science magazines, and popular science fiction, by watching Mr. Wizard, Flash Gordon, and other TV favorites, Braxton and his friends textured their lives with the larger-than-life images of experiment and technology. In the symbols of American imperial superiority, moreover, Braxton seemed to find an embodiment of extrahuman strength: rocketships and hot rods became stylized gestures of supernatural forces created by the hands of women and men. The urban folk art of the hot rod, celebrated in car-culture magazines and later by social commentators such as Tom Wolfe, became not only an emblem of power accessible to American youth, but a symbol of the mechanized urban-centered culture in which Braxton and his friends lived.[31] These personalized creations based on standardized commodities embodied teenage liberation as they celebrated American economic strength and myths of inventorly ingenuity. In the German-born scientist Wernher von Braun, Braxton found a boyhood hero. As director of America's fledgling space program, von Braun seemed to personify Braxton's conception of technological advancement. As such a personification, he may even have helped to provide coherence to the anonymous, urban-industrial culture in which Braxton lived.

It is important to recognize the extent to which Braxton had begun to form a patently urban worldview even at this early age. His recollections brim with references to street life, population density, feelings

30. Clarence Braxton, Sr., died in 1971.

31. Tom Wolfe, *The Kandy-Kolored Tangerine-Flake Streamline Baby* (New York: Farrar, Straus, and Giroux, 1965; Bantam, 1977). See especially the title essay on George Barris and "The Last American Hero," a profile of Junior Johnson.

of closure. The intensity of the urban environment became for Braxton a shaping influence, its compressed spatial and temporal character representing what Edward Relph has called in his study of the urban landscape a "[physical] expression of what we are."[32] According to David Harvey, this abstraction of the urban setting correspondingly intensified vernacularism. "While celebrating universality and the collapse of spatial barriers, [the postwar era] also explored new meanings for space and place in ways that tacitly reinforced local identity."[33] Significantly, Braxton's references to mediated culture, to magazines, newspapers, radio, television, and the phonograph, identify images that would become appropriated into the making of a personal black world. While a child living in virtual isolation, whose jaunts around the block or across the lower South Side made up most of his travels, Braxton typified urban youths at the time, drawing upon electronic media, the technological antennas of everyday life, as a means of transferring the spatially foreign into the local present.

In his book *No Sense of Place,*[34] Joshua Meyrowitz argues that postwar media played a principal, causative role in the hierarchical realignment of American life, creating new social and institutional appearances that altered previous perceptions of authority and power. As figures of authority (such as political leaders) grew more and more conspicuous and commonplace in everyday life, they accordingly lost much of their primacy and exclusivity. As a consequence, according to Meyrowitz, their demystified images blurred into the mass of mediated sameness that characterizes the electronic age. Electronic media homogenized our surroundings and experience (and accordingly perceptions of time and place), with the new technologies becoming the "common denominators that link all of us regardless of status and 'position.'"[35] While Braxton's neighborhood may have looked much the same as it did before the war, it had acquired a fundamentally new quality with the coming of the electronic age. Radio and particularly television drew from the outside and merged with the commonplace, glorifying the mundane while creating a sense of transparency and

32. Relph, *The Modern Urban Landscape* (Baltimore: Johns Hopkins University Press, 1987), preface.

33. Harvey, *The Condition of Postmodernity* (Oxford: Basil Blackwell, 1989), 273. Harvey speaks specifically of a 1970s space-time compression in the context of general observations of the modern/postmodern continuum.

34. Meyrowitz, *No Sense of Place: The Impact of Electronic Media on Social Behavior* (New York: Oxford University Press, 1985).

35. Ibid., viii.

interface.[36] Braxton's South Side became a world enlivened by a plurality of information, encouraging the blurring of previous hierarchies and dichotomies between the public and private, upper class and lower, black and white. On a national level, this new equilibrium would provide the framework for the rise of a popular expression stemming from the new prominence of black and working-class culture, which ultimately became a determining influence in the postmodern musical landscape.

III

In his seminal essay on the rise of rock 'n' roll, George Lipsitz presents a compelling argument for a class-based analysis of postwar musical change. Tacitly challenging race-specific models that position black artists in competition with white, "bad guy," musical thieves, Lipsitz, like Greil Marcus before him, shows that the formation of rock 'n' roll depended above all on cross-relationships between members of an interracial southern working class. The appeal of African-American music across race lines, according to Lipsitz, rested on its communal associations and traditional status as a form of cultural resistance. "As the power of government, corporations, and unions expanded at the expense of individual aspirations, methods of carving away limited spheres of autonomy by outwitting those in power became increasingly relevant, and white Americans turned to black culture for guidance."[37] More recently, Lipsitz has elaborated on the theme of crossover to construct an overarching theory of exchange. Employing Mikhail Bakhtin's concept of dialogics, he shows that stylistic development in rock 'n' roll depended on an ongoing process of musical give-and-take that ultimately subverted modernist concepts of hierarchy, repertory, and formalized "works."[38] Extrapolating from Lipsitz's perspective, it becomes clear that rock 'n' roll was not simply a highly

36. See Relph's analysis of "Landscapes in an Age of Illusions," in *Modern Urban Landscape,* 120–37.

37. Lipsitz, "'Ain't Nobody Here But Us Chickens': The Class Origins of Rock 'n' Roll," in *Class and Culture in Cold War America: A Rainbow at Midnight* (New York: Praeger, 1981; Bergin and Garvey, 1982), 196. Greil Marcus's *Mystery Train* (New York: Dutton, 1975) provides an early model for processes of racial and musical interaction, albeit with limited sensitivity to how ideological and racial constraints regulate dialogue.

38. Lipsitz, "Against the Wind: Dialogic Aspects of Rock 'n' Roll," in *Time Passages: Collective Memory and American Popular Culture* (Minneapolis: University of Minnesota Press, 1990), 99–132.

visible fad but a powerful cultural force that exacerbated shifts in social alignment as much as it served as a symbol for processes of change.

Even a quick look at the emergence of rock 'n' roll demonstrates the profound nature of the change taking place in popular musical culture. In the space of three years (roughly 1954–56), the United States witnessed a profound, lasting shift in the nature and orientation of popular music and musical aesthetics. As repertory moved from a body of musicals and torch songs appealing to a mature middle class to tunes rooted in the black vernacular, popular singers such as Bing Crosby and Perry Como, and songwriters such as Irving Berlin and Richard Rodgers, were forced to make room for an interracial corps of young, frequently southern-born musicians from modest backgrounds. While the traditional pop songs continued to thrive,[39] they now stood beside a previously unknown repertory of rhythm 'n' blues and jump styles that had grown out of a separate legacy of African-American music rooted in southwestern swing. The black formal properties of early rock 'n' roll have been commonly noted. They include twelve-bar blues forms, small groups of electric instruments and drums, and a singing style based in blues shouts and vernacular speech. But what made the difference was the activation of a kind of ecstatic energy and "dance-beat" dynamism that incorporates the rhythmic contours of black swing and speech into an affective physicality.[40]

The unprecedented visibility of black-based rock 'n' roll is part of what Cornel West has called the "Africanizing" of American popular music.[41] Following that line of thought, one can discern evidence of an Africanization or "blackening" of the formal character of rock 'n' roll itself. The appearance of a scaled-down group of timbrally distinct, electric instruments—guitar, bass guitar, saxophone or harmon-

39. Appearing alongside rock 'n' roll hits such as Bill Haley's *Rock around the Clock* were the strongholds of swing- and studio-orchestra pop: Mitch Miller (*The Yellow Rose of Texas,* 1955), Frank Sinatra (*Learnin' the Blues,* 1955), Nelson Riddle (*Lisbon Antigua,* 1956), Perry Como (*More,* 1956). See Joel Whitburn, *Billboard Top 1,000 Singles, 1955–1987* (Milwaukee: Hal Leonard Books and Billboard Publications, 1988), 53–54.

40. Albert Murray, "The Blues as Dance Music," in *Stomping the Blues* (New York: McGraw-Hill, 1976; Da Capo 1987), 181–200. Murray refers to black Americans as "dance-beat-oriented people . . . [who] refine all movement in the direction of dance-beat elegance" (p. 189). Cornel West discusses the affective physicality of the African-American music in "On Afro-American Popular Music: From Bebop to Rap," in *Prophetic Fragments* (Trenton: Africa World Press, 1988).

41. West, "On Afro-American Popular Music," *Prophetic Fragments.*

ica, drums—suggests something more than the influence of swing-band rhythm sections; it identifies a fundamental alteration of the popular-music ensemble, finding its source in the structures of African-American music. Liberal use of instruments and objects for coloristic effect, the appointment of melodic and harmonic instruments to fulfill percussive functions, timbral disparity between voices, linear or multilinear (as opposed to harmonic) construction, swinging, "elusive" phrasing that mimics black speech and movement—all share common linkages to a previous era, setting into form some of the defining elements of the African-American musical character.[42] In rock 'n' roll, these qualities have served as a basis for nonharmonic interaction: musicians have tended to accentuate coloristic difference through heightened rhythmic variation and activity, producing a complex web of interdependent voices. The basic blues harmonic pattern on which rock 'n' roll commonly relies—an African-American formal innovation—permits complexity to develop rhythmically, orienting performance more toward linear interplay than to harmonic progression. This multivoiced emphasis is in turn enhanced through vocal phrase asymmetry, amplification—which again accentuates timbral disparity—and seemingly perfunctory and banal instrumental solos that heighten rhythmic drama. The net effect is a continuous, rhythmically dynamic texture, a kind of emotionally heightened stasis that reflects, in historical terms, the music's origins in African-American oral culture, and, as a dramatic, contemporary challenge to European-oriented temporal orientations, its position on the fringe of an emerging post modern epoch.

The formal properties that identify the oppositional character of rock 'n' roll extend beyond its exaltation of the black vernacular. Of equal import is the dialogic nature that within the context of an African-American aesthetic ultimately countered racial specificity and notions of artistic or cultural center. In a compelling analysis of the

42. Olly Wilson argues that many of these qualities are characteristic of both West African and African-American musics. See "The Significance of the Relationship between Afro-American Music and West African Music," *Black Perspective in Music* 2:1 (Spring 1974): 3–22. Also noteworthy is Wilson, "The Association of Movement and Music as a Manifestation of a Black Conceptual Approach to Music-Making," *Report of the Twelfth Conference of the International Musicological Society, 1977 at Berkeley,* ed. Bonnie Wade and Daniel Heartz, reprinted in *More than Dancing: Essays on Afro-American Music and Musicians,* ed. Irene V. Jackson (Westport, Conn.: Greenwood Press, 1985). With particular reference to rhythm and bodily movement, see commentary on the ring shout in Marshall Stearns, *The Story of Jazz* (New York: Oxford University Press, 1956), 12–14; Sterling Stuckey, *Slave Culture* (New York: Oxford University Press, 1987), "Introduction: Slavery and the Circle of Culture."

formation of rock 'n' roll, Bruce Tucker argues that the dialogical character of the music extended beyond racial crossovers of working-class musicians; its subversion of hierarchical divisions and binary oppositions undermined the integrity of Western rational thought and, as such, suggests a compatibility with subsequent images of the postmodern.[43] In its challenge to fixed concepts of race, sex, class, culture, and region, early rock 'n' roll took the form of a radical "proto-postmodernism," a form of subtle musical resistance that disarmed conventional social categories and assumptions of official culture. The leading figures of early rock 'n' roll embodied categorical confusion: Chuck Berry demonstrated an intimate knowledge of white teen culture and suburban life as he projected the seamy, sexual aura of the exotic jook joint; Little Richard occupied the category of racial and sexual Other as the androgynous black minstrel (the self-proclaimed "King of the blues and the Queen, too") to mock middle-class rigidities—the culture of *Tutti Frutti;*[44] Elvis Presley drew inspiration from the racially ambiguous, Memphis cat culture as he transcended racial and cultural specificity in tunes such as Little Junior Parker's *Mystery Train*—an engaging exercise in subtly pulsating rhythms—and *Hound Dog*—a white-over-black cover of northern insights into southern black "originality."[45] Together these became profound forms of creative protest—in Tucker's words, "two-and-a-half minute avowals of social possibilities, strikingly affirmative forms of resistance."[46]

In sum, rock 'n' roll's radicalism took two forms. By foregrounding black musical elements it challenged conventional artistic hierarchies that placed European over American, northern over southern, white

43. Tucker, "'Tell Tchaikovsky the News': Postmodernism, Popular Culture, and the Emergence of Rock 'n' Roll," *Black Music Research Journal* 9:2 (Fall 1989): 271–95.

44. Ibid., 286. Working as a dishwasher in the Macon Greyhound bus station, Little Richard (Richard Penniman) "couldn't talk back to the boss, so instead of saying bad words I'd say 'wop bop a loo bop a lop bam boom' [the refrain of *Tutti Frutti*] so he didn't know what I was thinking. I would also sing *Tutti Frutti* to lighten the load." Notes to *Little Richard: The Specialty Sessions* (1989), 21. The tune became a popular "primitive" number in whites-only clubs, as the message once directed to Penniman's boss now appeared to critique as it entertained the dominant culture.

45. As Greil Marcus notes, the "black" sound of *Hound Dog* was composed by Leiber and Stoller, white, northeastern Jews, who sold it to Johnny Otis, a white rhythm 'n' blues bandleader commonly mistaken for an African American. First recorded by blues singer Big Mama Thornton, it received a rhythmically heightened treatment by Presley. Marcus, *Mystery Train,* 155.

46. Tucker, "'Tell Tchaikovsky the News,'" 282.

over black; by confusing the fixities of race, class, and gender it undermined the epistemological certainties that had defined cultural value according to traditional aesthetic absolutes. For Braxton, rock 'n' roll offered an added value. Its glorification of the black vernacular as a force of liberation would, ironically, enable him to employ that same vernacular to move beyond his own cultural boundaries and limitations.

Braxton vividly recalls his childhood love of rock 'n' roll and the impact it had made on his early life. He was, like many boys his age, a lover of the extremes of a musical style built on celebrations of excess. His favorites included an interracial mix of the most popular, the most flamboyant, and the most outrageous: Elvis Presley, Little Richard, Bill Haley. His special favorites were typically the most familiar: the Chicago-based Chuck Berry and the teenage singing idol Frankie Lymon, who projected an ingenuous, amateurish street style in the context of mass markets and high-fidelity recording. These artists became the first of Braxton's musical "heroes," as he calls them, his imaginary playmates who embodied the interface of the local black vernacular and the official cultural mainstream. With his real-life friends and with his brother, Juno, Braxton sang the same songs while standing on street corners, playing in the playground, and walking to school. Art on record and art in life cut across mediated boundaries as Braxton and his cohorts started composing their own versions of the repertory for casual rehearsals and classroom concerts.

It is quite common for children to make up their own songs and lyrics. But these boys had an added incentive: black urban pop was growing up, so to speak, right in their own backyards. Chicago stood, with New York, as a central force in black popular music, the home of several major artists and the institutions that recorded and supported them. According to the *Defender,* the South Side had become by 1956 "the hotbed for small singing combos."[47] Among them were the Clouds, the Hepsters, and the Enchanters, known mainly to local audiences, and the Platters, the Spaniels, the Moonglows, and the El-Doradoes, who had secured record contracts and enjoyed sizable reputations. Doo-wop, together with other styles of black urban popular music, was, quite literally, built into the structure of Chicago's black community. The music was performed in schools and the streets, and professionally in community theaters such as the Regal. It was

47. "Chicago Learns It Has Hot Quartets for Sale," *Defender,* national ed. (April 21, 1956), 15.

also produced and distributed by the local independent labels that lined "Record Row": United, King, Parrot, Chess, and many others, including the largest black-owned company of the 1950s, Vee-Jay.[48] Furthermore, doo-wop had made its way onto television and jukeboxes, while gaining an added boost from the city's black deejays. For Braxton and his friends, black urban pop had become a profound shaping influence, an ever-present source of coherence that cast the details of the everyday into an encompassing web of black memory and culture.

In symbolic terms, Braxton could virtually hear the identity of the black community fixed audibly in the range of singing and music-making that animated the South Side. These sonic images appeared not just in rock 'n' roll and rhythm 'n' blues, but in the obvious stylistic relationship between his musical loves and the traditional vernacular styles that coexisted in the same musical space. From the blues musician performing on the street he heard more than a song and a few choruses of licks; he encountered a musical rendering of the collective life of southern emigrés living in an alien urban world. As a choirboy in the family's Baptist church, Braxton did more than memorize gospel hymns at his mother's coaxing; he acquired a few pieces of the cultural puzzle that shaped an image of his people. The traditional repertories, together with their popular offshoots, provided glimpses into the cultural ethos of the black community, actualizing the identity of the urban American black. As vessels of acquired knowledge, they preserved Braxton's memories of early life in a complex symbolism of associations. Frankie Lymon's hit, *Why Do Fools Fall in Love?,* the gospel hymn *Old Rugged Cross*—a family favorite—and the blues shouts his mother sang with her sister at family gatherings became personal emblems of his culture, sacred/secular linkages that, like the songs of Mahalia Jackson, embodied a conception of blackness that has lived on in Braxton's memories of his childhood.

Music became, then, for Braxton, a kind of symbolic commentary through which he could observe and understand the perspective of black people. The popular styles he so deeply cherished and that occupy his attention still today, abstracted, in a kind of sonic code, the style and language of the South Side. Clifford Geertz has suggested that when art forms are vital to a culture, they "materialize a way of experiencing, bring[ing] a particular cast of mind out into the world."[49] For Braxton, and indeed for the Chicago community gen-

48. Robert Pruter, *Chicago Soul* (Urbana: University of Illinois Press, 1991), 3–12.

49. Geertz, "Art as a Culture System," in *Local Knowledge: Further Essays in Interpretive Anthropology* (New York: Basic Books, 1983), 99.

erally, black music suggested such a materialization. As a cultural icon, it provided black Chicagoans with a dramatic recasting of the urban experience, what Albert Murray has called in his definition of art "the ultimate synthesis and refinement of a life style."[50] African-American musics of postwar urban culture contained the elements of history and sentiment of the South Side. Musical style corresponded with life style: blues, rhythm 'n' blues, and other urban favorites of a "dance-beat people" expressed the ethos, the identity, and what had emerged by this time as the "soul" of Chicago's black folk.[51] For Braxton, black music was an embodiment of the African-American collective memory, of art as activity, of black peoples' social sense of being in the world. Every song he sang, every performance he heard, every record he listened to reinforced this perspective.

IV

In 1959, Braxton followed the path of his brother, Juno, and enrolled in the Chicago Vocational High School. Located on 87th Street in the southeast corner of Avalon Park, the high school had enjoyed a reputation for achievement and advancement, a place where working-class students of mixed races and ethnicity could learn a skilled trade and, with some luck, eventually secure steady work. While Braxton may have thought somewhat about pursuing a career in skilled labor, he has dismissed that possibility, recalling that he attended Vocational above all out of sheer love of technology. Beyond the sequence of courses in science, mathematics, and the humanities, Braxton favored shop classes, where he learned about electrical circuitry, fixing televisions, and reading the wiring schematics that would later inform the making of compositional diagrams. He also favored drafting courses, which developed his talents as an artist, talents that would show up in his famous diagrammatic picture titles of the 1970s. These studies were complemented with other hobbies that would interest future publicists, most notably his involvement in the chess club, which he headed in 1959, becoming its champion player in 1960.

Socially, moreover, the Vocational experience introduced Braxton to a new world, markedly different from the one he had known around his neighborhood. In the white neighborhood of Avalon Park, blacks were in a clear minority, representing about 10 percent of the student body.[52] Braxton here discovered firsthand the complexities of the

50. Murray, *The Omni-Americans: Black Experience and American Culture* (New York: Outerbridge and Dienstfrey, 1970; Vintage, 1983), 54.

51. Murray, *Stomping the Blues.*

52. According to Wirth and Bernert, the residents of Avalon Park in 1940 were

white world, an unfamiliar terrain that he had previously assumed to match popular media portrayals of middle-class life. Recalling frequent incidents, Braxton has referred to altercations not only between blacks and whites, but also among the ethnically diverse body of white students themselves. His memory of one particular incident—couched in uncharacteristic terms of innocence and tempered with a punning allusion to the minstrel stage—suggests how little he knew about the complex makings of the white world:

> [Before attending Vocational] I always thought white people were white people. Then I had an experience in my first year that I didn't quite understand. I was in English class, and this pretty young lady walked in and sat down. The two guys in front of me said, "Aw, this woman, she's nothing. She's Jewish." And I thought, first of all, how could they tell? All these white people look alike to me. And second, if she is Jewish, what does that mean? Is there a division that I don't know about?[53]

Much of the racial friction Braxton observed stemmed from the controversy over integration and expansion of the South Side. Altercations between Irish and Jews, Italians and blacks, Poles and Hispanics were emblematic of the racial and ethnic tensions in what a 1959 report by the U.S. Commission on Civil Rights called the most residentially segregated large city in the nation.[54] On a national scale, the conflicts reflected a new level of antagonism among the races as blacks took a renewed stand against unequal treatment in housing, jobs, and transportation. This "new black militancy" would meet with a swift backlash as racial struggle escalated and as America moved closer to the edge of what some feared would finally become an all-out black/white uprising. At that moment in 1960, after episodes in Montgomery, Little Rock, and Greensboro, after years of instability and struggle in the urban North, America seemed like a racial calamity waiting to happen, summed up in one national headline as "Everywhere: Tension."[55] Such deep-seated commitment to the oppression of blacks

---

mainly of Swedish, Irish, and German extraction. *Local Community Fact Book,* 65. Anderson and Pickering, moreover, show that the neighborhood had remained white into the late 1950s. *Confronting the Color Line,* map on p. 79.

53. Interview with Anthony Braxton (February 22, 1983).

54. Anderson and Pickering, *Confronting the Color Line,* 80.

55. "Everywhere: Tension," *U.S. News and World Report* (March 21, 1960), 72–75. For other examples of tensions during the period, see, among many others, "The New Fighting South," *Ebony* (August 1955), 69–74; "Boycott on Hollywood?" *Time* (December 2, 1957), 90; "Senator Russell Wants Negroes to Move," *U.S. News and World Report* (January 2, 1959), 14; "The South: Battle of the Buses," *Time* (June 18, 1956), 27.

must have seemed at first incomprehensible to Braxton, who was encountering racism personally for the first time. He soon came to realize, however, that racial conflict was endemic to all walks of American life, engendering a rightful skepticism that would remain with him over the years.

Yet perhaps most directly threatening to Braxton was the inner circle of gangs that had dominated West Side and South Side youth culture. Gangs symbolized status, rank, and identity through regulations of race, ethnicity, class, and gender; as such, they hardened prejudices that divided those within Chicago's lower and working classes. Most of the time youths entered gangs willingly, as early as eleven or twelve. At others—and particularly as gangs grew more violent in the 1960s—the members would enlist new candidates through threats and intimidation. Once members, youths entered into a kind of fraternity with its own social rituals and networks that reinforced solidarity and a sense of group identity. By remaining on the outside, Braxton and his friends sacrificed the privileges of that readymade clique. And by refusing to join, they sometimes even had to bear the burden of gang members' reprisals. "You were either in the gangs or you weren't," he reminisced. "And if you weren't in the gangs, you were really on the outside. I wasn't in on it. I was drawing pictures of rocketships."[56]

Braxton's position on the outside of gang life provides a fitting metaphor of his image of himself at the time. His reminiscences of adolescence return frequently to feelings of anxiety and confusion about the world in which he lived, a world dominated by opposition and conflict, by cliques and social groups, from all of which he inevitably felt estranged. Indeed, Braxton's newly acquired awareness of social and racial tensions seemed to encourage questioning of his own identity at a time when notions of ethnicity, race, class, and gender were consistently being challenged. This sense of anxiety no doubt was further compounded by the reproving glances of a white population that had collectively voiced the cutting challenge to all *Souls of Black Folk,* "How does it feel to be a problem?"[57] Reflecting on the

56. Interview with Anthony Braxton (February 22, 1983). For background, see Gerald D. Suttles, *The Social Order of the Slum: Ethnicity and Territory in the Inner City* (Chicago: University of Chicago Press, 1968); R. Lincoln Keiser, *The Vice Lords: Warriors of the Streets* (New York: Holt, Rinehart, and Winston, 1969); David Dawley, *A Nation of Lords: The Autobiography of the Vice Lords* (Garden City, N.Y.: Anchor Books, 1973).

57. W. E. B. Du Bois, *The Souls of Black Folk,* 15. See, for example, "When Negroes Move North, Many Problems of the South Come with Them," *U.S. News and*

period, Braxton echoes the remarks of various black writers who grew increasingly self-conscious and color-struck. Realizing that he was darker complected than other members of his family, Braxton soon began to notice the ads for skin creams and hair straighteners that appeared in black magazines and newspapers.[58] He also remembers becoming increasingly social and class conscious, to the point of joining a nearby Catholic church in order to meet the middle-class girls who worshiped there. Venturing into the white-dominated business world in downtown Chicago, Braxton would see the "towers of conspicuous administration"[59] where disparities of wealth, material, and well-being reinforced his have/have-not conception of American life. The supposed advances of "the race" reported in the mainstream press were now counterbalanced by everyday encounters with racism and a seemingly endless stream of reports of hostility and violent attacks from daily, small skirmishes to large-scale uprisings in Cicero, Trumbull Park, and Calumet Park.[60] Despite the notable resistances among a burgeoning corps of local black organizations and churches, the realities of urban life became for Braxton a source of anxiety, feelings which were intensified by the trials of adolescence and coming of age.

It was around this time—ca. 1959—that Braxton started playing and listening to jazz. While a good student, he soon realized that he had no real ambitions to learn a trade and consequently never took his vocational studies seriously. Music, on the other hand, gave definition and meaning to his life, providing a social and emotional center in an increasingly decentered outer world. The alto saxophone that his father bought for him became an extension of his creative self, the source of countless hours of activity as he played at home and in the school's stage band, the Melody Makers. Recalling that experience, he will-

---

World Report (April 13, 1956), 29–33. On p. 31, two arrows enclose a picture of a black man, supporting the caption, "This is Chicago's race problem." The caption was meant to refer to the chart below it.

58. For a published reference to teenage insecurities, see "Be Proud of the Negro Look," *Ebony* (April 1955), 58. The essay responded to a teen's letter of inquiry about how he might "improve" his facial appearance.

59. Relph, *The Modern Urban Landscape,* 168.

60. "The Rev" [Rev. David K. Fison], "How to Stop the Riots," *Ebony* (November 1957), 58–60, 62, 64, 66. Other reports include "Illinois: 'Nigger, Go Home,'" *Time* (July 7, 1961), 16; "Suburbia: High Cost of Democracy," *Time* (December 7, 1959), 23; "Race Trouble in the North, Chicago: Where Whites and Negroes Battle Again," *U.S. News and World Report* (August 9, 1957): 31–33; Warner Bloomberg, Jr., "Negroes in the North," *New Republic* (June 18, 1956), 13–15; "Races: Seven Months' War" [Trumbull Park], *Time* (March 1, 1954), 19; "Chicago: Race Troubles Return" [Trumbull Park], *Newsweek* (October 26, 1953), 44.

ingly elaborates on his enthusiasm for the decidedly white, conformist repertory, which consisted of light popular works by composers such as Neal Hefti, Sammy Nestico, and Henry Mancini. Those interests would be challenged (yet never entirely replaced) after hearing older students play the hard bop and soul jazz of Sonny Rollins, Benny Golson, and Art Blakey in sessions after school. Braxton's tastes seemed to straddle racial lines at a time when conventional social and artistic categories were being consistently challenged, when venues such as the Blue Note had departed from the segregationist norm by hiring blacks and admitting integrated audiences.[61] While listening to and learning from the albums of black hard-bop players, Braxton also pursued his interests in the white musical vein. Paying frequent visits to a local record shop a few blocks north of Washington Park,[62] he collected hard bop as well as cool, black as well as white, but remembers most fondly two albums by his special favorites: Ahmad Jamal's *Live at the Pershing* (1958) and Dave Brubeck's *Jazz at College of the Pacific* (1953). Of particular importance to Braxton was the alto saxophonist in Brubeck's group, Paul Desmond, whose languid, full-bodied tone would influence his own playing. As he learned about the variety of players at local clubs, as he read about the central place of Chicago in jazz history, and as he listened to the recorded evidence of that legacy on the programs of Marty Faye, Sid McCoy, and Daddy-o Daylie, Braxton began to imagine a career as a jazz artist.

Working actively toward that end, "of leaning on pianos and playing saxophone like Desmond,"[63] Braxton began taking private saxophone lessons with Jack Gell at the Chicago Musical College of Roosevelt University, where jazz had been a longtime formal presence.[64] Studying with Gell intermittently from 1959 to 1964, he acquired a sturdy foundation, developing strong reading skills, technique, and knowledge of repertoire in both the classical and jazz traditions. Gell, moreover, introduced Braxton to the music of other contemporary white jazz musicians. He found particular favorites in

61. In 1955, Chicago's Urban League cited Blue Note's owner Frank Holtzfiend for hiring artists and admitting patrons without regard to race. "Is Chicago the New Jazz Capital?" *Ebony* (December 1957), 96.

62. Braxton does not remember the name of the store. It may have been Maury Alpert's Met Records, on 58th Street, between Calumet and Prairie Avenues, only four to five blocks from his home.

63. Interview with Anthony Braxton (September 6, 1982).

64. "Chicago, the New Jazz Capital," *Ebony,* 99. The essay notes that Joe Segal, musician and concert producer, directed a jazz club and organized concerts under Roosevelt's auspices.

Lennie Tristano, Lee Konitz, Art Pepper, Stan Getz, and Warne Marsh, artists who would inform his playing for years. Around the same time, he recalls becoming fascinated with the complex arrangements of the Stan Kenton Orchestra, most notably Kenton's recording of Robert Graettinger's *City of Glass* (1951). It was also at this point that Braxton first heard early free-jazz recordings by Ornette Coleman and Cecil Taylor, lent to him by his friend's father. These made little impression on him, beyond curiosity about their anarchic surface.[65]

Braxton's perspective of the music world seemed to have changed markedly by the time he had developed an enthusiasm for jazz. His growing interest in the complexities of style suggest that he too believed jazz to be a serious art, whose subtleties could be appreciated only through effort and whose intricacies could be mastered only through hard work. Living in an age when complexity had become a principal element in the aesthetic equation, Braxton most likely would have defended the superiority of jazz on musical grounds. No doubt he had encountered this view among his older peers, who in turn repeated the positions of Chicago's professional jazz musicians. Turning the pages of jazz magazines and newspapers, moreover, Braxton would find another variation of the jazz-as-art perspective. In this version, the strains of black vernacularism that had once defined the music's oppositional center were recast into a consensus vision of a united mainstream. Originally a form of rhythmic resistance, bop and the postbop revitalizations of the 1950s had been transformed into a remarkable "classical" accomplishment, highlighted by a complex European-based harmonic language and a canon of virtuosic recorded solos.[66] According to the dominant themes in the literature, the young "modern" artist aspired above all to become what was known in jazz parlance as the "complete musician." While many black musicians did in fact hope to develop a sound theoretical understanding, strong reading skills, and perhaps even a knowledge of arranging, these goals stood far from the critical model, which, at its worst, amounted to a jazz version of the well-schooled performer of concert music.[67]

65. The Coleman album was *The Shape of Jazz to Come* (1959). Interview with Anthony Braxton (February 22, 1983).

66. *Down Beat* would elaborate on that canon by continuing to publish transcriptions of solo masterpieces that young players could duplicate and incorporate into their own playing. Among them, Coltrane's recording *Giant Steps* (1959) marked a pinnacle of sorts in the pursuit of harmonic and technical mastery.

67. Many jazz arrangers from the era were trained by concert-music composers. George Russell, Eddie Sauter, Lee Finegan, and John Carisi, for example, all studied under Stefan Wolpe. Institutional support for formal jazz study took place in Lenox,

Coverage from the 1950s shows that many of the musicians favored by jazz journalists had equated artistry with approaches and pedagogy grounded in the concert tradition. Billy Taylor, for example, spoke of performing jazz in "an artistic manner," while Red Rodney voiced his opinion that jazz was now a high art appropriate only for the concert hall. Concerns with history, canon, and tradition were surely on Stan Kenton's mind when he spoke self-servingly of the music's formal exhaustion and need of revitalization.[68] In Dave Brubeck, moreover, the architects of the mainstream found a personification of the newly classicized jazz music. An exceedingly popular performer with academic credentials and concert-music ambitions, Brubeck fit the critical image of an educated authority, which helped to counter the portrayals of jazz musicians as tortured, self-abusive romantics common to the period.[69] In articles and interviews through the 1950s—including in a cover story published in *Time* in 1954—Brubeck offered his personal interpretations of jazz history, reinforcing current notions of musical and aesthetic progress.[70] Such views ultimately encouraged some of the more overzealous commentators to reason that jazz was after all simply an American version of concert music. Jazz figures were not mere "entertainers," they argued, but in reality "introspective intellectuals who would rather read Gide and Sartre than venture into the

---

Massachusetts, and at the Berklee School of Music, which had been running regular advertisements in *Down Beat* for years. The magazine itself promoted formal educational advancement with frequent stories of jazz and academe in the late 1950s and early 1960s. A 1951 essay by a swing-era musician showed symptoms of increasing interest in formal study. See "Bud Freeman Says: It's Smart to Study Arranging," *Down Beat* (March 23, 1951), 15.

68. Sharon A. Pease, "Taylor One of Creators among Progressives," *Down Beat* (August 11, 1950), 12; Jack Tracy, "Make Jazz Respectable, Asks Rodney," *Down Beat* (June 2, 1950), 3; John S. Wilson, "Complete Break with Past: Stan," *Down Beat* (January 27, 1950), 1; "Progressive Jazz, Top Pianist Billy Taylor Defines Jazz, Shows Its Role in Contemporary Music," *Down Beat* (March 7, 1956), 11; "Group Twixt Classics, Now Erased: Hammond," *Down Beat* (May 7, 1952), 1, 4; "First-Rate Musicianship Now the Norm, Says Duke," *Down Beat* (December 2, 1953), 16.

69. During the 1940s, Brubeck had studied with Milhaud at Mills College. In the early 1950s, just after his move to Columbia Records and rising success in the jazz college circuit, he hoped to spend half his time composing concert music. He did manage to complete some concert music, composing, among others, a mass, an oratorio, a cantata, and solo works. "Jazz Fills Role of Classical Composition, Brubeck Learns," *Down Beat* (June 2, 1954), 2. "Brubeck Has Double Life as Jazzman, Classic Composer," *Down Beat* (December 3, 1952), 6.

70. "The Man on Cloud No. 7," *Time* (November 8, 1954), 67–76; Dave Brubeck, "Jazz Evolvement as Art Form," parts 1 and 2, *Down Beat* (January 27 and February 10, 1950), 12, 13 respectively.

smoke-laden interior of a night club."[71] Likened to a hip cadre of Franco-intellectual incarnates—creators of "our country's only original art form"—the new jazz artists would now be most properly heard in the auspicious setting of Newport, home of the New England elite.[72]

In short, published images of jazz had to a far greater extent than before the war taken the pedagogy and ideals of the classical tradition as a model for representation. As a consequence, many black musicians embraced these views, yet in most cases without losing track of the vernacular aesthetic center in which their art was grounded. In fact, publicist efforts to refashion jazz to fit middle-class images of proper concert practice seemed ultimately to strengthen the centrality of "blackness" in jazz. Having acquired new levels of authority and legitimacy, jazz musicians now consciously and effectively set the terms for what identified a black art. The paradoxically empowering effects of appropriation may help to explain why Braxton, a studious and intellectually curious young man, became so attracted to white college-set artists such as Brubeck during a time when many young black musicians resented the commercial success of cool and West Coast favorites.[73] Brubeck, Kenton, and Desmond, together with Jamal, Rollins, and Miles Davis, reinforced Braxton's view of jazz at the head of the totem of musical greatness as they further confused the racial categories to which many others still held closely. Surely the place of jazz in Braxton's aesthetic hierarchy would grow increasingly secure as he learned more and more about the music's history of innovations and innovators through a critical discourse that equated it with the concert tradition.

Wishing to pursue a career in jazz but lacking the experience and expertise to follow that path, Braxton bought some time by enrolling in Wilson Junior College after graduating from high school in 1963. At Wilson, he met several musicians—John Powell, drummer Jack DeJohnette, tenor saxophonist Richard "Ari" Brown—some of whom he played with in informal sessions. Chief among the Wilson contin-

71. "The Cool School, Modern Jazz Lovers Switch from Hot to Cool in Praising Top Musicians," *Ebony* (February 1955): 74.

72. "Newport Jazz Festival, Top Musicians from Dixieland to 'Cool' Play Concerts at Staid Resort," *Ebony* (October 1955): 70–76. Coverage in *Ebony* serviced an aim to improve the image of jazz among blacks. Yet it did so by exaggerating the European character of the music. In the mainstream white press, such representations encouraged massive appropriation, to the point where black artists were frequently trivialized and at times edged out. Many musicians certainly felt that when Brubeck appeared on the cover of *Time*.

73. Nat Hentoff, "Race Prejudice in Jazz," *Harper's* (June 1959), 74.

gent were his future colleagues in the Association for the Advancement of Creative Musicians: saxophonists Henry Threadgill and Joseph Jarman, and the bass player Malachi Favors. But it was another future AACM colleague, saxophonist Roscoe Mitchell—later the principal founding member of the Art Ensemble of Chicago—who would make a lasting impact on Braxton's musical life. Mitchell had returned from army service in West Germany in 1961, where he had been playing alto saxophone in military bands and, on his own time, in informal sessions. (A few of these were attended by the free-jazz innovator Albert Ayler.)[74] When Braxton met Mitchell in 1963, he was already a highly developed musician, who had been experimenting with free playing for over a year.[75] Through Mitchell, Braxton learned to appreciate Ornette Coleman, Eric Dolphy, Cecil Taylor, and other free-jazz musicians performing and recording in New York. Mitchell also helped Braxton to broaden his interests, encouraging him to study early bop players as well as the recordings of John Coltrane, a regular visitor to Chicago, with whom Braxton, like most young horn players, would become particularly impressed. Braxton's association with Mitchell and the others at Wilson brought him a step closer to the jazz life, teaching him about the opinions, tastes, and perspectives of Chicago's black musicians. At a particular session he received from Mitchell a memorable lesson on how far he was from reaching his artistic goal:

I went to this session on a Wednesday, I'll never forget it. People were whispering, "Roscoe is going to show up and play." [At that time] everybody bowed to Roscoe wherever we went. [And I wondered] why are all these people bowing to him? When we would play in sections, there was no difference between us. In fact I was a stronger reader in that period. I was a stronger technician. [But to these people] Roscoe was like a god or something. And when he came in, everything stopped. They started playing *Bye Bye Blackbird.* I could take five years to describe what happened but I will just sum it up by saying Roscoe started playing and I never heard anything like it. I got dizzy. The music was so incredibly beautiful, so *strange* because Roscoe was into sounds, even then. . . . Then I realized there was something happening that I didn't know about. Here I was trying to understand the records [by Ornette Coleman and Cecil Taylor] I had just bought, records which were, to me, very

74. Interview with Roscoe Mitchell (Madison, Wis., April 27, 1988). Mitchell recalls hearing Ayler play in a free style during one session, soloing on a blues.

75. Mitchell has played for me an unreleased private recording of a session from 1962 that included Malachi Favors, Alvin Fielder, and Fred Berry. Playing in a free style, the group sounded remarkably similar to the quartet featured on *The Complete Braxton 1971.*

strange, and I was still trying to decide if I liked them. And here is Roscoe who had already passed that point, and he had found his own voice! Suddenly I understood the difference between myself and Roscoe: I was a student and a good technician, but Roscoe was a *musician*.[76]

V

Following the path that shaped Mitchell's talent—and the talent of scores of musicians before him, including Desmond—Braxton left Wilson in mid-semester to join the army toward the end of 1963. After basic training at Fort Knox, Kentucky, he transferred to the Fifth Army Band, "one of the best marching bands in the Midwest," stationed at Fort Sheridan in Highland Park, Illinois, a few miles north of Chicago.[77] As a member of the band, Braxton learned a diverse repertory that ranged from Richard Wagner to Richard Rodgers, from Ferde Grofé to John Philip Sousa, which they performed in concerts and on weekly radio broadcasts. Other army functions required a more homogeneous repertoire: light concert works together with the march literature he had enjoyed since his childhood. As a forum for musical learning, moreover, the army contributed greatly to Braxton's development as an artist. It gave him a chance to reflect and ruminate, to plan his future, and to think seriously about the rewards and pitfalls of a career in music. Above all, it taught him that a life as a jazz professional would be no easy challenge. Braxton soon found out that many of the older musicians were not only abler readers than he, but were also stronger improvisers. The competition, in turn, sparked his ambition and inspired him to practice hard, often up to six hours a day. He also continued paying weekly visits to Chicago in order to study with Gell, while listening conscientiously to the music of Coltrane, Sonny Stitt, and other black jazz musicians who now seriously interested him. By continuing to learn the recorded solos of his favorite musicians Braxton began to develop a personal style, one that he characterizes as a merging of Desmond's lyricism with Coltrane's emotion, a style for which he would later be known.

It was socially, however, that army life had its greatest effect. Entering the closed social system of a recently integrated armed forces, Braxton participated in a progressive social experiment that had been applauded as an institutional challenge to the legacy of racism and Jim Crow. For some optimistic observers, the army promised to lead the

76. Interview with Anthony Braxton (February 22, 1983).
77. Ibid.

way toward the erosion of hardened racial barriers as soldiers learned to judge one another individually, beyond race and color. Having faced the illogic of racial prejudice, the argument followed, enlisted men and women would transfer their integrationist views into the mainstream upon return to civilian life.[78] While such an interpretation may have made some sense prior to the black-rights struggle, it would seem little more than farcical when Braxton made the transition at the height of the movement. Not only did he leave Chicago for the first time, he also became the first black in the Fifth Army Band. That experience would have dramatic consequences on his social and aesthetic development as he encountered, face to face, the realities of public life beyond the black community.[79]

Braxton could not have chosen a more inopportune time to enter the white-dominated military. By 1963, one hundred years after the signing of the Emancipation Proclamation, the black-rights movement had become suffused with new militance as blacks pitched their hopes high. Demonstrations and marches, which had been previously sporadic, swept the South that spring. Most notable among them was the Birmingham march, under the leadership of Reverend Martin Luther King, Jr., and the Southern Christian Leadership Conference (SCLC), during which 2,500 people—including King—were arrested. Hostile police tactics and, in May, the shooting of Medgar Evers, an NAACP leader in Mississippi, escalated tensions while reinforcing activist commitment. Three months later, the centerpiece of the movement, the March on Washington, took place on the national mall, where 200,000 people gathered in the name of jobs, freedom, and equality for blacks. During the next two years, black protest and racial conflict grew even more feverish as some members of the Congress on Racial Equality (CORE) and the Student Non-violent Coordinating Committee (SNCC), frustrated with white resistance and limited progress, turned toward more aggressive action. Their frustration echoed the tenor of the black community as a whole, which became enmeshed in violent disturbances in Chicago, New York, Philadelphia, and elsewhere. In Los Angeles, anger, hatred, and lost hope ignited a major revolt in the Watts section, which led to renewed violence and coun-

78. Charles C. Moskos, Jr., "Has the Army Killed Jim Crow?" *Negro History Bulletin* 21 (November 1957): 27–29.

79. Lt. Dennis D. Nelson, USN, "A Report on Military Civil Rights," *Negro History Bulletin* 16 (January 1953): 75–78; Gen. Mark W. Clark, "Does Integration Work in the Armed Forces?" *U.S. News and World Report* (May 11, 1956), 54–56; James C. Evans, "Integration, Differentiation, and Refinement," *Negro History Bulletin* 23 (April 1960): 151–52, 156.

terinsurgencies by police and hostile civilian mobs. Surely such incidents were frightening for Braxton as they were for his white colleagues, as he tried to find a place in army life.[80]

Braxton's memories of the first weeks at Fort Sheridan reflect the degree to which racial tensions had affected relations between blacks and whites at the time. Despite official claims of complete integration and racial equality, prejudice according to color seemed to Braxton still very real. He compares the band's initial reaction to the typical greeting many blacks received in Chicago's expanding neighborhoods, employing the metaphor of "the first black on the block: lockers overturned, horns hidden, [actions communicating the message] nigger go away, we don't want you."[81] Cultural and racial differences would, moreover, be underscored by differences in musical taste; Braxton remembers clashes with other soldier-musicians who favored a white, stage-band repertory. While also sharing a fondness for white players, Braxton seemed by then to have adopted, perhaps as an expression of resistance, a special allegiance to black artists. (It is also likely that many white musicians were more receptive to black jazz than Braxton remembers.) Such sense of loyalty to "the race" helps to explain the severity of his words about that past; he called the army on one occasion "the worst thing that ever happened to me," and related on another (upon return from Korea, where he was stationed briefly) his attempt to burn his uniform in a Seattle airport.[82] Social dislocation seemed to strengthen feelings of black pride, thereby reinforcing his budding tastes in bop, hard bop, and eventually free jazz. While it would oversimplify the process of learning to suggest that Braxton's fondness for the music of McLean, Rollins, and Coltrane developed directly from a new social sense of place, it is also more than coincidental that the army experience marked a pivotal change in his perspective. While continuing to listen to white saxophonists, Braxton had developed a new responsiveness to the sounds identified with his cultural heritage, acknowledging the rising presence and authority of the African-American people. For a musician coming from the rich musical background of Chicago, whose tastes were shaped by the world of a highly visible black vernacular, black jazz was something meant to be upheld and exalted. It not only reflected but embodied the

80. For background, see August Meier and Elliott Rudwick, *CORE: A Study of the Civil Rights Movement* (New York: Oxford University Press, 1973); Clayborne Carson, *In Struggle: SNCC and the Black Awakening of the 1960s* (Cambridge: Harvard University Press, 1981).

81. Interview with Anthony Braxton (February 22, 1983).

82. Interview with Anthony Braxton (August 21, 1983).

history and sensibility of a people who were collectively acting out for the first time on a national scale their anger over the inequities they had suffered for years.

It is noteworthy that Braxton has also acknowledged the salutary aspects of the army experience, recalling that over time he developed casual friendships with some white members. Operating within an isolated and transient subculture that could at moments transcend the codes of conventional society, Braxton and his colleagues ultimately learned to turn differences into a basis of unification. Opposing tastes and outlooks, once ridiculed or unspoken, were now joked about; cultural differences seemed over time actually to strengthen personal bonds. Braxton explains how his army experience made him even more receptive to the musical styles of white musicians:

> Listening to white musicians wasn't new to me. I grew up on Paul Desmond; Warne Marsh and Lee Konitz were my other heroes. But I was surprised by the racial feelings throughout the culture: whites didn't listen to black musicians, and most black musicians didn't listen to white musicians. I thought this was really far out. People were missing a lot of music. . . . So rather than put[ting] up some kind of ego wall and not acknowledg[ing] what I was seeing, [I tried] to be open and learn.[83]

Braxton's aesthetic eclectism typifies the liberal views of many music-loving youths in the postwar era. Living in a culture that celebrated on ideological grounds its own inherent diversity, casual listeners and musicians alike have frequently claimed an appreciation for widely varying expressions. The comment "I like all music," common to our era, reveals as much a flexibility in relating to unconventional sound worlds as a lack of strong critical opinion. In Braxton's case, it seemed as if an African-American proclivity to musical adaptation had motivated consideration of all that he encountered. Recalling early jazz musicians such as Jelly Roll Morton and Sidney Bechet, who grew up in the rich variety of New Orleans styles, Braxton remained open to the new while never forgetting his special fondness for innovators in the black tradition. One suspects, in fact, that Braxton's attraction to white practices reflected a procedure of reverse appropriation as he recast the foreign in order to make it familiar. That tendency, moreover, would be heightened in the context of a culture where stylistic fixities and identities had begun to be challenged. Braxton would be content for the time being to listen widely while pursuing his studies in jazz. As his political perspective grew increasingly radical, however,

83. Interview with Anthony Braxton (February 22, 1983).

he would more actively incorporate an eclectic range of styles to voice his personal reading of the cultural nationalist movement. This paradox would take creative form as Braxton began to craft an art based on opposing perspectives of musical globalism and Afrocentricity.

Taking advantage of the free education program offered to service men and women, Braxton attended school on the GI Bill. In 1964—and then against as a civilian in 1967 and 1968—he attended classes part-time at Roosevelt University in Chicago. His aim at first was to study music composition, for composition could offer another vehicle of expression. "I became aware of the significance of writing your own music," Braxton recalls, "because you can make it apply more directly [than improvisation] to your focus at a given time."[84] Following the standard curriculum, he attended classes in music theory, music history, sight singing, and, for a brief time, oboe. His devotion to academic studies described in interviews may be put into question, since he jumped from course to course and soon left school altogether. No doubt much of his restlessness stemmed from the nature of the academy itself. Braxton recalls that it was during a composition class that he realized music school would not provide him with what he was after. Coming from the world of jazz and popular music, he found it curious that his teachers and fellow students treated European music with such reverence. He felt that the emphasis given to European musical theory and the common-practice repertoire seemed narrow and limiting, for it represented only a small portion of the music heard in the United States. Braxton was particularly surprised, moreover, by the lack of attention his professors gave to jazz, a music that he considered highly complex and difficult to master. He elaborates on his impressions, recalling statements by John Cage, Robert Ashley, and other experimentalists who also questioned the supremacy of the European concert-music tradition:

When I was going to music school, many of the things that they would talk about I could not relate to: counterpoint or . . . Of course when I was going to school, [the teachers seemed to believe that] black people didn't exist. They didn't talk about relationships between Asian, African, and Western musics, they only talked about Gregorian chants. They stopped before Schoenberg. . . . I will never forget when I was studying composition. They would say: you can't have parallel fifths. And then they would play them and they sounded beautiful to me. But you couldn't have them because Beethoven didn't have them. The vitality that was so important to the music [of the classical

84. Interview with Anthony Braxton (July 12, 1984). Braxton is vague about the sequence of his studies over the five-year period.

era], through present-day so-called education, had become just a formulated phrase.[85]

Braxton's statement reflects the tendency of many American musicians to dismiss the whole of institutional musical learning, as if their artistry developed in spite of experiences in classrooms, student orchestras, and school bands. Yet it also expresses a justified resentment about the European bias of American musical education, which reaches back to the reforming efforts of Lowell Mason in the 1830s and 1840s as well as to the rise of German-influenced performing organizations and music schools after the Civil War. Confronting the narrow interpretation of "good music" characteristic of concert artists and professionals, Braxton began to recognize how difficult it would be to pursue a career in the marginalized field of jazz. Formal musical education, he now realized, was still dominated by the concert tradition, which was for many of those in positions of power the only true tradition despite the broad appeal of the popular arts among the masses. And because music of the classical realm found its primary support from an educated, white elite, Braxton came to believe that racism surely helped to explain why that music still dominated formal musical pedagogy. When he remarked in conversation about "not growing up until I came out of the army,"[86] he seemed to be speaking above all of his new awareness of the oppositions between musical worlds and the institutions supporting them. From his point of view, surely heightened by the racial tensions of the time, music-making in the United States reflected the general inequities of American life. He saw a rivalry between blacks and whites, between the haves and the have-nots, with patrons of classical orchestras still seeking to perpetuate an outmoded high rank and dominance at the expense of black expressions. While he has stated that he had at this point maintained a pluralistic love of all musics, one suspects that Braxton's real feelings were far more ambiguous, leading him at moments to position black music at the top of his aesthetic scale.

Significantly, Braxton's growing contempt for institutions of American musical life seemed to coincide with his active participation in

85. Interview with Anthony Braxton (September 6, 1982). According to Braxton's theory as outlined in the *Tri-Axium Writings,* Gregorian chant derived from African and Asian ritual musics, which he identifies together as "trans-African" and "trans-Asian progressionism" (cf. chapter 5, part 8). For the views of Cage and Ashley, see Cage, *Silence* (Middletown, Conn.: Wesleyan University Press, 1961); Cole Gagne and Tracy Caras, eds., *Soundpieces: Interviews with American Composers* (Metuchen, N.J.: Scarecrow Press, 1982).

86. Interview with Anthony Braxton (May 6, 1983).

Chicago's black-rights movement. Having grown up in the midst of a massive racial struggle that had radicalized an already politically conscious community—"the city from which the most incisive and radical Negro thought has come," observed Richard Wright in 1945—he was drawn into a movement that by the 1960s had animated the South Side.[87] Most important to Braxton was the Congress on Racial Equality, the Ghandian-based, direct-action organization founded in the midst of other activist groups in Chicago during the 1940s.[88] With his cousin, Rafiki Woodard, Braxton began attending CORE meetings during his weekly visits from Highland Park. By 1964, he had joined the organization at a time of extreme contentiousness within its ranks.[89] As a member, Braxton participated in CORE programs to combat racist policies in employment, housing, and education. Canvassing neighborhoods, participating in rent strikes, manning picket lines, he gradually developed a stake in Chicago's civil rights movement, witnessing its triumphs and ultimately, in response to savage brutality and enduring racial inequities, its turn toward violent action.

Most lasting on a personal level was Braxton's acquaintance in his late teens with a young woman who helped him to focus his intellectual direction. Politically astute and well-read, Shosana Ori introduced Braxton to a body of progressive literature that would form the basis of his political views. Together they read widely, pursuing interests in philosophy (Marx, Freud), fiction (Dostoevsky), and the occult. Through Ori and other friends on the South Side, moreover, Braxton came in touch with the perspectives of Du Bois, Garvey, Malcolm X, and other black intellectuals who had helped to define the African basis of the nationalist movement. After this episode, Braxton began in earnest to read on his own, particularly the novels of Richard Wright, Ralph Ellison, James Baldwin, and other black authors who made racial issues, and in Ellison's case, jazz, the subjects of their books.

Braxton's pursuits suggested a struggle for self-definition, for a personal identity that would mesh with his developing intellectual and creative interests. He found an early answer to that in CORE and in the community of young artists and activists on the South Side. Among Chicago's African-American artists and intellectuals, Braxton sensed a like-mindedness that reinforced his political views and ulti-

87. Wright, introduction to Drake and Cayton, *Black Metropolis,* xvii.

88. These included the Christian-pacifist Fellowship of Reconciliation, and the Council against Discrimination, the Catholic Interracial Council. Hirsch, *Making of the Second Ghetto,* 176.

89. Robert Weisbrot, *Freedom Bound: A History of America's Civil Rights Movement* (New York: W. W. Norton) 169.

mately made an impact on his creative direction. Increasingly, nationalist perspectives had become a shaping force in his musical world. While resisting exclusionist doctrine and the idea of a separate black state, Braxton began to pursue an artistic path that he felt expressed his true self, to build an art-world that celebrated individualism and blackness in the face of societal adversity. By reading radical literature and simply by growing more sensitive to the workings of the world, he would soon more fully recognize the limits to freedom of expression—particularly those imposed on an unschooled black musician. In the United States, a nation that, in the words of Harold Cruse, "idealizes the rights of the individual above everything else," even art had been "dominated by the social power of groups, classes, in-groups and cliques," leaving marginalized artists in a compromised position.[90] Aware of what he would be up against, Braxton grew increasingly committed to intellectual pursuits. In a world in which struggle seemed endemic to life, education was now, recalling a legacy of critical teachings from Frederick Douglass to Malcolm X, "a necessary part of the total picture."[91] This ideological commitment to learning ultimately vitalized Braxton's interest in the free-jazz movement, whose ironic mix of Afrocentric impulses and the rarefied language of modernism would be claimed as an emblem of the community of radically minded black intellectuals.

VI

Traditionally, jazz musicians have been more or less unmindful of the details of politics, owing perhaps to a deep-seated skepticism about what good the white-dominated political sphere has done for the African American. During the civil rights movement, however, musicians demonstrated a sympathy if not a commitment, performing at benefit concerts and speaking out publicly in the name of black rights. Principal among the early supporters were popular and mainstream artists who defended the still-dominant integrationist policies of the NAACP. Following the lead of Nat Cole, a longtime NAACP supporter during the 1950s, a few major figures—Duke Ellington, Sarah Vaughan, Dave Brubeck, Herbie Mann—lent their names to the civil rights movement through benefit performances for the NAACP in 1962.[92]

90. Cruse, *Crisis of the Negro Intellectual* (New York: Quill, 1967/1984), 7–8.

91. Interview with Anthony Braxton (February 22, 1988).

92. Leonard Feather, "On the Racial Front," *Down Beat Music '63*, 20–22. Ellington performed a benefit for the NAACP at the Metropolitan Opera House in 1951. See

Others—Count Basie, Art Blakey, as well as Ellington—declared their support of the sit-ins taking place throughout the South.[93] Around the same time, Dizzy Gillespie gave expression to what Leonard Feather called a turn toward a "new [jazz] militancy" when he publicly recalled personal racial incidents and sometimes sarcastically expressed "black anger" on stage.[94] The source of that anger was hardly new, of course. But increasing opportunities for musicians to voice their political opinions undoubtedly caused consternation among some writers who believed that issues of politics and music were best kept separate.[95] Already by the late 1950s, the commentary of a few musicians had acquired a more radical cast that seemed truer to the impassioned involvement of civil rights leaders. Charles Mingus had developed a reputation for his caustic—and perhaps, for some middlebrow audiences, frightening—statements against racism; his "Faubus" compositions (1959–1968), for example, ridiculed the former governor of Arkansas, Orval Faubus, known for his racist tactics. Mingus and others drew attention to their views by employing politically suggestive titles or by making artistic reference to an African background that, after emancipation from colonialist rule, had vitalized the African-American community.[96] Even earlier, black artists

---

Jack Tracy, "Here's News Capsule of Music World for 1951," *Down Beat* (January 11, 1952), 3. His pleas for NAACP support were covered in "Jackie, Duke Call for Support of NAACP," *Chicago Defender* (December 14, 1957), 22. In 1964–1965, moreover, jazz performances for political causes occurred sporadically, such as when Charles Mingus appeared at Town Hall to benefit the NAACP, and Ayler and Taylor played at the Five Spot to support CORE. By the late 1960s, political benefits by free-jazz musicians were common. For background, see Burt Korall, "Dissent within the Ranks," *Down Beat* (January 11, 1968), 15; "Black Order of Revolutionary Enterprise," *Down Beat* (July 24, 1969), 30; "Black Solidarity Festival," *Down Beat* (July 23, 1970), 30. A reference to Cannonball Adderley's and Gene Ammons's performance at a Chicago SCLC benefit appeared in the *Westside Torch* (October 24–31, 1969), n.p.

93. Nat Hentoff, notes to *We Insist! Max Roach's Freedom Now Suite* (Sweden: Amigo AMLP 810). This is a reissue of the original album on the Candid label.

94. Feather, "Jazz at the Crossroads," *Negro Digest* (May 1963), 88–89. (This is a reprint of an essay originally published in *Hi-Fi/Stereo Review*.) Gillespie called his recent African tour "apologies for the State Department" and mockingly warned his white audience: "You better be ready, 'cause we're fixin' to take over the world."

95. Ira Gitler voiced that opinion during a roundtable discussion on jazz and black protest, published as "Racial Prejudice in Jazz," *Down Beat* (March 15, 1962), 20:26.

96. Duke Ellington had made racism an issue already in the 1940s with his *Deep South Suite* (1946). In the 1950s and 1960s, moreover, Africa had become a symbol of black emancipation in several works, including Art Blakey's *Message from Kenya* (1953) and *Ritual* (1957), the latter inspired by a trip to Africa; Sonny Rollins's *Airegin* (1954) (Nigeria spelled backward); Randy Weston's *Uhuru Afrika* (1960) and *Music*

such as Art Blakey, Sahib Shihab (Eddie Gregory), al-Hajj Abdullah Rasheed Ahmed (Lynn Hope), and Ahmad Jamal (Fritz Jones) embraced a brand of African nationalism, converting to the Moslem faith. In certain cases, this conversion took the form of the radically separatist doctrine advanced by the Nation of Islam, an ironic choice, given orthodox Islam's strict prohibition of musical participation.[97] Perhaps most notable among politically active jazz musicians was, however, singer Abbey Lincoln. A collaborator with Max Roach on the historic recorded protest against pan-Africanist oppression, *We Insist! Freedom Now Suite* (1960), Lincoln had been well known in jazz circles for her advocacy of the African "roots" movement and dedication to black rights, a commitment expressed artistically on the release *Straight Ahead* (1961). In 1962, both Lincoln and Roach—subsequently partners in marriage—were given a chance to air their views during a hostile roundtable discussion with jazz critics affiliated with *Down Beat,* published in a two-part series as "Racial Prejudice in Jazz."[98]

---

from the New African Nations (1963); Max Roach's *Garvey's Ghost* (1961) and *Man from South Africa* (1961); John Coltrane's *Liberia* (1960) and *Africa* (1961); and Wayne Shorter's *Juju* (1964) and *Nefertiti* (1967). Mingus's *Pithecanthropus Erectus* (1956) paid tribute to theories of an African basis for humankind, popularized in 1959 by Louis B. Leakey. The allusions appeared in the wake of African tours by jazz musicians, beginning with Louis Armstrong's staged publicity appearances for Edward R. Murrow's *Saga of Satchmo.* A series of State Department–sponsored tours began with Wilbur De Paris's performances in 1957. See Nat Hentoff, "Jazz in Africa," *Nation* (January 4, 1958), 16–17; "Satchmo Is a Smash on the Gold Coast," *Life* (June 11, 1956), 38–39. References to domestic politics appeared in, among other works, Jackie McLean's *Let Freedom Ring* (1962), Andrew Hill's *Black Fire* (1963), Rollins's *Freedom Suite* (1958), and Nina Simone's and the New York Contemporary Five's homages to Medgar Evers, respectively *Mississippi Goddamn!* (1963) and *The Funeral* (1963).

97. "Moslem Musicians: Mohammedan Religion Has Great Appeal for Many Talented Progressive Jazz Men," *Ebony* (April 1953), 107–9. I thank Eltigani Gaafar Eltahir for calling my attention to this article and noting the irony of the Muslim musicians' embrace. See also C. Eric Lincoln, *The Black Muslims in America,* rev. ed. (Boston: Beacon Press, 1961/1973); Yvonne Yazbeek Haddad, ed., *The Muslims in America* (New York: Oxford University Press, 1991).

98. *Down Beat* (March 15 and 29, 1962); respectively, 20–26, 22–25. The discussion centered on Ira Gitler's criticism of Lincoln's LP, criticism Lincoln took to be racist. It is certain that Lincoln's career suffered from her political involvement, which many critics seemed to find inconsistent with artistic practice. Most likely they would have found such political expression unobjectionable if it expressed a more liberally centered viewpoint. Furthermore, Roach's equation of jazz, Africa, and protest appeared most overtly in two articles published in the Nation of Islam's newspaper, *Muhammad Speaks.* In the first essay, Roach writes: "Jazz actually was founded in African chants and songs. It began as an expression of the pain and suffering endured by chained,

The contentiousness of the exchanges appearing in the *Down Beat* report reflected the background of escalating racial, cultural, and aesthetic tensions that had, from the 1940s, pitted black against white, musician against critic. As white-oriented official culture came increasingly to dominate perspectives of jazz practice and conventions, as white musicians consistently fared better at obtaining the best jobs and recording contracts, many African-American musicians resisted what they deemed a broad-scale appropriation by recasting artistic correctness in the image of the black vernacular. "Real jazz," according to many practitioners, was now rooted in the images and styles of downhome blues and pentecostal churches, and more specifically in the elusive rhythmic and timbral character that has traditionally characterized black styles of movement and speech. "Soul jazz" became, as Nat Hentoff comments, an expression of "fierce pride" by those who had been "denied full acceptance as individuals outside of jazz," as well as a creative "fortress [that] excluded the squares and most white jazzmen."[99] By inverting a rigid, consensus-oriented critical category to favor the black cultural past, musicians such as Cannonball Adderley redefined the "mainstream" as something based in the African-American tradition. "Anybody who is familiar with my music," Adderley commented, "understands my feeling . . . about staying near the roots of the mainstream of the plant."[100] Significantly, some writers misinterpreted such concerns to mean the classic recordings of an institutionally framed past. For example, Nat Hentoff expressed surprise at how "shockingly little" musicians knew about jazz recorded history and speculated that their rejection of theory and classification related (illogically, it would seem) to a "fear of [stylistic] newness."[101] Albert Murray has suggested, however, that anti-academicism revealed not revolution but a spiritual aesthetic center:

> Even when some of those who aligned themselves with bop, cool, and the special extensions of John Coltrane and Ornette Coleman, for example, used to claim that the new music represented a new and even revolutionary message, they never really addressed themselves to the content of the new message, or the old one, for that matter. . . . But percussive incantation, purification,

---

innocent black men, women, and children deep in the dark, damp filthy holes of slave ships crossing the Atlantic." "Max Roach on Jazz: How Whites Made $Billions from Negro Art Form," *Muhammad Speaks* (December 15, 1962), 20–21; "Max Roach on Future of Jazz," *Muhammad Speaks* (December 30, 1962), 20–22.

99. Hentoff, "Race Prejudice in Jazz: It Works Both Ways," *Harper's* (June 1959), 76; "The Murderous Modes of Jazz," *Esquire* (September 15, 1960), 91.

100. Lerone Bennett, Jr., "The Soul of Soul," *Ebony* (December 1961), 112.

101. Hentoff, "Murderous Modes," 88–89.

and fertility rituals, and ceremonies of affirmation . . . are precisely what their work is very much about.[102]

Soul jazz, then, that seemingly playful and sarcastic expression commonly remembered by jocular (and often sexist) titles such as *Home Cookin'*, *Juicy Lucy,* and *Opus de Funk,* had been armed with the power of a ritualistic cultural past, thus securing it from the appropriative tendencies of a white-centered mainstream.

By 1965, critical speculation about the meaning of black musical creativity had shifted from soul jazz to free jazz, motivating new interest in the significance of the free movement as a social symbol.[103] Once judged more specifically on musical grounds, free jazz became a new source of speculation as writers began to draw links between the movement's strident language and the intimidating challenges of black militancy. Most notable among the critics were Imamu Amiri Baraka (LeRoi Jones) and Frank Kofsky, whose attacks on the critical community and a few white jazz musicians, set the tone for subsequent commentary.[104] Among performers, published discussions of politics and race typically focused on their own professional and economic difficulties, which they attributed to the preponderence of racist record producers and club owners rather than to the inaccessibility of their iconoclastic music. More outward-looking and outspoken was tenor saxophonist Archie Shepp, who advanced a radical and at times threatening doctrine that, he implied, represented the views of all black free-jazz musicians.[105] In a group of interviews and essays from 1965 and 1966, Shepp chastised the mainstream community, branding it racist while proclaiming free jazz to be above all the voice of rebel-

102. Murray, *Stomping the Blues,* 229–30.

103. It is noteworthy that Norman J. O'Connor complained about the lack of political initiative among jazz musicians in an editorial published in *Jazz* 4:9 (1965): 5. Leonard Feather made similar remarks in his essay "On the Racial Front," in *Down Beat's Music '63,* criticizing musicians for their "lack of militancy" (pp. 20–22). These comments suggest that free jazz had yet to be associated with radical politics.

104. Kofsky's positions appeared first in a series of essays published in *Jazz.* They were consolidated as a Ph.D. dissertation (University of Pittsburgh) and published as *Black Nationalism and the Revolution in Music* (New York: Pathfinder, 1970). Baraka's comments about the white saxophonist Frank Smith appeared in "Apple Cores #6," *Black Music* (New York: William Morrow, 1967).

105. Alongside the moderate interpretations of John Coltrane, Don Cherry, Albert Ayler, and John Tchicai, Shepp's claim of representing a musicians' consensus would appear exaggerated. See, for example, Mike Hennessey, "Cherry's Catholicity, a Kaleidoscopic View of Jazz," *Down Beat* (July 28, 1966), 14–15; Dan Morgenstern, "John Tchicai: A Calm Member of the Avant-Garde," *Down Beat* (February 10, 1966), 20–21, 49–50.

lion of the black people.[106] Ironically, Shepp's comments bear a resemblance to the racially questionable remarks of Norman Mailer, whose essay "The White Negro" portrayed jazz as the primal scream of an emasculated black male. As with Mailer's romantic inaccuracies, it was Shepp's equation of an antiwhite radicalism and free jazz that drew the most attention from the press, which had summed up the movement with the simplistic formula "Black, Angry, and Hard to Understand."[107]

Baraka, Kofsky, and Shepp advocated a musical brand of revolutionary nationalist opinion, and for that they have been much maligned in the jazz press. They called attention to issues many thought stood beyond the music, verbalizing the collective frustration of a community that had suffered greater inequality and more indignities than perhaps any other artistic group in recent American history. In many ways, their pointed commentary did much good. For example, it stressed the artistic stature of the free-jazz musician, it impressed upon jazz performers and listeners the desperate importance of the civil rights movement, and it exposed the severely limited range of a supposedly "objective" body of criticism. Furthermore, radical jazz criticism performed a musically specific service by underscoring the disparities between jazz and pop at a time when many seemed to confuse jazz culture with likenesses of the white hipster, portrayed at the height of mainstream appropriation as, for example, Jerry Lewis's *Nutty Professor*.[108] Yet in other ways, these same figures, however un-

106. Shepp, "A View from the Inside" (39–42, 44) and "Point of Contact: A Discussion," *Down Beat's Music '66*, 19–21, 24–26, 28–31, 110–11; "An Artist Speaks Bluntly," *Down Beat* (December 16, 1965), 11; "On Pugilism," *Jazz* 5 : 7 (1966): 7. In his essay "The Black Musician in White America," moreover, Larry Neal offered this counterpoint: "Recently musicians and writers like Archie Shepp and LeRoi Jones have referred to the music personified by Ornette Coleman and Cecil Taylor as 'revolutionary music.' I feel that this is an abuse of terms. The music . . . is not revolutionary in any manner that is socially observable. The music is exciting and extremely artistic. . . . However, in order for this music to become revolutionary, it must extend itself into the black community in a manner which, heretofore, it has failed to do." *Negro Digest* 16 : 5 (March 1967): 53.

107. A profile of the movement by Nat Hentoff appeared with that title in the *New York Times Sunday Magazine* on December 25, 1966. Hentoff began the article with Shepp and his polemics, later explaining that the movement had many meanings beyond the association with radicalism. It would seem that Hentoff's (or his editor's) desire for an engaging lead conflicted with his typically judicious reporting. Mailer's essay "The White Negro" was originally published in *Advertisements for Myself* (New York, 1954), 302–22, republished in *Dissent* 4 : 3 (Summer 1957): 276–93.

108. In the 1963 film, Lewis imbibed a potion that transformed him from the stereotype of the nerdy academic scientist to another, a slick-haired, cigarette-smoking,

wittingly, helped to defuse a movement they sought to empower. By taking on the role of spokespersons who declared free jazz a sonic expression of black power, they oversimplified the ideological dimensions of the music. This, in turn, permitted aesthetically conservative writers to ridicule the movement while maintaining a seemingly objective stance. Free jazz, that loud, "nonmusical noise," what later observers would call "the sounds of black protest," could be dismissed outright by simply repeating the claims of its representatives.[109]

A crucial element in the free-jazz aesthetic was the belief, shared by many in the circle, of the spiritual basis of the modernist jazz language. Investigating traditional associations between sound and the spirit that extend back to early slavery and perhaps even to an African past, these innovators gave new immediacy to the twin voices of protest and transcendence that, Lawrence Levine argues, share common roots in the sacred world of traditional African-American culture.[110] The identification of such linkages does not, however, affirm essentialist views of an aesthetic continuity stretching back to an ancient wellspring. Early free-jazz musicians were not African, musically, culturally, or otherwise; nor were, for that matter, any of their musical contemporaries in soul, funk, or blues. But they did draw from the image of blackness, from the elements of distinction that identify the African-American musical language (and most specifically, its linear orientation and body-imaging, ideologically elusive rhythms) to assert a sense of social and artistic self. By reclaiming sacred-sonic linkages

---

womanizing jazz musician. Compare this image to the versions of Braxton appearing in the jazz press during the 1970s (cf. chapter 6).

109. See J. L. Commoli and Philippe Carles, *Free Jazz/Black Power* (Paris, 1971); A. B. Spellman, "Revolution in Sound: Black Genius Creates a New Music in Western World," *Ebony* (August 1969), 84–89; Lloyd Miller and James Skipper, "Sounds of Black Protest in Avant-Garde Jazz," in *The Sounds of Social Change*, ed. R. Serge Denisoff and Richard Peterson (Chicago: Rand McNally, 1972). In these instances, the authors praise the music as they perpetuate negative stereotypes that equate free jazz with black rage.

110. Levine, *Black Culture and Black Consciousness* (New York: Oxford University Press, 1977), 49. Spiritualist associations appeared strongest during the antebellum period, when music, particularly the spiritual, stood centrally in everyday black rural life, confounding the sacred/secular dialectic that had dominated other sectors of Western culture. While Levine may rightly argue that black spiritual wholism collapsed after the Civil War, there is reason to believe that the sacred world has survived through music, secular or otherwise, to a greater extent than recognized. See Neil Leonard, *Jazz, Myth and Religion* (New York: Oxford University Press, 1988); Sterling Stuckey, *Slave Culture* (New York: Oxford University Press, 1987); John Szwed, "Afro-American Musical Adaptation," in *Afro-American Anthropology*, ed. Norman E. Whitten and J. Szwed (New York: Free Press, 1970), 219–30.

for their own uses, black artists underscored the traditional importance of a spiritual center in African-American performance, even if the contexts, meanings, and forms of that association have changed over the years.

In his early commentary on free-jazz practice, Ornette Coleman related views that seemed to owe to a spiritual belief in the emancipation of black music. Outlining his conception of a motivically and rhythmically generated music, he explained to Martin Williams that musicians should "play the music and not the background" if they hoped to enliven the emotional basis of jazz.[111] By "background" Coleman implied harmony, and his comments suggest that he had perceived this European element as a suppressor of the fundamental—and seemingly spiritual—timbral and rhythmic properties of traditional African-American music. Comparing musical expression with liberation, moreover, Coleman told Nat Hentoff, "I believe music is a free thing . . . as natural as the air we breathe." And in another instance, he stated emphatically, "When [a musician] tries to do the best he can his own way . . . he's just showing [that] God exists."[112]

Coleman's departure from harmony represented a kind of psychic autonomy from the constraints on which jazz had been previously based. He was perhaps the first among the free players to introduce the idea of improvisational freedom signifying cultural freedom, albeit in terms more poetic than overtly ideological. His linear-rhythmic orientation, which alluded to practices stemming from the New Orleans past, may be interpreted as an effort to revive African-American performance practices that had been lost, or at least repressed, during an era of increasing institutional control over the nature and reception of the arts.[113] Indeed, free jazz seemed above all to reassert practices based in the African-American legacy, notably the highly developed rhythmic properties that "elasticize the jazz language,"[114] at a time

111. Martin Williams, notes to *Free Jazz* (1960).

112. Hentoff, *The Jazz Life* (New York: Da Capo, 1975), 246. In his essay "To Whom It May Concern," *Down Beat* (June 1, 1967), Coleman asks: "Why don't we Americans, who have a duty to our neighbor and our mother country, get off this was-jazz [*sic*], race-jazz, poverty-jazz, and b.s. and let the country truly become what it is known as (God Country)—unless we fear God has left. . . . Maybe God will let us all go back home." For Coleman's elaboration, see Hentoff, "The New Jazz—Black, Angry, and Hard to Understand," 10.

113. Coleman makes reference to free music's association with the New Orleans tradition in his notes to *This Is Our Music* (1960) and (as told to Gary Kramer) *Change of the Century* (1959). See also Shepp's comments about the same musical relationship in the notes to Coltrane's *Ascension* (1965).

114. Hentoff, "Murderous Modes," 90. Such notions of elasticity refer to the elusive

when parallel reassertions of "blackness" were appearing in popular sacred musics (gospel) and the sacred-centered popular art of Little Richard, Aretha Franklin, and James Brown.

Coleman's early allusions to psychological and spiritual freedom prefigured—and may have even directly encouraged—commentary by others who drew direct associations between spiritualism, politics, and free jazz. In his impassioned appeals for a new musical spiritualism, for example, Albert Ayler called attention to the emerging nationalist implications of the free-jazz movement. Ayler had won the respect of many musicians and critics for taking Coleman's linear approach a step beyond its melodic-based, note-scale implications. In some of his best work, he achieved a kind of linear purity, creating solos based on sweeping flashes of color that revealed no clear pitch differentiation. The linear, collective orientation of his improvised music, together with its frequent allusions to the American musical past—appearing in the form of folk tunes and marches—suggested that he shared Coleman's interest in premodern and preindustrial expressions of the black heritage.[115] Ayler's departure from the constraints of scale, harmony, and form underscored his commitment to a "free, spiritual music" that "frees the mind" and enables one to "find out more about yourself." Departing from the harmonic conventions of bop, which repressed feeling, Ayler, like Coleman, sought to uninhibit emotional expression. "[Bop] was too constricting. . . . I've lived more than I can express in bop terms. . . . Why should I hold back the feeling of my life, of being raised in the ghetto of America. It's a new truth now."[116]

Nationalist and spiritualist oppositions to mainstream aesthetic conventions acquired a new resonance after John Coltrane joined the free-jazz ranks. Through his influence, a new generation of young players would embrace spiritualist interpretations of jazz that linked free playing with the music of Africa and black America. By the early 1960s, Coltrane, who was, with Sonny Rollins, the undisputed leader of hard-bop tenor saxophonists, began to move toward free playing, first with a recorded collaboration with Don Cherry, then through his

---

character of the signifying voice as well as metaphorically to the rhythmic contours of black dance. See, for example, Cecil Taylor's comment about re-creating dance movement in his piano performance practice. Bill Dobbins, "Cecil Taylor," *The New Grove Dictionary of Jazz,* 2:522.

115. On the album *New York Ear and Eye Control* (1964), Ayler introduced true collective collaborations that broke from the solo/rhythm orientation typical of free jazz, prefiguring the works on AACM recordings.

116. Nat Hentoff, "The Truth Is Marching In," *Down Beat* (November 1966), 16–18, 40.

scandalous "anti-jazz" experiments with Eric Dolphy.[117] On his recordings from 1965 to 1967, Coltrane wholeheartedly embraced free jazz, transposing his harmonically oriented "vertical" solo style into an ensemble conception emphasizing traditional African-American elements of rhythmic interplay and extremely dense, multilinear activity. Thick webs of static, pulsating texture provided a platform for rhythmically charged linear improvisations. The manic freneticism of Coltrane's music conjured up associations with the characteristically dense pulsations of tribal West African drumming, associations that Coltrane sometimes encouraged by employing a clatter of drummers, bass players, and extraneous percussion. Furthermore, the music's ritualistic intensity, heightened by allusions to the sacred world in titles and compositional programs, reinforced Coltrane's spoken message of Christian tolerance and spiritualism, often framed in the language of new-age, otherworldly exoticism.[118] Soft-spoken and serious, Coltrane conveyed a new image of the jazz musician, one that encouraged reflection, devotion, and commitment—revising good-times soul and sensuality into a kind of radical puritanism that befitted the severe, contentious climate of the era. While Coltrane himself never seemed to espouse radical politics—in fact he seemed spiritually and socially more akin to Reverend Martin Luther King, Jr., than to Malcolm X—his iconoclastic challenges to the musical mainstream communicated a signal of approval to those whose radical political beliefs were already firmly in place.

VII

Braxton's interest in free jazz heightened during this period of increasing political controversy and public spectacle. Stationed in Seoul, Korea, from 1965 to 1966, he acquired through the PX record store and parcels from his mother some of the ground-breaking recordings of early free jazz. He remembers most vividly Ornette Coleman's *Shape of Jazz to Come* (1959), Cecil Taylor's *Hard Driving Jazz* (1958), Bernard Stollman's ESP label (especially Albert Ayler's *Bells* [1965]), Archie Shepp's recordings with the New York Contemporary Five (1963), and John Coltrane's *Ascension* (1965). After having heard free jazz on and off for several years, Braxton now listened with new in-

117. *The Avant-Garde John Coltrane* (1960). For discussions of the "anti-jazz" controversy, see chapter 1, note 47.

118. Album titles such as *Love Supreme, Kulu Se Mama, Ascension,* and *Om* helped to inspire the spiritual cult that surrounded Coltrane at the time.

sight. A style once cacophonous and confused had become rich with meaning; he *felt* the music emotionally for the first time. This shift in taste might, in part, be the result of increasing familiarity: a forbidding style can after repeated listenings begin to make sense and inspire an intellectual appreciation. Yet to affect the listener so profoundly, it would need to convey something more. Given the social circumstances in which Braxton's interest developed, it would appear that his response reflected a changed attitude about art and perhaps about life in general. For many young black musicians, free jazz stood as a symbol of experiment and change, of a willingness to consider new orders, new musical worlds, after jazz had been thoroughly formalized into the conventions of "modern jazz" after bop. While perhaps appealing on multiple levels, political, cultural, and racial, free jazz seemed to have become for Braxton the sound of a generation that had been seized by the historic moment when blacks strived for social and spiritual liberation. Still, Braxton's receptivity to the more rarefied forms of black modernism can only partially explain his passionate response to another modernist art standing historically and musically well outside the realm of jazz. He describes the encounter in a vivid recollection:

> [In Seoul, Korea] I discovered Schoenberg. Until that time I had always thought of Western art-music as something only relevant to white people; it had nothing to do with me and my life. I played in the orchestra on clarinet, I played my part, I played my Bach, but it never touched me. I thought it was very pretty music, I could throw some words at it, but it wasn't really involved in my life. As long as [my teacher] was happy, I'd play what [he] wanted, and then I would go home and play *Scrapple from the Apple* because it had meaning for me. Experiencing Schoenberg['s Opus 11], however, suddenly made everything more meaningful. . . . It opened up the next whole aspect of my life. It affected me in as profound a way as anything has ever affected me. . . . It opened up the whole reality of notated music to me, something that I had never really been interested [in] before that time.[119]

A passion for Schoenberg's repertory might seem inconsistent with the musical learning and interests of most jazz musicians and with the social impressions those interests tend to communicate. One is hard put to find anything hip about Schoenberg, at heart a Viennese romantic, or about the *Three Pieces for Piano* (1909), early atonal works, which look back to the romantic as much as they peer forward into the modern. Yet in many ways Braxton was prepared for his encounter with the Opus 11 works. The establishment of the jazz mainstream had

119. Interview with Anthony Braxton (September 6, 1982).

enforced a vision of aesthetic absolutes, of tradition, of fixed forms and canonized masterworks. Furthermore, musicians such as John Lewis, Robert Graettinger, Stan Kenton, and Dave Brubeck, and third-stream composers such as Gunther Schuller, were conducting formal and compositional experiments that recall in intent if not in originality Schoenberg's own desire to strike out on a new path, while keeping tradition and its developmental forms and note-scale orientation intact. From Braxton's perspective, whose inherent catholicity inspired a wide-ranging search for new sounds and ideas, Schoenberg was closer to his interests than many contemporary jazz artists who seemed content with a routinized language and repertory that could only lead to predictable improvisational ends. In Braxton's view, Schoenberg, like Ornette Coleman and Eric Dolphy, had rejected tonality, creating an order based on line and rhythm, an order that seemed curiously consistent with the dominant musical elements of the African-American heritage, elements free-jazz musicians would exploit fully. While Schoenberg (like Coleman and Dolphy) stayed truer to harmonic considerations than his protégé Webern and the post-Webern serialists of the 1950s, his departure from functional harmonic relations opened up to Braxton a new musical world that seemed to complement and reinforce the rightness of his own creative direction.

Thus, for Braxton, jazz and concert music were fast becoming part of the same tradition, representing a kind of proto-postmodernist linkage consistent with the formation of the new musical balance. Arnold Schoenberg and Ornette Coleman were, from Braxton's perspective, musical soulmates inspired by the same creative muse: both spoke in a radical, artistic tongue that conflicted with the enforced homogeneity of mass cultural existence. Rejecting the categories that typically define American musical life, Braxton had begun to develop his own "tradition." In that tradition, "good music" expressed spiritual meaningfulness, reasserting the importance of the sacred world in African-American musical expression. As a nontechnical category, moreover, it could make room for Braxton's wide-ranging interests. "Good music"—what he would later call "creative music"—could be found in any style, identified subjectively by its ability, to borrow from the blues vernacular, to "speak the truth" (in a decidedly black voice) about the emerging postmodern condition. The most significant were those radical modernist or "restructuralist" (Braxton's term) expressions that vigorously exerted an intellectual vanguardism. This applied principally to Schoenberg and Coleman, but also to Braxton's earlier favorites, Frankie Lymon, Paul Desmond, Chuck Berry, and Warne

Marsh, who had recast jazz and pop into a new racially confused dialogic. Braxton's reworking of the categories of limitation paved the way toward his experimentalist activity. And he would find the institutional catalyst to pursue that direction upon returning to Chicago, where he would join a group of like-minded black musicians organized under the umbrella of the Association for the Advancement of Creative Musicians.

Muhal Richard Abrams (ca. 1967). Photo courtesy Terry Martin.

3 Musical Assertions of Black Identity

The Association for the Advancement of Creative Musicians

A spirit of radicalism animated artistic life on Chicago's South Side during the 1960s. Vitalized by the bounty of creative possibilities emerging from the new, postmodern landscape, black artists in a range of fields labored to create timely and distinctively African-American forms of expression. The most radical practitioners sought not simply to express blackness, but, with vanguardist intent, to strip away traditional principles and practices entirely. Aroused by nationalist sentiments overtaking black creative and intellectual circles at the time, these artists celebrated the distinctive qualities of African-American music and life, developing practices and aesthetics that departed from accepted standards of official culture. Their commitment to self-reliance and spiritual growth inspired a search for innovative artistic languages that would assert black identity; this commitment, in turn, led to the formation of grassroots organizations that could accommodate radical creative pursuits.

The previous chapter described the profound effect of American institutions on Anthony Braxton's early musical life. The church choir, the army orchestra, the record industry, and the jazz community all played influential roles in his creative development. Most important to Braxton's growth as a professional, however, were the small, ill-funded institutions on the South Side: they provided the key to his artistic self-discovery. And it was through the backing of one particularly virulent, anti-Western, and, at moments, antiwhite organization that Braxton shaped his experimental approach and radical sense of identity. The organization, which had turned American free jazz on its head by the early 1970s, began as a fledgling operation in a South Side community center where it was established as the Association for the Advancement of Creative Musicians.

I

The AACM originated from modest beginnings when a few well-established Chicago jazz musicians—the "elders" of the city's jazz youth—planned to launch an informal rehearsal band. At first, the band included tenor saxophonist Eddie Harris, pianist Muhal Richard Abrams, bass players Donald Rafael Garrett and Victor Sproles, and other local hard-bop musicians who welcomed new opportunities to perform. The ensemble rehearsed a few times in 1961, but soon disbanded over internal disputes. Abrams and Garrett, however, sought to revive the band by appealing to Harris and other established musicians—pianist Jodie Christian, drummer Steve McCall—and by inviting promising young South Side players to join in. Among them was drummer Jack DeJohnette, who brought along some of his friends from Wilson Junior College, most notably alto saxophonists Roscoe Mitchell, Joseph Jarman, and Henry Threadgill, and bass player Malachi Favors. Soon Abrams and Garrett had a core band that included many of the future leaders of the Chicago free-jazz movement.[1]

During 1961 and 1962, the makeshift ensemble rehearsed at a local South Side club, C. & C.'s, at 63rd Street, east of Cottage Grove Avenue, later at Abrams's house around the corner. Initially, they played arrangements worked out by Abrams and Garrett, perhaps somewhat based in free practice, but drawing mainly from the hard-bop styles that dominated the Chicago community at the time.[2] Both Abrams and Garrett had been members of a circle of former DuSable High School

1. Interview with Roscoe Mitchell (April 27, 1988). Mitchell notes that the band had been active when he returned to Chicago from the army in 1961. He recalls that other young musicians were in the band prior to his arrival. These included alto saxophonists Wallace MacMillan and Troy Robinson, tenor saxophonists Gene Dinwiddie and Maurice McIntyre (later Kalaparusha Ahrah Difda), trombonist and cellist Lester Lashley, bass player Charles Clark, and trumpeter Fred Berry. Mitchell also mentioned that Alvin Fielder (drums), Erskine Brody (trumpet), Eddie Harris, and baritone saxophonist "Van Johnson" (possibly William Van Allen) occasionally sat in with the band, while Abrams noted in an interview with Ray Townley that Herbie Hancock may have contributed a few arrangements. Townley, "Muhal Richard Abrams," *Down Beat* (August 15, 1974), 34. John Litweiler has reported that the band may have gone back to 1960 or even earlier, as some former members contend (written communication, June 13, 1992).

2. Initial efforts were said to have developed from Abrams's and Garrett's collaborative work from the late 1950s, which, Abrams intimates, drew from the recorded music of Ornette Coleman. Abrams explains that he and Garrett were treated with suspicion by the local players, who could not comprehend their radical ideas. See Townley, "Muhal Richard Abrams," *Down Beat*. Abrams's arrangements may also have been influenced by his recent studies of modernist concert music and the theories of Paul Hindemith and Joseph Schillinger, which he encountered while attending the Chicago Musical College (ca. 1947–1951). Schillinger's theories would later have a profound impact on jazz with the founding of the Berklee School of Music in 1954. See "Schillinger School Renamed for Berk," *Down Beat* (March 10, 1954), 14. On Schillinger and jazz, see S. Frederick Starr, *Red and Hot: The Fate of Jazz in the Soviet Union* (New York: Oxford University Press, 1983), 74–76.

classmates that included Johnny Griffin, Eddie Harris, and John Gilmore (the latter a mainstay in Sun Ra's Solar Arkestra since 1953), all accomplished bop musicians.[3] They looked mainly to Rollins, and particularly to John Coltrane, who, in the late 1950s, turned up periodically at Garrett's house—a musicians' meeting ground—when in town with the Miles Davis band.[4]

By 1963, musicians' comments suggest that Garrett and some of the older members who preferred hard bop began to distance themselves from the band—by this time named the "Experimental Band"—and Abrams accordingly assumed the principal responsibility for writing arrangements. One suspects that these arrangements had begun to move closer to the style described by John Litweiler in 1967: long, multisectional compositions defined by elaborate instrumental variety; rapid and abrupt rhythmic, dynamic, and textural successions; emphasis on multiple, disparate, instrumental voices that obscured any clear sense of tonality.[5] In time, Abrams explains, these early scores supplied the basis for the band's improvisations. He recalls that originally he had in mind an approach to group improvisation that could only be learned through written arrangements. Once the musicians had internalized that language, they were then able to build compositions without the aid of a score.[6] Eventually other members, notably Troy Robinson, Roscoe Mitchell, and Joseph Jarman, began to contribute to that musical ideal with their own arrangements.

Many young players were anxious to join the Experimental Band simply because they had otherwise few chances to play. While seasoned musicians could still find work in the clubs that dotted the North and South sides, younger artists were mostly out of luck.[7] At

3. Abrams had been a member of MJT+3 (with Nicky Hill, Paul Serrano, Bob Cranshaw, and Walter Perkins), one of the city's premier bop groups from 1955. John Litweiler, "Richard Abrams: A Man with an Idea," *Down Beat* (October 5, 1967), 26. The band recorded on the Vee-Jay label and performed regularly in local clubs. In 1960, it appeared opposite the Mal Waldron Trio at the Five Spot. *Village Voice* (February 3, 1960), 10. Garrett had played and recorded with several top-ranked Chicago leaders, including Ira Sullivan, Bunky Green, Roland Kirk, and Eddie Harris (all 1960–1962).

4. Valerie Wilmer, *As Serious as Your Life* (Westport, Conn.: Lawrence Hill, 1980), 138–39. Eddie Harris's occasional participations, reported by Mitchell, also suggest that the band was playing bop at the time.

5. John Litweiler, "A Man with an Idea," *Down Beat*. Litweiler has noted subsequently that the 1963 band may have stood more in between that mature style and a "third-stream music with a strong jazz bias" (written communication, June 13, 1992).

6. Litweiler, "A Man with an Idea," *Down Beat*.

7. The North and South sides offered a variety of jazz styles from dixieland to hard

best they could count on jobs at cocktail lounges, which supported organ/trio formats and commercial bands, or they might occasionally sit in during nonpaying sessions at the Archway, C. & C.'s, the Pad, and, on the West Side, Fifth Jack's. By 1963 matters had grown significantly worse as the club scene declined with the rise of rock and as the urban community that had originally supported jazz followed the movement out to the suburbs.[8] Within the next year or so, the professional jazz community was in shambles: virtually all of the well-known jazz forums had changed music policies (often to a disc jockey format) or had closed entirely. For the young musician starting out, then, the Experimental Band offered at least a forum for development, if not a source of paying work.[9]

---

bop. North Side clubs such as the Victory Club, London House, and Jazz Ltd. tended to favor piano trios, swing groups, or New Orleans revival bands. Popular South Side showcases—the Sutherland Hotel, Birdhouse, Roberts' Show Lounge, and McKie's Disc Jockey Lounge—featured postbop "modern" jazz by some of the best bands out of New York. (Bop could also be heard at Joe Segal's Showcase on the North Side.) Miles Davis, Cannonball Adderley, and Art Blakey, for example, appeared on a regular basis around the black belt, often for extended engagements. At the smaller South Side clubs—the C. & C. Lounge, the Coral Club, the Wonder Inn, Budland, the Archway Lounge—one usually heard from the best local talent. On a given evening club hoppers might stop by to hear from several well-known Chicago musicians, including Johnny Griffin, Ira Sullivan, Ahmad Jamal, Ramsey Lewis, Wilbur Ware, Sonny Stitt, and the new talent, Herbie Hancock. Or they might choose to follow other young players, such as Joe Farrell, Eddie Harris, and Jodie Christian, who were developing reputations of their own. In addition to regular club acts, moreover, musicians found playing opportunities in rehearsal bands, most notably the Dick Long band. Several of the public sessions were kept alive due to the efforts of Joe Segal. Segal organized sessions at the Pad, the Poodle, and the Gate of Horn. This picture of Chicago jazz, circa 1960 to 1962, is based on local coverage in *Down Beat* and the *Chicago Defender,* together with a perusal of jazz texts. See, in particular, Gene Lees, "Report on Chicago," *Down Beat* (February 18, 1960), 18–21.

8. Already in 1962 fears about the death of jazz—a recurring theme in the literature—began showing up in trade coverage. With reference to free jazz, see, for example, Jean P. LeBlanc, "Jazz: The Happy Sound Is Dying," *Esquire* (April 1962), 74–75. A follow-up discussion appears in the June issue (pp. 11–12).

9. My perspective on the situation has benefited from conversations with Dan Morgenstern and John Litweiler. Roscoe Mitchell has noted additionally that the situation in Chicago became particularly difficult after the city government instituted a policy whereby clubs' licensing fees were determined according to band size. Consequently, several clubs opted for "light music" duos and trios, which put the standard hard-bop quartets and quintets out of business. (Interview with Roscoe Mitchell.) For parallels in New York, see Martin Williams, "Jazz Clubs, Jazz Business, Jazz Styles in New York: A Brief History and a Cultural Lag," *Down Beat* (November 8, 1962). Reprinted in *Jazz Masters in Transition, 1957–1969* (New York: Macmillan, 1970; Da Capo, 1980), 89–93.

Abrams's influence on young Chicago players may also be attributed as much to his role as a charismatic figure as to the economic conditions of the period. By the time the band had acquired a stable membership in 1963, Abrams's house had become a meeting ground for young musicians, where they would in their spare time come to talk about music or anything else they had on their minds. They played and discussed their favorite jazz recordings, sometimes even bringing over albums in the modernist concert-music vein. ("We all had our favorite composers," Mitchell has remarked.) Abrams encouraged them to read, to educate themselves, to increase their awareness of factors outside the music world that directly affected their lives. He also inspired the musicians to develop their talents in the other arts: Jarman, for example, was by then writing poetry, while Mitchell rekindled his early interest in painting.[10] Abrams's guidance was a recipe for personal development, recalling similar messages being spoken by Reverend Martin Luther King, Jr., and traditionally by Chicago's black religious leaders. In particular, his views resembled those of John Coltrane, who provided a new, priestly image for the nation's jazz youth. Abrams led the young Chicagoans down a path of discovery, toward self-fulfillment, self-awareness, and self-respect. He underscored the importance of group solidarity as a means of survival, as a defense against a world of conflict and competition, in which blacks often received the raw end of the deal. Joseph Jarman speaks passionately of Abrams's ministerial influence in this frequently cited yet still poignant recollection:

> Until I had the first meeting with Richard Abrams, I was "like all the rest" of the "hip" ghetto niggers; I was cool, I took dope, I smoked pot, etc. I did not care for the life that I had been given. In having the chance to work in the Experimental Band with Richard and the other musicians there, I found the first something with meaning/reason for doing. That band and the people there was the most important thing that ever happened to me.[11]

Jarman's statement typifies the rhetoric of the AACM, which commonly describes Abrams in the most favorable terms and characterizes the Association itself as a cadre of selfless, benevolent musicians. Without questioning the sincerity of these reminiscences, one must wonder what took place beneath the surface of a public image of musical fellowship. As activists attempting to change the very nature of aesthetic understanding, the AACM members made sure to present

10. Interview with Roscoe Mitchell. Jarman eventually published a collection of his works as *Black Case*, vols. 1–2 (privately published, n.d.).

11. Originally quoted in J. B. Figi's notes to Jarman's album, *Song For* (1967).

their organization in the best possible terms. But as ambitious professionals seeking to make a living through their art, they surely ran into more conflicts than most members were willing to admit. In fact, one senses that the AACM of the 1960s was a caldron of conflict, fueled by contrasting opinions about art (bop vs. free), politics (separatism vs. integration), and the music business (careerism vs. a radical rejection of established institutions).[12] Yet if we keep in mind the inherent subjectivities of activist rhetoric, which at times forced some members to suppress their truest feelings, we can cut away at some of the mystery surrounding the AACM and move toward a more honest picture of the organization and its intents.

There is no doubt that Abrams's message had a profound effect on Chicago's black musical community: it tapped the wellspring of jazz talent, inspiring a generation of young musicians who would shape a new course in the music's development. With Abrams's encouragement, the members of the Experimental Band started developing their own free-jazz expressions in informal, small-group sessions at clubs and in private homes.[13] Many of these sessions took place at the Wonder Inn on Cottage Grove Avenue at 75th Street and at Fifth Jack's. Both clubs were frequented by many of Chicago's free circle, including Garrett, saxophonist Fred Anderson, a trumpeter nicknamed "Clanky," and members of the Sun Ra Solar Arkestra—notably John Gilmore, Pat Patrick, and Sun Ra himself—who returned periodically to their native Chicago.[14] As for working engagements, they were extremely rare, taking place mostly in South Side cafes, whether they played free jazz or bop. Even for a full ensemble, opportunities ap-

12. David Baker has recalled in conversation such contentiousness when he interviewed members of the AACM in the 1960s (telephone conversation, Spring 1990). See also Leslie Rout, "AACM: New Music (!) New Ideas (?)," *Journal of Popular Culture* 1:2 (Fall 1967): 128–40.

13. Already by 1962, Robinson was leading sessions with musicians both in and outside the band. Mitchell was performing with Donald Rafael Garrett and Gene Dinwiddie. Favors, Mitchell, and Berry were rehearsing regularly with a former Arkestra drummer, Alvin Fielder. Berry and Mitchell also performed in a quartet with bassist Scotty Holt and drummer Jack DeJohnette, whose formidable hard-bop credentials—DeJohnette had worked with Coltrane—gave credibility to the new music and encouraged others to explore the free-jazz language. Interview with Roscoe Mitchell; Terry Martin, "Blowing out in Chicago: Roscoe Mitchell," *Down Beat* (April 6, 1967), 21; Bill Smith, "Roscoe Mitchell," *Coda* (September 1975), 3–8. Moreover, Holt would later show up in Parisian press reports after other AACM members, including Braxton, had settled there. "Flashes," *Jazz Hot* (July/August 1969), 12.

14. Elaine Cohen, "Fred Anderson," *Coda* (August 1984), 18–20; interview with Roscoe Mitchell. Sun Ra had left Chicago by this time, settling with his Arkestra in New York in 1960.

peared infrequently, and usually amounted to appearances at the Abraham Lincoln Center, a South Side community center and future home of the AACM.[15]

By 1964, the broad-scale economic decline of jazz was making conditions difficult for even the most seasoned and popular musicians. Interpreting the lack of work as a form of racially motivated economic oppression, many artists started to discuss the idea of creating their own organization that would operate outside the reach of establishment control. Fred Anderson recalls such conversations taking place at Fifth Jack's as early as 1963.[16] But the idea truly got off the ground after Abrams met Phil Cohran, a former trumpeter with Sun Ra, then working on the West Side. Cohran was well respected in West Side jazz circles, a leader among young rhythm 'n' blues players, and someone who could summon musicians' support.[17] Despite their differences in taste, Abrams and Cohran sought similar social ends: the complete creative freedom and autonomy of the black musician. Accordingly, they started formulating guidelines for a performance organization run by the artists themselves. Engaging the help of Jodie Christian and Steve McCall, they spread the word around Chicago's black jazz community about their plan. Soon after, they scheduled the first formal meeting of the Association for the Advancement of Creative Musicians.[18]

II

The appearance of a musician-operated performance organization was surely greeted with skepticism by many commentators and enthusiasts, who typically assumed that administration and planning stood

15. Built in 1905, the center had served the community thereafter, maintained through the cooperation of the Chicago Housing Authority and the Department of Urban Renewal. It offered cultural and recreational activities to nearby residents and a meeting place and/or residences for several organizations, among them All Souls Unitarian Church, the Center for Inner City Studies, a planned-parenthood center, and Operation Headstart. In 1969, the center moved from its original location at 700 East Oakwood Boulevard to a new site at Pershing Road and Cottage Grove Avenue. See "Lincoln Centre Breaks Ground," *Black Truth* (February 14–28, 1969), 8.

16. Cohen, "Fred Anderson," *Coda,* 19.

17. Cohran was a notable influence on Donald Myrick, Tom Washington, and Maurice White. White and Myrick later formed the group Earth, Wind and Fire. Myrick is also the author of several books on jazz.

18. Cohran had played and recorded with Sun Ra's Solar Arkestra from 1957 to 1960, appearing on the privately issued Saturn LPs, including *Angels and Demons at Play* (Saturn 407).

antithetical to the concerns of most jazz musicians. Indeed, much of the romance about jazz relates to stories about musicians' unreliability, which writers and even some performers still report approvingly in chronicles and recollections. Yet observers have often failed to recognize other qualities of African-American life that seemed to encourage collective commitment. Self-reliance and self-help have long histories in the black tradition, extending back to antebellum slave cultures which perpetuated African-based social structures of communalism and group loyalty.[19] In music circles, communal consciousness remained especially strong, particularly through associations with the church and spiritual beliefs that transcended purely sacred boundaries.[20] In jazz, one may observe extensions of black communality in early New Orleans ensembles, which were frequently affiliated with mens' clubs, fraternal organizations, and even secret societies. Similarly, territory bands of the 1920s and 1930s were typically "commonwealth bands" that made professional decisions collectively and shared earnings equally. By the 1930s, jazz—or, more properly, swing—had become rigorously professionalized and institutionalized, producing a generation of highly ambitious performers who had to learn the ropes in an increasingly commercial business network. Still, the musicians' communal ethos survived even as they themselves became increasingly ambitious and individualistic. The institution of swing laid the foundation for the survival of cultlike in-groups, reinforced by language, perspective, and behavior. Confronting the realities of life in an essentially white-owned and -operated enterprise, black musicians, despite their obvious self-interests and personal goals, seemed to retain a commitment to a community identity as a means of providing mutual support. The commercial success of bands such as Basie's and Ellington's, for example, seemed to have as much to do with the leaders' abilities to maintain a balance between group solidarity and musical management as with the ensembles' strengths on musical grounds.[21] Certainly the endurance of Sun Ra's Solar Arkestra, an early Chicago-based free ensemble, owed to the members' unusual commitment to preserving the integrity of the collective "family."

19. Sterling Stuckey, *Slave Culture, Nationalist Theory and the Foundations of Black America* (New York: Oxford University Press, 1987), introduction: "Slavery and the Circle of Culture," 3–102.

20. Neil Leonard, *Jazz, Myth and Religion* (New York: Oxford University Press, 1987).

21. Artie Shaw's comments about the business of jazz are relevant here. See Shaw, *The Trouble with Cinderella* (New York: Farrar, Straus, and Young, 1952), 307–13.

Moreover, jazz musicians, black and white, had good reason to create their own music enterprises: they had been cheated and mismanaged by rapacious agents, managers, and record-company executives continually over the years.[22] While committed to their artistic pursuits, most musicians had traditionally left the handling of financial matters up to their agents, a practice that encouraged a long history of administrative underhandedness and double-dealing. By the late 1950s, however, the emerging civil rights movement seemed to ignite a new assertiveness as some musicians sought to reclaim control of their art. In 1960, for example, Charles Mingus and Max Roach staged a program counter to the Newport Festival at a nearby hotel. "The Rump Festival," the musicians explained, came about as a reaction to the racism and excessive commercialism they had observed in recent Newport programs. Featuring several top-ranked musicians, the festival proved a success, leading to other organizational efforts, notably New York's Jazz Artists Guild.[23] Another musicians' festival, organized under the provocative epithet "The October Revolution," produced a second offshoot, the Jazz Composers' Guild. This organization consisted of a racially integrated assemblage of many of New York's best free artists.[24] Neither organization lasted, a consequence, one suspects, of the highly competitive and alienated New York jazz environment. In Chicago, however, where identifications with southern communities had endured the upheavals of the migrations, where racial isolation fostered a closely knit musicians' circle, collective action seemed to stand a better chance of survival.

III

The AACM grew out of a series of meetings that took place first at Cohran's house and then at the Abraham Lincoln Center during the spring and summer of 1965. Initially, the meetings served mainly to attract prospective members and to determine whether such an orga-

22. Nat Hentoff, "The Apprenticeship and the Accounting," *The Jazz Life* (New York: Da Capo, 1961/1975), 46–59.

23. Roy Eldridge, Coleman Hawkins, Jo Jones, Kenny Dorham, and Ornette Coleman were among them. The Guild released two LPs, notably *Newport Rebels* (1960). Musicians' efforts to establish their own performance forums date back to Earl Hines and Louis Armstrong, who briefly opened a dance hall, the Usonia, in Chicago in 1927.

24. Dan Morgenstern and Martin Williams, "The October Revolution: Two Views of the Avant-Garde in Action," *Down Beat* (November 19, 1964), 15, 33; Robert Levin, "The Jazz Composers' Guild: An Assertion of Dignity," *Down Beat* (May 6, 1965), 17–18.

nization might work. These first gatherings attracted an eclectic mix of musicians from the communities of hard bop, free jazz, and rhythm 'n' blues. Mitchell recalls about thirty-five musicians in attendance at the meetings, many of whom had worked with Abrams in the Experimental Band. At the first meeting,[25] Abrams and Cohran led a discussion about their plan for the organization, soliciting views from the prospective membership. They agreed on a one-person, one-vote decision-making process, proceeding to establish a "corporate structure" with Muhal Richard Abrams as president and John Shenoy Jackson and Lester Lashley as administrators. They also drafted a preliminary outline of intent that expressed their principal aim of sponsoring performances by the members themselves. The initial charter stated that all members would be required to attend weekly AACM meetings and to pay weekly dues of one dollar. The funds would help to produce concerts, any profits being paid to the performing musicians. New members could join only after having been nominated by an AACM musician and receiving a majority vote. All members were encouraged to participate in weekly sessions and to play in the AACM big band, an outgrowth of the Experimental Band.[26] While members could play in bands outside the organization, they had to maintain a majority of AACM musicians in their own groups.[27]

Artistically, the AACM reflected Abrams's personal commitment to original music.[28] The style of that music, however, was never clearly specified in published accounts, owing perhaps to the organization's equal commitment to uninhibited creative expression.[29] Yet by the time the membership had stabilized in 1966, the AACM was above all a free-jazz organization, giving special emphasis to the brand of music Abrams, Jarman, Mitchell, and Robinson had been developing in the

25. According to Leslie Rout, the meeting took place on May 8. "The AACM," *Journal of Popular Culture,* 130. Rout's phrasing suggests that this may have been the date of the Illinois charter, which would put the meeting earlier.

26. In 1966, the band included Roscoe Mitchell, William Van Allen, Maurice McIntyre, John Shenoy Jackson, Lester Lashley, Charles Clark, Leonard Jones, Thurman Barker, and Sandra Lashley. "Jazz Musicians' Group in Chicago Is Growing," *Down Beat* (July 28, 1966), 11.

27. Ensembles were required to maintain at least 60 percent for groups larger than a quartet. Rout, "The AACM," *Journal of Popular Culture,* 139, n. 5.

28. Abrams reports that the first AACM concert included Jarman, Bill Brimfield (trumpet), Charles Clark, and Thurman Barker. John Litweiler, "Interview with Muhal Richard Abrams," *Chicago Reader* (May 9, 1975), 13. This has been verified by Fred Anderson. See Elaine Cohen, "Fred Anderson Interview," *Coda* (August 1984), 18–20.

29. At most, it was referred to as music in "an avant-garde style." See "Jazz Musicians' Group," *Down Beat,* 11.

Experimental Band.[30] Commercial recordings by AACM groups show, for example, that the musicians built upon the multisectional arrangements of the Experimental Band, identifying a direct link between Abrams's original conception and the members' subsequent realizations. Mitchell's first album, *Sound* (1966), suggests that he in particular played a principal role in shaping the AACM's improvisational conception. His approach, which departed from the solo orientation of New York free jazz, would help to define the Chicago style. Mitchell had developed these essentially organic, atonal procedures with Joseph Jarman and an influential AACM newcomer, trumpeter Lester Bowie. In fact, Jarman had been experimenting with related alternatives to creative expression after joining the Experimental Band in 1962. Perhaps best known are his aforementioned forays into poetry and applications of performance art, the latter drawing as much from the multimedia happenings of the late 1950s and early 1960s—and perhaps, with an ironic touch, from vaudeville—as from jazz. Eventually Mitchell, Jarman, and Lester Bowie joined with Malachi Favors in forming the Art Ensemble of Chicago, the musical-theatrical tour de force that became the AACM's flagship ensemble through the 1970s and 1980s.[31]

Published accounts suggest that by 1966 the AACM had stabilized with a membership of fifty musicians.[32] Organizational stability was largely an outgrowth of the Association's successes at producing regular concerts and intermittent performances in neighborhood bars and

30. There seems to have been some disagreement about the stylistic emphasis at the early meetings. In *As Serious as Your Life,* Valerie Wilmer reports that Eddie Harris spoke against the free-jazz emphasis, while many of the West Side musicians seemed to favor soul and rhythm 'n' blues. It is likely that those who lacked interest in the free orientation eventually dropped out. Discographic research shows, for example, that Jodie Christian was playing and recording regularly with Harris from 1967 to 1969 in and outside of Chicago, and it is likely he had left the organization by that time. By 1968, Cohran would devote his attention to another South Side project, the Affro Arts Theater. See ahead.

31. Descriptions of Jarman's theatrical performances appear in Rout, "The AACM," *Journal of Popular Culture.* The happening expressed a vanguardist rejection of objectified artistic forms, beginning with Cage's theatrical efforts at Black Mountain College in 1952. The genre was further developed in the late 1950s by Cage's students at the New School. See Allan Kaprow, *Assemblage, Environments, and Happenings* (New York: Harry Abrams, n.d.), and Michael Kirby, *Happenings* (New York: E. P. Dutton, 1965). Jarman collaborated with Cage for a concert, ca. 1966. Doug Mitchell, a participant in the performance, recalls that the collaboration was orchestrated by a student at the University of Chicago. (Conversation with Doug Mitchell, Baltimore, October 1991.)

32. "Jazz Musicians' Group," *Down Beat,* 11.

clubs, all of which provided for some steady, if poorly paid, work.[33] Through their own promotional means, AACM musicians advertised upcoming concerts around the South Side, posting signs in shops, in bookstores, and on billboards. Ads for concerts also appeared in local underground newspapers such as the *Kaleidoscope* and in black-community publications, notably the *Westside Torch* and *Black Truth*.[34] Furthermore, Chicago-based *Down Beat* provided intermittent coverage of AACM events. In its "Strictly Ad-Lib" column from November 17, 1966, for example, the magazine reported the AACM's upcoming fall concert schedule, listing performances by several band leaders.[35] Other reports indicated that the AACM had now boasted a surfeit of bands with fluid memberships that had emerged and endured because of the organization's unified efforts.[36] In reality, unity meant

33. Most typically performances took place at the Abraham Lincoln Center and the University of Chicago's Reynolds Club, a student lounge, which in 1966 sponsored Jarman's weekly open sessions. They were also held less frequently at the university's Mandel Hall, the Museum of African-American History, the Urban Progress Center, the St. John Grand Lodge, the Harper Theater, a makeshift space run by Troy Robinson, the youth-services center of the University Disciples of Christ Church (the Blue Gargoyle), and clubs such as the Hungry Eye, the Plugged Nickel, the Phamous Lounge, and the Happening. For a reference to the Museum of African-American History (located at 38th Street and South Michigan Avenue), see Bill Smith, "Roscoe Mitchell," *Coda* (September 1975), 3; for the Urban Progress Center (at 64th and Greene streets), see "Strictly Ad Lib, Chicago," *Down Beat* (June 30, 1966), 15; for the St. John Grand Lodge, see "Strictly Ad Lib," *Down Beat* (February 10, 1966), 16–19, 51; for the Harper Theater, see Terry Martin, "Blowing out in Chicago," *Down Beat* (April 6, 1967), 21. Robinson's space at 76th Street and Cottage Grove Avenue was mentioned by Roscoe Mitchell during our interview. For a reference to the Hungry Eye on North Wells Street, see "Ad Lib," *Down Beat* (October 6 and November 3, 1966), respectively, 12, 42–44; 12–13, 46–50; to the Plugged Nickel, interview with Roscoe Mitchell; to the Phamous Lounge and Reynolds Club, personal conversation with John Litweiler (September 1988) and Litweiler, "Heard and Seen, Anthony Braxton," *Coda* (March 1967); to the Happening, "Ad Lib," *Down Beat* (November 17, 1966), 48–53.

34. For example, Joseph Jarman at the Blue Gargoyle, *Kaleidoscope* (April 11–24, 1969), 6; Leroy Jenkins's String Quartet at Afro-American Expo 68, *Torch* (November 30–December 13, 1968), 5; Phil Cohran and David Moore at Black Arts Festival honoring Malcolm X, *Black Truth* (May 15–30, 1969), 6.

35. The list included Troy Robinson, Roscoe Mitchell, Joseph Jarman, Allan Joiner, Richard Abrams, and former Sun Ra saxophonist Virgil Pumphrey (Absholom Ben-shlomo). For subsequent reports see *Down Beat* issues February 10, 1966; June 30, 1966; July 28, 1966; October 6, 1966.

36. Some of the other AACM bands included Phil Cohran's Artistic Heritage Ensemble, the Leroy Jenkins String Quartet, the Gerald Donovan (Ajaramu) Quintet, and the Anthony Braxton trio and quartet. Reports of the Artistic Heritage Ensemble appeared frequently in the *Torch*. It called Cohran and his group "the most popular performers of Afro-American music now in the city." "Phil Cohran at BBR," *Torch* (August

fraternity prior to the women's movement and despite public claims of egalitarianism; a trio led by Amina Claudine Myers and occasional participation by Sandra Lashley, Fontella Bass, Sherri Scott, and dancer Darlene Blackburn represented the extent of the Association's female representation.

Down Beat's coverage reveals that the AACM's social ambitions had developed hand in hand with its musical successes. Initially devoted to the purely practical matter of finding work for its musicians, the organization had soon expanded its program to address social issues relating to the status of the black jazz artist in American society. Abrams elaborated on some of these aims in a profile from 1966.[37] After explaining the Association's commitments to "original music" and "genuinely individual expression from each musician," he then outlined some of its newest aims.[38] These included a grassroots fundraising campaign to finance the training of AACM musicians and a program offering musical instruction to black teenagers.[39] Abrams also underscored the AACM's intent to correct the persistent negative stereotypes of the jazz musician, which had defamed the black heritage and hindered artistic growth. Above all, Abrams reported, the AACM sought "to set an example of high moral standards for musicians and to return the public image of creative musicians to the level of esteem which was handed down from past cultures." These aims, together with plans "to stimulate Spiritual growth in Creative artists," "to uplift the public image of Creative Musicians," and "to uphold the tradition of elevated, cultured Musicians handed down from the past" originally appeared in the AACM's charter. They were subsequently published as excerpts in several accounts and reprinted in their entirety in the notes to Joseph Jarman's *As If It Were the Seasons* (1968).

The AACM's guarded reference to a cultured musical tradition be-

22–September 5, 1968), 11. Donovan's band was listed in a *Down Beat* "Ad Lib column from October 6, 1966, 12, 42. In a retrospective on the AACM, moreover, John Litweiler recalls: "The excitement of the AACM's early years was unmistakable. It seemed that fresh new voices were appearing continually . . . so that Richard Abrams's big and small bands, and a dozen others as well, were continual parades of talent." "AACM's 10th Anniversary: Voices in the Wilderness," *Chicago Reader* (May 9, 1975), 12.

37. "Jazz Musicians Group in Chicago Growing," *Down Beat* (July 28, 1966), 11.

38. Abrams said, "We could play a tune like *Body and Soul* forever and not express what *we* feel—only variations of what the original composer felt." The membership's commitment to expressing a collective self thus shows up from the beginning.

39. Litweiler, "Muhal Richard Abrams," *Chicago Reader* (May 9, 1975), 13. The AACM also sought donations in the form of used instruments from residents and shopkeepers around the South Side.

trayed the centrality of blackness as a defining artistic category. From the start an affirmation of blackness was basic to its goals.[40] The organization was founded by blacks to perform black music. Self-motivated and self-reliant, it sought to foster a rarefied form of black artistic modernism that could not hope for support from outside sources. Nor did the membership seek such support. The AACM stood decidedly against accepting grants from formal institutions, which they believed would only perpetuate the paternalistic treatment they, as black artists, sought to overturn.[41] The musicians organized and promoted their own concerts. They enlisted the help of Chuck Nessa, a local record producer, who established a series of AACM recordings on Robert Koester's blues label, Delmark Records.[42] Abrams, moreover, created a music-publishing operation, Richarda Music, to publish members' original works.[43] The AACM's commitment to self-direction expressed a tacit condemnation of the performance and production environments black musicians had endured over the years. "The music," Mitchell told Terry Martin, "is not a sideline for other people's folly. [But] in the clubs, that's what it [has been]."[44] For the more radically nationalist members, the AACM engendered a form of racial separatism: it would be a microcosm of the new black nation.[45] Through its own concerts, its own promotional mechanism, its own promoters, its own publishing arm, the AACM hoped to transcend the white-dominated corporate structure on which the music had previously depended. In a special report on the AACM, published in the black literary journal *Black World* in 1973, Abrams and John Shenoy

40. "In Chicago, the meaning of black power was felt in everything." A comment attributed to Leroy Jenkins by Valerie Wilmer in *As Serious as Your Life,* 149.

41. Later, the AACM would be a recipient of support from the National Endowment for the Arts.

42. The arrangement came about after Mitchell met Chuck Nessa, a Delmark employee and friend of critics John Litweiler and Terry Martin, at an AACM concert. Nessa convinced Koester to record Mitchell's *Sound,* the first Delmark release in 1966. (Interview with Roscoe Mitchell.) As a blues label, Delmark included, among other artists, Junior Wells, Magic Sam, Luther Allison, and Mighty Joe Young.

43. Litweiler, "A Man with an Idea," *Down Beat,* 41.

44. Terry Martin, "Blowing out in Chicago: Roscoe Mitchell," *Down Beat* (April 6, 1967), 20–21.

45. Leslie Rout refers to Gordan Emmanuel (Emanuel Cranshaw), brother of Bob Cranshaw, as a "white" vibraphonist who was a member briefly. Rout, "The AACM," *Journal of Popular Culture.* Moreover, after Kalaparusha's and Braxton's nomination of John Gilmore, a white pianist attending the University of Chicago, the organization reevaluated its racial policies, prohibiting the introduction of nonblack members. Conversations with Litweiler (January 7, 1991) and Anthony Braxton (March 1992). Emmanuel appeared on Abrams's album *Levels and Degrees of Light* (1967).

Jackson spoke openly of the organization's commitment to cultural nationalism. Referring to the black artist as a "cultural missionary," they wrote:

> The Black creative artist must survive and persevere in spite of the oppressive forces which prevent Black people from reaching the goals attained by other Americans. . . . For years the mass-media scavengers have stolen and feasted on Black creativity, literally forcing ersatz art on the total American community in general and the Black community in particular. . . . The AACM is attempting to precipitate activity geared toward finding a solution to the basic contradictions which face Black people. . . . [It] intends to show how the disadvantaged and the disenfranchised can come together and determine their own strategies for political and economic freedom, thereby determining their own destinies. This will not only create a new day for Black artists but for all Third World inhabitants; a new day of not only participation but also of control.

The AACM's achievement as a stable, working organization could not have come about without a strong commitment from its membership, and that commitment surely would not have developed without inspiration from the black-rights movement. Civil rights initiatives fueled the AACM, providing it with a compelling institutional model consistent with the Association's own social doctrine as well as a framework for voicing that doctrine in public. The civil rights example taught the members that collective action could promote personal goals, a concept that complemented their communal concerns and that, as will be seen, was expressed symbolically in the AACM's approaches to improvisation. CORE, SNCC, and even the SCLC were, in their view, saviors of the black community, assuming a spiritual/activist role once assigned exclusively to the church, a role and an action that made meaningful the musicians' creative lives. While some radicals may have questioned the effectiveness of the SCLC's and CORE's early integrationist philosophies, the major black civil rights organizations stood nonetheless as symbols of promise and hope for the African American. For if nothing else, the commitment and conviction of leaders such as King, Floyd McKissick, Stokely Carmichael, and religious activists Elijah Muhammad and Malcolm X had helped to raise the dignity and self-respect of the black people.

That commitment, of course, had touched the hearts of many Americans. But it carried special meaning for the black citizens of Chicago, who lived in what had become the principal center for northern civil rights activities. From the early 1960s, Chicago's black community supported several grassroots organizations that had been working to improve local housing and educational conditions. (It is likely that the AACM's plan for a youth music school grew out of the black community's educational programs.) Activism on the part of these groups, organized under the umbrella of the Coordinating Council of Community Organizations (CCCO), and supported by several local leaders—including members of the black clergy—had by 1963 become a regular feature in city politics and in the pages of the local press. In 1964, two school boycotts, the CCCO's "Spotlight Campaign" on public schools, its successful voter-registration program, and a massive Illinois Rally for Civil Rights—two days after the passing of the 1964 Civil Rights Act—provided unprecedented attention to the grievances and concerns of the black community. By 1966, the significance of Chicago to the black-rights movement had escalated when King established the SCLC's headquarters on Chicago's West Side. Its campaigns from that year, Breadbasket, PUSH, and (with the CCCO) the Chicago Freedom Movement, together with numerous short-term projects, garnered support from much of the black community, even if its more ambitious plans (including a march into Cicero) faltered under Mayor Daley's pressure.[46] Among Chicago's youth, the presence of such operations seemed inadvertently to exacerbate a turn toward activism as demonstrations and racial clashes grew increasingly violent.[47] From 1966 and through the decade, the civil rights movement heightened to a pitched intensity, reinforcing a sense of commitment to nationalist policies among many black Chicagoans. The movement also inspired the musicians of the AACM, who shared a similar commitment but toward an artistic end, one that they felt would celebrate and ennoble the heritage of black people.

IV

A survey of the black-oriented literature from the mid-1960s reveals the extent to which social-rights issues had transformed the city. Radical newspapers such as the *Truth,* the *Black Liberator,* and the *Struggle* carried critiques of political affairs and essays on activist groups such as the Committee for Independent Political Action, the

46. David J. Garrow, ed., *Chicago 1966: Open Housing Marches, Summit Negotiations, and Operation Breadbasket* (Brooklyn: Carlson Publishing, 1989); "Boycott Buses," *Torch* (December 19, January 2, 1968), 8; Dempsey Travis, *An Autobiography of Black Politics,* vol. 1 (Chicago: Urban Research Press, 1987).

47. A minor incident touched off a riot (or, from the participants' perspective, a rebellion) on the West Side in 1966. Riots also occurred in 1965 and would again in 1968 after King's assassination.

Chicago Freedom Movement, and the W. E. B. Du Bois Freedom Center.[48] More moderate journals, including the *Defender* and the *Southside Bulletin,* stayed closer to the reporting of major events from the arrival of Reverend King in Chicago to the SCLC's various efforts. Representing the middle ground, the *Torch* and the *Negro Digest* published profiles of prominent civil rights leaders, such as the Reverend Jesse Jackson (head of Operation PUSH), while also running poignant indictments of official powers, notably a photo essay on the 1968 riots.[49] As a cultural journal, moreover, the *Negro Digest* regularly advertised books by black writers and products depicting black themes. The conspicuous presentation of works with contentious titles and images of desperate life on the South Side—David Lytton's *The Goddamn White Man,* Ronald Fair's *Hog Butcher,* Paul Crump's *Burn, Killer Burn!*—gave voice to the passions and commitment of a readership whose lives embodied in a self-referring cycle the experiences on which these journals were reporting.

Newspaper coverage also shows that the AACM's self-help platform mirrored the efforts of other grassroots organizations committed to the advancement of the African-American heritage. Several South Side galleries, notably the Afam Gallery and the Art and Soul Workshop, produced shows by black artists,[50] while a cluster of black-owned galleries on the Near South Side gave special attention to African-American innovators, earning the title of the black "Gallery Row."[51] In music, the South Side Community Center, the Blackyard (House of UMOJA), the Museum of African-American History, and the Afro-American Dance and Culture Club scheduled regular events that complemented the institutionally backed radio programs of

48. The *Struggle* (January 18 and January 31, 1966), 4, 8. A list of these and other publications appears in James P. Danky, comp., *Undergrounds: A Union List of Alternative Periodicals* (Madison: Wisconsin State Historical Society, 1974).

49. The essay depicted the Chicago riots following King's assassination, together with images of a police/teenage struggle from 1966. "Aftermath Chicago" (April 12–26, 1968), 3; "New Black Organization" (October 18–31, 1968), 7; "SCLC and Teamsters Coordinate a Scavenger Program" (November 10–24, 1967), 2; all in the *Torch.* Coverage in the *Negro Digest* made reference to Sterling Stuckey's Amistad Society and the International Organization for People of African Descent. *Negro Digest* (November 1966), 19, 29; "Perspectives" (September 1966), 41.

50. *Torch* (December 19, 1968–January 2, 1969), 9; *Negro Digest* (August 1969). The Afam show included works by Murray N. de Pillars, a friend of Braxton for whom *Composition 8A* (1968, *For Alto* 1/3) was dedicated.

51. "Perspectives," *Negro Digest* (August 1967), 84. These appeared together with their white counterparts, as described by Lynne Warren in *Alternative Spaces: A History of Chicago* (Chicago: Museum of Contemporary Art, 1984).

WGRT and WVON.[52] Phil Cohran founded another South Side institution, the Affro (*sic*) Arts Theater, as a counterpart to the AACM, known colloquially as "the shrine of blackness . . . medium of black knowledge and entertainment."[53] Located on Drexel Boulevard, just a few blocks from the Lincoln Center, Affro Arts sponsored a range of performances, most of which were oriented toward black rhythm 'n' blues and soul. It also staged workshops, symposia, black radical theater, and political events, including a benefit for Imamu Amiri Baraka in 1968.[54] Most closely resembling the AACM was the Organization of Black American Culture (OBAC), also housed at the Abraham Lincoln Center.[55] OBAC sponsored and promoted an annual program on local black artists as part of its commitment to the creative expression of the black experience. In a 1967 program of "Black Experientialism," OBAC presented performances by several Chicago artists, including painter Jeff Donaldson, poet David Moore (Amus Mor, a frequent AACM collaborator), AACM singer-dancer Sherri Scott, and the Fred Humphrey Quartet. In February 1969, it had launched a literary journal, *NOMMO,* which published works by local writers.[56] The OBAC's list of goals recalled those of the AACM. The organization sought to

52. *Torch* (September 5–19, 1968), 9, 16; (November 1–14, 1968), 14; *Negro Digest* (February 1967), 49–50. "Umoja" is the Swahili word for unity. The call letters of WVON stood for "voice of the Negro." The station was owned by the Chess brothers, founders of Chess records. See Robert Pruter, *Chicago Soul* (Urbana: University of Illinois Press, 1991), 12–17.

53. Cohran's Artistic Heritage Ensemble and the Pharaohs (most likely a gathering of Cohran's former sidemen) served as house bands. *Torch* (August 21–September 15, 1968), 11; *Black Truth* (January 2–15, 1969), 6. See also "Affro-Arts Theater and Black Experience," *Torch* (August 9–21, 1968), 3. In an "Open Letter from Affro-Arts," Cohran stated, "We provide both a sounding board of black opinion and a medium of black knowledge and entertainment." *Torch* (July 25–August 8, 1968), 4. The building would later become the headquarters of the El Rukn gang.

54. The theatrical works included Marvin X's *Take Care of Business* and Jimmy Garrett's *We Own the Night. Black Truth* (March 14–27, 1969), 11. Baraka was sentenced to two and a half years in prison for his role in the Newark riots. "Benefit Jones," *Black Truth* (February 2–16, 1968), 3. Reports on other events appeared in *Black Truth* (February 28–March 13, 1969), 11; (January 2–15, 1969), 6.

55. In an effort to evoke the resonance of West African dialects, the acronym was pronounced "oh-bah-say."

56. "NOMMO Is Here!" *Black Truth* (March 14–27, 1969), 3. A collection of *NOMMO* literature was published as *NOMMO: A Literary Legacy of Black Chicago,* ed. Carole A. Parks (Chicago: OBAhouse, 1987). The concept of NOMMO—the driving power of life—was popularized and romanticized in Janheinz Jahn's *Muntu: An Outline of the New African Culture* (New York: Grove Press, 1961).

work toward the ultimate goal of bringing to the Black community indigenous art forms which reflect and clarify the Black Experience in America. [OBAC seeks] to reflect the richness and depth and variety of Black History and Culture. [It also hopes] to provide the Black Community with a positive image of itself, its history, its achievements, and its possibilities for creativity.[57]

Increasing awareness of the black contribution became a principal concern for many of Chicago's African-American arts organizations, whose campaigns for self-determination mirrored the efforts of political activists. Radical black artists sought to construct a new social reality, a new cultural era that would lead blacks away from what they believed to be a materially obsessed and corrupt white world. One can safely assume that they possessed their own elements of corruption. And, unless one is willing to accept the premise that these musicians had, as African progeny, transcended the socialization of America, then it follows that they shared many of the same patterns of behavior that orient Western capitalist culture. As activists, however, they could stand together with conviction in the name of the "true" black cultural ethos, maintaining a position they believed to be morally and aesthetically superior to that of whites.

Black radical artists had created a curious cultural role reversal. Inverting the assimilationist ideal of the SCLC, which tacitly acknowledged white cultural domination, these artists undercut the longstanding aim to achieve social parity by simply proclaiming blackness superior to the American social norm. Black cultural nationalism would provide an antidote to black peoples' perpetual alienation, a way of putting an end to what James Baldwin called in *The Fire Next Time* "the horrors of the American Negro's life [for which] there has been almost no language."[58] Inspiration and sustenance toward that political end would come from the black cultural heritage, more specifically from the artists' conceptions of the communalism and "spiritual" aesthetics of precolonial Africa.

Allusions to Africa abounded in Chicago's black community through the 1960s, showing up typically in coverage of politics, literature, art, and fashion. As noted in chapter 2, the emancipation of black African nations had captured the imagination of America's black communities, which consequently grew to expect more for themselves here in the United States. By the mid-1960s, the African

57. "Happenings: Culture Consciousness in Chicago," *Negro Digest* (August 1967), 85–89.

58. Baldwin, *The Fire Next Time* (New York: Dell, 1962/1988), 95.

rebirth had entered black popular culture, and by mid-decade it had consumed it, prompting stylistic celebrations in dress and "Afro" hairstyles. Among the black literati, the *Negro Digest* helped to fuel interest by advertising books about Africa and publishing a regular column, "The African Scene," beginning in July 1963.[59] As the "Black Is Beautiful" campaign reached national proportions by the mid-1960s, Africa assumed a regular presence in Chicago's cultural life. New shops such as the African Look and the African Lion supplied trappings of African exotica.[60] Forums such as the Auditorium Theater and the Museum of African-American History sponsored courses and lectures on the African heritage together with performances of African dance.[61] At times these manifestations of a new black awareness seemed to be little more than superficial expressions of fashion, and certainly some of the AACM members could have been drawn to them out of mere curiosity. Yet for others the image of Africa had become a vital influence that had reshaped perspectives of the purpose and value of art.

Indeed, for many cultural activists, Africa provided proof of the moral and artistic superiority of black people. Such "proof," it was believed, could be seen when comparing Africa's tribal cultures to the decaying condition of the West. According to these observers, the previously celebrated technological, industrial, and scientific successes of the Western world had led down a path of decline, a sentiment that had been shared by many white intellectuals since the initial crisis of modernity. By seeking to raise humanity above the natural world, Western culture, many nationalists believed, had sacrificed the sense of communalism and spiritualism preserved in the pan-African cultural progeny. Of course black nationalism was a partner in this overarching "Western culture," and as such, may be construed as an extension of modern uncertainty about the quest for an enlightenment through reason.[62] Nonetheless, in the mythology of Africa—and, for

59. By 1962, African fashion had already generated comment in the *Negro Digest*. See Peter Pan, "Stop Faking African Culture" (November 1962), 16–20; Horton Floyd, "How to Spot a Phony Intellectual" (March 1963), 28. Appearing under the category "Africana" were ads for books, notably Colin Turnbull's *The Lonely African* and *The Art of Africa*.

60. *Torch* (January 19–February 2, 1968), 2; (September 1966), 44.

61. In August 1965, the *Negro Digest* published a preview of the First World Festival of Negro Arts, which took place in Dakar, Senegal, in April 1966. A photograph of the AACM collaborator, Darlene Blackburn, striking an African dance pose, appeared in the *Torch* (September 5–19, 1968), 16.

62. Such views of an African cultural supremacy appear as early as the 1820s. See

that matter, in the everyday lives of many black Americans—they had identified real alternatives to the American social norm. Black culture's legacy of community closeness challenged the ideology of a fiercely competitive, capitalist state; its devotion to religious life, whether tribal or Afro-Christian, offered an antidote to the atheism of an alienated urban existence. The black tradition, from its romantic African past to its new-world incarnations, offered a way out of the cultural cycle stemming from Europe, an alternative to a belief system that many artists felt had been imposed on American culture rather than having grown up from within.

The vision of black cultural superiority acquired intellectual buttressing from the nationalist literature that had been circulating in the South Side arts community for years. The studies helped to shape an orally transmitted version of history that placed the African progeny at the forefront of cultural and spiritual achievement. Particularly noteworthy were the theories of an African basis to Western culture, popularized through the historical literature of Joel A. Rogers and George G. M. James, the revisionist interpretations of Albert Cleage and Maulana Karenga (Ronald Everett), and the supremacist rhetoric of Elijah Muhammad and Malcolm X.[63] In many of these studies, Africa appeared at the helm of Western cultural and artistic development; some even suggested that major historical figures presumed to be white—notably Ludwig von Beethoven—were in fact of black African extraction.[64] Versions of these theories became widely

---

George Frederickson, *The Black Image in the White Mind: The Debate on Afro-American Character and Destiny, 1817–1914* (Middletown: Wesleyan University Press, 1971), 13. See also Sterling Stuckey, *The Ideological Origins of Black Nationalism* (Boston: Beacon Press, 1972).

63. J. A. Rogers, *World's Great Men of Color* (published privately, ca. 1947; rev. ed., New York: Macmillan, 1972); *100 Amazing Facts about the Negro, with Complete Proof* (1957; St. Petersburg, Fla.: Helga M. Rogers, 1985); *Africa's Gift to America: The Afro-American in the Making and Saving of the U.S.* (New York: published privately, 1961). George G. M. Jones, *Stolen Legacy: The Greeks Were Not the Authors of Greek Philosophy, but the People of North Africa, Commonly Called the Egyptians* (New York: Philosophical Library, 1954). Elijah Muhammad, *Message to the Blackman* (Chicago: Muhammad Mosque no. 2, n.d.). Albert Cleage, *Black Messiah* (New York: Sheed and Ward, 1968). For a general account of these histories see Martin Bernal, *Black Athena: The Afroasiatic Roots of Classical Civilization*, vol. 1: "The Fabrication of Ancient Greece, 1785–1985"; vol. 2: "The Archaeological and Documentary Evidence" (New Brunswick: Rutgers University Press, 1987/1991).

64. J. A. Rogers, *Sex and Race*, vol. 3, 306–9; *World's Greatest Men of Color* (privately published, 1947), 538. Dominique-René De Lerma has conducted a thorough

accepted in arts circles around the South Side, sometimes showing up in the content of artists' works. In this way, nationalist literature fueled the growth of a private belief system that supported what many considered to be the moral imperative of their own creative expression.

Acknowledging the vast contingencies of cultural change as well as the discursive limits to our range of knowing, the most singleminded nationalist arguments must be seriously questioned in their applications to both history and the arts. For what today would be called an Afrocentric aesthetic can only reflect an inherently Western mindset that relies on an essentialist category of "black art" to construct a code of expressive exclusion. Indeed, the proclamations of black aesthetic greatness suggest that few artists had discarded the delimiting categories of Western critical evaluation, which enabled them to invert high culture's absolutes, placing black artifacts above those of whites. Such modernist rigidities might say more about the crisis of black identity at that moment than about the reality of an "authentic" African culture. "By rewriting history and culture to suit their own needs," John F. Szwed has observed, "such new Afro-American leaders also inadvertently join their own black-American parents in finding [an authentic] Africa an unsatisfactory ideological home." And as Lewis Nkosi remarks in a related insight, "It is interesting that the further back the African artist goes in exploring his tradition, the nearer he gets to the European avant-garde."[65] Of course, these artists were not historians, nor should they be observed as such; as creative activists, they looked the other way when potential inconsistencies could mar the effectiveness of their rhetoric. Accordingly, it would be wrongheaded to suppose that such inconsistencies lessen the movement's importance on artistic grounds, any more than Bach's belief in Jesus Christ or Kandinsky's spiritualism placed limitations on their significance as artists. Searching for a way out of the established dictates of mainstream culture, Chicago's radical black artists came to believe, quite earnestly it would appear, that their art spoke African. And regardless of their "purity" and historical accuracy—matters increasingly in dispute today—these beliefs inspired something quite pro-

investigation of this theory in "Beethoven as a Black Composer," *Black Music Research Journal* 10:1 (Spring 1990): 118–22.

65. John F. Szwed, "Discovering Afro-America," in *Black America*, ed. Szwed (New York: Basic Books, 1970), 290; Nkosi, *Home and Exile* (London: Longmans, 1965), 113. I thank Sandy Adell for calling my attention to Nkosi's insight.

found. They supplied an aesthetic basis and source of inspiration for the artistic renaissance that overtook black Chicago during the late 1960s.

V

An African-inspired cultural nationalism became the official position of the AACM, whose membership—particularly those aligned with Abrams—envisioned an immutable, pan-African musical legacy transcending cultural and historical categories. "Creative music" or, less euphemistically, as later defined by the Art Ensemble of Chicago, "Great Black Music," was a dialect of the mother tongue, a creation with African origins that had been spiritually preserved in the slave culture of the United States. Evoking images of the musician-seer of tribal Africa, many AACM musicians spoke in priestly terms of black music's spiritualism, which, they believed, revealed a kinship with the ancient myth-makers, the original cultural guardians of the black people. Malachi Favors, the Art Ensemble's "resident specialist" on Africa, helped to introduce many members to nationalist conceptions of black history and culture, which he had acquired through years of independent reading.[66] Favors has also been credited with inspiring the AACM's well-known use of "little instruments" (makeshift and exotic percussion instruments, both hand-held and stationary), which, Muhal Richard Abrams explained, "had to do with our thoughts regarding African instruments."[67] Moreover, Favors's performance makeup, which consisted of colorful facial paints,[68] originally expressed, according to Leslie Rout, the bass player's nationalist commitment to "Egyptian philosophy" and the return of black peoples' control of the known world.[69] Afrocentric philosophy helped to raise the status of the black musician in the eyes of the AACM membership. By reviving connections with tribal Africa, the black musician had

66. Jurg Solothurnmann, "Insights and Views of the Art Ensemble of Chicago," *Jazz Forum* (May 1969), 31.

67. Giddins, *Ridin' a Blue Note* (New York: Oxford University Press, 1981), 194. Litweiler speculates that it was Roscoe Mitchell who introduced the instruments, which he had been employing by 1966. Such an innovation is hard to pinpoint and may well have developed collaboratively (written communication, June 13, 1992).

68. These were subsequently adopted in performance by Jarman and the Art Ensemble's drummer, Don Moye.

69. Rout, "The AACM," *Journal of Popular Culture* 1:2, 128–40.

become, in the words of Askia Muhammad Touré (Rolland Snellings), "[a spiritual] holdover from our ancient past. . . . The major philosopher [and] cultural hero of the Black Nation."[70]

Available evidence suggests that the AACM's members, like many of their artistic cohorts on the South Side, had embraced nationalist reinterpretations of Western history with conclusions firmly in place. They sought support of their contention that previous white historians—and white people generally—had underrated African contributions, and they repeated versions of arguments by Rogers, James, and other writers to defend their points of view. By referring to historical events, they legitimized their version of history in academic terms at a time when the rhetoric of black activism had caught the attention of the press and had begun to gain backing in some segments of academe. And by arguing that jazz and Western culture derived from Africa, they elevated the status of black music, giving it historical respectability, with jazz becoming a principal component in the survival of a newly invented, ancient African "classical tradition." These efforts to defend publicly their conception of creative music suggest that some AACM members were looking beyond the closed aesthetic system that the most fervently separatist musicians had hoped to perpetuate. Indeed, the beliefs were, in the end, views of creative activism, forced to fit, somewhat illogically, with the values and classicist notions of a high jazz art in which the movement was inevitably grounded. In some cases the beliefs may have served careerist motives, particularly in light of the decision of certain members, Braxton included, ultimately to abandon the Association's ideals in favor of professional pursuits in Europe. How to maintain a commitment to cultural nationalist doctrine while pursuing one's own professional goals would prove to be a recurring, if unspoken, dilemma for several members of the organization.

The AACM's notion of African-based creativity was intimately linked with a collective concept of aesthetic spiritualism. "Spiritualism" became the foremost aesthetic criterion for identifying greatness in art. In an interview with John Litweiler, Abrams spelled out some of these spiritualist notions that had been developing among the musicians since the early years of the Experimental Band.[71] He told Litweiler that life is a balance between two fundamental aspects, the

70. Askia Muhammad Touré, "We Are on the Move and Our Music Is Moving with Us," *Liberator* 5 (October 1965); "The Crises in Black Culture," *Journal of Black Poetry* 1:8 (Spring 1968). Both reprinted in *Black Nationalism in America,* ed. John H. Bracey, Jr., August Meier, and Elliott Rudwick (New York: Bobbs-Merrill Co., 1970).

71. Litweiler, "A Man with an Idea," *Down Beat,* 23, 26, 41.

"concrete" and the "abstract." Musicians who seek spiritual transcendence are drawn more toward the latter aspect, an unknown region beyond the boundary of accepted thought. For Abrams and his followers, "transcendence" referred to a kind of intellectual and emotional catharsis. Yet it also defined something else: devotion to aesthetic spiritualism would improve political awareness. The act of experimental music-making would teach musicians about "the lies [black] people have been told," while providing a mechanism for them to "break out of" the mindset that goes hand in hand with spiritual and cultural oppression. The point of complete transcendence was what Abrams called the "spiritual plane," where, through collaborative creation, intuition and intellect meet.

The AACM's concept of aesthetic spiritualism had ultimately extended from its commitment to black self-reliance. Spiritualism celebrated African notions of community and ritual, revamping them to suit a contemporary American end. A commitment to collective action on both artistic and social levels would, it was believed, improve one's chances for personal gain. By working together for a common good, the AACM musician, as Roscoe Mitchell put it, would learn "to deal with [one]self as an individual."[72] Collective improvisation itself offered a pathway toward self-improvement; it served as a kind of musical group therapy during which the performers exposed the depths of their creative psychologies.[73] Aesthetic spiritualism represented a confluence of observations on African musical practice with a countercultural quest for self-expression and spiritual freedom. Learning to "let go" musically affirmed their African-inspired theories of catharsis through a process that resembled social encounter, mixing metaphors of tribal trance ritual and psychotherapy. Equating spiritualism with free expression revealed, moreover, something about the sensibility of the radical free-jazz musician who displayed a propensity for change, a willingness to take chances in the name of aesthetic and personal progress. "Change is synonymous with any conception of the deity," Abrams explained to John Litweiler.[74] As a mechanism for self-

72. Martin, "Blowing out in Chicago," *Down Beat* 20–21.

73. Mitchell recalls his turn toward free jazz as a struggle against musical repression: "After I began to really listen to this music, I would be playing and feel the urge within myself to play things I would hear, and I fought it for a long time because I wasn't really sure that this was what was happening. Then after I stopped fighting, it just started pouring out." Martin, "Blowing out in Chicago," *Down Beat,* 21. Abrams, moreover, envisioned his big-band scores as "psychological plots." Litweiler, "A Man with an Idea," *Down Beat,* 26.

74. Litweiler, "AACM's 10th Anniversary: Voices in the Wilderness," *Chicago Reader,* 12.

discovery, change also lies at the heart of the African-American concept of hip, which is traditionally associated with irony, cunning, and an inscrutable character.[75]

It is in the African-American heritage that one finds the principal cultural foundations for the AACM's spiritualist aesthetics. As noted earlier, images and rituals of religious life have survived the course of African-American history, persisting as a kind of cultural anachronism within the context of a highly secularized and rational West. "The masses of Negroes may increasingly criticize their church [and] may develop a more secular outlook on life," wrote E. Franklin Frazier, "yet they find in their religious heritage an opportunity to satisfy their deepest emotional yearnings."[76] Such retentions of spiritualist symbolism live on in African-American music, expressing what David N. Baker has called the "humanizing influence" of its emotive properties.[77] Lawrence Levine and Sterling Stuckey have traced these retentions to an early historical background in studies of landmark significance; Charles Keil and John F. Szwed have, in turn, supplied important supporting evidence of modern continuities in secular musics—what Keil calls the "spiritualist ideology" of the blues. In jazz, moreover, ecstatic experiences growing out of the black vernacular have provided a sturdy, if somewhat discrete, frame of reference for musical interpretation, as previously observed by Albert Murray and Amiri Baraka, and explored exhaustively by Neil Leonard.[78] Southern-

75. David Dalby speculates that "hip" originates with the Wolof verb and agentive suffix, *hipi-kat,* meaning "a person who has opened his eyes." Dalby, "Americanisms that May Once Have Been Africanisms," the *Times* (London) (July 19, 1969), 9; reprinted in *Mother Wit from the Laughing Barrell,* ed. Alan Dundes (Jackson: University of Mississippi Press, 1973), 138.

76. E. Franklin Frazier, *The Black Church in America* (New York: Schocken Books, 1964), 73.

77. See Richard Abrams, David N. Baker, and Charles Ellison, "The Social Role of Jazz," in *Reflections on Afro-American Music* (Kent State University Press, 1973), 101–10.

78. Levine, *Black Culture and Black Consciousness* (New York: Oxford University Press, 1976); Stuckey, *Slave Culture.* While Levine and Stuckey differ about the extent to which the antebellum sacred world and the African past pervade the present, they share a belief in the formative role of the sacred experience in the making of the modern black musical character. Keil, *Urban Blues* (Chicago: University of Chicago Press, 1968); Szwed, "Afro-American Musical Adaptation," *Afro-American Anthropology,* ed. Norman Whitten and Szwed (New York: Free Press, 1970), 219–30; Murray, *Stomping the Blues* (New York: Da Capo, 1976); Baraka (LeRoi Jones), *Blues People* (New York: William Morrow, 1963); Leonard, *Jazz Myth and Religion* (New York: Oxford University Press, 1987). See also David Evans, "Black American Music as a Symbol of Identity," *Jazz Forschung* 13 (1981): 105–16.

born AACM musicians such as Leo Smith and Fred Anderson had first-hand contact with music in vernacular settings; others, including Malachi Favors, Alvin Fielder, and Leroy Jenkins, have recalled particular musical experiences in the black church. Yet even those raised in urban, essentially secular environments such as Chicago, that extension of the cultural South, would have encountered in their daily lives a creative ideology informed by conceptions of the sacred.[79]

Spiritualism as an aesthetic category might seem hopelessly subjective to the formalist critic who seeks to put a finger on the musical attributes of artistic greatness. Yet that kind of identification was precisely what the AACM musicians (and many traditional jazz players) were trying to avoid. While recognizing differing levels of originality and technical ability, these musicians sought to do away with critical efforts to objectify art, a practice that they considered alien to their African-based notions of art merging with life. According to the AACM's logic, once the critic isolates qualities of greatness, the life essence of the music is destroyed. Such skepticism about critics and their analytical categories has a long history in jazz culture, reflecting a mode of resistance firmly rooted in the African-American heritage.[80] Free-jazz musicians, however, turned this African-American aversion for constrictive labeling into a principal component of their ideological platform. "Black people produce and white people package," remarked drummer Andrew Cyrille, objecting to institutionalized labels; "we are more or less a race of consumer employees."[81] Rejecting the term "jazz" altogether, Ornette Coleman protested, "I still have that 'black jazz' image, I'm an entertainer who's supposed to exist on

79. Most members had been raised in Chicago, typically on the South and West sides, where, "like all dark people," as Leo Smith has remarked with only slight exaggeration, they learned to make music at church with their families. For example, Leroy Jenkins learned to play violin in his family church; Alvin Fielder recalls performing in gospel groups; Malachi Favors lived the sacred life as the son of a preacher. Smith himself was born in Mississippi, the son of a bluesman. Fielder has remarked about the AACM, "It was like a church—it *was* my church." See Wilmer, *As Serious as Your Life,* 113, 117.

80. Levine, "Black Laughter" and "Secular Song as Protest," *Black Culture and Black Consciousness;* Henry Louis Gates, Jr., *The Signifying Monkey* (New York: Oxford University Press, 1988); Houston A. Baker, Jr., *Blues, Ideology, and Afro-American Literature* (Chicago: University of Chicago Press, 1984). This calls to mind Ellington's well-known objections to the term "jazz." He preferred broad categories of "good music" and "bad music." In a conversation with Nat Hentoff, he recalls that in the 1920s he proposed to Fletcher Henderson that they promote the term "Negro music." Hentoff, *Jazz Is* (New York: Avon Books, 1976), 30.

81. Valerie Wilmer, *As Serious as Your Life,* 225.

a certain level and that's it."[82] According to many AACM musicians, the destruction of the black cultural essence has been the aim of criticism all along. Leo Smith argued, for example, that critics have created rules and labels in order to set limits on black musical expression.[83] Echoing Smith's claim, the Art Ensemble of Chicago suggested to a group of writers for *Jazz Hot* that it was whites who applied labels to black musical genres.[84] From the AACM's perspective, acceptance of established critical categories would only perpetuate the injustices and repression black musicians have had to endure over the years. Accordingly, terms such as "Great Black Music," "Creative Music," and "spiritual plane" offered a way out of that trap, setting up new boundaries constrained only by the limits of one's own musical imagination.

Yet it would be hard to ignore the contradiction between the musicians' efforts to distance themselves from Western artistic notions while simultaneously pursuing exceedingly Western, progressivist artistic goals. There is no doubt that the AACM players embraced modernist views of style and greatness. They valued originality; they recognized virtuosity; they looked up to the same jazz "masters" honored by the critical community. Quite clearly, they, knowingly or not, acknowledged the critical standards and measures in which jazz, as an American form of "popular entertainment," had been situated over the years. Indeed, these standards provided the basis for the edifice of black classicism they had constructed as a buttress against an encroaching, dehistoricized postmodernism. Clearly the AACM had a right to argue against the categories and constraints commentators have typically imposed on the art form. Yet it would be foolhardy and to some extent racist to propose that these musicians had internalized a constructed African aesthetic to the point where they no longer heard or thought as Americans.

Recalling the commentary of early free-jazz musicians, Abrams and Mitchell have shown that the AACM had some clear ideas about how aesthetic spiritualism could be expressed musically. According to their view, "spiritualism" and "the spiritual plane" were metaphors for a brand of collectively improvised music that exceeded the constraints of harmony. "Cats that play bop are more [often] concerned with things like chords and changes rather than spirits," explained Roscoe

82. Richard Williams, "Ornette and the Pipes of Joujouka," *Melody Maker* (March 17, 1973), 22–23.

83. Wilmer, *As Serious as Your Life,* 114.

84. Philippe Gras, Daniel Crux, and Marc Bernard, "A.A.C.M.," *Jazz Hot* (October 1969), 18.

Mitchell. While acknowledging that spiritualism could surface in harmonic music, he maintained that "in free music you are dependent on the spirits because you don't want to fool with those chords."[85] Abrams offered a similar view when outlining his concept of a concrete/abstract dualism. Equating harmony with the emotional and the "concrete," he proposed the theory that "the concrete can't sustain a progressive-type mind." "Melody," on the other hand, which he associated with the abstract, "generates a purely mental atmosphere" that may induce "mind expansion."[86] Driving melody is rhythm, the second element of the spiritual. Unlike harmony, which in spatial terms translates as "vertical," rhythm is time-oriented or "horizontal." According to Abrams and Mitchell, then, harmony stood as an aesthetic barrier that restrained black musicians in their search for spiritual unity.[87] As the principal component of European-based music, it became a metaphor for white cultural dominance and oppression: harmony was a sonic reconstruction of the disciplining practices that had objectified black difference, of the rationalism that had stifled African spiritualism. In rhythm and melody, on the other hand, the musicians identified formal attributes that stressed the communal, multilinear orientation of West African musics and traditional African-American styles from early spirituals to skiffle bands to blues. Aesthetic and social concerns would be joined in a compositional procedure that made group awareness a fundamental part of successful music-making.

Recorded performances by AACM bands bear out these observations. On the title track of Abrams's first album, *Levels and Degrees of Light* (1967, 1/1), slow, sustained melodic improvisations performed first by vocalist Penelope Taylor, then by Abrams (playing clarinet), supply the principal pitched material of the work. Shimmering cymbal rolls and oscillating vibraphone swells accompany the improvised lines, creating a sonic texture that evokes images of Eastern exotica and that, in reflecting the musicians' embrace of both modernist and black-based sound worlds, recalls early modern "exotic" works, such as Maurice Ravel's *Asie*. On Abrams's *Young at Heart* (1969, 2/1), the quiet clatter of little instruments and plucked piano strings provides a backdrop for Leo Smith's nontonal and often ame-

85. Martin, "Blowing out in Chicago," *Down Beat*, 21.

86. Litweiler, "A Man with an Idea," *Down Beat*, 26.

87. Abrams did not attempt to explain the occasional appearance of harmony in AACM performances, nor did he address why he offered lessons in it as part of the AACM program. It is likely that the musicians had recontextualized it to fit an aesthetic centralizing texture and rhythm.

lodic trumpet introduction. On *My Thoughts Are My Future—Now and Forever* (*Levels* 1/2), a frenetic pulse and Abrams's dense, percussive piano textures (suggesting the influence of Cecil Taylor) support a nontonal, free-jazz improvisation. Linear-oriented, coloristic effects also appear in Abrams's *The Bird Song* (*Levels* 2/1), where a wash of percussion effects and instrumental imitations of bird sounds make punning reference both to Parker and the ornithological interests of Dolphy and Messiaen. The allusions also revive, in abstraction, the signifying potential of the bird reference in jazz, as outlined in Ralph Ellison's famous discussion of the Blue Devils Orchestra's *They Picked Poor Robin Clean*.[88] Here, the bird as trickster, the in-the-know observer, provides commentary through rhythmically enlivened textures to challenge mainstream musical orthodoxies. Underscoring the resistant character of *The Bird Song* is the poetic introduction by Amus Mor (David Moore). Blending references to Africa with poetic images of life on the South Side, Mor transcends the limits of historical and temporal distance to promote an exalted, unified blackness. The performance is cast in a dense, reverberating haze that mimics the acoustics of a church cathedral.[89]

On other AACM recordings, linear and rhythmic emphases are presented in the form of chordless and pulseless group compositions in which the members of the rhythm section become equal partners in collective collaboration. On works such as Joseph Jarman's *As If It Were the Seasons* and *Song for Christopher* (1968, *As If It* 1/1, 2/1), and Roscoe Mitchell's *The Little Suite, Sound* (1966, *Sound* 1/2, 2/1), and *Congliptious* (1968, *Congliptious* 2/1), traditional instrumental functions give way to an egalitarian group exploration of sound color or what Mitchell calls sonic "atmospheres." Through a kind of organic unfolding, textural colors emerge, evolve, fade, and reemerge in a kaleidoscopic panoply of percussion and wind instrumental sounds. Lacking a harmonic platform, the musicians work instead from group example, building their improvisations from the musical style and the mood that the preliminary written sections or head arrangements set up. Subsequently, they perform in a collective, constructivist fashion, according to the rhythmic, motivic, and stylistic character of the ensemble's collaborative ideas. Quiet, percussive sounds inspire gentle bowing or subtle mouthpiece noises; flashes

88. Ellison, "On Birdwatching," *Shadow and Act,* 231. Gates elaborates on the essay in *Signifying Monkey,* 104–5.

89. Bob Koester notes that the echo was added at Abrams's request. Will Smith, "Muhal Richard Abrams, Young at Heart/Wise in Time," *Down Beat* (December 9, 1971), 18.

of periodic, rhythmic propulsion lead to hard-swinging, energized blowing. Sometimes a particular musician will stand out, during which times the others accompany. At other times, all players perform in parallel, creating a noninteractive, multilinear web. Instability here suggests the quality of "spatiality," developing from the performance's abstract style and lack of formal, syntactical order.[90] Extending the metaphor, spatiality calls to mind the image of free-floating—or, recalling Braxton's phrase, of being "firmly planted in mid-air"—which, as a mode cut loose from mundane, earthly fixities, evokes the sacred.[91] Rhythmically, moreover, spatiality is enhanced as performers establish a perpetual state of unpredictability that intensifies motion. Heightened rhythmic sense, in turn, suggests an abstraction of swing, reasserting images of dance and bodily movement that inform the character of African-American music.[92] One hears another African-American impulse in the sheer range of percussion. More fundamental than exotic allusions to tribal Africa, the AACM's "little instruments" recall the makeshift sound sources of an earlier time in black history, celebrating through modernist abstraction the black vernacular musical legacy.

Perhaps most remarkable about the AACM improvisations is the process by which these dynamic structures are produced. The improvisations *work,* and they work because of the performers' uncanny ability to discern interesting improvisational pathways during the moment-by-moment act of creation. The musicians are constantly faced with decisions of where to begin and end phrases and sections, when to play and not to play. And they make these decisions to shape a composite texture, while also paying attention to signs of where the improvisation might lead. Such acute sensitivity developed from years of continuous ensemble playing and perhaps more generally from the collective orientation of African-American musical practice, which has been documented at least as far back as the invention of the spirituals.[93] It also pays tribute to the organization's communal ideal, which

90. Robert Morgan, "Musical Time/Musical Space," *Critical Inquiry* 6 (Spring 1980): 527–38.

91. The association of abstraction with the sacred has informed modernist art since Mondrian and Kandinsky. Interestingly, Kandinsky's *Black Relationship* appears as the cover of Braxton's album *Six Compositions: Quartet* (1981).

92. Olly Wilson, "The Association of Movement and Music as a Manifestation of a Black Conceptual Approach to Music-Making," in *Report of the Twelfth Congress, Berkeley 1977,* ed. Daniel Heartz and Bonnie Wade (Basel: Bärenreiter/American Musicological Society, 1981), 98–113.

93. Levine, "The Sacred World of the Black Slaves," *Black Culture and Black Consciousness,* 25–30.

may explain the quality of anonymity one hears in some of the early AACM improvisations: at moments of true union, the performers offer convincing evidence that they have achieved their ultimate aesthetic end, having melded together their respective musical personalities into an all-encompassing, spiritually unified whole.

The rejection of harmonic and tonal practices in the name of spiritual and ideological freedom, then, lies at the heart of the free-jazz movement. These notions to lead the music away from traditional tonal practices first appeared with the work of Coleman, Taylor, Ayler, and Coltrane, and then reached an apex with Chicago's AACM. The revitalization of jazz through advances in the areas of texture and rhythm reflected a sensitivity to contemporary West African practices as it reinforced ideological identification with the recently emancipated African states. Furthermore, the appearance of specific formal traits, notably a linear-oriented textural heterogeneity, suggests that these procedures may relate to early practices transplanted in the colonial era.[94] Yet regardless of the possible African linkages, what seems most relevant to the present discussion is the music's basis in patterns associated with the African-American tradition. In *The Jazz Tradition,* Martin Williams contends that jazz, at its root, is foremost a rhythmic-based art that finds its source in the musical legacy of black America.[95] Free players seem to have drawn from these indigenous practices as a way of reasserting qualities of blackness in a new form of artistic expression. As musicians seeking to make a new generational statement, they cast an art form that gave voice to black distinctiveness through qualities of rhythm and line, qualities that traditionally eluded imitation by whites. Reflecting their stature as serious artists, moreover, they restyled these elusive features by appropriating the abstract, nontonal sound world of modernism. By association, then, free jazz had become aligned with modernism's creative intelligentsia, even as their appropriative efforts allowed them to maintain a certain vital distance.

94. Olly Wilson, "The Significance of the Relationship between Afro-American Music and West African Music," *Black Perspective in Music* (Spring 1974), 3–21. Wilson has expanded on this view in "Musical Analysis of African-American Music," paper presented at the Society for Ethnomusicology preconference symposium, Oakland, Calif. (November 7, 1990). Moreover, Robert Farris Thompson has argued that African rhythmic conceptions have oriented the character of certain African-American visual expressions, in *The Flash of the Spirit* (New York: Random House, 1983; Vintage, 1984).

95. Williams, *The Jazz Tradition,* rev. ed. (New York: Oxford University Press, 1983). This position is put forth in the introduction and then explored in a series of critical essays.

VI

Early free-jazz musicians have typically denied that modernist concert music influenced their art, most likely out of fear that their creative efforts would be explained away as weak imitations of white cultural achievement. Yet, while it is true that white musicians have repeatedly won glory at the expense of black innovation, it would hardly aid the black musicians' cause to deny that free music has drawn heavily from modernism. In fact, such denials have more often produced the opposite: they have perpetuated a rather perverse vision of the jazz tradition as a cloistered, self-contained community, insulated from the broader musical culture and world of ideas. In fact, jazz musicians have always been musically wide reaching, continually drawing their sources from outside the tradition, from pop, from the concert repertory, from any area of musical interest. In the 1950s, as musicians grew increasingly self-conscious of their positions as artists, they began to borrow liberally from concert styles and practices. By the 1960s, free musicians had transformed the modernist aesthetic for their own uses, recasting it to assert a specifically black-oriented artistry. In this way, the development of free jazz may be seen as a kind of dialogue taking place between white and black in the context of artistic modernism, a dialogue not unlike the parallel give and take appearing in the realm of rock 'n' roll.

Ornette Coleman was one of the first to embrace the language and ideas of musical modernism. His theoretical formulations of harmonic unison and harmolodics, for example, appear to stem from Boulez's concept of *aleatory,* and his application of concert musical elements to jazz grew out of early studies with Gunther Schuller, together with his involvement in Schuller's thirdstream sessions of 1960.[96] For Coleman, however, modernist theory appeared to serve above all as an elaborate justification for his original, iconoclastic art.[97] Cecil Taylor,

96. Coleman's concert works include *Forms and Sounds for Wind Quintet* (1965), *Saints and Soldiers* (1967), *Inventions of Symphonic Poems* (1967), and *Skies of America* (1972). He appeared on Schuller's recording *Jazz Abstractions,* a serial work.

97. Coleman's reference to "aleatoric" bass lines appears in A. B. Spellman, *Black Music: Four Lives* (New York: Schocken Books, 1966), 123–24. "Harmonic unison" is an ambiguous term to which Martin Williams referred in his notes to *Free Jazz.* "Harmolodics," on the other hand, is a concept that remains cloaked in obscurity. Coleman gave this definition in *Down Beat:* "Harmolodics is the use of the physical and mental of one's own logic [*sic*] made into an expression of sound to bring about the musical sensation of unison executed by a single person or with a group. Harmony, melody, speed, rhythm, time, and phrases all have equal position in the results that come from the placing and spacing of ideas." Coleman, "Pro Session: Prime Time for Har-

on the other hand, acquired a formal knowledge of the concert tradition in the academy, having attended the New England Conservatory from 1952, where he studied early modern repertories, including those of his special favorites, Stravinsky and Bartók. (Taylor has said, "Bartók showed me what you can do with folk material.")[98] In his *Enter Evening,* he openly embraced European postwar modernism and perhaps even a particular composition: Stockhausen's *Zeitmasse,* which he had heard in 1964.[99] Yet more often, Taylor's modernism took the form of a rhythmic propulsiveness and kinetic energy that supplanted traditional qualities of swing. Further, his technical essays, which betray a familiarity with the "scientific" theoretical literature of contemporary composition, owe equally to the rhythm and musical metaphors of contemporary black poetry, suggesting a complementary oral discourse.[100]

Other early free-jazz musicians have demonstrated similar familiarity with musical modernism: Eric Dolphy was an admirer of the work of Schoenberg, Satie, Varèse, and Stockhausen as well as a collaborator with concert composers; Don Cherry expressed enthusiasm for the concert repertory, including Stravinsky's *L'histoire du Soldat;* Sunny Murray created a performance procedure that drew consciously from the work of Cage, Boulez, Stockhausen, and Varèse; Don Ellis, a white trumpeter tangentially affiliated with the movement, actively explored the music of Harry Partch.[101] The particular nature of these borrowings testified to the analytical orientation of the free-jazz musician, who took an interest in the most intellectually engaging musical

molodics," *Down Beat* (July 1983), 54–55. In his essay on Coleman for *The New Grove Dictionary of Jazz,* moreover, Gunther Schuller suggested that harmolodics is based on the superimposition of the same musical phrase (or phrase relatives) in varying keys, producing a kind of polytonality and heterophony. But Coleman's definition of "unison" as "one's own voice" (*Down Beat,* 54) suggests that it may be just as appropriate to think of harmolodics as a theoretical poetics akin to Braxton's musical system.

98. Spellman, *Black Music,* 28.

99. Ibid., 34.

100. See Taylor's notes to the album *Unit Structures.* His musical poetry appears most forcefully as *Chimampas* (1991).

101. Vladimir Simosko and Barry Tepperman, *Eric Dolphy: A Musical Biography and Discography* (Washington: Smithsonian Institution Press, 1971; Da Capo, 1979), 12; Litweiler, *The Freedom Principle: Jazz after 1958* (New York: Morrow, 1984), 72. Dolphy appeared on Schuller's recording of *Abstraction* and participated in the ONCE Festival of avant-garde music in 1964. See Gilbert Chase, *America's Music,* 2d ed. (1966), 664. Robert Levin, "Sunny Murray: The Continuous Cracking of Glass," *Jazz and Pop* 4:5 (1969): 52–55. For information about Cherry, see Dan Morgenstern, "John Tchicai, A Calm Member of the Avant-Garde," *Down Beat* (February 10, 1966), 20–21, 49–50.

advances of the era. Yet each of these artists actively recast the dominant styles into a personal musical vocabulary that placed the black musical legacy at the forefront.

Modernist innovation may have even moved free-jazz musicians to revitalize the linear character of their African-American–based music. From the turn of the century, concert composers had been exploring alternatives to the harmonic basis of Western art music through experiments with new timbres, textures, and forms based on temporal strictures. Preserial atonalists and bitonalists such as Skryabin, Stravinsky, and Schoenberg (before 1912) gave special emphasis to compositional experiments with sound color and rhythm in their early modern works. By the 1910s, the French composer Erik Satie had identified duration as a principal formal constraint; in *Choses vues à droite et à gauche (sans lunettes)* (1914) and later works such as *Socrate* (1918) and *Relâche* (1924), he relied on phrase and section lengths to define compositional structure. By midcentury, moreover, textural and temporal explorations had become the overriding compositional interest for nonserial modernists such as Varèse and the later sound-mass composers, Penderecki and Ligeti, who sometimes applied such parameters to regulate the style and architecture of their works. Satie's own antiharmonic conception had made by this time an indirect impact on American experimentalists, largely through the example of John Cage, who held up the former's approach as a historical precedent for his own time-generated, compositional structures. In "Defense of Satie," Cage's controversial lecture delivered at Black Mountain College (1948), he paid tribute to the French composer while charging that Beethoven's harmonic influence "has been deadening to the art of music."[102]

For serialists, nonserial modernists, and experimentalists alike, harmony had been cast out as the Cassandra of musical invention, prompting composers to give greater emphasis to tone-color exploration and rhythm in their filling of the musical space. The elements central to the modernist style seem to have been absorbed into jazz, appealing to artists who recognized linkages between the liberation from conventional tonal-music parameters (scale, harmony, meter, etc.) and the black-centered concern for musical freedom. With free jazz, black music and modernism achieved a level of structural syncre-

102. "Satie Controversy" and "Defense of Satie," *Musical America* (April 1, 1950 and December 15, 1950), reprinted in *John Cage: Documentary Monographs in Modern Art*, ed. Richard Kostelanetz (New York: Praeger, 1970). See also "Erik Satie," *Art News Annual* (1958), reprinted in *Silence* (Middletown: Wesleyan University Press, 1962), 76–82.

tism, in which likenesses from both musical worlds encouraged stylistic merging.[103] These interactions were motivated above all by the musicians' desires to express abstract artistic concepts at a time when the aesthetic constraints of traditional culture were being unleashed. While high modernism had previously reinforced conventional aesthetic hierarchies, it had also been traditionally associated with a left-of-center artistic elite whose values complemented the oppositional views of many jazz musicians. Accordingly, by embracing modernism, free-jazz artists would distance themselves from the assimilated mainstream world while affirming musically their ties to the African-American heritage.

For the AACM in particular, the embrace of modernism serviced the musicians' cultural nationalist ideals. Modernism provided an artistic bulwark that reinforced their separatist defenses against the values and aesthetics of the white world. In this sense, the early AACM fit Peter Bürger's definition of "avant-garde" as a movement that sought to distinguish itself institutionally from the accepted social and aesthetic position of a dominant class.[104] Ultimately, however, the musicians' hope of maintaining a separatist aesthetic proved a social failure, once the leading figures—Bowie, Mitchell, Jarman, Threadgill, Braxton, and eventually Abrams himself—began to enter the jazz mainstream. That step seemed to fracture the organization, upsetting those with stronger separatist convictions. And although the AACM has survived, the success of the most celebrated bands and musicians has made it into something different from when it held high hopes of creating a nationalist musical culture, a dream that may have seemed more obtainable at the time than it does from a distance today.

Mapping Out an Experimental Music

News of Chicago's vanguard arts movement reached Anthony Braxton while he was still stationed in Korea, where he had been transferred in 1965 to the Eighth Army Band. In letters from friends and his cousin, Rafiki Woodard, he had heard about the revitalizing efforts of organizations on the South Side, and, in particular, about the AACM's initiatives in the name of black musical freedom. The stories seemed

103. A theory of African/European syncretism in North American music appears in Richard Waterman, "African Influence on the Music of the Americas," in *Acculturation in the Americas,* vol. 2, ed. Sol Tax (Chicago: University of Chicago Press, 1952; Cooper Union, 1967), 207–20.

104. Bürger, *The Theory of the Avant-Garde* (Minneapolis: University of Minnesota Press, 1984).

Anthony Braxton (*right*) with Joseph Jarman in Chicago's Hyde Park (ca. 1968). Courtesy Anthony Braxton and Joseph Jarman. Photographer unknown.

to have given some hope and comfort to a young man who by this time felt alienated from the army's musical fraternity, which, as he perceived it, had treated with suspicion his interest in musics challenging mainstream aesthetic norms. No doubt such suspicions reflected in a general way broad social and cultural differences between Braxton and the others, differences that music tended to reinforce. Braxton's recollections of a trying and sometimes painful final year in the service help to explain why he was so anxious to join the AACM upon his return to Chicago in the fall of 1966. On his first day back, he called Woodard, who told him about an AACM concert at the Abraham Lincoln Center. At the concert he saw an old friend, Roscoe Mitchell, who introduced him to some of the Association's members. Mitchell then agreed to sponsor his initiation into the organization. Braxton had become a regular AACM member by the end of the year.

As an AACM artist, Braxton upheld many of the same political and aesthetic views embraced by his colleagues. He shared their aversion to established institutions and, at meetings and in conversation, learned about the Association's philosophy of "creative music." Furthermore, from Malachi Favors and others he heard the specifics of Afrocentric theory as he encountered during the course of his AACM experience the spectrum of radical opinion. Inevitably, Braxton's conversations with other AACM musicians took place while playing, discussing, and listening to music. As a result, theories of aesthetics and social change developed hand in hand, as part of the same intellectual complex, with "creative music" representing the dominant ideology of the organization.

Most influential on Braxton's musical development was Muhal Richard Abrams. His teachings reinforced the aesthetic views that Braxton had already come to embrace, as they helped him to shape his thinking about the position of black art in American life. Musically and intellectually, Braxton learned through Abrams to trust his instincts, to follow his passions, to pursue openly and freely interests that would contribute to his creative ends. He received from him encouragement to listen widely, to compose his own music, and to develop an approach that, complementing the organization's commitment to radical innovation, would express his own personal character. Taking to heart Abrams's teachings, Braxton followed a course that ultimately exceeded even the radicalism of the AACM, pursuing simultaneously a range of interests. He listened to and transcribed recorded performances of Coltrane, Dolphy, Coleman, and other jazz innovators. He studied scores of Schoenberg, Varèse, Webern, Stockhausen, and Xenakis; these inquiries eventually led to an informal AACM study group that included trumpeter Leo Smith and, at times, Roscoe Mitchell and Joseph Jarman. In addition to analyzing scores, Braxton read standard histories of jazz and modern concert music. One of these appears to have been William Austin's *Music of the Twentieth Century* (1966), a seminal study in its acknowledgment of jazz as serious art. Another was John Cage's *Silence,* which, Braxton reports, "blew me away."[105] As a complement to this search for knowledge and understanding, Braxton also began to read intensively in philosophy and religion, first on his own—mainly cult books on mysticism and Daisetz Suzuki's and Alan Watts's studies of Zen—then formally as a part-time student at Roosevelt University.

Abrams's instruction paved the way for Braxton's experimental initiatives, for an expression that would ultimately exceed conventional social, stylistic, and racial categories. That pursuit was reinforced by the message of the AACM, which had institutionalized the equation of musical modernism and the belief in the creative potency of the black

105. Interview with Anthony Braxton (May 5, 1983).

musician. Somewhat ironically, the AACM inspired Braxton to pursue his divergent musical interests, even as other members focused theirs more specifically on jazz. By acknowledging the Association's cultural nationalist doctrine, Braxton could intellectually justify his disparate musical loves, from marches and rhythm 'n' blues to concert music and free jazz; they would represent, according to Braxton's thinking, a confluence of vital, black-derived artistry. "Creative music," then, would identify an array of radical expressions that, paradoxically, transcended racial limits while responding to impulses thought to emanate from an ancient African creative wellspring. In narrow, artistic terms, one wonders if "creative music" defined, at this point, simply all the musical loves of an intellectually curious and flexible young man.[106] Yet in practical terms, the AACM's notion of creativity had legitimized Braxton's ventures into the concert realm and his attempts to bridge the gap between musical modernism and jazz. It supplied "proof" of the aesthetic equivalence of jazz and concert music, and accordingly, of high and low art, equivalences that Braxton had believed in for some time. As such, it offered a basis for developing a creative voice that spoke symbolically of a new era of black intellectual and cultural advancement, during a time when many radical African Americans, like Braxton, believed the traditional social structures and aesthetic preconceptions that went hand in hand with them could be overturned.[107]

It is also important to recognize that the AACM interested Braxton for another more practical reason: his options were undoubtedly few. With the jazz scene in such a dismal state, there were only occasional opportunities for professional employment, whether one played dixieland, mainstream, or free. Scarcity of jobs was compounded by the condition of separatism that had afflicted the community, making circumstances difficult for musicians on either side of the racial fence. With the AACM, however, Braxton would have a chance to gain

106. "You can list my influences as being Paul Desmond and then Ornette [Coleman], Eric Dolphy, Jackie McLean, Karlheinz Stockhausen, Miles [Davis], James Brown, and the Chicago Transit Authority," Braxton told John Litweiler. Liner notes to *Three Compositions of New Jazz* (1968).

107. Gifford, "Chicago: The New Music," *Jazz and Pop* (January 1969), 40–44. In his notes to *Three Compositions,* John Litweiler begins: "'We're on the eve of the complete fall of Western ideas and life values,' says Anthony Braxton, one of the newest generation of musical prophets. 'We're in the process of developing more meaningful values, and our music is a direct extension of this. We place more emphasis on the meaningful areas of music, and less on artifacts—'art facts' meaning today's academic over-emphasis on harmonic structure, chord progressions, facility, mathematics, the empirical aspects of art.'"

experience performing with some of the best jazz musicians in Chicago. His recollections suggest that this reason was as important as the motivations of aesthetics and ideology. At the time Braxton was a young, intellectually engaged musician who had become entranced by the sound world of modernism, and who, while displaying serious political opinion, had only begun to appreciate the complex relationship between those tastes and the radical politics he upheld. Shortly, however, Braxton's views would connect more directly with his aesthetic perspective, influencing the character of his music-making and defining the creative path he would follow.

I

Over the ensuing thirty months of regular membership in the AACM, Braxton charted out the major musical directions he would pursue over the next twenty-five years. At times his actions suggested a principal commitment to contemporary practices in free jazz. At others they took the form of works best fitting the description of concert music. Yet it was the creative partnership of jazz and modernism that ultimately established the true character of Braxton's music, and that posed the most serious challenge to the way in which critics had previously described improvised art. By integrating the elements of nontonal concert music and free jazz, often in complex, formally elaborate ways, Braxton established the groundwork for the creation of a similarly double-sided aesthetic stemming from his inculcation of the AACM's cultural ideology with an emerging affinity for globalist artistic values.

Braxton's professional activities ranged widely. As a sideman, he worked with several AACM bands, including those led by Roscoe Mitchell, Gerald Donovan, and, most often, Muhal Richard Abrams. As a leader, he performed at the Abraham Lincoln Center, the Phamous Lounge, the University of Chicago, and, on the West Side, the White Elephant. Personnel would vary, but most often included saxophonist Maurice McIntyre (Kalaparusha Ahrah Difda), bassist Charles Clark, and drummer Thurman Barker.[108] Complementing this work in vanguard music were his occasional performances with pop

108. Interview with Anthony Braxton (May 6, 1983). Hans Wachtmeister reports that Leroy Jenkins often joined this quartet. He also notes that Braxton performed with AACM groups led by Gerald Donovan as well as Abrams. *A Discography and Bibliography of Anthony Braxton* (Stocksund, Sweden: Blue Anchor Bookshop, 1982), 54. A photograph in the March 1967 issue of *Coda* (p. 28) shows Braxton performing with Jenkins, Lester Bowie (trumpet), and Leonard Smith (drums).

and blues musicians, playing with Sam and Dave, accompanying the Dells, and performing with a rock orchestra. While these sessions were prompted above all by financial need, they also called attention to Braxton's wide-ranging artistic interests.[109]

Reviews by John Litweiler appearing in *Down Beat* and *Coda* suggest that Braxton and his AACM collaborators often worked in the high-intensity style developed by Coltrane and his followers.[110] Yet a commercial recording from the period reveals that Braxton had been moving away from Coltrane, even while acknowledging his influence. On *My Thoughts Are My Future—Now and Forever,* a track from Abrams's first Delmark album, *Levels and Degrees of Light* (1967, 1/2), Braxton played an extended solo that introduced the aggressive, complex style for which he would later be known. The performance is as powerful as it is distinctive. Braxton combines the rhythmic drive, virtuosity, and extreme-register distortions of Coltrane's approach with rhythmically and melodically intricate phrases suggesting the music of Ornette Coleman. Avoiding a fixed tonal center, he shapes an improvisation that builds on dramatic fluctuations of contour and rhythm. Phrases often contain wide intervallic leaps that mimic the "pointillistic" contours characteristic of many postwar atonal works. Compression and collapse of melodic rhythm through shifts from rapid, staccato lines to slow, legato phrases, and from accelerando to ritardando, heighten the sense of disruption that nontonality and a frenetic tempo create. Braxton's approach is acutely modernist, conceptually akin to the early ensemble works of Varèse, in which pitch repetition, nontonality, fragmentation, *Klangfarbenmelodie,* and rhythmic intensity similarly create the sonic illusion of fluctuating speed. These elements effect a dislocation that characterizes art avoiding traditional forms of coherence. In Braxton's case, dislocation appeared to serve a specifically aesthetic-ideological end as a form of creative resistance. Applying the musical resources of white and black realms, he constructed an art that eluded the classifications of both.

Braxton's early playing put into practice a sensitivity to radical design that he had acquired while studying concert music and the free jazz developing in Manhattan. He realized early on that he could not match an innovator like John Coltrane on his own terms, and rather than trying to "out–*Giant Steps* Coltrane,"[111] as he put it, he would

109. Philippe Carles, "Braxton: Les Regles du jeu," *Jazz Magazine* (France) (December 1972), 20.

110. Litweiler, "Heard and Seen: Anthony Braxton," *Coda* (March 1967), 28; "Caught in the Act," *Down Beat* (May 18, 1967), 25–26.

111. Interview with Anthony Braxton (September 6, 1982).

try to develop an approach that grew out of his own strengths and interests. Continuing to analyze conductors' scores and to transcribe solos, Braxton began to notice similarities that reinforced his belief in the aesthetic equivalence of the best of modernist concert music and jazz. In particular, he observed that for both the composer and the improviser, contour and phrase structure mattered most in the determination of style—elements that, he would later argue, are traceable to a global mystical structure.[112] Expressing a decidedly jazz-oriented view, Braxton concluded that linear contour contained the imprint of artistic originality. The most creative, the most spiritually enlightened musicians, regardless of genre or idiom, devised the most inventive phrasing. They were the true innovators or, once again, the "restructuralists." Accordingly, Braxton reasoned that if he were to pursue the same path, he too would have to find a personal voice. That assumption encouraged him to reach beyond the confines of jazz in order to develop phrase structures and rhythmic conceptions in marked contrast to those employed by previous artists.

Braxton's commitment to radical innovation expressed an essential tendency among twentieth-century African-American artists to contradict previous assertions of black creative inferiority, and particularly the claim that blacks in literature, in the construction of spirituals, in culture generally, had merely imitated white expression.[113] In jazz, stylists from Louis Armstrong to Lester Young to Billie Holiday to Sarah Vaughan have been celebrated by white observers precisely because of their ability to create improvisational approaches of supreme originality, and such outside recognition has reinforced measures of value within the musicians' community as well. Yet there is reason to suspect that musicians' concerns about originality refer as much to the creation of a distinctive *rhetorical voice,* in the tradition of orally centered black arts, as to the fulfillment of the progressivist preoccupations of the jazz press. It is precisely this devotion to the African-American legacy of "storytelling" soloists and to a black

112. See discussions of *The Tri-Axium Writings* in chapter 5, part 8.

113. See, for example, George Pullen Jackson, *White Spirituals in the Southern Uplands* (Chapel Hill: University of North Carolina Press, 1933). In his seminal survey of "primitive musics," moreover, Richard Wallaschek writes: "There still remains to be mentioned one race which spread over all America and whose musical powers have attracted the attention of many Europeans—the negro race. . . . I think I may say that, speaking generally, these negro-songs are very much overrated, and that as a rule they are mere imitations of European compositions which the negroes have picked up and served up again with slight variations. . . . A closer examination [shows in] fact that they [are] not musical songs at all, but merely simple poems." Wallaschek, *Primitive Music* (London: Longmans, Green, 1893), 60.

Anthony Braxton in a studio rehearsal at Delmark Records, Chicago (ca. 1967). Photo courtesy Terry Martin.

propensity for revising the master texts of American musical culture that led Braxton to embrace modernism and to invent phrasing and rhythmic conceptions in marked contrast to those commonly employed by jazz artists. As such, Braxton's voice would develop from its black roots not only as a critique of the categories of official culture but of jazz and "black music" as well.

II

Searching for new ways, new ideas, or what he would later call "languages" for articulating a distinctive personal approach, Braxton became increasingly committed to the study of concert music, to the point where he began composing works in the styles of his favorite composers. Originally didactic exercises meant to enhance his work in improvisation, these compositions set a new course in his creative development and one with which he has remained over the years. From a distance, Braxton's early concert works showed signs of youth, of a budding artist finding his way in a new language. The compositions are nonetheless important to this analysis because they reveal how Braxton had already begun to develop a personal, idiosyncratic approach, an all-encompassing experimentalism that would set the stage for subsequent artistic linkages.

In his first concert work, *Composition 1* ("Piano Piece No. 1," 1968), Braxton made an obvious attempt to meld into a tonal work stylistic attributes stemming from the atonal music of Schoenberg and Stockhausen.[114] A perusal of the first page of the score in figure 3.1 shows that Braxton provides frequent tonal references, both in his application of triadic elements and reiteration of C♮ and F♮ pitch centers. At the same time, his reliance on chromaticism and neighbor-note couplings often obscures tonality, recalling, for example, Schoenberg's preserial, expressionist compositions. One may also note stylistic elements—displaced intervals spanning the keyboard, frequent shifts in time-signature, successions of pitches of brief duration, continuously varied dynamic markings—that suggest properties attributable to the 1950s serial works of Stockhausen. In a second piano work, *Composition 5* ("Three Pieces for Piano," 1968), Braxton again acknowledges his concert-music models, most notably in

114. Braxton typically employs nonverbal picture titles to refer to most of his compositions. In discussing these works, I employ the composition numbers that he has assigned to them in his catalog. The actual titles appear in Appendix A. The significance of the nonverbal titles is discussed ahead and in subsequent chapters.

Figure 3.1. First page of *Piano Piece No. 1*. Courtesy Anthony Braxton.

applying a quasi-serial ordering over strong tonal underpinnings. Similar stylistic attributes and references to the modern European repertory appear in other concert works from the period, notably *Composition 7* for orchestra (1969) and *Composition 12* for woodwind quartet (1969).

In time, Braxton's experiments had become something more than mere didactic exercises and in certain instances suggested the coalescence of a new stylistic genre. By the time he had started *Composition 10* (1969), a solo piano work, he had clearly viewed his notated music as something distinct from his efforts in improvisation. The piece in figure 3.2 consists of nine pages of what Braxton calls "symbolic notation": a collection of lines, dots, asterisks, abstract shapes, and geometric figures. Each notation refers to a specific performance procedure (open clusters, sustained tones, quick attacks, trills, etc.) that loosely constrain an otherwise highly flexible and openly interpretive work. Braxton may be emulating here the practices of John Cage, Earle Brown, and Morton Feldman, whose unusual notations had become well known in composers' circles. Furthermore, the performance instructions to arrange the nine pages in any order and to play each notation for any length of time recall, among other works, Cage's *Variations II* (1961) and Stockhausen's *Aus den Sieben Tagen* (1968), both of which require the musicians to determine the form of a performance. The following year, Braxton would compose another work employing symbolic notation in an effort to make direct reference to similar experiments by Stockhausen. In *Composition 14* (1970) for solo instrument he printed his symbolic notations on a single 16 by 24 inch page. The layout recalls Stockhausen's *Klavierstücke XI* (1956), in which an array of discrete ideas appears on a 21 by 37 inch roll of paper. Although the latter piece is based on traditional notation, it, like *Composition 14,* instructs the performer to play the motives in any order.

But to place Braxton's symbolic works squarely in the concert tradition misses the point of their signification. As abstractions of the traditional, notated score, Braxton's pieces foreground the importance of flexibility and revision; while relying on concert procedures, they frequently privilege the performer's interpretation, and, as a matter of course, identify improvisation as a centering impulse. Furthermore, by replacing serial rows and chance procedures with a mix of squiggly lines, starlike asterisks, and connect-the-dot directions, Braxton appropriates a modernist forum for a kind of pop-culture stylistic play. These symbols orient the image of popular script—comic books, adolescent doodling—into the context of "serious" musical

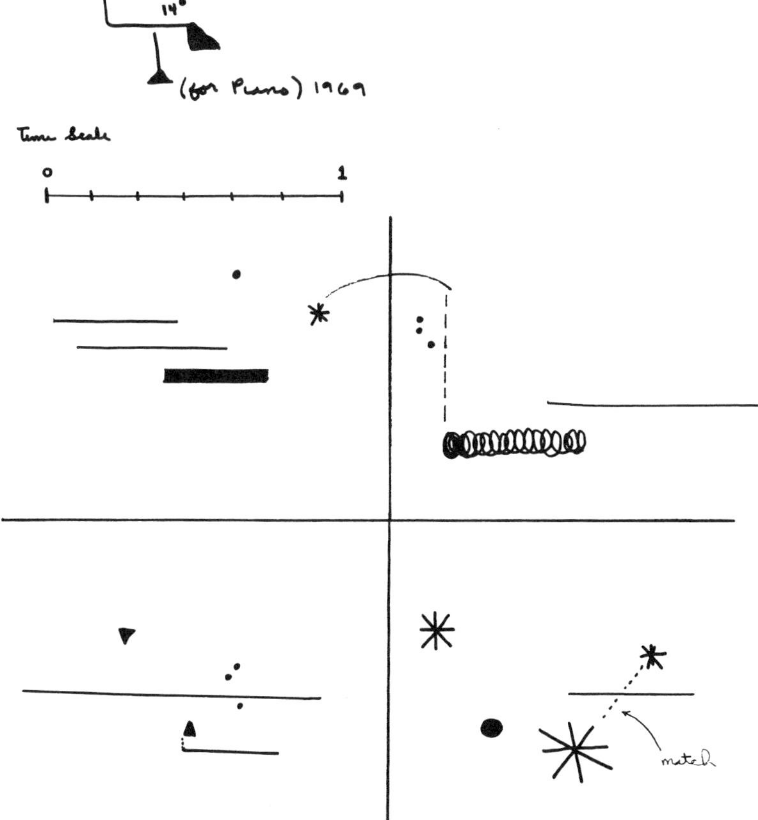

Figure 3.2. A page from the score of *Composition 10.* Courtesy Anthony Braxton.

composition. They are Braxton's way of refiguring formal methods, notations, and compositional techniques according to the whims of personal taste.[115]

Working simultaneously on opposite sides of the musical fence, then, Braxton had established the basis of his musical practice. He would be both a composer and a performer, a creator who relies on personal, idiosyncratic notations and preperformance concepts as well as a spontaneous music-maker who shapes improvisations with a vocabulary partly derived from his compositional studies. As he increasingly perceived an emerging union of his disparate practices, Braxton

115. Similar figures appear in *Composition 1,* where a star is positioned seemingly for no musical reason.

began somewhat tentatively to combine these two worlds in a single work. For example, in *Composition 3* (1968) for eleven instruments and *Composition 11* (1969) for "creative orchestra" or big band, he experiments with simple couplings of jazz and a marginal atonality. The first work suggests instrumentally the genre of modern chamber music, but that association is partially undermined by the inclusion of a double-bass and drum rhythm section. The second work marks a return to a jazz medium, while employing symbolic notation and the loose performance interpretations that Braxton had learned from his concert-repertory studies. Together these efforts suggest a coalescence of musical worlds that would soon overtake Braxton's art. They also represent a convergence of another kind: the union of jazz and concert music reflected the erosion of traditional categories of genre and style, along with the critical standards that went hand in hand with them. Braxton's experimentalism had become a true vanguardism, an "Africanist art," he would call it, surviving in the language of European modernism. As it was nourished by an accumulation of oppositions, black experimentalism would voice a doubleness that stretched across Braxton's creative life, helping to explain the contradictory social position of vanguardist turned celebrity that he would eventually occupy.

III

The early fusions of concert music and jazz reached an apex of abstraction with Braxton's works for improvising ensembles. In these, he directed his efforts to radicalize jazz-based expression by reconceptualizing the character of ensemble performance right down to the processes that guide improvisation. The improvisations reveal again a predisposition to iconoclastic experiment and a commitment to overturning accepted definitions of art and aesthetics. They are, quite simply, period pieces that reflect the vanguardist preoccupation of many 1960s American artists. Yet because some of these works were recorded on jazz labels, they were judged according to measures that did not always accurately represent the artist and his intent.

Braxton's improvisations took two forms. One paid a direct formal tribute to the revolutionary innovations of the American experimentalists; the other carried to an extreme the radical pursuits of Roscoe Mitchell and the Art Ensemble, transforming that style into a sound form suggesting the modernist chamber works of postwar Europe. Viewed collectively, Braxton's ensemble improvisations were a music against method, exercises in aesthetic revision that were meant to challenge standard definitions of art. In their most extreme form, the "works" were not works at all but rather socially usable events—what Walter de Maria has called "meaningless work"[116]—that would, according to Braxton, encourage "everybody . . . to bring something into [the activity] from whatever occupation."[117] Braxton's aim to "free the music" from the conventions of the concert hall and the role of the musician-specialist were as much extensions of the art-as-life doctrines of Cocteau, Duchamp, and Cage as expressions of a black vernacular sensibility championed by the AACM. Furthermore, his belief that "the notion behind the music is just as important as the music itself"[118] recalled the viewpoints of many conceptual artists as it did the philosophical views of Abrams and his musical offspring.

Braxton's experiments with the fundamentals of ensemble improvisation took place at a time when the radicalism of Cage's message had, for that historical moment, begun to challenge the authority of America's traditional musical institutions. It was as if the anticanonical aesthetics of experimental artists had taken a grip on the world of concert music, leading to a questioning of the assumptions that had previously driven art-making in the United States. In the most traditional settings, conventional approaches enjoyed preeminence, and high-culture's authorities exercised their power in many of the most conspicuous presentations. Yet there were also indications that the impact of the Cagean avant-garde might actually topple art from its pedestal, particularly in the contentious and volatile political climate of the 1960s. Cage's message had changed musical practice and teaching not only at the artistic extremes, but within sectors of the academy as well. Europe, which had traditionally set the course for American concert-music innovation, was now following his lead, much to the consternation of those American composers and patrons who wished to uphold traditional artistic conventions.[119] Cage, whom Peter Yates called in 1963 "the most influential living composer today,"[120] had upset the hierarchical order by giving voice to the antirational, the antisystematic, and, by positioning so centrally an indeterminacy chal-

116. Walter DeMaria, "Meaningless Work," in *Esthetics Contemporary,* ed. Richard Kostelanetz (New York: Prometheus Books, 1978), 240–43. De Maria defines meaningless work as "work that does not make you money or accomplish a conventional purpose," such as putting blocks into a box or digging a hole and filling it.

117. Robert Levin, "The Third World: Anthony Braxton and the Third Generation," *Jazz and Pop* (October 1970), 12–14.

118. Ibid.

119. Cage's fame motivated Gunther Schuller to challenge publicly (in the *New York Times*) the European notion that Cage represented the character of American music. See Calvin Tomkins, *The Bride and the Bachelors* (New York: Penguin, 1968), 138.

120. Chase, *America's Music,* 2d ed. (1966), 72.

lenging Enlightenment-based theories of causation, the postmodern. This new balance defines the context in which Braxton's critique of standard jazz practice must be observed.[121]

Three compositions from 1969 show Braxton traveling full circle, drawing from the improvisational experiments of Larry Austin, Steve Reich, Alvin Lucier, and other jazz-influenced experimentalists to create platforms for spontaneous music-making. In his guidelines to *Composition 9,* a kind of work song for four performers, Braxton instructs each performer to complete a simple task: shovel coal for several minutes. The sounds of the performers' actions were to be picked up by contact microphones attached to their shovels and broadcast over a public address system. The notes to the composition indicate that electronically synthesized sound would accompany the performers' work.[122] In a second work, *Composition 6G,* recorded in Paris on the album *B-X°/N-0-1-47A* (1969, 2/1) with Leroy Jenkins, Leo Smith, and guest drummer Steve McCall, the ensemble introduces an element of vernacular playfulness into serious musical practice, creating anassortment of sounds by releasing air from balloons. The level of technique and the continuity of form become subordinate to an imaginative exploration of the timbral and coloristic potential of "found objects." On *In the Street,* from the album *This Time* (1970, 2/6), moreover, Braxton's group moved a step closer to an art of the everyday. As the title suggests, the ensemble took its music out of the recording studio and into what sounds like the streets of Paris.[123] Conversation, sirens, car horns, yells—at one point a musician shouts "Yeah, play that thing," recalling Bill Johnson's famous cry in King Oliver's *Dippermouth Blues* (1923)—and sporadic instrumental phrases are heard against the background of the sound of an automobile engine. To John Cage's question "Is a truck passing by music?"[124] Braxton answered an unequivocal yes by employing a similar sound as the framework for group improvisation. *In the Street* recalls works by Cage, Pauline Oliveros, and George Brecht, performances by Musica Elettronica Viva, and events by multimedia artists whose efforts simi-

121. Gates discusses the relationship between indeterminacy and a vernacular-grounded black aesthetic in *The Signifying Monkey,* 32, 129–30. Further, Cage's theories probably helped to legitimize the AACM's antiformalist perspectives when concert-music's experimentalists began to encounter them in the late 1960s.

122. The composition has never been performed.

123. Since one hears only the rumble of an engine, it seems likely that the piece was recorded in a studio or garage. The work is not identified by a composition number.

124. Cage, "Communication," *Silence,* 41.

larly reflected an attempt to remove art from the preoccupations of formal composition.[125] It also refers to the insouciant, parodical works of Jelly Roll Morton (*Sidewalk Blues,* 1926), Clifford Brown (*Parisian Thoroughfare,* 1954), and Charles Mingus (*Foggy Day,* 1956), which similarly re-create the sounds of the street.

In each of these works, Braxton challenged the formalist notion of an objectified artwork—"sound in time," as he calls it—to create sound in "all time," a proposed sonic accompaniment to daily life.[126] Passive listening would be replaced with active participation, and artistic acts would become, for everyone, the centerpiece of a utopian social existence. Braxton's desire to bring together art and life into a meaningful creative whole paid tribute to the radical vanguardist aesthetics of the 1960s. Yet by foregrounding the sound of a rumbling engine and employing obviously phony sounds of the street he seemed also to be mocking Western vanguardist aesthetics at the same time that he upheld them. Braxton's vanguardism, then, may be taken as an extreme effort to acknowledge modernism as he distances African-American music from the strictures of Euro-Western thought. More self-consciously, Braxton's populist art may have had another, private meaning. By placing work within the context of art, as he did in *Composition 9* and in a second piece for performers in a steel yard, Braxton exalted the labor of the working class, the way of life of his family and boyhood friends. Through art he could externalize the beauty and meaningfulness embodied in their everyday lives.

V

If the experiments in artistic vanguardism marked the extreme of Braxton's improvisational departures, the collective compositions of his AACM trio came close to that extreme while still maintaining semblances of jazz practice. In these works, which appeared on Braxton's first record, *Three Compositions of New Jazz* (1968), and beside the previously discussed experiments on his later Paris albums, *B-X°/*

125. Particularly noteworthy is Frederick Rzewski's (a founding member of MEV) *Street Music,* published in *Source: Magazine of the Avant-Garde* 3:2 (1969): 41. In the same year, New York performance artists planned a series of urban activities, including *City Day,* an event for fifty participants, and *Street Works,* realized in four summer productions. See Dore Ashton, "A Planned Coincidence," *Art in America* 57:5 (September–October 1969): 38. Lucy Lippard, *Six Years: The Dematerialization of the Art Form* (New York: Praeger, 1973), 91, 117.

126. Liner notes to *Three Compositions of New Jazz* (1968).

N-0-1-47A (1969) and *This Time* (1970), the European-based constructs of harmony and melody were abandoned for what he considered to be the fundamental "universal" elements of music: "sound, rhythm, silence, and space."[127] Distancing himself from the most constraining mainstream conventions, Braxton created an improvised music showing clear ties to early concert-music modernists, and particularly to the works of Edgard Varèse, who also sought openly to challenge, in the concert vein, traditional forms and syntaxes. Closer to home, the trio works suggested stylistically the improvisations of Roscoe Mitchell's Art Ensemble, as they did the rhythmic/textural centeredness of traditional African-American music. Interestingly, it was Mitchell who publicly advocated in 1966 a performance approach owing to experimentalism, and particularly to Cage, in a call for the elimination of all melodic, harmonic, and formal conventions.[128] But it was Braxton who most successfully realized the Cagean dictum and who most radically challenged the constraints distinguishing concert music from jazz.

An examination of Braxton's works for trio shows the extent to which he had departed even from the musical conventions of the AACM. In these works elements of jazz appear as abstractions within a sound world evoking postwar atonal composition. The spontaneous, formal flexibility of the Art Ensemble gives way to predetermined, yet circumlocutory, development; jazz timbres and phrasing are supplanted by a stark, almost bloodless landscape of disparate, unrelated elements. While glimpses of tonality appear, textures thicken and thin somewhat, and instrumental colors change, the pieces lack the formal coherence, the drive, and the direction one expects from jazz. They are static, owing perhaps in concept if not in form to the dense, thick-textured works of John Coltrane and other free-jazz players from the 1960s. Yet this quality of stasis differs from that found in New York free jazz, for it can claim none of the raucous intensity that characterizes the East Coast style of playing. Nor does it contain the dynamism and rapid successions of contrast found in other AACM

127. Quoted in Leo Smith's liner notes to the Arista reissue of *The Complete Braxton 1971*. Braxton has acknowledged in conversation that the album title was inspired by Schoenberg's *Three Pieces for Piano* (Opus 11), the work that had initiated his interest in concert music.

128. Mitchell states: "*Sound* is a composition that deals, like I say, with sound, and the musicians are free to make any sound they think will do, any sound that they hear at a particular time. That could be like somebody who felt like stomping on the floor . . . well, he would stomp on the floor." Martin, "Blowing out in Chicago," *Down Beat,* 21.

improvisations. Operating without a rhythm section, a harmonic accompaniment, or a timekeeper, working with middle-range instrumentation—alto saxophone, violin, trumpet—that disrupts the treble/bass polarity of harmonic tonal music, Braxton's trio succeeded in overturning the fundamentals of jazz practice. The trio works are purposeful exercises in detachment, suggesting the nondevelopmental qualities Jonathan Kramer has identified in radical concert music as "moment form."[129] Above all, Braxton's group succeeds in creating this sense of dislocation and non-evolution by self-consciously attempting to avoid musical interaction (call/response), which is, with rhythm, a fundamental element defining jazz.

Since jazz is above all a linear-based (or better, multilinear) musical language, successful performances require musicians to respond to one another and to contribute through improvisation to the coherence of the musical statement. As an oral musical language, moreover, jazz establishes coherence through change: a discernible, directional, and clearly developing form is the by-product of an active and varied collective effort. In most AACM bands—and in jazz generally—the performers respond to each other's musical statements. In Braxton's trio improvisations, however, the musicians, particularly Braxton, purposely try not to interact. Often the trio's principal instruments and its "little instruments" are juxtaposed in order to create an aural assemblage suggesting what Braxton would later call "collage improvisation." Taped conversation, the "droning monotony"[130] of Braxton's extremely rapid saxophone lines, honks of bicycle horns, harmonica sounds, and rhapsodic violin phrases are placed in "open space" (Braxton's expression) without conforming to the character of the accompanying sounds. Simultaneity, discontinuity, and breakdown of form replace the developmental principles of jazz. Like the collage art of Picasso, Schwitters, and Rauschenberg, the trio works similarly disrupt linear musical discourse without making, as David Antin writes about collage, "a commitment to explicit syntactical relations between elements."[131] From this perspective, Braxton's music for trio seems to have more in common with the tape pieces of Pierre Henry and John Cage or the live electronics of the Sonic Arts Union than it does with the interactive improvisations of jazz. At the same time, it

129. Kramer, "Moment Form in Twentieth-Century Music," *Musical Quarterly* 64:2 (April 1978): 177–94.

130. Ekkehard Jost, *Free Jazz* (Graz: Universal Edition, 1974; Da Capo, 1981), 174. Jost refers to Braxton's lack of rhythmic differentiation in the compositions.

131. Antin, "Modernism and Postmodernism: Approaching the Present in American Poetry," *Boundary* 2:1 (Fall 1972): 106.

maintains an essential linkage with traditional African-American expressions in its reliance on the centralizing characteristics of improvisation, multilinearity, and vocally oriented timbral exploration.

Take for example Braxton's recording of "Composition 1" from the album *This Time* (1970, 1/1).[132] In it one hears an impressive variety of combinations that pay tribute to the AACM's sonic explorations; what is missing is the rhythmic spirit and sense of movement that drives most jazz. New hues and colors appear, disappear, and then often reappear against the background of a new timbral setting. From moment to moment the aural palette changes, and the listener is treated to ever-varying combinations of sounds. The opening texture of contrabass clarinet, violin, trumpet, and drums gives way to a patchwork of timbres dominated by the repetitive sweeps of the sopranino saxophone and sprinkles of colorful sounds from a whistle, a bicycle horn, and a glockenspiel. These new sounds appear against the established timbres of the trumpet and drum set. Seconds later the texture changes again when the violin reenters, and the "sound machine" (taped sounds of a party), trombone, triangle, and percussive tapping replace the sopranino saxophone and trumpet. Yet because the musicians are also attempting to avoid interaction, more is missing than swing; the piece also lacks the sense of continuity one typically finds in jazz works. As an improvised version of moment form, "Composition 1" effectively challenges the notion of form evolving from logical development.

Interestingly, Braxton's trio improvisations do sometimes appear to be built with analogies to jazz in mind. On the most basic level, works such as "Composition 1" articulate standard jazz form, following a three-part ABA design, with A representing the respective seventy-five-second and twenty-second preplanned sections that frame a series of improvisations. When Braxton takes the lead, his energetic playing sparks interaction, offering faint glimpses of the kinetic energy produced in hard-driving jazz. Also central to a black-oriented aesthetic are the elements of satire and humor that appear throughout. Braxton's "sound machine" (the term itself mocking the arcane vocabulary of modern technology and science fiction), the playfulness of "little instruments," the comic grumblings of the contrabass clarinet, are ways of exerting control over an appropriated style, serving to distinguish these works from some of the more self-serious and literal mon-

132. While identified on the album as "Composition 1," this work has no relation to the piano piece *Composition 1*. It does not appear in Braxton's catalog.

uments of the European tradition. Even in as austere and static a work as *Composition 6E* (*Three Compositions* 1/1), Braxton keeps both feet on the ground, leading the piece with mock formal, vocal interplay that feigns the seriousness of concert-music choral singing.

Thus, Braxton's collage improvisations impart the ethos and spirit of jazz as they mask overt stylistic associations. Multivoiced textures, improvisation, solos, and an ironic sense of musical play are at the core of these works, while the style itself suggests the disconnected abstractions of modernist concert music. Braxton's integration of jazz and concert music appears too oppositional to classicist perspectives to be called thirdstream art. Yet in many ways he shares a stylistic kinship with Gunther Schuller, John Lewis, Dave Brubeck, and other composers whose elaborate arrangements established the formal, if not aesthetic, frame for later jazz/concert-music experiments. These resemblances grew more apparent as Braxton began to involve preconceived elements and structures as he plotted out his improvisations prior to performance, a procedure that showed up most dramatically in the music for unaccompanied saxophone.

VI

Much has been made of Braxton's almost bullish resolve to advance his unaccompanied solo improvisations, an approach that for many seemed to exist somewhere between oddity and aberration. From the jazz critic's vantage, Braxton's solo repertory seemed, in the scheme of things, to make little historical sense. In 1968, there was no clearly established genre of unaccompanied horn playing in jazz, and Braxton, who was busily exploring the depths of an arcane and highly cerebral musical logic, showed little interest in accommodating the uninitiated listener or in improving comprehension. Yet within the context of Braxton's creative world, the music for saxophone played a vital role, representing the aesthetic linchpin of his work as an artist. These compositions marked a convergence of sorts, consolidating the styles and influences that had guided his music-making and that would shape its future course. To be sure, the solo saxophone repertory of the late 1960s was hardly the work of an uncompromising nonconformist rebelling for rebellion's sake; the music existed quite logically at the heart of Braxton's experimentalism.

It is somewhat ironic that Braxton's earliest solo works were acts of imitation, fulfilling a performance requirement of all AACM members. According to Joseph Jarman, Muhal Richard Abrams expected all musicians in the Association to perform at least one unaccompanied solo concert.[133] Abrams believed the exercise would enhance the musicians' understanding of musical form by forcing them to create a coherent musical structure on the spot. As a working pianist, Abrams had undoubtedly learned the value of unaccompanied playing over years of solo experience. And as a seasoned professional, familiar with jazz on record, he may have been aware of the recorded solo precedents of Coleman Hawkins, Sonny Rollins, and Eric Dolphy, whose innovations provided ready models for budding stylists.[134] Occasionally, the AACM's solo concerts led to some interesting artistic results, most notably an album highlighting unaccompanied performances by Roscoe Mitchell, Lester Bowie, and Malachi Favors, and released under Mitchell's name on the Nessa label as *Congliptious* (1968). More often, the unaccompanied solos served mainly as didactic exercises that were intended to improve musicianship and ensemble performance. Yet for Braxton solo playing assumed a prominent place in his creative world, developing as much from the wealth of historical precedents in concert music as from the limited examples in jazz. He explains:

> I had been really affected by Schoenberg, Ornette Coleman, and other restructuralists who did things their own way. Eventually, I began trying to find a way of putting together music on my own terms, just as they did. I remember hearing Schoenberg's *Opus 33* and *Opus 11,* hearing Stockhausen's *Klavierstücke XI,* and thinking to myself, "Why can't I use the saxophone as my piano," since as a pianist I wasn't technically advanced enough to play what I wanted to play. From that point [I] used the saxophone to develop ideas for my work and to solidify my aesthetic. And in an improvisational context, I followed [Schoenberg's and Coleman's] lead as I began to do solo saxophone concerts.[135]

The saxophone repertory, then, marked a new plateau in the development of Braxton's musical thought, representing a true union of the aesthetic dichotomies traceable through his musical life. These works brought together, on the one hand, the spontaneity of New York free jazz with, on the other, sound colors and textures of musical modern-

133. Peter Kostakis and Art Lange, "Joseph Jarman Interview," *Coda* (December 1977), 3.

134. Hawkins, *Picasso* (1948); Rollins, several, beginning with *It Can Happen to You* (1957); Dolphy, *God Bless the Child* (1961). Jimmy Giuffre performed on "solo clarinet" at the October Revolution concerts. Jost, *Free Jazz,* 84. Sidney Bechet's multitrack "one-man band" recordings of *Sheik of Araby* and *Blues of Bechet* (both 1941) are noteworthy precedents.

135. Interview with Anthony Braxton (September 6, 1982).

ism and careful preperformance planning of formal composition. The unaccompanied works were not, like most of their solo jazz precursors, simply improvisations performed without the benefit of a rhythm section; nor were they rehearsed solos extracted from a big-band or other ensemble context. Braxton's unaccompanied performances were, as they are still today, distinct, autonomous entities—compositions in their own right—that operated according to preconceived forms and employed materials stemming from a range of modernist musics. The solo improvisations, as fusions of the compositional and stylistic realms of concert music and jazz, epitomized the black experimental artwork.

Braxton's turn toward models in concert music took place after an embarrassing public performance. During his first solo concert, at the Abraham Lincoln Center in 1967, he took the stage and started improvising freely, without a set of chord changes, a core, or even incipits of main themes. Lacking a means of stimulating his musical imagination, he quickly ran out of ideas. Braxton had fallen into the same trap that had encumbered many players before him and that had motivated the AACM's search for new approaches to improvisation. Long, high-powered saxophone improvisations played without the benefit of harmonic support had become a stylistic norm in free jazz after John Coltrane adopted the practice in the early 1960s. While Coltrane had an inspiring rhythm section that set a foundation for his playing, as well as a personal gift for constructing vivid and imaginative extended solos, many jazz musicians possessed neither the same quality of musical support nor the same level of talent. Braxton soon realized that if he were to perform successfully without even a rhythm section, he would need to create a new way of organizing his ideas. He set out to devise a method of selecting different materials for each performance that could produce a varied repertoire of compositions:

> I didn't want to give a concert and just play saxophone for five hundred hours; I wanted to find a way of presenting materials and separating things so I wouldn't repeat myself through the whole evening. So I began to create musical ideas beforehand so that I would have different problems to deal with in each composition. That was the basis of my music and those were my intentions.[136]

The preperformance procedure with which Braxton planned his solo works developed out of the analyses he was conducting at the time. As noted previously, he learned through his studies of phrase

136. Interview with Anthony Braxton (February 17, 1983).

shapes that contour was a defining feature of style for both the composer and the soloist. Hoping to acquire a "restructuralist" voice that could match those of master musicians, Braxton started to experiment with contours on the saxophone and to draw them on paper. Then he reversed the procedure: after outlining visual contours, he translated them on the saxophone. For performances, Braxton would often make a list of these contours, assigning a musical idea to each. These "line notations," as he called them, corresponded to Western interpretations of pitch height and timbral width: lines moving upward denoted rises in frequency, while shapes of increasing thickness indicated a higher density of partials and noise (see figure 3.3). The arrangement of these items in a specified order beforehand was what he called "conceptual grafting." And the collection of sixty ideas or "languages" he eventually developed would represent the principal material of his entire solo and ensemble repertory.

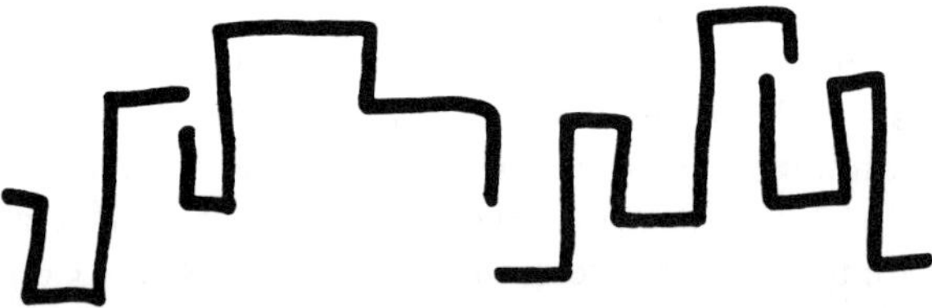

Figure 3.3. "Line notations" for *Composition 77A*. Courtesy Anthony Braxton.

An examination of the motivic and formal properties of the early saxophone works bears out some of the strategies Braxton put into practice. On his album *For Alto* (1968), Braxton employs a panoply of elements or "languages." Yet the striking originality of each solo exposes an intent to design works according to the particularities of a few musical ideas. *Composition 8A* "to John Cage" (1/2), for example, is a study based on quick tremolo motives taking varied forms and intermixed with legato phrases.[137] On the other hand, *Composition 8C* "to Kenny McKenny" (3/2) explores multiphonic sound colors: from gravelly, thick-textured overblowing to rich, coloristic sustains to shrill, high-register effects. *Composition 8A* "to Murray de Pillars" (1/3) abstracts and reorders the harmonic pattern of the

137. In his catalog, Braxton refers to an entire album side as a single composition, and the discographies of de Craen/Janssens and Wachtmeister follow that practice. However, the tracks may have been originally conceived as autonomous units and grouped together only when Braxton became intrigued with multisectional works in the mid-1970s.

twelve-bar blues cycle, lengthening four-bar phrases, disrupting harmonic patterns, and frequently departing from the cycle altogether. In *Composition 8B* "to Leroy Jenkins" (4/1), moreover, Braxton shapes an improvisation around a single-pitch repetition, varying tone, attack, volume, tempo, and rhythm in order to effect the splintered "pointillism" of Webern's late works. And in *Composition 8C* "to Susan Axelrod" (3/1), he builds a solo on long, extended lines that sometimes grow to feverish intensity, while at other times re-creating the banality of a legato scale exercise. Stylistically, Braxton reveals a commitment to Coltrane's solo playing, particularly in the rapidity—if not in the design—of his circumlocutory phrases and in his exploitation of the extreme ranges of the horn. One can also identify a lyricism and timbre evoking Desmond's playing, which makes for dramatic effect when juxtaposed against mercurial free-jazz figurations or, as one occasionally hears, the rapid, quicksilver chromaticism of Ornette Coleman. While disparate elements of free jazz often mingle during a performance, Braxton also seems to take pains to separate and distinguish the materials he employs, whether they be motives or allusions to jazz favorites.

The solo saxophone improvisations, then, involve procedures of great originality and conceptual import. From a musical standpoint, however, the recordings suggest that Braxton had not yet come to terms with the formal problems inherent in solo composition. There is no doubt that Braxton, at twenty-three, was a masterful improviser with remarkable technique and a powerful musical imagination. Particularly striking was his ability to shape highly complex and dislocated configurations, first introduced on Abrams's *My Thoughts*, which would, when constrained by precompositional structures or the quartet format, produce remarkable results. But within the context of the early unaccompanied solo improvisations, Braxton's approach suffered from a lack of clear structural provision. Even as a close listening reveals interesting ideas and a degree of internal logic, the solos themselves do not accumulate enough on their own to produce an engaging, memorable experience. It is perhaps telling that Braxton's best efforts appeared in *Composition 8A* "to Murray De Pillars" (1/3), the blues work, and during the first minutes of *Composition 8B* (4/1), the repetition piece in which he established clear formal guideposts for the listener. One might argue that Braxton's lengthy, formally obscure solos developed from a vanguardist irreverence toward mainstream art or even reveal an attempt to emulate the perceived stasis and cyclicity of West African music. Surely, *Composition 8A* "to Cecil Taylor" (1/4), a nineteen-second piece consisting of a single, sustained tone, poses a challenge to the traditional conception of the work of art in its dadaesque tribute to the banal. Yet even if Braxton had been attempting a subversive musical act, in the context of a commercially released album it loses power and presence, ultimately coming across—and despite sincerity of intent—as less "Africanist" than self-indulgent. Certainly Braxton himself recognized the limitations of his extended approach in the coming years, judging from the recorded efforts on *Live at Moers 1974* and *Alto Saxophone Improvisations 1979,* in which he takes pains to establish formal coherence.

From a historical perspective, *For Alto* is important in providing insights into the artist's creative intentions. The works show that Braxton had already developed an original, musicianly voice that distinguished him from other artists working in the improvisational idiom while servicing his commitment to the black cultural legacy. The solo works, like so much of his repertory, affirmed the dual importance of originality and revision so central to the African-American tradition. Like Count Basie and other master musical signifiers, Braxton, in a single work, "recapitulated the very tradition out of which he grew and from which he descended."[138] However, in his all-embracing desires to mix postmodern ecumenicalism with black-centered revisions, Braxton makes all he encounters his own. By borrowing and absorbing he transforms the foreign into the familiar, constructing an artistic integration in the image of his own constituted, subjective self.

Braxton's penchant for diversity and idiosyncrasy would also lead him to explore, as a matter of course, a variety of precompositional procedures. Planning similar to the unaccompanied saxophone music would soon show up in his ensemble works, revealing tendencies to the African-American background to integrate into music elements and expressions of everyday life. Number patterns, the repetitions of a firefly's light (the "cobalt" compositions), the configuration of a chess move became methods of structure and forms of coherence in the planning of his works.[139] Braxton's procedures were those of an artist seeking to define his own musical world, "his own terms," as he puts it, drawing from the modern while playfully parodying its distance

138. Gates, *Signifying Monkey,* 123–24.

139. The chess moves that guide several of Braxton's works may have been initially motivated by Cage's *Reunion* (1968) for amplified chessboard or his *Fontana Mix,* in which transparent sheets inscribed with lines and dots set the parameters for creating a tape piece. Similar processes are described in Cage, "Composition," in *Silence,* 57–61. The standard abbreviations that identify chess moves (for example, B-N5, N-KB3, KR-Q1, etc.) closely resemble Braxton's formula titles, discussed ahead.

from everyday life. Over time they would give way to a creative system based on an idiosyncratic reconstruction of the values and properties inherent in concert music and jazz.

The world of modernism had become by this time a powerful and even daunting influence for Braxton, who sought to emulate his concert-music idols without losing a firm grip on his African-American past. His studies of scores inspired him to build structures modeled after the innovations of Stockhausen and Boulez; his reading of analytic literature influenced the language he would employ when speaking publicly about his art: technical-sounding references to "cell complexes," "stochastic processes," and "conceptual grafting" recalled the theoretical languages of contributors to *Music Forum, Die Reihe,* and *Perspectives of New Music.* Later on, Braxton's difficult language would be called confused and convoluted, and perhaps rightly so. More important, however, is the sentiment it expressed: a rejection of conventional discourse and its "rational" wisdom in the name of an oddly self-reflexive, spiritual expression nourished by theories of the avant-garde and African past. Seeking to unify the anti-Western character of his music and methods, Braxton created, in the form of picture titles, idiosyncratic abstractions of his vigorously oppositional creative world. These would become the subject of considerable public scrutiny, which both drew him into and ultimately alienated him from the jazz world.

VII

In their earliest form, the nonverbal titles were called "formula titles" and modeled after the notations of chemists and mathematicians (figure 3.4). According to Braxton, they originally conveyed no specific meaning, but rather were intended to pay tribute to those composers who inspired his interest in structural complexity and formal invention. Braxton explains that his foremost concern was to create an emblem that would distinguish his music from that of the jazz tradition.

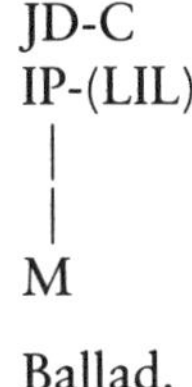

Figure 3.4. Picture title for *Composition 8K* (ca. 1968).

"When I first began to title my music differently," Braxton has said, "I didn't just want to call it 'Braxton's Blues.' I wanted to find a way to refer to the music that was in accordance with who I am."[140] And Braxton found the way in the arcane visual formulas and diagrams that expressed his allegiance to the world of contemporary concert music while also paying tribute to the pantheon of scientific heroes whom he had admired since his boyhood. The titles were, as Robert Farris Thompson has commented, a way of "saying, 'I mean to be taken seriously . . . here are summaries of our creativity in code.'"[141] The creation of titular codes intended for public scrutiny underscored Braxton's resistance to the burdens and expectations of the musical mainstream. These abstractions were his metaphors for a private world in which the rules of the consensus had no place.

The formula titles are also significant because they provide another manifestation of the creative elusiveness that pervades Braxton's art. On one hand, the titles expose Braxton's serious nature and his desire at the time to assume the posture of the concert artist. On the other, they express the concerns of an unschooled composer working in isolation, whose playful revision of high-modernist theory led to a rich crop of homegrown inventions. In this way, the picture titles are not unlike earlier signifying gestures appearing in jazz titles, from Louis Armstrong's *Struttin' with Some Barbecue* (1927) to Earl Hines's *Jelly, Jelly* (1940) to Lester Bowie's *Jazz Death?* (1968).[142] Braxton has made reference to the latter half of this particular dualism, noting that at first the titles were playful symbols for private use:

> When I started titling my works visually, I really didn't know what I was doing. Many of the formula titles were just my own way of referring to a work. I didn't know that they would present a problem in the future. I didn't realize that at a certain point people wouldn't be able to refer to the music. I wasn't really even thinking about those kinds of things. At the time I didn't think anyone was going to listen anyway.[143]

Of course Braxton had the opportunity to adopt more conventional, verbal titles as he became better known. He chose not to, perhaps to encourage public notice, but above all to assert the black vanguardist aesthetic that would drive his life and work. Braxton had

140. Interview with Anthony Braxton (September 6, 1982).

141. Thompson, "Notes (8 Pieces) Source a New World Music: Creative Music" [review of pamphlet by Leo Smith], *Coda* (November 1975), 11.

142. Direct references to signifying appear as the Big Three Trio's *Signifying Monkey* and Count Basie's *The Jungle King* (both 1947).

143. Interview with Anthony Braxton (February 2, 1984).

during these years laid the groundwork for a musical system that grew out of his experiences in the Chicago avant-garde, and the titles would enforce and advertise the oppositional character of his aesthetic views. Their peculiarities and ambiguous meanings implicitly challenged traditional jazz lovers to interpret with conventional means this highly unconventional art. The titles, then, reflected Braxton's position on the fringe, resisting singlehandedly the categories that had typically defined "popular" African-American musical practice. Their primacy within his aesthetic expression underscored his commitment to pursuing a direction that ran counter to the norms of mainstream musical life. That commitment precipitated a period of travel, learning, and exploration as he struggled to make a career in a business whose values conflicted with his experimental ideals and unconventional notions of artistic identity.

4 New Musical Convergences: Paris and New York

By 1969, the Chicago movement that originally inspired Braxton's embrace of an oppositional aesthetic had become an obstacle to his burgeoning artistic ambitions. If the Association for the Advancement of Creative Musicians had held determinedly to its ideal of a separatist creative program, it had failed in a practical sense to provide its membership with the self-sustaining economic network it had originally sought to create. Despite its admirable sense of loyalty to "blackness," the AACM could ultimately supply few performance opportunities. Of these, most, after a brief flourish, were typically attended by only a small scattering of people, forcing Braxton and the others to rely on modest day jobs, family support, or other means.[1] To some of the most ambitious members, moreover, the Association's aesthetic commitment probably seemed increasingly hopeless and perhaps even naive. Looking to the future for a career in jazz, they had met face to face with the reality of making a living in the music business, a world in which success required concessions to the market. For those holding to the strictest vanguardist and nationalist principles, such requirements precluded the possibility of measurable professional gain at a time when promoters were seeking new ways to revive the music's eroding appeal.

The situation in the AACM seemed to mirror the fate of other grassroots organizations on the South Side, which had become increasingly fractious centers of dispute and indignation. The disarray of organizations such as the Coordinating Council of Community Relations (CCCO) reflected the state of the civil rights movement generally, whose energy had already begun to evaporate after the failed attempts of Reverend Martin Luther King, Jr., and the Chicago Freedom Movement to revive the South and West sides.[2] Over time, the situation would worsen, especially in 1968, when the assassinations of King and

1. For example, Braxton worked for a Pepsi Cola bottling plant and for the Roosevelt College library; Mitchell took a job at United Parcel Service.

2. Alan B. Anderson and George W. Pickering, *Confronting the Color Line* (Athens: University of Georgia Press, 1986), 351–52.

Robert Kennedy, and the massacre of Black Panthers on Chicago's West Side, made black power seem less a solution than, as Robert Weisbrot writes, "an alternative utopianism for embittered idealists."[3] Braxton's comments from that year, which appeared in an AACM profile weeks after the police riot at the Democratic National Convention, encapsulized the tensions between the ideal of artistic liberation and the reality of social repression that all creative activists were facing: "What I'm doing needs freedom, man, [but] the closer I get to what I feel it is, [the more] I realize the pressure of the city—whatever [its] contribution to my own personal inspiration—is liable to cut me down."[4]

Braxton struggled with other kinds of ambivalences and tensions, to be sure. For example, he has remarked repeatedly that he had grown skeptical of the AACM's specifically black orientation and romantic vision of the African experience, yet he would also wholeheartedly embrace highly controversial, revisionist interpretations of the African basis of European musical history. Furthermore, while championing musical and spiritual brotherhood—"the complete freedom of individuals in tune with each other"[5]—and advocating a transcendental art that would overcome differences in race and culture, he also spoke out hyperbolically and in a caustic language about the racist character of whites.[6] Braxton's ambivalences are noteworthy not simply to challenge the status of veritable sainthood with which his most zealous advocates have wished to endow him; they are also important for what they reveal about his artistic personality. His commitment to creative "freedom" and resistance to style-specific labels

3. Robert Weisbrot, *Freedom Bound: A History of America's Civil Rights Movement* (New York: W. W. Norton, 1990), 206.

4. Gifford, "Chicago: The 'New' Music," *Jazz and Pop* (January 1969), 40–41. Braxton has said that while he enjoyed working with his AACM quartet (Leroy Jenkins, Charles Clark, Thurman Barker; Frank Gordon and Kalaparusha sometimes added), the city's music scene was insufficient to sustain them. "I think what really happened was that I kind of came to a crossroads. . . . Because of the intensity of the scene in Chicago, there were no opportunities to make a living. We could give concerts, but we would get three people or so." Interview with Anthony Braxton (May 6, 1983).

5. Litweiler, notes to *Three Compositions of New Jazz* (1968).

6. Braxton's comments, while certainly open to challenge, nonetheless provide considerable insight into the difficulties of musical representation. He said to Brian Case: "One of the most sophisticated weapons that white people have come up with would be language—words—a mono-dimensional language used to evaluate and distort a multi-dimensional music. The whole idea of words to justify or validate creativity is uniquely Western, and it has nothing to do with what's really happening. . . . White people who define have not been able to kill it, though they have been able to suck from it—Swing Period, Ragtime Period—these are siphoned off the music and used as the diversion of the hour." Case, notes to *B-X*^{0}*/N-O-1-47A* (1969).

seemed to reflect an aversion to rigid, totalistic thinking, appearing once again as artistic dualisms that define paradoxically a global and Afrocentric experimentalism. This same ironic tension would even occupy the course of his career. In the 1970s, he would pursue a black-centered vanguardism in the context of the commercial music business, seeking to find a place in a world that stood for beliefs clearly inimical to his own.

I

The AACM's efforts to maintain organizational unity collapsed in May 1969, when four of its senior members—Roscoe Mitchell, Joseph Jarman, Lester Bowie, and Malachi Favors—left for Paris. Their exodus, in turn, precipitated the departure of Leroy Jenkins, Leo Smith, and Braxton a month later.[7] While apparently still committed to a black vanguardism that rejected the classification of "jazz," these musicians also sought the social recognition that the jazz world could provide. More practically, they hoped for a chance to make a living in music, something that was clearly unavailable in the United States at the height of racial antagonism and the revolution of rock music. Paris, on the other hand, seemed to afford some potential for success, having provided opportunities for African-American artists and musicians since the 1910s.[8] For Braxton, the city offered as an added attraction a rich and dynamic concert culture, highlighted by the concert series, the Domaine Musicale, organized by Pierre Boulez.[9] Once

7. Braxton stresses that he left Chicago on his own, with Jenkins and Smith following, as if to disassociate himself from that cooperative. Furthermore, Steve McCall, a founding member of the AACM, had moved to Paris in 1967, which may have encouraged the others to follow. Braxton has noted to me and to others that a chance meeting with McCall on the day of his arrival helped him to get acquainted with the city. For background, see John Litweiler, "Three to Europe," *Jazz Monthly* (November 1969), 20–22; "Chicago Exodus: AACM Members off to Paris," *Down Beat* (June 26, 1969), 14.

8. American jazz had appeared in Paris since 1918, when Louis Mitchell's Jazz Kings performed at the Casino de Paris. The list of subsequent appearances is a long one, ranging from elder figures such as Sidney Bechet and Albert Nicholas to swing and bop artists, including Don Byas, Kenny Clarke, and Bud Powell, to more recent innovators, notably Johnny Griffin and Phil Woods. For general background, see Chris Goddard, *Jazz away from Home* (New York: Paddington Press, 1979); Whitney Balliett, "Panassié, Delaunay, et cie," in *Jelly Roll Jabbo and Fats* (New York: Oxford University Press, 1983), 3–15. For details about American free musicians in Paris, see ahead.

9. Boulez turned over conducting responsibilities to Gilbert Amy in 1967. The organization ceased activities in 1973 and was eventually superseded by the Institute de Recherche et de Coordination Acoustique/Musique (IRCAM) in 1976.

settled in Paris, he would seek out musicians and artists affiliated with the Domaine, with hopes of arranging performances of his music.[10]

Coverage in local magazines from 1969 shows that Parisians enjoyed a variety of jazz performance venues featuring a diverse range of international talent. Clubs such as the Blue Note frequently showcased top-ranked French bandleaders (Michel Terrioux, Michel Roques, and the Parisian favorite, Georges Arvanitas), while the strongholds of dixieland, the Caveau de la Huchette, the Slow Club, and Caveau de la Montagne, presented professional and semiprofessional groups specializing in New Orleans and early popular styles. Other nightspots, the Chat qui Peche, the Cigale, Cameleon, Gill's Club, and a few of the city's concert halls—the Pleyel, the American Center, L'O.R.T.F.—gave top billing to American artists visiting or living in Paris. The most notable of these performances were faithfully chronicled by a well-informed and frequently critically astute community of jazz writers working for *Jazz* and *Jazz Hot*.[11]

Appearing alongside coverage of conventional styles were profiles and reviews of the leading figures in American free jazz, often as a complement to album releases and local performances. The strength of coverage in proportion to the occasional reporting in the American press paid testimony to the appeal of the free style among French jazz lovers, particularly after the success of Ornette Coleman's European tour in 1965.[12] French interest would soon be heightened once native musicians such as Jef Gilson, Jacques Coursil, Michel Portal, and François Tusques (who recorded an album entitled *Free Jazz* under his own name in 1966) began to adapt and revise American approaches into an emerging European style. By the late 1960s, several new- and

10. Braxton has described in interviews his frustration with Boulez and the Domaine. (Interview with Anthony Braxton, July 12, 1984.)

11. See listings in *Jazz Magazine* (France) and *Jazz Hot*. Americans living and working in Paris at the time included Kenny Clarke (with Francy Boland), Phil Woods, Benny Waters, Bill Coleman, and Philly Joe Jones. Touring musicians, notably Stan Getz, Jimmy Heath, Hank Mobley, Max Roach, Cannonball Adderley, Lee Konitz, Noah Howard, and Frank Wright, appeared during the course of the year.

12. Gunther Schuller, "Ornette Coleman," in *The New Grove Dictionary of Jazz*, 229–31. Coleman appeared in Paris in November 1965. Concert performances were also scheduled for Brussels, Berlin, Helsinki, Stockholm, Copenhagen, and Bremen. See "Ornette in London, Plans Extended Stay Outside of U.S.," *Down Beat* (September 23, 1965), 17; P. Nahman, "En Angleterre, premier triomphe european pour Ornette Coleman," *Jazz Hot* (October 1965), 7–8; M. Van Peebles, "Tête-à-tête avec Ornette," *Jazz Magazine* (France) (December 1965), 26–31. Albert Ayler, moreover, performed in Paris clubs while stationed in France from 1960 to 1961. His records, together with those of Coleman and Cecil Taylor, were readily available in France from the beginning of the movement.

old-world alliances were appearing in clubs and on record as a veritable flood of American artists descended on the city, leading Daniel Caux to remark, is this the "smashing entrance of the new thing to Paris?"[13]

Caux's comment appeared in the context of a report on the Art Ensemble of Chicago (AEC), the newly formed quartet of AACM arrivals and among the most celebrated free performers in Paris.[14] Already in June 1969, Mitchell and his colleagues had been enthusiastically greeted by the French critics' circle, which seemed to be aware of their importance to the Chicago movement and of their contributions to free practice. Within weeks they were appearing in concerts at the Théatre du Lucernaire and the American Center (which sponsored the Premiere Festival de Free Jazz et de Nouvelle Musique), and recording material for four albums: *A Jackson in Your House, The Paris Session, The Spiritual,* and *Tutankhamun.* By the end of the year, they would record three more, while performing regularly in France, Belgium, and West Germany.[15] Coverage of the performances appeared in reviews and musician profiles, during which the artists, now as AACM representatives, announced to an enthusiastic French audience the Association's aim to "represent the dignity, intelligence, creativity, and beauty of black people."[16]

Early reports on Braxton typically appeared in the context of reviews of the AEC and AACM. In a celebratory essay about the Art Ensemble's performance at the Théatre du Lucernaire, for example, Caux advised his readers to attend Braxton's upcoming concert with Leroy Jenkins.[17] Subsequent articles made mention of Braxton's presence in Paris, while an interview with Bowie, Jarman, Jenkins, and others included a photograph of the saxophonist. The visibility led to some notable opportunities both as a leader and as a sideman. In early July, he played in the first of a series of collaborations with Günter

13. Caux, "Informations, Actualities France," *Jazz Hot* (July/August 1969), 8. The new faces in free jazz included Alan Silva, Marion Brown, Steve Lacy, Sunny Murray, Don Cherry, and Steve McCall, together with extended appearances by Archie Shepp, Ted Curson, and Coleman. The German artists Günter Hampel and Joachim Kühn moved to Paris around the same time.

14. Founded in Chicago as the Roscoe Mitchell Art Ensemble, the group changed its name after arriving in Europe. Working occasionally with Steve McCall and other percussionists, the ensemble brought in Don Moye permanently in 1970.

15. For a comprehensive list of its recorded works, see Eddy Janssens and Hugo de Craen, *Art Ensemble of Chicago Discography* (Brussels: New Think, 1983).

16. Lester Bowie, "A.A.C.M.," *Jazz Hot* (December 1969), 24.

17. Caux, "Informations, Actualities France, Le délire et la rigeur de l'Art ensemble de Chicago," *Jazz Hot* (July/August 1969), 8.

Hampel, the German vibraphonist, in concert and at a record session in the Netherlands.[18] Returning to Paris, Braxton recorded with Jacques Coursil, a brilliant black French trumpeter, who had recently returned from a stay in New York, where he had taken part in a session with French and American musicians.[19] "Within two weeks," Braxton has commented, "I had money for an apartment and to go out and have *poule* and *frites*. I was really very lucky."[20]

Particularly important in launching Braxton's European career was a concert at the Salle de la Mutualité, where the trio appeared alongside the Ornette Coleman Quartet, the Art Ensemble, and bands led by François Tusques and Bernard Vitet. Sponsored by *Jazz Hot,* the concert gained valuable advance publicity, including a full-page ad in the magazine's September issue.[21] The publicity spawned additional coverage, as writers reported regularly on Braxton's subsequent performances with the AEC, with his own group in Paris, and at the Amougies Festival in Belgium.[22] At Amougies, moreover, Braxton met Frederick Rzewski, the American composer and renowned interpreter of modernist piano music (notably, Stockhausen's *Klavierstücke*), who was at the time performing with his improvisation group, Musica

18. Braxton met Hampel after the saxophonist's first European performance with the AEC. The festival took place June 27–29. Paul Allessandrini, "Jazz on the Grass," *Jazz Magazine* (France) (September 1969), 9. In an interview with Nat Hentoff, Hampel described the close association he and Braxton had developed that summer. "Günter Hampel: An Introduction," *Jazz and Pop* (July 1970), 25–27. The album appeared on Hampel's newly formed Birth label as *The 8th of July 1969*. It was a watershed recording in attracting American critical attention to a distinctive style of European free jazz that had departed from the model established in New York. Hampel had already been working with other American musicians, notably Marion Brown, with whom he recorded in May. The same group, which included Willem Breuker, Arjen Gorter, and the Americans Steve McCall and Jeanne Lee, recorded again that day under the name of Breuker's Instant Composers Pool.

19. Guy Kopelowicz, "Un Américain de Montmartre, Jacques Coursil," *Jazz Hot* (April 1969), 32–33; Philippe Carles, notes to *Jacques Coursil: Way Ahead* (BYG Actuel 19; 1969). The New York session was released under Alan Silva's name as *Lunar Surface* (1969).

20. Interview with Anthony Braxton (May 6, 1983).

21. Braxton has confirmed the rumor that he and the others prepared and ate a meal as part of their performance. They also played "conventional" instruments ("chicken, trumpet, a hot plate, etc."). Conversation with Anthony Braxton (September 18, 1992).

22. Pierre Cressant, "O.C. et la Centrifugueuse," *Jazz Magazine* (France) (October 1969), 15; Cressant, "Ornette Coleman," *Jazz Hot* (October 1969), 6–7; Jean-Max Michel, "Amougies Free," *Actuel* 9 (December 1969), 18–23, 56–57. An ad for the Actuel Festival appeared in *Jazz Hot* (October 1969). Radio concerts of the AACM were noted in *Jazz Hot* (November 1969), 42.

Elettronica Viva. Braxton also met Archie Shepp, the controversial spokesman of New York's free-jazz community, who enlisted him for a recording session with Philly Joe Jones in December.[23]

Despite the considerable attention given to Braxton's appearances, many French writers seemed puzzled by his most iconoclastic music and sometimes candidly admitted being so. While a few, such as Laurent Goddet, would later champion the artist, most at this point could offer few stylistic observations and little critical insight.[24] Skeptics, moreover, were often deliberate in their objections to Braxton's applications of concert music, even as such objections drew strong responses from avid supporters. In his article "Apropos du Groupe d' Anthony Braxton," Caux recalled an incident during which an offhand comment ignited a heated debate. At a gathering of critics, he declared that Braxton's trio was "subversive" in its efforts musically "to turn its back on the audience." The comments were swiftly challenged, inspiring Caux to devote the entire article to an explanation of his remark. At one point he confided: "This music still creates problems for me; however I am never able to detach myself from it," while at another he admitted being "perplexed [by] the rhythmic conception of the ensemble." But Caux also went on to argue that Braxton's music represented a new direction in the jazz tradition. Comparing the trio performances to the experiments of John Cage and his principal pianist, David Tudor, Caux wrote: "I sense that it is not only a question of these musicians arranging their jazz to the likes of Cage and Tudor. . . . That is to say that the undeniably [Euro-]Western references only serve, in my opinion, as a springboard for 'another thing.'"[25]

English and American criticism expressed similar tentativeness, and at times seemed vehemently opposed to the most overt jazz/experimental-music linkages. In an article that introduced Braxton and the AACM to English-speaking European listeners, John Litweiler maintained his earlier praise for the artist, but took exception to what he considered to be the "academic and arbitrary" character of por-

23. The album appeared as *Archie Shepp/Philly Joe Jones* (1969). With Rzewski were Richard Teitelbaum and Alvin Curran, members of Musica Elettronica Viva. Rzewski's version of Stockhausen's *Klavierstücke No. 10* appears on Heliodor Wergo 2549016 (1969).

24. For example, Laurent Goddet, "Anthony Braxton: Saxophone Series F," *Jazz Hot* (September 1972), 26.

25. Daniel Caux, "A Propos du Groupe d' Anthony Braxton," *Jazz Hot* (November 1969), 8–9. Translation by author.

tions of *Three Compositions of New Jazz* (1968).[26] Others criticized the record directly for its application of modernist practices. Writing in the August 1969 issue of *Coda,* Brian Blevins reported that the improvisations on the first side were "clinical" and "fragmented," owing a resemblance to "Webernesque pointillisme."[27] Lawrence Kart contrasted the performances on *Three Compositions* to the superlative improvisations of Roscoe Mitchell's Art Ensemble, but vindicated Braxton somewhat by focusing his attack on the other performers, Leroy Jenkins and Leo Smith, and by noting that the album did not accurately demonstrate Braxton's talent.[28] Two other critics, Jack Cooke of *Jazz Monthly* and *Jazz and Blues* (both UK) and Will Smith of *Jazz and Pop,* elaborated on themes appearing in the early criticism. In his May 1970 review of *Three Compositions,* Cooke echoed Kart's claim that Braxton's self-conscious musical modernism was a pale imitation of the style forged by Roscoe Mitchell: "Braxton and his men don't have the persuasive way with [collective improvisation] that Mitchell's group has; there's a thinness of texture and hesitancy in development that has all the marks, it seems to me, of a style imposed from the outside rather than, as in Mitchell's case, growing up from inside the group."[29] Will Smith also found the album unsuccessful, but for a more specific reason: "The failure of Braxton's own album is that it lacks a rhythm section and thus has little impetus. The music is rather like the wanderings of contemporary 'serious' composers—cold, detached, and somewhat static."[30]

Braxton's European releases and collaborations fared better. In a *Down Beat* review, Lawrence Kart lauded Hampel's *8th of July* (1969), noting that "Braxton once again plays with the gorgeous lyricism that marked his earlier efforts."[31] Smith called the second trio

26. Litweiler, "Three to Europe," *Jazz Monthly* (November 1969), 20–22.

27. Blevins, "Anthony Braxton," *Coda* (August 1969), 18–19.

28. Kart, "Anthony Braxton: Three Compositions of New Jazz," *Down Beat* (November 14, 1968), 20.

29. Cooke, "Anthony Braxton: Three Compositions of New Jazz," *Jazz Monthly* (May 1970), 18.

30. Smith, "Chicago: Winds of Change," *Jazz and Pop* (April 1970), 20. Of the early writers, only Barry McRae was complimentary about *Three Compositions,* offering considerable praise based on a thorough listening of the recorded material. McRae, "Anthony Braxton: Three Compositions of New Jazz," *Jazz Journal* (April 1970), 27.

31. Kart, "Record Reviews," *Down Beat* (December 11, 1969), 18. Kart compared the album to Hampel's collaboration with Marion Brown—"a pretentious attempt to incorporate into jazz the sonorities and methods of the European classical avant-

album, *B-X°/N-O-1-47A* (1969), a "musically fertile offering . . . a far more dynamic and convincing expression than the earlier record," while reporting that it still suffered from a lack of rhythmic verve and dynamism. Smith also remarked on Braxton's own improvement: "Already a dramatic voice on the first album, [Braxton] has shed his influences for the most part here. A supremely lyrical player, he performs with a great, free beauty on all his instruments."[32] Jack Cooke, moreover, believed that the compositions on Braxton's third album, *This Time* (1970), demonstrated a successful balance of experiment and convention. In the earlier works, Cooke reported, Braxton "never seemed entirely at ease with [Jenkins and Smith] and seemed often to be trying to work towards a more conventional themes-solos-themes basis." On the new release, a collective unity had been established, "giving his music a confidence and sureness it never had before."[33]

While favoring the strong efforts from the Paris sessions, most writers were clearly resistant to Braxton's most radical departures from the strictures of mainstream jazz. Perhaps a sound criticism could be launched against the *Three Compositions,* which, of the early albums, contains more suggestion of potential than realization of perceptible intent. But the published commentaries failed to supply an appropriate basis of criticism, and as such, revealed more about the writers' own preconceptions and limitations than about the faults of the works themselves. For example, Cooke's argument that a jazz style must grow from within some ill-defined creative wellspring imposed rigid developmental processes onto a music whose tradition has been shaped by repeated "outside" influence. Smith's comment, in particular, lacked credibility unless one dismisses an entire genre of postwar music-making as mindless "wanderings." Yet despite their failings, these criticisms contained no obvious malice, racist or otherwise, as Braxton, deeply offended by the early reports, has contended.[34] What they do reveal is the crisis of convergence in the arts at a time when stylistic strains were clashing and intersecting, and when the hierarchical distinctions between jazz and popular, classical and jazz, art and folk, highbrow and lowbrow, were eroding.

---

garde"—and Braxton's earlier efforts, which were to him "the American equivalent of such affectation, squandering his considerable gifts."

32. Smith, "Record Reviews: Anthony Braxton, B-X° /N-O-1 47A," *Jazz and Pop* (September 1970), 54.

33. Cooke, "This Time," *Jazz and Blues* (March 1972), 25.

34. Robert Levin, "Anthony Braxton and the Third Generation," *Jazz and Pop* (October 1970), 12–14.

II

Down Beat's reporting from the period suggests a general concern—if not a preoccupation—with the heightened erosion of mainstream common practice and the insistent survival of free jazz. Elder musicians such as Albert Nicholas, Lenny Tristano, Teddy Wilson, Zoot Sims, and Tommy Vig were, for example, predictably unimpressed with free playing, voicing, in frequently nostalgic recollections, a preference for the music of the past. Still, their comments were encouraged and faithfully reported in "The Blindfold Test" and elsewhere, as much, one suspects, to bolster magazine sales as to perpetuate a conservatively framed vision of the jazz tradition.[35] Many critics, on the other hand, had come to terms with free jazz by the late 1960s, and spoke favorably of performances that advanced Coltrane's stylistic innovations and Coleman's reinterpretation of the organically evolving, interactive nature of ensemble playing. Yet the most formally obscure performances still often met with rebuffs, not only from jazz critics, but also from rock commentators such as Alan Heineman, who occasionally demonstrated an aesthetic provincialism reminiscent of mainstream writers.[36] Even established critics sometimes appeared

35. Mike Hennessey, "Albert Nicholas, from New Orleans to Paris," *Down Beat* (June 12, 1969), 17; Lars Lystedt, "The Unchanging Perfection of Teddy Wilson," and Alan Surpin, "Lennie Tristano: Feeling Is Basic," both *Down Beat* (October 16, 1969), respectively, 15; 14, 30. The latter titles attribute qualities of stability and permanence to the music. Nicholas himself suggested continuity through longevity. After referring nostalgically to the "real [jazz] creators," the early musicians of New Orleans, Nicholas commented: "Yeah, those were beautiful, happy days. But I can't see very much beauty in some of this free jazz. . . . I admired the energy, but there was nothing in it musically. It was noise. They didn't tell me anything." In "The Blindfold Test," moreover, musicians would respond to unidentified recordings that seemed meant to elicit colorful responses. For Vig, columnist Leonard Feather mixed obscure selections of free (Sun Ra) and early fusion (Charles Lloyd, Roy Ayers, Jazz Crusaders) with similarly inappropriate recordings by Kenton and Gabor Szabo. (He did include one work by Phil Woods at the end.) A frustrated Vig remarked: "I'm extremely sorry you played so few things that I liked; things like Coltrane, Albert Ayler, Miles Davis, Lee Konitz, Milt Jackson, etc., or anyone with swinging original, beautiful ideas, high aims and pure music." See "Blindfold Test," *Down Beat* (March 20, 1969), 34. For Zoot Sims's reaction to *Aum,* a track on Pharoah Sanders's album, *Tauhid,* see *Down Beat* (January 8, 1970), 8.

36. Alan Heineman, "Albert Ayler, New Grass," *Down Beat* (July 24, 1969), 18. Heineman's comments usually addressed the static nature of free jazz rather than the tonal distortions that offended traditional critics. He called Sun Ra's performance at the Boston Globe Jazz Festival "anarchy . . . a thundering (in both senses) bore. . . . The whole set was one long what? Space Suite one supposes." Heineman, "Caught in the Act," *Down Beat* (May 1, 1969), 36. Reviewing Chick Corea's album, *Now He Sings,*

in retrospect on unsteady aesthetic ground when they faced performances that lay beyond their interests and expertise. Such was the case when Lawrence Kart, in an otherwise thoughtful review of Günter Hampel/Marion Brown collaboration, remarked: "Theirs is a music based almost entirely on sonority, and its relation to Brown's is that of a noise element a la John Cage—an uninvolved, complicating factor, like a pebble in your shoe."[37] Furthermore, free playing would often take it on the chin when artists reinforced its associations with radical politics, even while those very associations seemed to attract attention from the press. Heineman's review of Archie Shepp's *Three for a Quarter, One for a Dime* (1966) reflected as much frustration with Shepp's politics as with his music, an equation the writer advanced in a vituperative harangue.[38] Even *Down Beat* editor Dan Morgenstern, one of the more thoughtful commentators on the music of the era, ran into trouble for his strong and, to some, unwarranted words about the Jazz and People's Movement, an activist musicians' group.[39]

Critiques of jazz-rock hybrids—what would later be known as the dominant type of "fusion"—showed strong resemblances to the criticisms of free playing.[40] As writers provided regular coverage of rock-based styles in order to satisfy advertisers and to boost circulation, they repeatedly sniped at a musical adversary that, they believed, had undermined established notions of fine art. In many instances, the comments echoed charges launched from both the left and right against mass culture and populist youth movements, with which rock music was intimately connected. From the common critical vantage, it seemed as if America's new generation of jazz players and listeners had been corrupted by the banal effects of the rock 'n' roll band, which,

Now He Sobs, moreover, he wrote: "It's motion without direction, a sumptuous chocolate icing with no cake. I *think.*" *Down Beat* (May 29, 1969), 20–21. The following year, the French Jazz Academy voted Corea's album "Record of the Year." "Ad Lib," *Down Beat* (April 30, 1970), 42.

37. Kart, "Marion Brown/Günter Hampel, *Gesprachsfetzen,*" *Down Beat* (May 29, 1969), 20.

38. Heineman, "Three for a Quarter," *Down Beat* (September 18, 1969), 25.

39. For Morgenstern's comments, see "It Don't Mean a Thing," *Down Beat* (December 10, 1970), 13. For a response, see Andrew Cyrille's letter to the editor, *Down Beat* (January 21, 1971). Cyrille wrote: "As artists, to be aware of the things that control our lives externally, like politics, economics, and culture, is essential to our very being. . . . We feel that racism is at the core of the reason why more black jazz musicians are not seen on television, heard on radio, or are commercially successful." See discussion of the Jazz and People's Movement ahead.

40. The fusion label referred mainly to jazz/rock hybrids but could also be applied to other stylistic linkages.

despite its African-American roots, had diverged too far from the principles of Western artistic practice.[41] Speaking of the "venerable institution" of the big band, John McDonough lamented that Steve Allen and Oliver Nelson had sold out to the "current fads from the rock sound," while in a second essay, Pete Welding lambasted Muddy Waters for denigrating another venerable institution, the Chicago blues band—in itself a composite of downhome and urban performance practices and instrumentation—with "instrumental effects associated with the new rock."[42] In his film review of the Monterey Pop Festival, moreover, Ira Gitler enlisted the popular theme of the "generation gap" to explain the gulf that separated rock's youthful philistines from the arbiters of good taste.[43] Dan Morgenstern echoed these views as he also supplied insights into the fascistic potential of rock in comments reminiscent of early Marxist criticism.[44] Most blatantly expressing the gulf between youth and middle-aged tastes were the coy, barbed remarks of certain elder writers who failed to grasp the style and humor of the rock era. Writing about Miles Davis's second billing behind The Band, for example, Leonard Feather assumed a tone of

41. Dan Morgenstern, *Down Beat*'s editor in 1969, has indicated in conversation that the majority of the magazine's readers were teenage or in their early twenties. In an essay on Duke Ellington, moreover, Leonard Feather noted in passing that the average *Down Beat* reader was twenty-three years old. By 1969, its record-review sections were headed by rock or rock-oriented albums. For example, on May 1, the section led with Blood Sweat and Tears; on May 15, it featured Canned Heat, the Outlaw Blues Band, and the Colwell-Winfield Blues Band.

42. McDonough, "Spotlight Review" (March 6, 1969), 22, and Welding, "Record Reviews" (April 3, 1969), 29–30, both in *Down Beat.*

43. Gitler wrote: "Let this be a warning to the over 30s—and the under 30s with taste—find a better way to spend your time and money. . . . Canned Heat has a good beat; the Who's drummer is a heavy clod, and Janis Joplin looks like a big, beige baby having a conniption fit. . . . The Who breaking up their guitars and Jimi Hendrix breaking and burning his after some puerile sexual gesturing certainly does nothing to confirm the theory of the rock pundits that this music has raised American popular culture to the level of art." "Film Review: Pop Flop," *Down Beat* (May 29, 1969), 14.

44. "Rock, Jazz and Newport: An Exchange," *Down Beat* (December 25, 1969), 22. The exchange between Morgenstern and Heineman was one of the most reasonable and informative from the period. Heineman noted convincingly that Morgenstern, while open-minded and thoughtful, was judging rock according to jazz standards. Morgenstern, on the other hand, argued that rock music succeeds through volume in order to "obliterate everyday reality and its concomitant responses in place of which it offers a total environment of its own." At another point, Morgenstern commented: "Rock today is a gigantic business, controlled and manipulated by the very forces its metaphysical and 'philosophical' and political underpinnings oppose. It represents another victory for the good old American system, which turns everything marketable for profit into a commodity, and it has long since been socially neutralized."

square, reproving condescension as he remarked: "It's a Barnum and Bailey world, a world in which Jimi Hendrix, the Who, the Guess Who and the God Knows Who are playing at giant bowls."[45]

Some of the criticisms launched against the most self-indulgent or commercially inspired free and fusion performances were certainly well deserved. At a moment when the most radical innovators were questioning the traditional bounds of art and aesthetics, opportunists and conscientious artists alike seemed to blur into a murky haze that confounded even some of the most diligent observers. Facile attempts to color jazz with quirky pop jingles and insipid rhythms may well have properly drawn ire, since these attempts showed weaknesses from practically any critical vantage, save the most patently assimilationist and middlebrow. Yet many other criticisms developed not from sound interpretation of patterns of stylistic change, but rather from dogmatic assertions of personal taste, whether they be based in rock, fusion, bop, swing, or dixieland. Indeed, some of the shrillest attacks seemed to express above all the frustration of writers and their readers who longed for a bygone era, a pre-postmodern world that could only exist in tellingly selective reporting of the New York jazz scene and nostalgic-toned features on "The Good Old, Brand New, Multitalented Mel Tormé."[46]

In sum, the contradictions inherent in *Down Beat*'s reporting were symptomatic of the condition of crisis in the arts by the late 1960s. As rock music overwhelmed all other popular expressions and institutions, as radical experiment became the order of the day, observers, still prone to discrete, unilinear models of style, had reason to believe that traditional genres, values, and notions of art were rapidly deteriorating. Accordingly, fears of the "death of jazz" were revived as members of the community cast aspersions on both fusion and free as they blamed the traitorous former stars of the mainstream, Miles Davis and John Coltrane, for contributing to the music's economic hardships.[47]

45. Feather, "The Name of the Game," *Down Beat* (October 15, 1970), 11. In "TV Soundings," *Down Beat* (January 22, 1970), 11, Feather complained about Sly Stone's "sledge hammer drums." Occasionally, letters from readers questioned the commentary of the staff writers. See, for example, "Chords and Discords," *Down Beat* (October 2, 1969), 6.

46. Ira Gitler, "Chasin' the Apple," *Down Beat* (March 6, 1969), 18. The table of contents read, "Gitler pursues the New York jazz scene." The "scene" featured Ruby Braff, Red Norvo, and the Newport Allstars. Feather, "Mel Tormé," *Down Beat* (November 13, 1969), 14–15. The nature of the commentaries precluded youth appreciation of these important talents.

47. Reports of the music's decline appeared throughout the decade and particularly

Even musicians' objections to the term "jazz" seemed to reflect the general disintegration of traditional style. Initially raised on grounds that it perpetuated a racist subtext, the objections also expressed a general confusion about what constituted a clearly defined and separate musical style. More than a decade after Cecil Taylor's and Ornette Coleman's performances at the Five Spot publicly introduced the free movement, definitions of genre seemed more confused than ever. Looking further back into the past provided little additional help. For if the past could define an essence, it was not a living one, since "classics" survived at this point only in the form of semiprofessional repertory performances or on historical recordings. Even solid mainstream playing, which a few years earlier would have been applauded, seemed now no longer to satisfy. Reporting on Lou Donaldson's album *Midnight Creeper* (1968), an album that featured two proficient artists, Blue Mitchell and George Benson, Chris Albertson lamented, "If jazz has stagnated, it is sessions such as this that prove it. . . . We have enough blowing sessions to last us quite a while. I hope the future will bring us more *growing* sessions."[48]

III

Despite his early successes in the European jazz scene, Braxton had already begun to make plans to return to the United States by late fall of 1969. It is likely that while Paris afforded him a few opportunities, his situation was by no means a secure one. There was considerable dissension in Braxton's trio, fueled by the mixed reviews it had received from the French critical ranks, while the group's colleagues in the Art Ensemble were gaining wide notice and performing regularly throughout Europe. Furthermore, New York was still the center of

---

at moments where mainstream aesthetics seemed particularly threatened. A sample of the bounty of literature includes: Leonard Feather, "Is Jazz Committing Suicide," *Melody Maker* (September 15, 1962), 20–21; "What's Killing the Coast Concerts," *Down Beat* (March 30, 1961), 14–15; "Is Jazz Dead" [survey of critical opinion], *Jazz* (October 1965), 21; Arnold Shaw, "The Dilemma in Jazz," *Jazz* (April 1965), 9; Bill Quinn, "Lou's Blues: Alto Saxophonist Lou Donaldson's Gloomy View of the Future," *Down Beat* (February 9, 1969), 16; Ralph Gleason, "How to Reach Young Audiences," *Jazz and Pop* (February 1969); Thomas Tolnay, "Jazz Will Survive: J. J. Johnson," *Down Beat* (May 28, 1970), 16.

48. Chris Albertson, "Record Reviews," *Down Beat* (March 6, 1969), 25. See also Albertson's criticism of Ray Bryant as "a mainstream-type pianist" who needs to "say something new." *Down Beat* (May 15, 1969), 25. Such an attitude helps to explain his enthusiasm for Braxton's Artista releases in the mid-1970s (cf. chapter 6).

jazz activities, particularly for those in the free movement, and despite the economic difficulties American performers and showcases were facing. By staying with Ornette Coleman, who had invited Braxton to visit when they met in September, he would be provided further entrée into the New York scene—having already met many musiciansin Paris—and perhaps, Braxton may have thought, help in finding work.

New York seemed ideally suited to Braxton's creative inclinations. Diversity and pluralism have traditionally been defining features of the city's cultural character, but it seemed that by 1970 it had exceeded even the most celebrated portrayals of an urban American mosaic. Artistically, New York seemed, even from a safe historical distance, quite maddening as expressions not only flourished but intersected and collided. Ads and concert reviews from the time of Braxton's residence show that the city hosted an assortment of activities that paid testimony to its reputation as the cultural and musical nexus of contemporary American life. In the *Village Voice, Hi-Fi/Musical America, Jazz and Pop,* and other New York–based journals, critics were discussing the various manifestations of stylistic convergence, from classical to pop, modernism to rock, and East to West.[49] References to alliances and meetings between Mauricio Kagel and Buell Neidlinger, Luciano Berio and Paul McCartney, Benny Goodman and Peter Serkin, Rahsaan Roland Kirk and Frank Zappa, Andy Warhol and the Velvet Underground, Ornette Coleman and the Living Theater, Jimmy Giuffre and the Jean Erdman Dance Troupe, reflected the explosion of interaction that had now animated New York's downtown cultural life.[50] Ralph Berton's New York Rock and Roll En-

49. David Hamilton discussed the fractured lines of classical and pop as part of a series of essays on postwar music (the other authors are Roland Gelatt and Lukas Foss). For Hamilton's comment, see "A Synoptic View of New Music," *Hi-Fi/Musical America* (September 1968), 41–60. Passing references to stylistic convergences appeared scattered across the literature. Examples include: Martin Williams's comments on sitar-playing studio guitarists in "Bystander," *Down Beat* (February 5, 1970), 11; contemporary East-West interfaces in Carman Moore, "Music from India," *Village Voice* (March 19, 1970), 28. In popular magazines, essays by and about Stockhausen and other vanguard composers were also symptomatic of the erosion of genre. See, for example, Karlheinz Stockhausen, "An Open Letter to the Younger Generation," *Jazz and Pop* (December 1969), 22–24; R. Unwin, "The New Spiritual Era of Stockhausen," *Melody Maker* (May 29, 1971), 22; "Electronic Composers," *Jazz and Pop* (December 1969), 32–34.

50. A picture of McCartney chatting with Berio appeared in Hamilton, *Hi-Fi/Musical America* (September 1968), 49; reference to the jazz bass player Buell Neidlinger's

semble's fusion of classical and jazz, David Rosenboom's phantasmagoria of electronic sounds at the Electric Circus rock club, and Salvatore Martirano's amalgam of jazz, rock, and experimental music in the antiwar performance work, *L's GA,* similarly reflected the emerging realignment of style and genre.[51] Rich and dynamic yet confusingly conflicted, the fluxus of creative action had become the order of the day; with the appearance of Pierre Boulez to lead the New York Philharmonic, it had even affected the cloistered preserves of the classical elite. If the scores of middle-class nostalgia bands and stage shows suggested a conspicuous challenge to this musical mosaic, they also seemed like an appropriate background to a musical culture built upon patterns of groundless, decentered opposition.[52]

Braxton arrived in New York in January 1970, staying at Coleman's Prince Street loft for several weeks, and then moving to his own apartment in Greenwich Village.[53] At that point, Coleman, at work on his harmolodic theory of improvisation, had opened his loft to public performances and frequent private gatherings, through which Braxton was introduced to many of the musicians and artists in the community.[54] Furthermore, at East Village coffeehouses and black perfor-

concert of works by Kagel and LaMonte Young appeared in *Down Beat* (March 5, 1970), 34; Giuffre's performance with Erdman was reported in the *Village Voice* (April 30, 1970), 30; Goodman appeared with Serkin, performing Weber, Brahms, and Messiaen. *Village Voice* (April 30, 1970), 30. Ornette Coleman collaborated with the Living Theater in 1967, both on stage and for the film, *Who's Crazy.*

51. "L's GA" referred to Lincoln's Gettysburg Address, the subject of the performance. *Village Voice* (February 5, 1970), 29. Also noteworthy was the ad in the *Village Voice* for Max Neuhaus's New Year's performance work that encouraged citywide participation. The ad instructed readers to call WBAI on New Year's Eve with "some sound." Their offerings would then be broadcast over the air around midnight. *Village Voice* (January 1, 1970), 34. Stephen Ruppenthal, "David Rosenboom," in *The New Grove Dictionary of American Music,* 93–94.

52. Boulez conducted the New York Philharmonic from 1971 to 1977. His appointment created considerable controversy among a community of supporters repelled by his serial/modernist inclinations. For dixieland performances and show listings, see ads for Jimmy Ryan's, the Red Onion, the Red Garter, and the Roosevelt Grill in the *New Yorker* and *Village Voice* throughout 1970.

53. Braxton made at least one trip back to Chicago during this period, appearing at the Blue Gargoyle on February 6. "Strictly Ad Lib," *Down Beat* (March 19, 1970), 13. He has told me that he stayed with Coleman for six months (January through June). That would suggest that he lived in the Village for only two more, since he left New York in August.

54. These included visits by the artist Frederick Brown, Braxton's friend from Chicago, who provided the cover art for his 1976 Arista album, *Duets* (with Muhal Richard

mance spaces such as Studio We, Braxton could hear performances by artists who frequented Coleman's loft.[55] And at clubs such as the black-owned and -operated Pee Wee's on Avenue A and Slugs on East Third Street, he could see top-ranked musicians, including Cecil Taylor, Pharoah Sanders, McCoy Tyner, and Sun Ra, who appeared with his Arkestra on Monday nights. Visits to mainstream clubs, notably the Village Vanguard and the Village Gate, would round out Braxton's listening, offering a chance to observe an impressive assortment of bop and postbop innovators.[56]

The mood in the New York jazz environment surely must have tested Braxton's skepticism about black radical sentiments at a time when race seemed to define musicians' circles and relations. At Studio We and Slugs, black musicians had established closed circles defined by racial difference that excluded most white musicians seeking employment or simply curious about goings-on.[57] Organizations such as the Harlem Music Center were attempting, along the lines of the AACM, to provide a community base for black performers and young musicians, while the Collective Black Artists and Black Order of Revolutionary Enterprise asserted an exclusionist ideology that, however justified, exacerbated racial tensions in the jazz community.[58] Tensions

---

Abrams). John Howell, "New York: Painting the Blues, Fred Brown's Vivid Panorama of the Black Experience," *Elle* (June 1990), 26–28. Braxton claims that Coleman was performing frequently at this point. These were most likely private sessions in the loft circuit, since magazines reported that he had appeared rarely. See "Ad Lib," *Down Beat* (April 30, 1970), 40; "Ad Lib" (at the Village Gate), *Down Beat* (August 20, 1970), 12.

55. It is not clear to what extent Braxton was performing with New York musicians at this point. One suspects that the actual sesssions were limited. He told me that he never played with Coleman when they lived together.

56. Thelonious Monk, Miles Davis, Roland Kirk, Bill Evans, Gil Evans, and the Chicago drummer Jack DeJohnette all appeared at these clubs from January to June. A report on East Village clubs appears as Joe Klee, "East Village Club Marks Anniversary" (Pee Wee's Cafe), *Down Beat* (February 18, 1970), 8.

57. An interview with James Dubois, Milford Graves, Noah Howard, Juma Sultan, and others affiliated with Studio We appears as Chris Flickers, "The New York Musicians Organization," *Jazz Hot* (November 1973), 12–14. Recalling visits to Slugs and downtown lofts around this time, Richard Beirach has stated that whites could expect to encounter hostility from black employees, patrons, and musicians. "I can tell you many, many personal experiences of extremely strained relationships with blacks. This was especially true in clubs in the Lower East Side like Slugs." Beirach went on to say that he found this reception understandable, given the racial discrimination that black musicians had endured. Interview with David Leibman and Richard Beirach, New York (March 3, 1980).

58. The center was founded in 1969 by Herbie Hancock. See Robert D. Rusch, "CBA Conference Seeks Unity of Black Artists," *Down Beat* (July 20, 1972), 10–11;

were further compounded by the accusations of the Jazz and People's Movement and Black Artists for Community Action—the latter headed by Archie Shepp—which challenged the limited coverage and support of jazz by foundations and television programs.[59] The membership of the J&PM represented the opinions of many black artists who resented the limited playing opportunities and dependence on a predominantly white audience.[60] While Braxton was sympathetic to the activist sentiments of musicians such as Shepp, he had grown increasingly wary of the way in which race had served both sides as a category of exclusion.[61] As he became more and more accepting of activities outside the realm of jazz, he would pursue more vigorously creative avenues that critiqued the viability of race to define aesthetic and social difference.

Helpful to Braxton's experimental pursuits was his reacquaintance with Frederick Rzewski and the members of the Rome-based improvisation group, Musica Elettronica Viva. In early 1970, MEV had returned to the United States for an East Coast tour that included a concert in the New York area.[62] While in Manhattan in May, Rzewski

"Black Solidarity Festival" and "Black Order of Revolutionary Enterprise," *Down Beat* (July 23, 1970), 30. Similar collectives existed in the other arts, notably the Black Artists Group, the Nafashi Film Studio, and Takis's Art Workers Coalition. The latter staged protests in the name of underground and black artists. John Perreault, "Whose Art," *Village Voice* (January 9, 1969), 16; Elton Fax, *Black Artists of the New Generation* (New York: Dodd Meade, 1977), 115.

59. For background on the BACA, see Robert Levin, "Third World," *Jazz and Pop* (January 1971); for discussions of the Jazz and People's Movement, see *Down Beat*, October 10, November 12, and November 26 (all 1970); April 1 and May 27 (1971).

60. Oppositional critiques came not only from the free circle but from musicians of every ilk, including Miles Davis, the high priest of jazz. In one instance, Davis argued that the label "jazz"—"a white man's word"—was tantamount to calling a black person "nigger." Chris Albertson, "The Unmasking of Miles Davis," *Saturday Review* (November 27, 1971), 68. In the same essay, Albertson reported that Davis had forfeited half of his earnings for a New York performance to cover $2,000 worth of tickets for inner-city blacks. See also Davis's comments on the distinctions between black and white musicians in John Burke's "Festival in Black," *Rolling Stone* (May 31, 1969), 26.

61. "Shepp Big Band Stars in Coltrane Tribute," *Down Beat* (August 20, 1970), 12. Braxton has expressed his views of Shepp in interviews. The change in his outlook—or enhancement of an already ecumenical nature—has been confirmed by David Liebman, who met Braxton in the summer of 1970. Liebman remembers Braxton's proclamations of a spiritually oriented ecumenicalism, encouraging a group of white musicians to emulate the organization of the AACM. See "Free Life Communication: A Model of Change," a chapter in my master's thesis on avant-garde jazz (M.A., University of Michigan, 1981).

62. See Michael Parsons, "Sounds of Discovery," *Musical Times* (May and July

attended a reunion performance of the Braxton trio—billed the "Creative Construction Company"—held at the Judson Hall "Peace Church" on Washington Square.[63] After the concert, Rzewski suggested that Braxton begin rehearsing with MEV. A few weeks later, he joined the ensemble for a tour of the Midwest.[64]

The collaboration with MEV initiated a pronounced shift in Braxton's artistic direction. After having worked almost exclusively in the context of a musical community committed to black-centered expression, he would not explore a new experimental brand of spontaneous music-making with a group of white, Ivy League–educated concert artists who could demonstrate little or no experience in jazz performance.[65] Yet the disparity in musical learning and cultural background mattered less than their shared interest in pursuing an improvised art that suffused "serious music" with the egalitarianism of the vernacular. With the MEV, Braxton gained a chance to develop an expression that would transcend the hierarchical framework separating traditional forms of creative activity.[66]

Since its formation in 1966, the MEV had been experimenting with a variety of performance situations that radically departed from the traditional practices and experiences of the concert hall. Most typically they presented a form of improvised music that expressed, in both style and performance procedure, a vision of musical creativity as boundless collective action. By engaging in spontaneous "free form" improvisations that mixed electronic music with "natural," acoustically generated sounds, the MEV shaped sonic portraits of its ideal of creative communion, evoking images of a compassionate so-

---

1968), 29–30, 644–45; Michael Nyman, "New Music," *Musical Times* (December 1969), 1268–70. E. Safford, "Living Electronic Music in Providence," *American Music Digest* (December 1969), 14–15. The tour included a performance at the Brooklyn Academy of Music in February. For a review, see "Musica Elettronica Viva," *Hi-Fi/Musical America* (May 1970), 20–21. Rzewski also performed at a March concert at the Whitney Museum. "Whitney Avant-Garde," *Hi-Fi/Musical America* (June 1970), 25.

63. The performance was also recorded and released as *Creative Construction Company,* volumes 1 and 2 (1970). This name has been incorrectly applied to the previous trio, which appeared publicly as the Anthony Braxton Trio.

64. The tour included a residency at Antioch College in Ohio. "Promotional Biography," Arista Records (clippings files, the New York Public Library, Lincoln Center).

65. MEV's cofounders were Frederick Rzewski (B.A. Harvard, M.A. Princeton), Alvin Curran (B.A. Brown, M.M. Yale), and Richard Teitelbaum (M.M. Yale).

66. Rzewski's piece, "Street Music" (1968) may have inspired Braxton's *In the Street* and suggested the direction he would pursue on his first European recordings. See Rzewski, "Street Music," *Source: Magazine of the Avant-Garde* 3:2 (1969): 41.

cialist world. Furthermore, by collaborating with untrained musicians, including audience members invited to participate onstage, the group aggressively defied traditional binary oppositions that separated art from life, musician from listener, performer from composer, and musician from musician. In his program notes to an appearance at the Brooklyn Academy of Music in February 1970, Rzewski outlined the group's aesthetic doctrine: "Our music is meant to be useful. We are interested in rediscovering and applying all of the divine and healing properties which music has been known to possess ever since man can remember. . . . Our music is not meant to impress people, but to liberate them."[67]

Rzewski's comments captured the spirit of the experimental movement, which stood committed to the upheaval of classicist ideals, often through theosophic revisions of artistic practice. As a cultural symbol, the movement represented a challenge to the mythology of Western moral and cultural superiority in an era of civil rights conflict, global imperialism, and nuclear brinkmanship; as a reassessment of the very nature of the creative act, it paid tribute to the profound impact of Cagean aesthetics at the height of the 1960s vanguard movement. Already a powerful force when Braxton first encountered his writings in 1966, Cage was by the end of the decade the certified brahmin of the postwar avant-garde, the leader who had empowered a generation of artists in all fields to break from the restrictive norms of European practice. In music, he was principally responsible for initiating a grand challenge not only to traditional forms of coherence and control, but to a romantic ideology that privileged white male composers over the making and experiencing of art. The inherently radical character of the experimental aesthetic led composers, as a matter of course, to create in countless ways. While some applied alternative systems, others created unorthodox performance situations that, like the early "open forms" of Earle Brown, transcended the conventional bounds defining artistic practice. Members of the Sonic Arts Union (Alvin Lucier, David Behrman) and independent figures such as Max Neuhaus, Allan Bryant, and Christian Wolff similarly questioned the legitimacy of commonsense classifications, such as those separating musical instruments from "functional," everyday objects. Appropriating artifacts of suburban and rural environments in the act of open-ended collective performance, they created musical experiences in which the only ref-

67. Carman Moore, "MEV Pool," *Village Voice* (March 5, 1970). Details of a selection of MEV compositions appear in *Source* 2:1 (1968).

erent to traditional aesthetic circumstances was the stage itself.[68] Among an artistically radical contingent of experimentalists, moreover—represented, for example, by the "primitive" ceremonies of Pauline Oliveros—aesthetic experience depended above all on the effectiveness of achieving social communion through ritualistic performance. In this instance, celebrations of art-life intersections effectively eliminated regard for the formal outcome or necessity of "the work."[69] Other artists, such as Philip Glass, Steve Reich, and notably Terry Riley, whose *In* C (1965) helped to vitalize the experimental movement, remained committed on the integrity of the score. Yet their static repetition works also contradicted traditional concepts of balance and formal design, while questioning, through the application of banal melodic patterns attributable to popular music, standard equations of teleological logic, complexity, and aesthetic value.

What united all of these creative efforts was a vernacular ethos that celebrated everyday activity and performance practices of the nonprofessional. Whether glorifying artifactual emblems of the folk, romanticizing the "purity" of a distant, exotic Other, or exalting with static abstractions the simple elegance of popular song, these composers looked to territories outside the concert world not simply to color a traditional art but to liberate their artistry from the aesthetic preconceptions on which creativity had been previously grounded. They were committed, like Harry Partch, an earlier borrower from vernacular sound worlds, not "to be straight jacketed [*sic*] by anyone . . . [but rather] to be *completely free*."[70] The flurry of live performance works often drew inspiration from the liberating potential of traditional African-American music, as the frequent application of grassroots instruments exalted the mythic innocence of "the folk." Embrace of vernacular forms, moreover, suggested not only the vitalizing effects of Cage's vanguardism but the power and influence of popular music similarly informed by black performance practices. The preponder-

68. Robert Ashley, *In Memorium Kit Carson,* and Max Neuhaus, *Public Supply,* draw from commonplace technologies of the home (respectively, televisions, radios, telephones). Lucier's *Chambers* for "environments," Robert Erickson's *Cardenitas,* Allan Bryant's *Pitch Out,* and Alvin Curran's *Home-Made* employ found objects that evoke a grassroots image of rural life. Wolff's *Sticks* calls for sticks to be picked up and struck against objects and themselves at random. See "Living Electronic Music in Providence," *American Music Digest* 6 (1970): 14–15.

69. For background on Oliveros's *Rosemoon* and *Psi Star Psi d Tau Equals One,* see G. Von Gunden, *The Music of Pauline Oliveros* (Metuchen, N.J.: Scarecrow Press, 1983). Oliveros's *Psi Star* was published in *Source: Magazine of the Avant-Garde* 4:1 (January 1970).

70. Kyle Gann, "Hobo Saint," *Village Voice* (May 22, 1990), 90. Emphasis added.

ance of improvisation referred specifically to the impact of black urban forms, which had led to alterations of concert music since Satie's early experiments with ragtime. As such, experimentalism offered an obvious compatibility with Braxton's own creative ambition to explore formal processes of composition while preserving improvisation and the language of modernism as his spiritual-aesthetic center.

Collaborating with the MEV, Braxton had the opportunity to meet and socialize with many of the leading artists in the experimental movement.[71] Through Rzewski, he met Glass and Reich, with whom he rehearsed occasionally during the summer of 1970.[72] Trips to Wesleyan University to visit Richard Teitelbaum led to a meeting with John Cage, performances with the Sonic Arts Union, and separate appearances with David Behrman, a Sonic Arts cofounder and entrepreneurial prime-mover of experimental music.[73] Behrman's relationship with Larry Austin, editor of *Source: The Magazine of the Avant-Garde* and a principal advocate of experimental improvisation, helped Braxton to secure publication of *Composition 17* for string quartet in 1971. Its appearance represented the magazine's first publication of a work by a black artist. It also affirmed Braxton's position in the experimental-music community, leading the way toward other alliances and associations. Commenting about the period, Braxton has remarked: "By that time it became clear to me that I did not want to be remembered in only one context. I came to understand that I wanted to be involved in a broader area of creativity, and as such, I didn't want to limit myself by just performing jazz. Not to mention I simply was curious and attracted to what people like Glass and Behrman were doing."[74]

71. It is noteworthy that the downtown area had become a physical manifestation of new artistic alliances since the early free sessions at the Five Spot, a favorite meeting place for vanguardist writers and artists. Nearby on Tenth Street, a scene had also developed, documented by Harold Rosenberg in "Tenth Street: A Geography of Modern Art," in *Discovering the Present: Three Decades in Art, Culture, and Politics* (Chicago: University of Chicago Press, 1973). In the 1950s, Cage's "Bozza Mansion" on the Lower East Side was the scene of early loft performances. See Calvin Tomkins, *Against the Wall: Robert Rauschenberg and the Art World of Our Time* (New York: Doubleday and Co., 1980), 99–100.

72. Glass substantiates this in Keith Potter and David Smith, "Interview with Philip Glass," *Contact* (Spring 1976), 26. The experience inspired Braxton's genre of *Kelvin* works, of which *Composition 26E,* recorded on *Saxophone Improvisations Series F* (1972, European release only), was dedicated to Glass.

73. Teitelbaum was studying for the Ph.D. and had created the World Band, a group of Western and non-Western musicians that performed from 1970 to 1972. Behrman, producer of experimental music for Columbia Records, was a founding member of *Source: Magazine of the Avant-Garde.*

74. Interview with Anthony Braxton (February 2, 1983). This statement may be

Yet despite these successes among the experimentalists, Braxton would ultimately pursue most fervently his opportunities in the context of jazz. For while the experimental movement, on one level, may have affirmed his commitment to an iconoclastic improvised music, it also, on another, excluded him from the social world and professional opportunities—club dates, record sessions, critical attention—of an aspiring jazz-based artist. Moreover, it is likely that the improvisational approaches of experimental musicians, in the end, seemed inappropriate for an artist whose conception of performance had taken shape in jazz. If experimentalism drew inspiration from the vernacular, its desire to exceed the boundaries between artist and audience, between art and life, contradicted an aim grounded in the black vernacular—in blues, in the preacher's sermon, in the cutting contests of Harlem and Kansas City—to develop a personal artistic voice. Indeed, Braxton's comments from the period suggest that he had grown skeptical about some of the ideals of the experimentalists, who had conceptualized an impersonal vanguard aesthetic attributable to the vernacular rather than letting such procedures develop from the character of real-life relations and situations. During his first major interview in a jazz magazine, Braxton, in addition to a profusion of admiration, had this to say about John Cage, the leading figure of American experimentalism:

> There are a lot of things Cage hasn't come to terms with. His music is almost all intellectual, all conceptual. . . . I met Cage once and we talked about this. I was telling him that when you look in this life you see trees and rocks, but you also see people—people exist, egos exist . . . and if that's true then his music isn't really reflecting nature as much as he thinks it is, because people are just as much a part of nature as rocks and trees.[75]

Braxton's attraction to the subversive implications of modernism would make certain his pursuit of an abstract compositional style, and his developing political-creative interest in advancing an ecumenical art based in black aesthetics would help to ensure his continued involvement with Rzewski, Teitelbaum, and other experimentalists. But in the 1970s, he would also explore ways of articulating a radical artistic conception that, while showing no true allegiance to any particu-

---

compared with Joseph Jarman's comment from the period: "The critics have called it avant-garde, they've called it the new thing, but we have only one name for it: Great Black Music." Valerie Wilmer, "Caught in the Act," *Down Beat* (June 25, 1970), 26.

75. Robert Levin, "The Third World: Anthony Braxton and the Third Generation," *Jazz and Pop* (October 1970), 12–14.

lar community or genre, nonetheless underscored his attraction to and familiarity with jazz music's circle of culture.

IV

The catalyst for Braxton's recommitment to jazz was a chance meeting then subsequent collaboration with pianist Chick Corea. After the same "Peace Church" concert where he had been reacquainted with Rzewski, Braxton also crossed paths with Jack DeJohnette, a former Wilson Junior College classmate who was, at the time, performing with Miles Davis.[76] DeJohnette suggested that they visit the Village Vanguard, where Corea, who had recently left Davis, was opening with his new trio.[77] By the end of the evening, Braxton was sitting in with the band. The session, in turn, led to further collaborations with Corea, bass player Dave Holland, and drummer Barry Altschul, at the pianist's loft on 19th Street. Toward the end of the summer, Braxton had formally secured a place in the band, eventually renamed—to advance its supposedly collective orientation—Circle.[78]

From August to October 1970, Circle developed its improvisational approach in a series of performances and sessions on the East and West coasts. A premier concert at New York's Upstage recording loft was followed by a session for its first album, *Circulus* (1970), and subsequent engagements in San Francisco and Los Angeles. After completing work toward a second album in October, the group embarked on a six-month tour of Europe. Performances in West Germany, France, Belgium, Italy, and England received considerable attention, prompting the release of *A.R.C.* (1971), together with two live albums and, later, a London studio session under Braxton's name.[79] In March,

76. DeJohnette had also appeared previously on Corea's album *Is* (1969).

77. An advertisement in the *Village Voice* noted that the trio would premiere on May 19, on a double bill with Roy Haynes. See ads from May 14 and May 21, 1970. Discographical evidence confirms Braxton's recollection, showing that the "Peace Church" concert also took place on May 19.

78. According to *Down Beat*'s "Strictly Ad Lib" column from September 17, 1970, Braxton sat in during the August 2 concert. His appearance in the *Circulus* session on August 21 suggests that he had joined the group by then. Dave Liebman recalls that Holland and Corea also had lofts in his building on 19th Street and frequently rehearsed there (interview with David Liebman and Richard Beirach).

79. The second album was released as *Circling In* (1970). Braxton's album, *The Complete Braxton 1971,* is discussed later in this chapter. *A.R.C.*, moreover, is a Scientological acronym for affinity, reality, communication, which together refer to understanding. According to L. Ron Hubbard, A.R.C. "has come to mean good feeling, love, or friendliness, such as he was in ARC with his friend." See Hubbard, *Dia-*

the band returned to the United States, where it recorded *Gathering* (1971) and appeared in clubs in Boston, New York, and California.[80]

Braxton's affiliation with Circle provided him with an opportunity to explore experimental approaches to improvisation while maintaining a secure footing in jazz practice. The band represented a partnership between musicians attuned to the language and aims of vanguard experiment, yet whose grounding in jazz assured likenesses in approach and intention.[81] Furthermore, Circle's advocacy of the free-jazz mix of black spiritualism and countercultural ideology would complement Braxton's own developing aesthetics. In particular, they all shared a commitment to a jazz-centered, black-based modernism that would *extend* traditional African-American associations of art and the sacred. Combining the intensity of jazz with the collage-like abstractions of atonal music, then, Circle would be for Braxton the perfect match, supportive of his radical artistic aims while reinforcing his commitment to the traditional values and ethos of jazz.

Stylistically, Corea's previous experiments with jazz/modernist linkages were chiefly responsible for setting the band's creative direction. His first record, *Tones for Joan's Bones* (1966), shows that he had acquired a firm grasp of Latin music and bop, which inspired a personal approach based on long stretches of rapid, rhythmically complex, melodic line. By the time of his second release, *Now He Sings, Now He Sobs* (with Roy Haynes and Miroslav Vitous, 1968), he had transposed this melodic approach into a more-or-less free language.

netics and Scientology, Technical Dictionary (Los Angeles: Publications Organization, 1975), 20.

80. American coverage of Circle appeared principally in *Down Beat* (January 7, February 4, March 18, May 27, and July 22, 1971). See also Richard Williams, "Dave Holland Forms Circle," *Jazz and Pop* (February 1971), 25–27. For European coverage, see Denis Constant, "La Quadrature du Cercle," *Jazz Magazine* (France) (March 1971), 7; Bernard Loupias, "Un Cercle parfait," *Jazz Hot* (April 1971), 23; Gudrun Endress, "Circle, " *Jazz Podium* (Germany) (February 1971), 53–55, 68; Arrigo Polillo, "Festival del Jazz a Bergamo," *Musica Jazz* (Italy) (May 1971), 15–19.

81. Altschul was a longtime associate of Paul Bley, while Holland worked formerly with Miles Davis. Early recordings of the trio show that it had already begun to embrace modernist practices prior to Braxton's arrival. On *The Song of Singing* (1970), the band plays in a highly interactive modal and frequently nontonal style, exploring coloristic invention in the context of an engaging free improvisation. On *Toy Room* and *Nefertiti,* it extends bop practices and intensity while articulating a free language; on *Ballad I* and *Ballad II,* the musicians stress timbral variety in a style that pays tribute to modernist concert music. Also noteworthy is Corea's solo on Marion Brown's *Afternoon of a Georgia Faun,* which interplays conventional elements (notably chords built on fourths) with an atonal modernist language.

Corea's rhythmic verve highlighted these performances, in which a driving percussive articulation seemed to vary the resonance of each tone. His reliance on scalar and harmonic pentatonisicm—typically, as chromatically shifting left-hand comping—augmented qualities of tunefulness even as it confused tonal bounds. Similarly, his preference for long, breathlike phrases effected balance while tending to obscure formal order. Later recordings show Corea further advancing modernist procedures that upset this tenuous balance between anarchy and order. On the albums *Is* (1969) and *Circling In* (1970), and particularly on the track *Fragments,* which featured Holland and Altschul, Corea leads an effort to combine an assortment of unrelated melodic and rhythmic elements into a cubistic, nontonal juxtaposition.

Circle's supporting musicians were also solid contributors. Of chief importance to the rhythmic conception of the band was percussionist Barry Altschul. As an accompanist, Altschul functioned as a sensitive ballast to the lead instruments, at times playing with a frenetic intensity that seemed to heighten tension and accentuate Corea's fractured, disjointed style. To be sure, Altschul was an artful and subtle performer who could interlace a barrage of sharp attacks with momentary pauses and rapidly changing dynamics in the context of a single phrase. He was also a remarkably flexible artist whose ability to change rhythmic and dynamic directions on a dime created a background of explosive kineticism that evoked the illusion of simultaneous compression and expansion of musical time. In quieter passages, Altschul enhanced the rhythmic texture with colorful sound sources from brake drums to bull roarers to finger cymbals to tam tam. His ability to vary roles consistently from ensemble driver to sound colorist and accompanist, while still maintaining a sense of animated rhythm, seemed to vitalize the band's playing, setting it apart from many lesser-inspired free groups.

Channeling the rhythmic energy of piano and percussion, Dave Holland provided the essential link. A virtuosic melodist with unbridled energy and impeccable sense of time, Holland succeeded both to enhance and temper the ruptured rhythmic assertiveness of Altschul's most energized moments while frequently, as a secondary lead voice, complementing Corea's own melodic/percussive gifts. Together the members of the trio created a rhythmically dynamic texture, whether reaching the height of percussive intensity or working within a tense, pulseless space. As it shifted from riotous energy playing to deep calm to clamorous collective interaction, the ensemble created, in a musical language of abstraction, interfaces of tension and relaxation that traditionally define swing.[82] It was this quality of perpetual and seemingly unresolved musical energy that characterized the rhythmic approach of the Circle band.

As a trio, Circle would have remained one of the premier New York–based free ensembles of the post-Coltrane era. With the addition of Braxton, however, it more actively explored the extremes of modernist abstraction while still operating, as its instrumentation and performance practices reflected, within the bounds of the bop legacy. In particular, Braxton contributed to the ensemble a fundamentally new formal and rhythmic dimension, frequently increasing the level of abstraction to the point of parody. In its turn, Circle provided Braxton with a forum for testing the boundaries of jazz while always honoring the music's most fundamental strictures. The procedure by which he went about this deserves close attention here, for it would orient his subsequent approaches both as a soloist and as an ensemble leader.

Earlier discussions have shown that, as a soloist, Braxton sought to transcend the conventional parameters of traditional tonal music—scale, harmony, meter, and melodic balance—by employing a highly disjunct nontonal language that highlighted rapid, abrupt shifts in motive, rhythm, and tempo. With Circle, he exaggerated the extremes of this language to a point suggesting a kind of stylistic fracture, while taking pains to provide coherence, either by establishing formal markers during the course of an improvisation or by highlighting preset compositional structures (typically the outlines of song form). Braxton's particular use of extremes, whether in the form of phrasing cut loose rhythmically from the accompaniment, corny, marchlike stilted passages, or abstract coloration in the context of straight-ahead ensemble playing, reflected a continued effort to impose his personal stamp on jazz performance in keeping with the revisionist practices of African-American oral arts.

On the Paris version of *There Is No Greater Love* (1971, 4/1), for example, Braxton takes a three-chorus (I–III) alto saxophone solo that transforms Isham Jones's standard into a vehicle for an arresting, rhythmically charged performance. Formally, Braxton makes a point of establishing a general sense of order by marking off the beginnings and ends of phrases across an AA′BA″ form.[83] Within particular sections, however, he relies on stylistic elements that subvert formal

82. André Hodeir, "The Phenomenon of Swing," *Jazz: Its Evolution and Essence* (New York: Grove Press, 1956), 195–209.

83. The superscripts (A′, A″) serve only as reference points to particular sections rather than as indications of stylistic variation.

clarity. These range from furious, pointillistic sprays that at once acknowledge the musical styles of Webern and Dolphy; to collections of disjunct motivic fragments that break in midphrase (particularly in chorus IIA); to rapid streams of slurred, coarse-toned chromaticism that mimics the artistry of Ornette Coleman (IIA″ and into IIIA); to temporal compressions of rhythmic articulation against a steady beat (IA″). The consummate revisionist, Braxton acknowledges the formal bounds in which "jazz" performance takes place while recontextualizing them in a sound world reflecting his own learning and interests.

At certain moments in the solo, Braxton's subversion of convention approaches mocking satire.[84] Most noteworthy are the places where he introduces a series of highly unconventional "pointillistic" ideas against a gently swinging, walking bass line. The deliberate incongruity pokes fun at the swing convention and ultimately the "sweet" era from which *Greater Love* originates. Particularly satirical are Braxton's stiff, rhythmic passages, which exaggerate the uniformity and order of the march, appearing in the context of a relaxed, swinging accompaniment. Here parody serves at once to exaggerate and repress musical dislocation: like a stifled scream, it signifies one extreme (confusion and incoherence) by articulating another (the literalness of the march). As Braxton continues to work the idea, the instability builds into a surrealist *Affect* that ultimately enhances qualities of abstraction.[85]

Similar procedures appear in other examples preserved on record. On the Paris version of *Nefertiti,* for example, Braxton juxtaposes a range of musical parodies to create an absurdist confusion. Working with no preset constraints, he once again highlights stilted, dotted-note march rhythms and pointillistic motives against an undercurrent of gentle lyricism. Then he shifts to another extreme, playing rapid passages that transcend rhythm-section tempo. This inversion of effect, from a lumbering rhythmic squareness to an intentional, remarkably precise rushing of the beat, effects a profound emotive drama that intensifies the vividness of the overall performance.

But perhaps best characterizing the techniques of musical revision and parody is Braxton's solo performance on *Starp,* from the album

84. This technique might explain a reviewer's comment: "If there was anything approaching a flaw in the group unity, it was Braxton. Though he played superbly much of the time here, there were occasions when his direction seemed at odds with the group thought." Will Smith, "Paris Concert," *Down Beat* (March 1, 1973), 22.

85. A similar effect occurs on the German version of *There Is No Greater Love* (1970, 2/1), where a modified single-note repetition encompasses the first eight bars of Braxton's opening solo.

Circling In (3/1). Here, he accentuates these same vertiginous qualities by casting the performance as a series of sonic ambiguities and oppositions. While nondialectical, antihierarchical opposition would by definition seem to disrupt a sense of structure, in this context it appears to support it; the "form" of Braxton's solo depends on the calamitous energy that the continual process of construction and deconstruction produces. In the opening passage, for example, Braxton initiates at a moderate tempo an atonal ascent in a pointillistic contour. Just as quickly, however, the phrase changes course and moves rapidly downward. Proceeding, the line never reveals a clear direction or sense of resolution. Like a run-on sentence, it lumbers on relentlessly, finally reaching a conclusion when it reverses direction again with an upward flourish. In the next succession of ideas, Braxton initially steadies the performance, beginning with a sustained tone that suggests the possibility of an ordered progression. Yet that logic is also undermined as he departs from developmental process, gliding back and forth from a nearly inaudible, whispered tone to a loud, overblown attack. Next, he follows a similar pattern, working a pair of free-floating pitches to outline the extremes of the dynamic range. As the ensemble accompaniment becomes more assertive, Braxton's playing grows to a feverish, dramatic height. He seems to reach toward a state of musical convulsion, of interacting stylistic and dynamic extremes, as if to recall the transpositions of fast lines and moments of silence appearing in the head. *Starp* is surely one of Circle's most arresting performances, highlighting a strange yet entrancing mix of indeterminacy and virtuosic control. As the musicians unleash a powerful, chaotic explosion of multidimensional sound, they also maintain a sense of rhythmic precision that achieves the paradoxical sensation of performative cohesion through formal collapse.

Undergirding Circle's artistic commitment to individualistic, radically free expression was its involvement in the Church of Scientology.[86] Founded in 1953 by L. Ron Hubbard, the Church had attracted a considerable following among an American youth who sought alternatives to traditional religious orthodoxy.[87] Its emphasis on the spiri-

86. Corea was most certainly involved in the movement by 1969, when he recorded *Is,* whose title alludes to the Scientological concept of isness, "an apparency of existence brought about by the continuous alternation of an as-isness." L. Ron Hubbard, *Dianetics and Scientology, Technical Dictionary,* 218. On another track, Corea mixes metaphors of Scientology and cultural nationalism: the title of the track, *Jamala,* is a Swahili term for courtesy, which is consistent with the Scientological behavioral code.

87. Roy Wallis, *The Road to Total Freedom: A Sociological Analysis of Scientology*

tual pursuit of self-knowledge for the good of the community gave institutional endorsement to social nonconformity, presented in a fascinating assemblage of psychotherapy and Eastern mysticism. The application to art of Scientological interpretations of the self-in-community was no doubt appealing to Braxton, who had shaped a compatible black-based aesthetic spiritualism in the AACM, and who, by then, had begun to reinterpret further the most radically separatist views espoused by many of his former Chicago colleagues. Soon he would join his new associates in formally pursuing Scientology's rite of passage, reaching the advanced introductory level, Grade Four.[88]

In a *Down Beat* interview published in April 1969, Corea outlined an aesthetic that anticipated Circle's spiritualist ideals while suggesting the influence of his earliest Church encounters. Likening collective improvisation to "séances," Corea called for a unified approach to free-jazz performance—what he would later describe as an agreement of "universes"—that would restore to the music its oral ethos, while also distancing it from the objectifying tendencies of the critical establishment.[89] His refusal to provide a biography for the interview or, in another setting, to grade performances for "The Blindfold Test," underscored the egalitarian orientation of his musical values as it voiced resistance to the historical framing of artistic innovation.[90] Furthermore, Corea's comments suggested that he had applied the Scientological dichotomy of personal growth and social communion to the act of collective musical performance. Celebrating the virtuosic yet highly interactive nature of jazz, he seemed to believe that the most successful performances were those in which reflective, individualistic artists attained high levels of group communication. Recalling at a later time the experience of the *Paris Concert,* Corea spoke poetically of

---

(New York: Columbia University Press, 1977), 128. See also L. Ron Hubbard, *Scientology 0–8: The Book of Basics,* 4th ed. (Los Angeles: Church of Scientology of California, 1975); Hubbard, *Dianetics: The Modern Science of Mental Health,* 2d ed. (Los Angeles: Bridge Publications, 1985).

88. Lock, *Forces in Motion,* 88. Braxton left the organization around the time that Circle disbanded. He had espoused Scientological beliefs at the time of his interview with François Postif, in which he referred to the ARC triangle, printed with the essay. "KFQ4-6F," *Jazz Hot* (April 1971), 14–17.

89. Corea outlined his theory of universes during an appearance in Leonard Feather, "The Blindfold Test," *Down Beat* (November 26, 1970), 30. In an interview with Larry Kart, "The Chick Corea File," *Down Beat* (April 3, 1969), 21–22, Corea mentions musical séances, adding: "I've been involved in some situations where the music has taken itself into letting it all out, just playing whatever may be at hand rather than trying to create 'gems of music.'"

90. Kart, "The Chick Corea File"; Feather, "Blindfold Test," *Down Beat.*

"sharing, creating, loving, freely giving . . . romping together in a shared and real world of each others' wildest creations . . . to be what we are as spiritual beings . . . [while] always knowing who you really are."[91] Communication as such became the operative word, and the "freedom" of modernist abstraction the vehicle for true communion. Circle would actualize what Ralph Ellison has called in his definition of the jazz ethos "an art of individual assertion within and against the group," an expression for which improvisation serves "as [a] link in the chain of tradition." Scientology's spiritual ideals would further strengthen these communalistic concerns, affirming the contradiction of self and selflessness that causes every musician to "lose his identity even as he finds it."[92]

Recorded evidence shows that Circle developed and advanced this strategy of African-American music-making as a complementary symbiosis of individual expression vs. collective interaction. Whereas mainstream ensembles mediated such practices by relying on conventional forms and procedures, Circle, by operating in a free language, succeeded in creating a kind of concentrated purity of the jazz ethos. In the context of group performance, the musicians' assertions of self tended to heighten the level of interaction: imaginative ideas and their articulation meshed at a level of precision and depth that stood virtually unmatched in the "energy" improvisations commonly heard in New York lofts. The disparity of performance procedures, moreover, ranging from unaccompanied solos to chamber duets to an assortment of quartet arrangements, created continual shifts in timbral character and density, while the ever-changing state of performer interaction imparted similar fluctuations in melodic/rhythmic texture. Changes in the nature of improvisational interaction seemed, in fact, to be one of the chief determinants of style and procedure, growing out of the call/response paradigm of the African-American tradition.

Circle's improvisational procedures may be observed as a typology of relationships growing out of Scientological and African-American individual/group dichotomies. At their most basic, the procedures outline a series of performance roles, from interactive to noninteractive, from hierarchical (solo or "lead" vs. accompaniment) to nonhierarchical ("collective").[93] Interactive hierarchical relationships (e.g., solo with rhythm section) are most common to jazz and appear frequently

91. Notes to *Circle: Paris Concert* (1971).

92. See Ellison, *Shadow and Act,* 234.

93. I use "soloist" to define the traditional improvisational role and "leader" to describe the dominant voice of a more egalitarian, interactive improvisation.

in Circle's recorded performances. Sometimes accompaniment provides general support to the lead voice; at others, it interacts in a particular way, emulating the soloist, answering his phrases (e.g., "trading fours"), initiating new directions, or even opposing lead statements. In the rare instances where a noninteractive hierarchy occurs—rare because hierarchy typically enforces interaction—the soloist (usually Braxton) appears disconnected from and almost oblivious to the rhythm section's accompaniment; as noted previously, these typically constitute a form of parody. Nonhierarchic interaction, on the other hand, embodies the "freeness" of free jazz and is often identified with the rather vague term "collective." Given the vast range of potentially collective relationships, it is useful to identify the most common types occurring in Circle's performances. At moments, instrumentalists may work imitatively or oppositionally, as if engaged in a musical sparring match. In some instances, motivic contrasts provide support, or what might be called a kind of symbiosis. Less common are "constructive" and "communal" interactions, the former where musicians construct phrases collectively by alternating and interacting—a form of *Klangfarbenmelodie*—the latter where time and meter give way to a blanket of nearly static tone colors. Communal procedures identify the periods of true union and intimacy, the points at which musicians seem to transcend rules and constraints to reach a "spiritual" height. They can be contrasted to a final type of improvisation, which is neither interactive nor hierarchic, identified by moments of loud, "energy" playing. In these, musicians seek to create a different kind of stasis, built upon a dense clustering of impersonal, unrelated sounds.

Circle's German-concert version of Dave Holland's *Toy Room/Q&A* shows how the group applies these techniques in performance.[94] The composition is an extended, multisectional improvisation whose chief consistencies are the themes that identify two main movements. The first, *Toy Room,* begins with a simple, folklike melody (played in octaves by piano and bass) that descends sequentially as it fluctuates between F major and D minor. The melody of *Q&A* also develops sequentially from a major mode, but its rapid compression of tempo and phrase length creates a condition of unresolved tension, establishing a suitable basis for the ensuing frenetic, free blowing. It is in the question and answer of *Q&A* where the most involved collectivity appears.

94. *Toy Room* can also be heard on *The Song of Singing* (1970), while *Toy Room/Q&A* appears on *Paris Concert* (1971).

From the beginning, Circle's manner of solo expression and group interaction seems to vary from moment to moment. After an introductory piano solo, Corea leads the group toward the theme and then onward to a hierarchical improvisation in which he receives general support from the rhythm section. Quickly, he increases the level of rhythmic intensity through rapid flourishes of highly chromatic, staccato runs and energetic left-hand comping. Altschul, in turn, complements Corea's actions by launching an explosion of fragmented drum attacks that initiates a new direction as it energizes ensemble performance. In the second section, Holland and then Braxton (playing flute) effect a contrast from the previous intensity by working in imitation to produce a nonhierarchic melding of sound. Shortly after, a resumption of tension appears through the absence of tempo and time: Altschul and Holland pause while Braxton and Corea engage in a counterpoint of brief, rapid atonal flourishes that vacillate between imitation and symbiosis. When the drums and bass reenter, they elevate, through imitation, the fractured "pointillism" that Corea and Braxton (having shifted to sopranino saxophone) had previously established, while increasing the sense of textural contrast by rapidly shifting instrumentation. Allusions to and then statement of the *Q&A* theme introduce a section of intense, wildly free improvisation, now with Braxton leading the way. The ensuing improvisation explores the extremes of intensity, coloration, and texture through an elaborate sequence of instrumental couplings.[95] A return to energy playing, accelerated by Corea's rhapsodic flourishes encompassing the entire keyboard, reestablishes a texture appropriate for a restatement of the *Q&A* theme.[96]

V

While performing with Circle in London in February 1971, Braxton recorded a session of his own compositions, subsequently released as *The Complete Braxton* (1971). The range of instruments, instrumen-

95. These couplings include: bass/bull roarer/pennywhistle/percussive attacks on piano strings; piano/tambourine/kazoo/bass, with Holland evoking the haunting tones of the *dijeridoo;* duets of bass/sopranino saxophone and bass/drums.

96. Similar operative procedures appear in the Paris version. At this point, the band had become more adept at instrumental interaction, the result of six months of additional performing experience. Here they respond directly to each others' ideas, not only emulating the lead player's style, but at times composing constructively. Yet what the German version lacks in interaction, it gains in fire and vigor, making for a satisfying (and this writer's preferred) performance.

tal combinations, and performance practices appearing in these works reflect Braxton's experiences with Circle, and the appearance of Holland and Altschul on the album reinforces that connection. What makes a noticeable difference is Corea's absence, which clears the ensemble texture while greatly reducing rhythmic intensity and drive. As a consequence, the sense of musical space increases, stretching the sonic canvas to encourage textural experiment and to provide greater room for Braxton's solo efforts. The addition of trumpeter Kenny Wheeler enhances the change further, his nervous, introspective style effectively offsetting Braxton's energetic playing. Compositionally, moreover, Braxton's quartet pieces mark a new progression in his efforts to implant modernist practices into jazz, presented as an imaginative display of unconventional approaches. In each work, Braxton invents a different set of rules that serve to define instrumental roles and stylistic practices. Rather than quirky reorientations of standard jazz performance, these compositional designs develop from deep-level stylistic linkages that supply a context for the ensuing improvisations. Imaginative and sometimes elaborate, the compositions demonstrate once again Braxton's aim to widen the powers of his expressive voice in an encompassing embrace of his prior creative experience. The interplay of jazz and concert music in Braxton's own playing sets up yet another level of stylistic linkages that create a reciprocal relationship between the specifics of the solo and the composition itself.

In *Composition 6A* (2/1), Braxton alters conventional performance practices to an extent that obscures clear jazz associations. In the opening "head" section, he replaces tune and song form with a series of unfolding A-major arpeggiations separated by brief moments of ensemble improvisation. While hardly tunes as such, their melodicism and tonal centering maintain a stylistic consistency familiar to the standard repertory. As an accompaniment to the head and subsequent solos, moreover, Dave Holland sets down a walking bass line, as is typical in postbop practice. While Holland's bass line (supplied in notation) serves a jazz function as a regulator of tempo, its brisk, staccato outline of chromatic contours effectively undermines the rhythmic elasticity necessary for swing. Abrupt, emotionally tense, and marchlike, the bowed bass line becomes the stylistic fixture of the work, supplying background accompaniment in the solo sections.[97] Interestingly, its peculiar energy, complemented by Altschul's series of disconnected flourishes, creates another kind of rhythmic drive, which

97. In his catalog, Braxton identifies *Composition 6A* as an "arco march."

inspires one of Braxton's more memorable solos. Moving from sustained tones to virtuosic sweeps, from soft, high-register attacks to pronounced low-register distortions, all the while interlacing extended statements with abrupt pauses and brief interjections, Braxton creates again with oppositional extremes in order to build a rhythmically stylized, cubistic juxtaposition.

Composition 6I (3/1), on the other hand, shows clear likenesses to conventional jazz performances in which a notated head prepares for a series of accompanied solos. Indeed, a first hearing suggests bop: Braxton and Wheeler play a fast unison theme built on a sequence of straightforward, two-bar motives. Melodically, however, the theme relies heavily on intervallic relations that confound harmonic movement and tonal certainty. Fluctuating between ambiguous, diminished-scale figurations, "open," perfect intervals (fourths and fifths), and chromatic, marginally tonal ideas, the written line acts as a kind of distorting filter that brings tonality in and out of focus. The first two motives in figure 4.1, for example, establish a conventional call/response sequence, and follow more or less the same contours in measures 1–4.[98] The "call" outlines an inherently unstable C-diminished scale that ends with a downward tritone leap; the response alternates chromatic couplings to close with another descending figure, this time a cadential, E♭ to E♭, octave jump. Clearly the theme is going somewhere, yet the ambiguity of the harmonic information (and the essentially chromatic movement of the bass line) leaves direction unclear. Measures 5–6 provide a resolution of sorts, as the new motive alters melodic contour and reverses the cadential turn upward. Still, tonality remains tentative because of the lack of clear harmonic outline. Descending stepwise from B♭ to E♭, and then upward to D♭ in leaps of a perfect fifth and fourth, the motive, in its repetitions, suggests several potential centers (E♭, G♭, D♭) as it hovers, unresolved, between the tonal cracks. When the melody finally moves, it shifts centering unexpectedly to an A♭, whole-tone arpeggiation, appearing on record against an A♮ bass pedal. And when a clear tonal center on A♮ finally appears in measure 9 (redefining the bass voice as an anticipatory pedal), a melodic tag shifts the center to A♭ (m. 13). The final ending (m. 14), which clearly establishes D♭ against a new D♭ bass pedal, nevertheless remains tentative, given the lack of a clear harmonic resolution.

In *Composition 6J* (1/2), Braxton creates a formal opposition on a

98. The recorded performance sounds an octave lower. Note also that the first pitch, C, sounds a minor third lower; in measure 7, the first pitch, F, is not played, while the second E is played as an E♭.

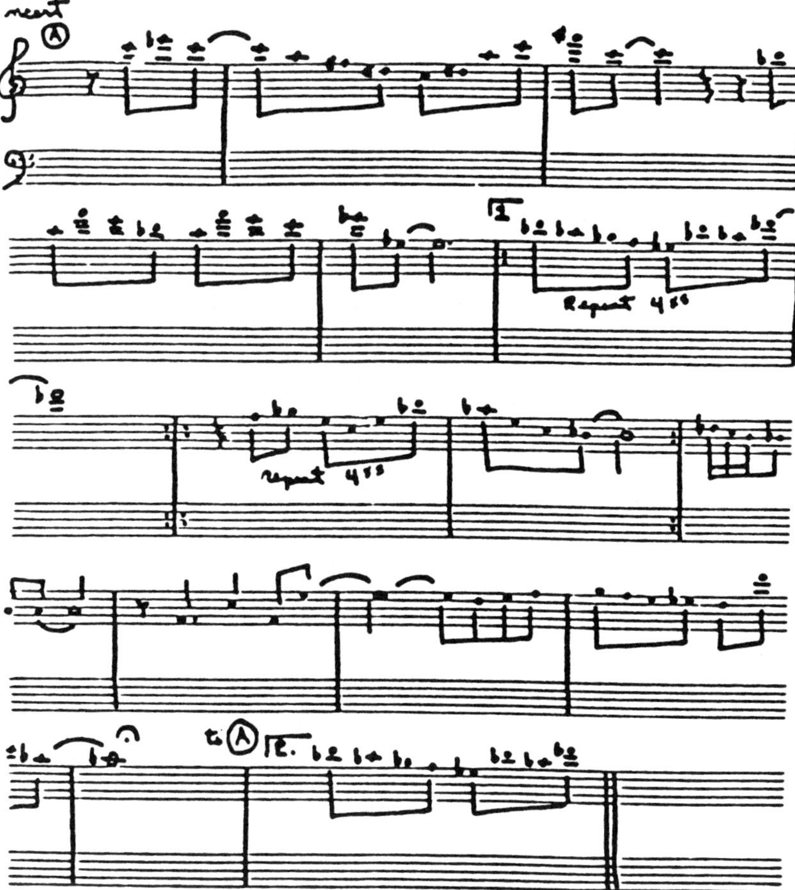

Figure 4.1. Braxton's manuscript of *Composition 6I*. Courtesy Anthony Braxton.

grand scale: as a preface to improvisation, notations serve to structure an extended section or "head movement" that functions more or less as a piece in itself.[99] Characterized by a five-minute melodic section transposed against quiet, shimmering gong and cymbal sustains, the movement abandons all recognizable qualities of jazz, excepting perhaps the instrumentation and initial unison playing. More than a form of exotic coloration, the percussion accompaniment provides a shimmering rhythmic underpinning, dense and highly active in its chang-

99. The break in surface noise on the recording betrays editing, suggesting that the head and the subsequent improvisation were recorded separately.

ing vibrational subtlety. After nearly three minutes, Holland joins Altschul, playing a plaintive arco descent that increases the degree of rhythmic oscillation. This effects a haunting contrast against the slow, nearly static statements of Braxton and Wheeler (playing clarinet and harmon-muted trumpet). Here the melody is also characterized by an opposition between chromatic lines and perfect intervals (fourths and fifths), demonstrating once again Braxton's penchant for tensions between lyricism and tonal ambiguity. In the improvisation, moreover, the ensemble engages in a lengthy exploration of the timbral possibilities established in the head movement. The absence of a piano or another harmonic instrument liberates the musicians, who replace the momentum of rhythm and swing with a complex, ever-changing array of orchestrational coloration. Holland invents a remarkable variety of textures by employing an assortment of bowing techniques. Altschul makes imaginative use of coloristic devices, interjecting set drumming with an assortment of hand-held and makeshift instruments: maracas, brake drums, thundersheet, mbira, bull roarer. Braxton explores the gamut of his expressive voices, changing from style to style and instrument to instrument—first alto saxophone, then contrabass clarinet, soprano saxophone, and flute—in a mix and match that virtually charts out the coloristic range of woodwind instruments. As a total frame of sound, the collective sequence evokes spatiality through abstract sound color as it articulates materiality through the use of "natural," acoustic instruments. As such, it calls to mind radical painterly abstraction—for example, the globs of (material) paint in Jackson Pollack's (spatial) "action paintings"—while maintaining a sensitivity to the individual/group dichotomy grounded in traditional jazz.

Other works on the album display similarly heightened levels of compositional invention in contexts more closely aligned with modernist concert music. In *Composition 6L* (4/1), a duet for soprano saxophone and piano, Braxton and guest pianist Chick Corea adapt atonality and the lyricism of gospel in a plaintive elaboration recalling works such as Webern's *Five Songs* (Opus 3) and Lennie Tristano's *Digression* (1949). In another duet, *Composition 6K* (1/1), the musicians work with percussive swatches of line to build a vivid and at times seemingly anarchic improvisational assault based on intensity and speed. In two solo efforts, an unaccompanied contrabass clarinet solo and an overdubbed saxophone "quartet," Braxton again ranges freely. In the first, he opposes the lyricism of jazz with a coy allusion to the opening bassoon solo of Stravinsky's *Rite of Spring;* in the second, he settles into a section of oscillating melodic/rhythmic stasis that recalls his *Kelvin* repetition series (named after the British chemist

Lord Kelvin) and the early "minimalist" studies of Terry Riley and Philip Glass. In *Composition 4* for five tubas (3/2), moreover, Braxton moves to stylistic and registral extremes in order to explore rhythmic properties and tone color in the context of a multisectional composition. Written in graph notation, the composition, as in some early studies of Morton Feldman, specifies rhythm and tonal contour, while leaving exact pitch choice to the performer. By subordinating pitch to the parameters of rhythm and timbre, both of which are commonly identified with African-American expression, Braxton again acknowledges the enduring influence of the black tradition, masked in the stylistic sound world of modernism.

Taken as a whole, the *Complete Braxton* sessions provide a valuable look into Braxton's early style, a style that became the formative basis for his subsequent quartet performances. The album exposes the depth of his creative talents and particularly the imaginative ways in which he fused seemingly unrelated elements and processes. As a soloist, he had by then established a mature voice, melding elements of lyricism and abstraction into one of the most dramatic styles of the 1970s. As a composer, he had broadened his expressive potential by successfully integrating unconventional materials with improvisation, to the point where the quartet became a kind of laboratory for formal experiment and multi-instrumental invention. The imaginative way in which Braxton had confounded conventional expectations betrayed his dedication to radical artistry as it voiced a parallel commitment to a creative "functionalism" servicing social and political change.

Corea, on the other hand, had come to question the practical value of the modernist approaches, and it is probable that his involvement in Scientology, which encouraged acceptance and tolerance over radical activism, was a determining factor in this change. Whereas Braxton, who ultimately rejected Scientological orthodoxy, believed that musical challenges to conventional perceptions would naturally lead society to a higher level of knowledge, Corea felt that only through a familiar language could musicians hope truly to communicate.[100] It was this shift in perception that led Corea increasingly to feature jazz standards in Circle's performances and to record two solo albums of lyrical music.[101] And it was this difference in opinion—a contemporary recasting of the historical vanguard/Marxist opposition—that fi-

100. Lee Underwood, "Chick Corea: Soldering the Elements, Determining the Future," *Down Beat* (October 21, 1976), 14.

101. *Piano Improvisations,* volumes 1 and 2. At some points, particularly in *Picture 3* and *Picture 6* (both volume 1), Corea continues to experiment in an atonal, modernist idiom.

nally motivated him to disband Circle in order to chart a new musical direction in jazz-rock.

Yet despite these personal differences with Corea, Braxton's ten-month association with Circle proved pivotal to his professional and creative development.[102] Through it he gained considerable public and critical attention, and soon he would be mentioned together with the leading saxophonists in free jazz. Public recognition, in turn, enabled him successfully to negotiate the release of a 1968 session as *For Alto* on Delmark Records and to attract the attention of *Down Beat*'s reviewers and "Blindfold Test." Particularly noteworthy was the interview he granted while still touring with Circle, conducted by Robert Levin for *Jazz and Pop*. In the article, Levin provided Braxton with his first chance to present his views as he introduced the persona of the cerebral eccentric.[103] Documenting the wide-ranging interests of this "classically trained," "extraordinarily bright and articulate young man," Levin underscored Braxton's vanguardist opinions while implying that he may well be jazz-music's first certified intellectual. In vivid discussions about the spiritual and political concerns of the AACM, the systematic procedures of modernism, and his essentially poetic "mathematical systems" of composition, Braxton advanced publicly the arcane creative world that would later attract so much curiosity and attention. Underscoring the boundlessness of his musical interests, he made frequent reference to a spectrum of influences and innovators—Miles Davis, Arnold Schoenberg, Lee Konitz, Anton Webern, Duke Ellington, John Cage—calling the latter pair "the [two] most important composer[s] in the country today."[104] At one point, Braxton voiced his hope for the development of a truly vanguardist music in a rhetorical style that acknowledged a debt to Rzewski and his AACM past as it paid tribute to the iconoclasm and wit of Satie, Cocteau, and Cage: "I want to make music that is socially usable, and from which there can be direct results. Like I dig watching shoemakers, watchmakers, ceramicists, work. I wish my art could be as useful as theirs is—I wish somebody could put tea or coffee in my music, or put their feet in it."[105] Later, he elaborated on this appeal by challenging the

102. Braxton recalls that the group broke up suddenly as tensions mounted between Corea and himself. The catalyst, he claims, was Corea, who abruptly dissolved the group, leaving Braxton and the others stranded in Los Angeles.

103. Levin, "Third World," *Jazz and Pop* (October 1970), 12–14. The interview was reprinted in the German magazine *Jazz Podium* in April 1971.

104. Levin, "Third World," 13.

105. Ibid., 14. This comment recalls, in particular, Cocteau's vanguardist proclamation in reference to Erik Satie: "Not music one swims in, nor music one dances on;

very notion of art and the artist, while giving voice to the teacherly role of the vanguard composer:

I'm afraid of being a "musician" in the sense that society defines it—that is, of separating art from life or of being in the music *business*. . . . I think the whole idea of art is something that Western culture has introduced so that it can be used on evil trips. Like Western music was originally just a toy for rich people, something for the king to talk shit about. I feel that potentially *we all are* the music, our lives are art in the purest sense. . . . Of course, I can see how right now we need "artists" as such, to help show people that they are artists too, to show them what's meaningful. Consciousness is the most valuable thing that can be communicated right now—making people aware of themselves.[106]

In practice, however, Braxton seemed to be pursuing two paths at once. Among free-jazz artists and experimental composers, and in the private world of his composition notebooks, he could plot out musical mechanisms that might initiate social and perceptual change. Yet as a professional, he was clearly drawn to visible and institutionally regulated forums of expression. Braxton probably considered such opportunities to perform with Shepp and Corea as something beyond the domain of "business"; they offered little money and provided mainly a chance to express and communicate, not unusual desires for any social being. But these associations would eventually take him into the world of the mainstream and its networks, which, by nature, ultimately draw aesthetic expressions toward a safer middle ground. Braxton has acknowledged this tension, yet, significantly, he fails to see its relevance, despite the obvious effects it has had on his career.[107] Such a puzzling reaction might be a reflection of an artistic consciousness that had learned long ago to devalue white-oriented institutional opinion even as artists must rely on the same opinions for public representation. Over the course of the decade, the subtleties of that consciousness, that identity, would be articulated further as Braxton pursued, first as an independent experimentalist, then as a contracted artist with Arista Records, the entire range of his creativity.

---

music ON WHICH ONE WALKS." "Cock and the Harlequin," *Call to Order,* translated by Rollo Myers (New York: Haskell House, 1974), 18.

106. Levin, "Third World," 14.

107. In an interview with Bill Smith (*Coda* [April 1974], 5), he remarked: "But by the very nature of the system that we live in, once something creative is established, they find a way to turn it into a spectacle." In our own discussions, however, he claimed not to see the relevance of my study of his reputation. "Braxton's Reputation," *Musical Quarterly* no. 4 (1986): 503–22.

5 Defining a Black Vanguard Aesthetic

Prelude: French Critical Responses

The elusiveness that had come to characterize Anthony Braxton's experimentalism would inspire a flowering of invention when he returned to the liberating environment of Europe. Recognizing once again the constraints under which musicians associated with jazz were forced to operate at the height of rock music's appeal, Braxton opted for life in Paris, which, despite its cultural incongruity for a South Side urbanite, provided far greater options then he could have hoped for in the United States. Indeed, for an artist whose creative personality had been built upon mutability, discontinuity, and the ironic, a return to Europe seemed entirely fitting: Paris, the modern center of Western high culture, would become, paradoxically, the ground base for an emerging vanguardism that mediated oppositions between aesthetic globalism and Afrocentricity.

Prior to his return, Braxton had already been something of a curiosity in Parisian jazz circles. As previously observed, his early recordings, most notably *Three Compositions of New Jazz* (1968), had generated a minor debate about his artistic legitimacy and ultimately, one suspects, about the true nature of jazz after the free movement (cf. chapter 4). That debate would resume after Braxton's startling performance with Circle in February 1971 showed the critical mass, and in particular, writer Bernard Loupias, that this cerebral black experimentalist, seemingly enraptured with European modernism, was also a formidable free-jazz soloist.[1] In an essay published in the April 1971 issue of *Jazz Hot,* Braxton formally voiced his commitment to pursuing "the interpenetration of these two music[al realms]," while demonstrating once again a range of knowledge encompassing both jazz and European modernism. Leading the essay with references to mathematics, philosophy, and an absurdist picture title that, he claimed, symbolized the meaninglessness of contemporary life, Braxton seemed to be pandering to a historical European fascination with the exotic and primitive—in which Africa and African America were historically

1. Loupias, "Un Cercle Parfait," *Jazz Hot* (April 1971), 23.

synonymous—just as he revealed his own casual assumptions about the French as existential.[2]

Thickening the plot and enhancing visibility were the published reviews of Braxton's album *This Time* (1970) as well as his performances on Jacques Coursil's *Black Suite* (1969) and Marion Brown's controversial album *Afternoon of a Georgia Faun* (1970).[3] Whereas Philippe Carles, reviewing *This Time,* distinguished Braxton from "energy" artists such as Cecil Taylor, Jean Echenoz devoted much of his review of the latter recording to Braxton's dramatic and, at moments, "terrifying" bass clarinet playing. The performance, according to Echenoz, suggested that he was on a course of becoming "an essential, immense musician." Also noteworthy were reports from the United States about a recent release of Braxton's unaccompanied saxophone performances that, while garnering praise from critics, was publicly denounced in a *Down Beat* "Blindfold Test" by saxophonist Phil Woods.[4] French writers and musicians would have their own version of unaccompanied solos with which to contend after the release of *Recital Paris '71,* recorded during a respite from Circle's tour in January. A favorable review of the album appeared in *Jazz Hot* just as Braxton was settling in again in late fall 1971.[5]

Benefiting from this early critical attention and the sense of anticipation it engendered, Braxton quickly received several opportunities

2. Braxton (as told to Francis Postif), "KFQ, 4—6F," *Jazz Hot* (April 1971), 14–17. The published title, *KFQ4—6F,* does not appear in Braxton's catalog of works. It may have served as an example of his titling method rather than as an identification of a particular composition.

3. Gérard Noel, "Afternoon of a Georgia Faun," *Jazz Hot* (April 1971), 34; Alain Gerber, "Afternoon of a Georgia Faun" *Jazz Magazine* (October 1971), 43; Jean Echenoz, "Black Suite," *Jazz Hot* (July/August 1971), 29.

4. Joe H. Klee, "For Alto," *Down Beat* (June 24, 1971), 18. Responding to Braxton's performance, "To Artist Murray de Pillars" (*Composition 8A, Stage* 2), Woods remarked: "That was terrible, I can't imagine the ego of a person thinking they can sustain a whole performance by themselves, when they can't really play the saxophone well. . . . It should be called 'the trill is gone.' If you're going to try and play—and it's a classically-oriented way of playing, that kind of sound he's trying to get—you should have the training to carry it off. It's not jazzy, it's not classical . . . it's dull . . . it's not well done, he doesn't breathe properly. . . . There's a lot of primitives that play and get a lot of exciting music; but this is such an ego trip, that you can think you're that much of a bitch that you can do a solo album." Feather, "Blindfold Test," *Down Beat* (October 14, 1971), 33. During an earlier test, Harold Land, commenting about the same track, praised Braxton's technique and control while noting that he "didn't get any emotional reaction to it." *Down Beat* (June 24, 1971), 26.

5. Bernard Loupias, "Recital Paris '71," *Jazz Hot* (December 1971), 33–34.

to perform on the concert stage. In December 1971, he appeared in four concerts at the American Center and Cinéma Le Vézelay, playing solo on one occasion and leading impromptu groups of European and American musicians on the others.[6] He also recorded a series of duets with Joseph Jarman, subsequently released on Delmark as *Together Alone,* which looked back to performance approaches first developed in the Association for the Advancement of Creative Musicians. In 1972, Braxton continued to receive attractive offers, making appearances as both a soloist and leader of duets and quartets at the Palace, the Second Festival of Free Jazz de Colombes, the Musée d'Art Moderne de la Ville de Paris, and the American Center. In March, for the Festival de Chatellerault, he assembled a fourteen-member ensemble to celebrate Scientological notions of "isness" with "Project Is" (*Composition 25*), a work in twelve parts. This performance was eventually released as *Creative Orchestra Music 1972* on Ring. In November, it was re-created at the American Center for a concert titled "Forms," then again in May 1973 in a truncated version at the Théâtre de la Cité Internationale.[7] Recordings of unaccompanied improvisations and quartet works also appeared, together with reunion sessions with Günter Hampel in April 1972 and with Dave Holland and Barry Altschul in New York in late November. An earlier collaboration with Holland and Altschul had taken place the previous spring, when Braxton returned briefly to the United States to perform at New York's Town Hall and Carnegie Recital Hall and to appear in a workshop sponsored by the Jazz Composers' Orchestra Association.[8] Favorable responses to these events led to distinctions from *Down Beat* and Japan's *Swing Journal.*[9]

Having established a reputation as one of Paris's foremost jazz-oriented improvisers, Braxton seemed no longer to have to hustle for regular work. While by no means financially well off and still needing to perform regularly in Parisian outposts and festivals, he could now

6. Laurent Goddet, "Braxton au Centre Américain," *Jazz Hot* (January 1972), 25; Denis Constant, "Jazz en Direct, Anthony Braxton," *Jazz Magazine* (France) (February 1972), 41. On December 4, he appeared with Bernard Vitet, Beb Guérin, and Noël McGhie; the December 20 group included Joseph Jarman, Alan Shorter, Oliver Johnson, and dancer Dawn Jones.

7. Alex Dutilh, "Pas D'entrechats pour Braxton," *Jazz Hot* (June 1973), 22.

8. Braxton may have also been commissioned at this point to compose music for the film *Paris Streets* for the Massachusetts Institute of Technology.

9. *Down Beat* critics voted Braxton second in the category "Talent Deserving Wider Recognition." He assumed the first position in 1973 and again in 1974. *Swing Journal* (Japan) awarded its 1973 Gold Disque to *Town Hall 1972,* according to "Biography: Anthony Braxton," Arista Records' publicity manuscript.

find the time to devote more attention to composition. Supporting these activities was the formal residency at the American Center, where he enjoyed a regular performance forum as well as private study in electronic-music composition with Jorge Arriagada. Working at the Center in 1973 and then at his home in the Cité des Arts in 1974, Braxton wrote for several genres: solo piano, unaccompanied saxophone, quartet, electronic tape, and film; the latter was prepared as an improvisation with Antoine Duhamel for Philippe Condroyer's film *La Coupe á Dix Francs.*[10] From September 1973, moreover, he began to set aside time to begin a series of essays in response to "what I felt to be deliberate mis-information about black creativity and black creative dynamics."[11] These would eventually become the three-volume, 1,700-page literary tome, *The Tri-Axium Writings.*

Appearances abroad enhanced Braxton's cosmopolitan life in Paris while also helping to advance his developing reputation. When not at his new home composing and performing, he seemed to be showing up at some far-off free-jazz festival or experimental outpost. After spending three weeks in Tokyo, where he recorded with the celebrated Japanese musicians Masahiko Sato, Keiki Midorikawa, and Hozumi Tanaka, Braxton returned to Paris to take part in a series of engagements.[12] In June, he performed in Toronto and then traveled to Denmark to teach at the Vallekilde Jazz Clinic. After more work and concerts in Paris, he headed to Umbria, Italy, to appear in the city's annual festival, and then to Copenhagen to perform and record sessions that were released as *In the Tradition,* volumes 1 and 2.[13] Appearances with guitarist Derek Bailey at London's Wigmore Hall[14] and as both soloist and leader of a new assemblage of his 1971 quartet at the Moers Festival in Moers, West Germany, further occupied a feverishly busy schedule that Braxton describes in this colorful recollection:

I had been living in Paris when [clarinetist and producer] Kunle Mwanga [George Conley] and I decided to go to Japan. We saved our money and went

10. According to David Meeker, *Jazz at the Movies,* rev. (New York: Da Capo, 1981), the film was produced in 1975. However, Arista's publicity manuscript, "Biography: Anthony Braxton," notes that Braxton participated in the film in 1973.

11. *Tri-Axium Writings,* vol. 1 (published privately, 1985), ii.

12. This may have taken place at the invitation of *Swing Journal* (Japan) or Nippon Columbia, which recorded *Four Compositions 1973.*

13. For volume 2, Braxton substituted for the intended saxophonist, Dexter Gordon. Charles Mitchell, "Record Reviews, Anthony Braxton," *Down Beat* (October 7, 1976), 20.

14. Bailey had joined Braxton and his Paris quartet for a performance the previous year. Martin Davidson, notes to *Braxton and Bailey: Live at Wigmore.* This double album is a reissue of the original Emanem releases.

over there on one-way tickets—I was a very aggressive young man! After spending a while in Tokyo, we sold the tapes of my Town Hall concert and that's how we got back to Paris. When we got back, we paid our bills, and then went off to America. Then we lost all of our money there and we had to raise cash to get back to Europe. I was living like a rat. We had no money but we were traveling all over the world. I traveled with two garbage cans, orchestra bells, a contrabass clarinet, all these different horns, and my "little instruments." And we were changing continents every other week. It was a crazy period. It was far out.[15]

French observers seemed greatly fascinated with Braxton's efforts to widen the constraints under which the improvising musician operated. By and large, they accepted as legitimate the terms that Braxton had defined for his art at a time when many American writers still maintained rather chauvinistic positions about the immutability of the mainstream style. In reviews of concerts and record releases, the French circle typically set Braxton apart from his colleagues in the 1960s free movement, suggesting that his radicalism indicated an entirely new direction. "Placing to the side those established norms that have already been assigned to 'free jazz,'" wrote Paul Gros-Claude, "Anthony Braxton has deliberately distinguished himself from the musicians of his generation, asserting himself as the rare, dignified artist who will succeed innovators of the past decade."[16] In order to underscore his uniqueness, moreover, writers highlighted the wide stylistic variety that his experimentalism was taking. Writing in *Jazz Hot,* Alex Dutilh suggested that "if one seeks to analyze this music one must break through a barrier. The usual concepts are inoperable here. Moreover, the danger (and failure) of a traditional analysis would be to reduce Braxton to a composite of the 'already known.'"[17] Braxton himself helped to advance this opinion, first by underscoring in interviews the disparity of genres in which he operated, and then by demonstrating their differences in concert. Most notable of these was the "Forms" concert, during which he presented a cross section of his eclectic ouevre. He also helped to orient Bernard Loupias's formal analysis of *Recital Paris '71,* which centered on Braxton's expressed aim

15. Interview with Anthony Braxton (July 12, 1984). The Town Hall tapes were released on Trio Records (1971).

16. Gros-Claude, "Les Dingues du Palace." *Jazz Magazine* (France) (March 1972), 22. Gros-Claude's comment was reprinted a month later in Jean Echenoz and Bernard Loupias, "Anthony Braxton," *Jazz Hot* (April 1972), 4. Translation by author.

17. Dutilh, "Anthony Braxton à l'American Center," *Jazz Hot* (January 1973), 24. The "already known" would include "Cage/Dolphy/Ayler/Konitz/Parker etc." Translation by author.

to pursue simultaneously several divergent paths.[18] In his review of *The Complete Braxton,* Michel Lequime showed a similar fascination with the way in which Braxton's eclecticism enhanced the complexity of his compositional efforts: "If [*The Complete Braxton*] doesn't possess the same level of strange, almost hypnotic fascination as *Series F,* it does possess a higher degree of the same range of qualities: an extremely precise formulation of musical thought, wide variety of improvisation, and especially, admirable richness of composition."[19]

Particularly fascinating to the analytically oriented French writers was Braxton's commitment to formal structure. Essays commonly demonstrated a sensitivity to Braxton's efforts to create complex multisectional works, which would be discussed in some instances in fairly rigorous and analytic terms. The most comprehensive of these was Maurice Gourgues's article about the controversial recordings for unaccompanied saxophone in which works were classified according to standard typologies of rhythm/tempo, melodic character, and form.[20] Braxton's own efforts to distance himself from "free jazz," a label that he felt obscured his concerns about structure and form, seemed to encourage critics to seek out new analytical methods. It is possible that Braxton's embrace of formalism and modernism may have been welcomed by French critics because such linkages put European innovation in a better light at a time when world-class Continental jazz was just beginning to develop. If they, in their enthusiasm, seemed at times to take too literally Braxton's claims of having shaped an art according to the disciplines of mathematics, science, and philosophy, these critics also demonstrated a legitimate appreciation of his commitment to creative experiment. Indeed, French critics, it could be argued, showed greater sensitivity than their American counterparts to the traditional notion of jazz as a mutable, changing process of invention rather than as a solidification of a classic repertory.

Three interviews with Braxton fleshed out the picture of the composer-instrumentalist in the early 1970s. As opportunities for publicity rather than analyses of an aesthetic, the articles provided, in the main, documentation of Braxton's background, interests, and opinions about other artists. Typically, the essays provided standard information about Braxton's Chicago childhood, his early musical

18. Loupias, "Anthony Braxton, 'Recital Paris '71,'" *Jazz Hot* (December 1971), 33.

19. Lequime, "Anthony Braxton: The Complete Braxton," *Jazz Hot* (March 1973), 25. Translation by author.

20. Gourgues, "Anthony Braxton, Antibes 23–28 Juillet," *Jazz Magazine* (France) (July/August 1974), 50–53.

tastes, and his membership in the AACM. Occasionally, Braxton offered some fresh insight, such as his reference to early work with the Dells and Sam and Dave, his commitment to Scientology, and his belief that his music was "filled with the spirit of the blues."[21] Especially noteworthy were his remarks about the symbolic nature of free jazz. While first suggesting that it represented many aspects of the world order, he went on to argue that above all free jazz reflected life in the black ghetto.[22] Both global and specific to the African-American experience, Braxton's ideas matched the dichotomies of his aesthetic overall. However, when the discussion turned to jazz critics, rock stars, and record companies, he could see in only one dimension. The persons and institutions of power, Braxton charged, had appropriated expressions such as black gospel music for personal financial gain.[23] Interestingly, Braxton's criticism of Futura for printing an insulting caricature of him in the liner notes to *Recital Paris 1971* appeared in the same journal that, in the following month, featured this exotic African-American intellectual with his face nearly flush to a chessboard.[24] A similar photo decorated the cover of the April 1972 issue of *Jazz Hot,* this time with Braxton, wearing wire-rimmed glasses, contemplating a chessboard while smoking his pipe.

Realizing the Experimental Totality

Braxton's European critical success proved to have a lasting impact on the development of his career. Professionally, it gave an obvious boost to his emerging reputation, increasing performance opportunities and eventually motivating his return to the United States in 1974 as an artist contracted with Arista Records. Even more important, however, were the benefits this visibility would have for his growth as a composer and musician. Having earned the French critics' stamp of approval, he could now explore as a working artist the various creative avenues he had begun to define. On occasion, he could also take advantage of his new prominence to arrange commissions for special

21. Respectively, Philippe Carles, "Braxton: Les Regles du jeu," *Jazz Magazine* (France) (December 1972), 18–21; Echenoz and Loupias, "Anthony Braxton," 4–6; Braxton and Postif, "KFQ, 4—6F," 14–17. See also Philippe Carles: "Braxton: Le Jazz est une Musique Dangereuse," *Jazz Magazine* (France) (November 1972), 13–17.

22. Braxton and Postif, "KFQ, 4—6F," 17.

23. See, for example, Braxton's comments about the public portrayals of Janis Joplin and the appeal of *Jesus Christ Superstar* in Carles, "Braxton: Les Regles," 19–20.

24. Braxton's criticisms appeared in Carles, "Braxton: Le Jazz," 14. The photo was published in Carles, "Braxton: Les Regles," 21.

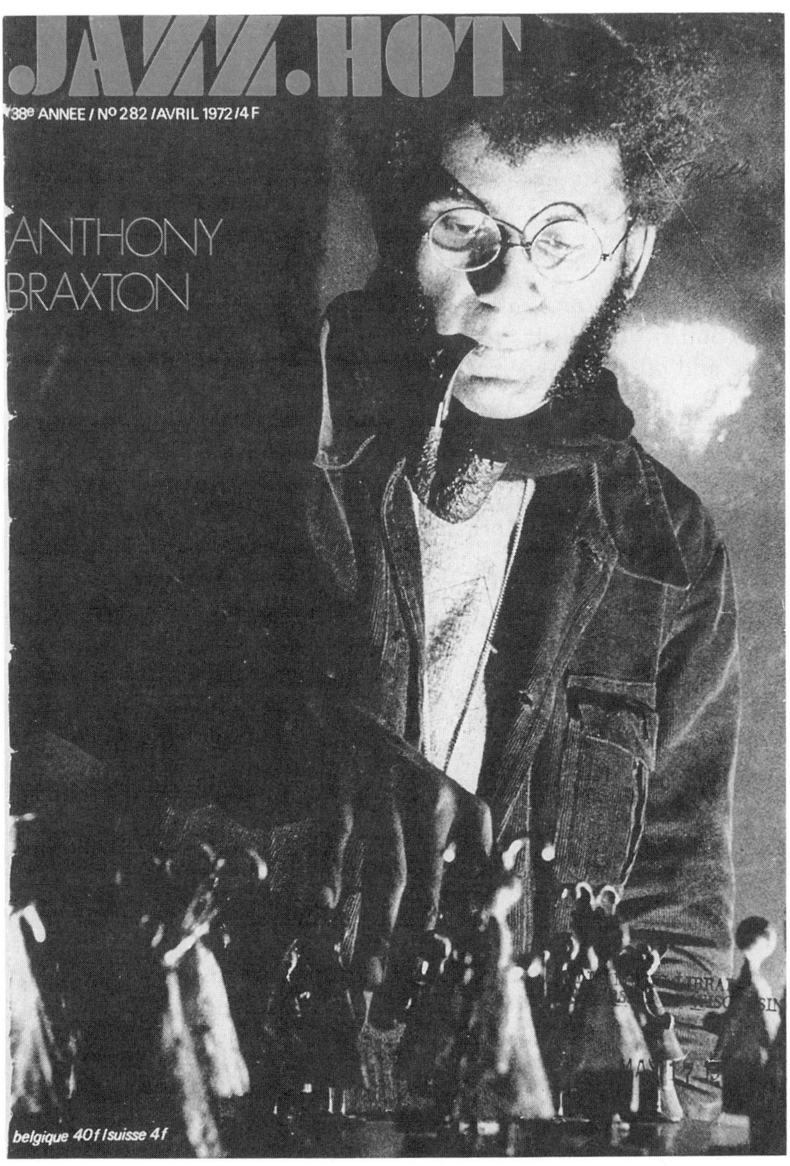

Cover page of the French magazine *Jazz Hot,* April 1972.

recording and performing ensembles in order to test compositional and performance ideas. The recordings that document these explorations range across a decade of activity when Braxton was methodically mapping out the breadth of his artistic vision. Extending over a broad terrain of style and experience—from his Paris years to his departure from Arista Records—these performances reveal how Braxton sought continually to refashion his art according to an evolving conception of vanguard practice. They flesh out the totality of his black experimentalism.

The matter of *musical identity* becomes enormously important in this context, for it helps to explain the motivations for Braxton's diverse and often idiosyncratic explorations. The documented releases provide a close look at a period of enormous growth and productivity, when Braxton, moving dexterously in and out of disparate settings, spun a web of highly original, experimental approaches. These approaches were, he explained, nothing less than "what I am as a musician, a person."[25] More than an eclectic assortment of interesting elements and ideas, they suggested a logical consistency built on a series of oppositional modalities: composition vs. improvisation, control vs. freedom, order vs. indeterminacy, lyricism vs. abstraction, tonality vs. atonality, jazz vs. concert music, black vs. white. From work to work, rarely would the listener encounter one without the other. And given Braxton's proclivity for abstracting musical practice, these modalities ultimately led to the development of a vast network of systematic relations. Yet whereas the notion of opposition would typically suggest a dialectical network, Braxton's dualisms seemed ultimately to derail logic as such. Contradicting the implications of hierarchy and center attributed to system, Braxton would, with each effort to create definition, make another to subvert it. In the practical situation of a performance, a stylistic commitment at one moment would give way to another; organizational logic, compositional plans, and specifics of style were being continually constructed and deconstructed, as a matter of course. Ultimately, Braxton would even subvert the logic of the system itself. By the late 1970s, he had granted his "language music"—the saxophone motives (cf. chapter 3)—a "functional" equivalent: a theosophical enterprise built upon the ambiguous relationship of globalism and Afrocentricity.

This is not to suggest that Braxton's system-making was ultimately a clever ploy to mask a trickster's machinations. His commitment to structure, musical logic, and system were very real, and carried with

25. Conversation with Anthony Braxton (July 1991).

them legitimate, nearly vital, meaning. Indeed, structure and system seemed essential to Braxton's artistic identity. Yet as a "restructuralist," he also took pains to elude all constraining definitions, particularly those that would seem to identify a central impulse. For Braxton, empiricism, structure, and logic expressed a vanguardist program to recast all associations and specifications, whether grounded in concert music or in jazz. That process would enable a kind of ironic freedom as he revised conventional programs to extend a repertory, once again, "firmly planted in mid-air." "Restructuralism," then, became Braxton's way of recasting existing expressions according to the centrality of his black creative voice. In the end, that centrality, that "deformation of mastery," in Houston A. Baker, Jr.'s, phrase, would be a dual centrality, and ultimately a decentering, that reflected the quality of doubleness that stretches across his creative work.[26]

I

Having established a case for an aesthetics of ambiguity, it might seem appropriately ironic if not downright confusing to claim that Braxton possessed an artistic center, after all. Yet in a practical sense, the unaccompanied saxophone music was precisely that: the creative realm where he would return to reconsider artistic direction, to plot out new ideas, to perform without social constraint—by himself. Previous discussions have shown that the earliest unaccompanied meditations sacrificed compositional execution for an exceedingly personal commitment to performance freedom. By the early 1970s, however, Braxton seemed to have harnessed their potential to give a more effective, communicative voice to one of the most radical expressions in contemporary American musical art. By situating himself between the realms of the concert soloist and the jazz improviser, Braxton had carved out a defining space for asserting his art of indirection. Many of the finest recorded moments would be documented on a series of albums produced in the United States and in Europe. The best of these show how successfully he had realized a dramatically original artistic conception, while close scrutiny of a cross section of performances demonstrates how the notion of "work"—and ultimately his conception of his artistic self—remained essentially fluid.[27]

26. Baker, *Modernism and the Harlem Renaissance* (Chicago: University of Chicago Press, 1987), 15.

27. Braxton also recorded solo piano music for the album *Recital Paris '71*. Dedicated to David Tudor, the performance recalls stylistically modernist piano works from

Stylistically, Braxton's unaccompanied solos express a diversity of composerly intention. Works such as *Composition 26A, Composition 26J* (1972, *Saxophone Improvisations Series F* 1/2 and 1/3), and *Composition 26H* (1974, *Solo: Live at Moers* 1/2) seem best described as concert-jazz ballads, for they integrate a lyrical jazz approach with features commonly associated with concert practice.[28] The works suggest, for example, the slow movement of a classical sonata. More distinctive, and often more successful, were the marginally tonal inventions that develop a principal motivic gesture: the scalar explorations of *Composition 77B* (*Moers* 1/3) or the chromatic figurations of *Composition 26E* (*Moers* 2/1). In some cases, Braxton took such an approach to an anarchic extreme. *Composition 26G* (*Moers* 2/3) relies on a single element—a controlled, pinched squeal created by biting down on the reed—as a way of usurping form in the name of a ninety-second exploration of subtle rhythmic and timbral variation. As it liberates improvisation from the constraints of structure, the performance also transcends overt patterns of coherence typically associated with oral composition.

But it is a third approach, in which Braxton engages in an elaborate exploration of atonality and coloristic collage effects, that deserves close scrutiny here. In these instances, the quality of coherence develops not so much from traditional concerns about order and balance, but rather from an ability to involve the listener with an ever-changing array of rhythmic and motivic devices. In their most elaborate, extended settings, preconceived structural outlines do appear, defining Braxton's formal conception of "the work." It is the complex interplay of motivic invention and compositional development that identifies the most lasting examples of Braxton's unaccompanied solo style.

A good introduction to Braxton's atonal solo work is his version of Duke Ellington's *Come Sunday* (*Recital Paris '71* 1/1). Keeping with the character of the standard (with Ellington's "impression of Sunday peace and religious quiet"), Braxton begins with a soulful, languid interpretation of the melody, which calls to mind the most melancholy passages of gospel as it makes oblique reference to the style of Johnny Hodges.[29] Then, after a transitional section that introduces many of

---

the postwar era. And despite Braxton's technical limitations, the performance proves remarkably effective.

28. Precise, note-to-note articulation, timbral consistency and clarity, strict adherence to major/minor scalar patterns, etc.

29. Ralph Ellison, *Shadow and Act* (New York: Random House, 1964), 218. Braxton dedicated the piece to Hodges.

Braxton's most familiar turns of phrase, the performance moves somewhat abruptly into a lengthy exposition of fluctuating timbral coloration. Whereas similar abruptness had previously suggested impressive technique without a developed sense of compositional execution, here Braxton demonstrates an impressive command of his materials as well as a sound compositional ability to weave formally coherent juxtapositions. At first, he integrates overblown, low-register "Texas Tenor" honks with quiet, high-register gestures that vaguely allude to the original melody. In a second section, he explores these elements while providing glimpses of melody at the middle range of the instrument. Subsequently, he conducts a lengthy investigation of key tremolos, multiphonics, extremely rapid phrases, single-pitch repetitions, and a battery of other techniques that create a patchwork of ever-shifting, rhythmically active sounds and ideas.[30] Never does he labor too long down a single improvisational path; while flashes of free virtuosity frequently appear, they are always met with a run of contrasting ideas that preserve a sense of fluidity, complexity, change. Indeed, what vitalizes the improvisation is Braxton's accomplished sense of musical opposition: by creating striking contrasts in range, attack, volume, and timbre he maintains a remarkably consistent sense of dynamic tension. Clearly by this point Braxton had not only internalized a rich sonic vocabulary but had also acquired the compositional skill to develop and integrate these ideas during the act of improvisation. He had now in the unaccompanied genre successfully realized his dual conception of the spontaneous music-maker and preperformance planner. Braxton, the skilled soloist, could also maintain an equivalent sensitivity to matters of coherence during the act of unaccompanied improvising.

A comparison of three performances of the same composition offers insight into how formal matters influenced Braxton's conception of the unaccompanied musical "work." *Composition 26B* was composed for a performance at the Palace of Fine Arts in San Francisco in 1971.[31] Braxton recorded the work twice while living in Paris: on *Saxophone Improvisations Series F* (1972) and *Live at Moers* (1974), and then again on the Arista release, *Alto Saxophone Improvisations 1979* (all versions were performed on alto saxophone). At first glance, the versions seem to vary significantly. "1972" is an extended, free improvisation (17:45), characterized by a free-ranging exploration of

30. A similar procedure appears in *Composition 8I* (*Series F* 1/1) where Braxton creates a complex oppositional interplay in the spirit of early solos such as that on *Starp*.

31. Liner notes to *Saxophone Improvisations Series F*.

nontonal gestures and motives. "1974," on the other hand, is much shorter (8 : 10) and operates according to more conventional written procedures (phrase symmetry, cadential preparation, etc.). "1979" (ca. 7 minutes), the most staid, controlled, "textual" version, consists of eight clearly articulated sections, each separated by a period of silence.[32] Closer inspection reveals, however, that each performance depends on a related family of materials. "1972" employs a free mix of multiphonics, key slaps, extreme high-register attacks, low-register distortions, and, most significantly, quiet tremolo attacks in the context of a slow melody, what Braxton calls the "staccato language."[33] "1974" operates as five loose sections, each of which develops a particular element: (1) the tremolo technique; (2) tone repetition and rapid phrases; (3) multiphonics with vocal overtones; (4) rapid phrases with descents to D♭ repetitions; and (5) a return to tremolo techniques. Similarly, "1979" highlights a different stylistic element in each of eight sections as it gathers together and reinterprets previously articulated ideas: (1) slow, nearly precious melodies played with the rapid tremolo, "staccato"; (2) sharp, dramatic descents to a loud bottom-register D♭; (3) rapidly articulated repetitions appearing at different pitch levels; (4) multiphonic coloration of phrases; (5) upper register, held-tone "squeals" and repetitions; (6) extended periods of rapid phrases and interaction of repetition, multiphonics, and vocal sounds; (7) repetitions at variable pitch centers; and (8) recapitulation of the melodic style of section 1.

Comparison of the versions shows that there are consistencies in the articulation of these elements that help further to define all three as the same composition. Figure 5.1 outlines the loose formal structure guiding the versions and sequence of ideas. The figure shows that all three versions begin with a slow, highly controlled, tremolo melody in the "staccato language," followed by a contrasting loud, energetic period. The low-register distortion—a timbral/rhythmic device—is introduced in these second sections, and predominates in "1972" and "1974." In the main body of the works, Braxton juxtaposes the primary materials freely and in any order. At climaxes and during periods of intensity, however, fast lines, multiphonics, and pop-tongue ideas often work together to accentuate rhythmic drive.[34] These sections are

32. "1979" is titled *JMK-730, CFN-7.* Braxton does not explain the discrepancy between the titles.

33. *Composition Notes,* Book B (published privately, 1988; distributed by Frog Peak Music, Hanover, N.H.), 197–98.

34. The pop-tongue effect resembles slap tongue. It is created by drawing quickly

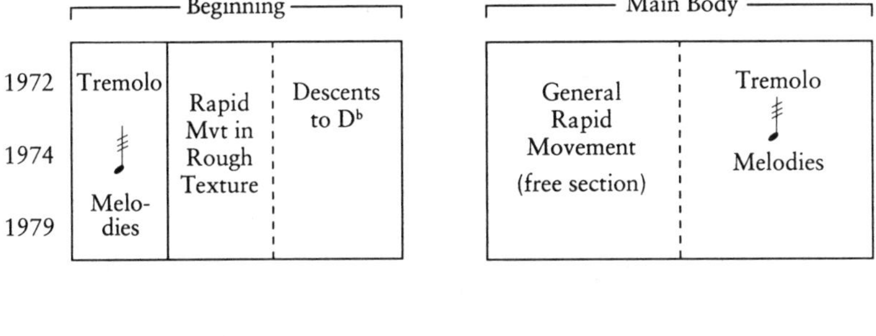

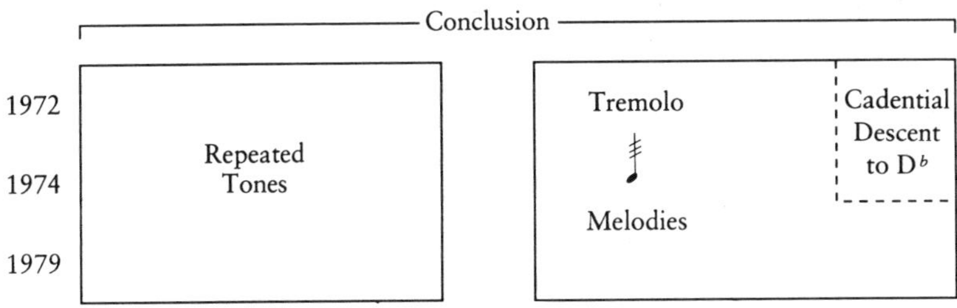

Figure 5.1. Framework guiding three versions of *Composition 26B.*

typically completed with contrasting low-register distortions, which increase rhythmic tension. As a complement to the energetic periods, slow tremolo lines are reintroduced in varying degrees throughout each version. Toward the end of the improvisations, moreover, other similarities appear. In "1974" and "1979," Braxton follows the highly charged statements with an extended section of rapid, high-pitched repetitions based on the tremolo technique. In "1972," the repetitions occur earlier; a lengthy period of slow, wavering lines in the "whinnying" style of Albert Ayler takes their place as a prelude to the final passage. Finally, Braxton's statement on the pitch repetitions themselves is different in each version. In "1972," he positions the pitch groupings against a low E♭ drone to suggest the quality of a British Isles bagpipe. In "1974," he varies the pitch center of each set of repetitions, while on "1979" he increases the number of repetitions per pitch. The versions also end somewhat similarly, with "1972" and

on the mouthpiece. I am indebted to a former saxophone student at Michigan, whose name I have since forgotten, for clarifying this distinction.

"1974" resting on a low-register D♭; the formally essential tremolo figures appear near the ends of all versions.

This comparison of three versions of *Composition 26B* shows that Braxton, despite his fondness for abstraction and performance flexibility, also had some specific notions about what formally constitutes a solo work. In each, he built his improvisation on preset materials and a loose structure, what he would call, by the mid-1970s, compositional "schematics" (see sections 4–5 ahead). Beyond this basic strategy, however, Braxton observed few performance constraints. In fact, what made these pieces work—and gave each its own personal character—was as much his ability to maintain a coherent sense of melodic/rhythmic direction as his commitment to the specifics of form. The precomposed materials helped to set limits on the improvisation and to suggest a direction the solo might take, yet the actual course would be determined only when Braxton began to perform. In jazz parlance, the recorded versions may be likened to a series of "takes" of the same tune, since both tunes and Braxton's languages provide similar modes of improvisational support. Yet whereas conventional jazz improvisations redefine and revise against a known, preexisting item, Braxton's solos revise the revision: they transform an already adapted and abstracted nonrepresentational language as they make reference to practices grounded in the black rhythm 'n' blues tradition. From such a vantage, Braxton's performances voice qualities of indirection characteristic of traditional black oral arts, as they reflect a commitment to system and logic in the act of performance. "Structure" serves as a vehicle for preserving musical identity while enabling a forum for free-ranging, radical experiment.

II

As an accompanied soloist, Braxton incorporated the sound, style, and languages of his solo saxophone music into conventional ensemble formats. In the context of his most accessible "mainstream" compositions, the abstractions create an ambiguity consistent with the oppositional character of his work as a whole. Simple time signatures, standardized rhythm-section arrangements, and tonal modalities provide a background of conventionality that heightens the radicalism of his solo approach. In this way, the mainstream performances appear at moments to be the *most* radical of his recorded work.

Of special interest is the way in which Braxton responds to chord progressions or "changes" in a conventional mainstream setting. In most cases, the changes serve as intermittent points of reference rather

Anthony Braxton playing contra alto clarinet in a concert rehearsal during the mid-1970s. Photo courtesy Bill Smith.

than as concrete, formal blueprints. Such is the case on *You Go to My Head* (1972, *Donna Lee* 2/1), where song form, melodic contour, and a relaxed, ballad tempo gently constrain an essentially open-ended improvisation. Similarly, on *All the Things You Are* (*Town Hall 1972* 1/3), he presents a remarkable interpretation that pays heed to phrase structure and form, if not always to the mechanics of the harmonic progression. Performing Parker's *Donna Lee* (*Donna Lee* 1/1), moreover, Braxton initially stays close to the changes as he confounds their regulation of rhythm and time. Crafting fluctuating sweeps of disjunct line in rapid-fire succession, he "compresses" phrases by purposely and exactingly rushing pulse.[35] In the second chorus, he begins to veer from the changes, moving even farther in the third. By the fourth, he has departed entirely from the tune, excepting hints of the melody and its phrase structure, which signal the return of the theme.

Among the most accessible of Braxton's early conventional performances are his interpretations with Dave Holland of show tunes, film songs, and other standards, appearing on the albums *Trio and Duet* (1974) and *Five Pieces 1975*. On Kern and Hammerstein's *The Song Is You* (*Trio* 2/1), Coots and Gillespie's *You Go to My Head* (*Trio* 2/3), and Kahn and Brown's *You Stepped out of a Dream* (*Five Pieces* 1/1), Braxton observes song form and chord progressions, largely because Holland's harmonic attentiveness and remarkable sense of four-square propulsive time encourage a more straightforward interpretation. On *Embraceable You* (*Trio* 2/2), he acknowledges the legacy of unconventional revisions of Gershwin's popular song—notably, the recordings of Parker and Coleman—in a haunting, exploratory performance. Also noteworthy are Braxton's performances on *In the Tradition,* volumes 1 and 2 (1974), where he maintains a free stylistic stance as he pays tribute, in a series of standard renditions, to a few of his favorite song composers.

Yet in most recorded circumstances, Braxton preferred to highlight original compositions. The most accessible of these, small-group works such as *Composition 23D* (*New York Fall 1974* 1/3; *Moers Quartet* 4/2), share close similarities with the lyrical, rhythmically subdued character of cool. Others, such as *Composition 6N* (*Town Hall* 1/1), are more oriented to bop, presenting a tuneful head before a fiery improvisation. In still other mainstream-centered works, Braxton's written tunes maintain a balance between jazz accessibility and modernist abstraction. *Composition 23M* (*Four Compositions 1973* 2/1), for example, presents a blur of "pointillistic" phrases and an

35. Braxton does much the same in the initial statement of Parker's theme.

abundance of disjunct intervals (notably major sevenths and minor ninths) to create a modernist veneer against the conventions of tonal movement, 4/4 time, and AABA form. The interplay of pointillistic abstraction and common-time conformity imparts a quirky, light-hearted, and very nearly silly character that in turn gives prominence to the idiosyncrasies of Braxton's alto solo. *Composition 69G* (*Seven Compositions* 1/1, *Performance 9/1/1979* 2/1) also exercises pointillistic techniques in a virtuosic display of instrumental dexterity. Here, Braxton and trombonist Ray Anderson find their way through an intricate, fast-paced theme that alternates between chromatic movement and wide, disjunct leaps. The calamity of virtuosic sound accelerates the sense of forward motion in a series of engaging, hard-swinging solos. A final example in this quick reference to small-group accessibility is *Composition 40F* (*Seven Compositions 1978* 1/2). This work alludes to serial composition by highlighting two, two-measure themes based respectively on eleven- and ten-note pitch classes. Yet the sense of formality that the serial method may evoke is quickly dispelled by the stiff, amusingly awkward arco bass accompaniment, which parodies both "serious" composition and Braxton's own "intellectual" persona.[36]

Composition 23B, which led off the debut album on Arista, *New York Fall 1974,* offers a close look at how Braxton employs modernist devices to personalize an otherwise conventional jazz performance. Scored for a standard quartet (alto saxophone, trumpet, bass, and drums) and played at a breakneck tempo, the theme to *23B,* despite its elongated AA′BA form, seems securely fixed in postbop practice.[37] Harmonically, the composition recalls earlier works in Braxton's repertory, such as *Composition 6I* (*Complete Braxton* 3/1; cf. chapter 4), which maintains melodic tension between two potential centers or "tonics." Here, tonality fluctuates between G♯ minor and its relative, B major, creating an unsteadiness that is exacerbated by ambiguous scale structures (whole-tone/chromatic) and sequences played so fast that one can barely recognize a harmonic outline. After the theme, Braxton plays a two-minute solo that reinforces the same tensions

36. Such irreverent play is subsequently only heightened when the band launches into a vigorous free improvisation. The shift from stiff-collared, serialist imitation to a heated exposition in rhythm creates a contrast so striking as to suggest a kind of signifying on the theme overall. A copy of Braxton's notation of the theme and its respective pitch classes appears together with several other original scores and transcriptions as examples in my Ph.D. dissertation (University of Michigan, 1985).

37. Fifty-six bars long, *23B* exceeds standard song form. Moreover, its twenty-two bar B section operates more like a formal counterbalance than a bridge.

between formal/stylistic stability and moment-by-moment tonal/harmonic ambiguity. While operating within the confines of "accessibility" prescribed by Arista, he continually challenges conventions with an amalgam of practices that seem virtually to turn coherence and predictability inside out.

From a broad perspective, the solo stresses structural outlines. After an early expository section of melodic and rhythmic invention, it moves to a midsection of rhythmic repetitions and sequences. These rhythmic patterns build tension toward a climax during which Braxton lets loose a flurry of overblowing, multiphonics, and noise effects. A final period of swinging, scalar playing closes the performance. Braxton also takes care to distinguish form by pausing between phrases and by beginning each with a melodically, timbrally, or rhythmically distinctive idea.

In the construction of individual phrases, however, Braxton favors stylistic opposition and difference. The transcription in figure 5.2 shows that the initial phrases consist of distinct and frequently discrete elements that exist in a fluctuating compression and extension of musical time. In phrase one (I: mm. 1–10), Braxton immediately places the listener off balance by phasing a three-beat, eighth-note figuration against a duple, 4/4 meter (mm. 1–2). Subsequently, the tenuous consistency that the repetitions provide is also undermined as Braxton patches together a series of brief unrelated ideas: a quick, coarse-textured glissando to D♭ (m. 3); an awkward, almost timid staccato figure that, after a pivotal A♭, takes on a new rhythmic appearance, seeming to float above the pulse (mm. 4–5); a rapid spray of notes (m. 6) that gives way to a melodic, yet similarly off-balance, closing phrase (mm. 7–10). In phrase two (II: mm. 12–23), collage effects and rhythmic-temporal instability are even more apparent. Beginning with a rapid scalar figure emphasizing B♭, Braxton complicates the melodic rhythm to create the illusion of a slowing of the pulse (m. 13). Subsequently, he obscures time, direction, and order by consistently eluding down beats, changing tone color (especially D♭, m. 14), and varying pitch length and contour, all the while keeping step with the ensemble's strict, four-square accompaniment. Stable, yet rhythmically diffuse, intervallic movement (m. 15) gives way to a motivically related passage that hovers above the pulse (mm. 16–18); a coarse-textured descent to D♭ zigzags its way back to accentuations of B♭ (mm. 19–20). A final gapped motive signals closure by providing a glimpse of rhythmic definition and tonality (A-minor inversion), while keeping time out of balance with a new infusion of "pointillistic" of leaps and syncopations (mm. 20–23).

Figure 5.2. Author's transcription of *Composition 23B,* phrases I and II.

Similar oppositions appear in many of the subsequent phrases, as Braxton, like a gifted pitcher working his way around a batter, continues to trick the listener by employing a remarkably diverse battery of contrasting materials.[38] The technique evokes, from moment to mo-

38. On the recording, note particularly those prior to the rhythmic repetitions of phrases five and six.

ment, a schizophrenic collapse of temporal continuity, a quality that Frederic Jameson has ascribed to radical postmodernist art.[39] Yet one need not look beyond the black tradition for suggestions of a similar practice. Alteration and revision of line are characteristic of oral expressions ranging across the African-American legacy, from the dramatic, storytelling innovations of Louis Armstrong and Sarah Vaughan to the virtuosic vocalizations of Aretha Franklin and James Brown. More generally, it refers again to the signifying nature of most jazz instrumental practices as it isolates an African-American expressive concern—reaching back to early blues shouters and preachers—with "personal voice."[40] Whereas most black artists adhere deliberately to conventions of tonal music while articulating this characteristic of indirection, Braxton manages much the same in a nontonal language while providing traditional jazz listeners with the markers and formulas they have come to expect in an improvisation. As such, he satisfies onlookers' expectations while eluding those constraints in a language built upon creative resistance.

III

More overtly expressing Braxton's desire to integrate compositional planning with performance were his alternatives to traditional song form. While sharing a kinship with standard tunes and changes, these pieces, written principally for his small, touring ensembles, replace the conventional constraints of jazz improvisation with a series of alternative structures. Among the best known of the alternative forms are the "Kelvin" compositions. In these, Braxton replaces chord changes with complex, rhythmic patterns which, in turn, orient the character and phrasing of the improvisations.[41] During a performance, musicians rely on the rhythm as they would a melodic theme: stated liter-

39. Jameson, "Postmodernism and Consumer Society," in *The Anti-Aesthetic,* ed. Hal Foster (Bay Press, 1983), esp. 118–25.

40. Cornel West suggests that musicians and preachers are the supreme creators in the African-American oral tradition, innovators of black personal voice. Recalling Gramsci, they represent black America's "organic intellectuals," the narrators and myth-makers of the African-American experience. West, "The Dilemma of the Black Intellectual," *Cultural Critique* 1: (Summer 1985): 109–24.

41. Recorded versions of the Kelvin compositions include *73° Kalvin* [*sic*] *Variation 3* (*Circle, Paris Concert* 2/3), *73° Kelvin* (*Wildflowers* 2/1), and *106 Kelvin M-16* (*Solo Moers* 2/2). Kelvin principles also orient portions of the performance of *Composition 55* (*Creative Orchestra Music 1976* 2/2). Braxton has catalogued most of his Kelvin works as *Composition 97.*

ally or in paraphrase, it offers a point of reference in the context of a collective, atonal improvisation.[42] In another instance, Braxton adapts a constraint associated with concert music for a similar rhythmic effect. *Composition 23G* (*Five Pieces* 1/3, *9/1/1979* 4/1) for jazz quartet relies on what Braxton calls a "gravallic basic" to outline the rhythmic dimensions of the performance. This arresting, spasmodic bass-drum accompaniment abstracts the complexities of hard-driving swing as it recalls the isorhythmic orientation of "ground-bass" ostinatos of Baroque passacaglias, chaconnes, and grounds. The transcription in figure 5.3 shows that while the "gravallic" differs from conventional song-form schemes, it follows, like chord changes, a cyclical pattern: after eighteen and a half bars, the rhythm repeats, continuing throughout the saxophone and trumpet solos. Thus, in both the Kelvin and gravallic works Braxton asserts rhythm as a principal constraining factor even as he sometimes turns to concert music to accomplish that task.

In his experiments with march form, Braxton recrafts some of the genre's most familiar stylistic conventions in a lighthearted revision of the music of his childhood and army years. *Composition 69M* (*Seven Compositions* 1/3), for example, employs two common march elements: key shifts to the relative minor and a relative-minor "break," replete with characteristic secondary dominant motion. Undermining the sobriety of these literal formulas, however, is an ironic subtext: "oom pah" ($\hat{1}-\hat{5}$) rhythmic figures that gradually invert and, as a matter of course, subvert the down beat (from $\hat{1}$ [C♯] to $\hat{5}$ [G♯]). Tempo and rhythmic control are also challenged by the articulation of compressed, rapid phrases that confound the regal rhythmic character of martial music. *Composition 69H* (*Seven Compositions* 2/2), moreover, makes obvious references to the march. Its arpeggiated melodies, drum rolls, and stereotyped rhythms (♩♩♩ (triplet 3) ♩♩♩) are all common march conventions, while the implied duple meter, rondo form (AA B A C A D AA), and A-theme repetitions reinforce those associations.[43]

42. Braxton's reference to Kelvin may be as much a voice of protest as an assertion of scientific authority, when recalling Ralph Ellison's *Invisible Man:* "I wanted peace and quiet, tranquility, but was too much aboil inside. Somewhere beneath the load of the emotion-freezing ice which my life had conditioned my brain to produce, a spot of black anger glowed and threw off a hot red light of such intensity that had Lord Kelvin known its existence, he would have had to revise his measurements" (New York: Random House, 1952/1972), 253.

43. Unlike conventional marches, the B, C, and D themes highlight improvisations. *Composition 69H* also appears on *Performance 9/1/1979* (4/2) under a different picture title.

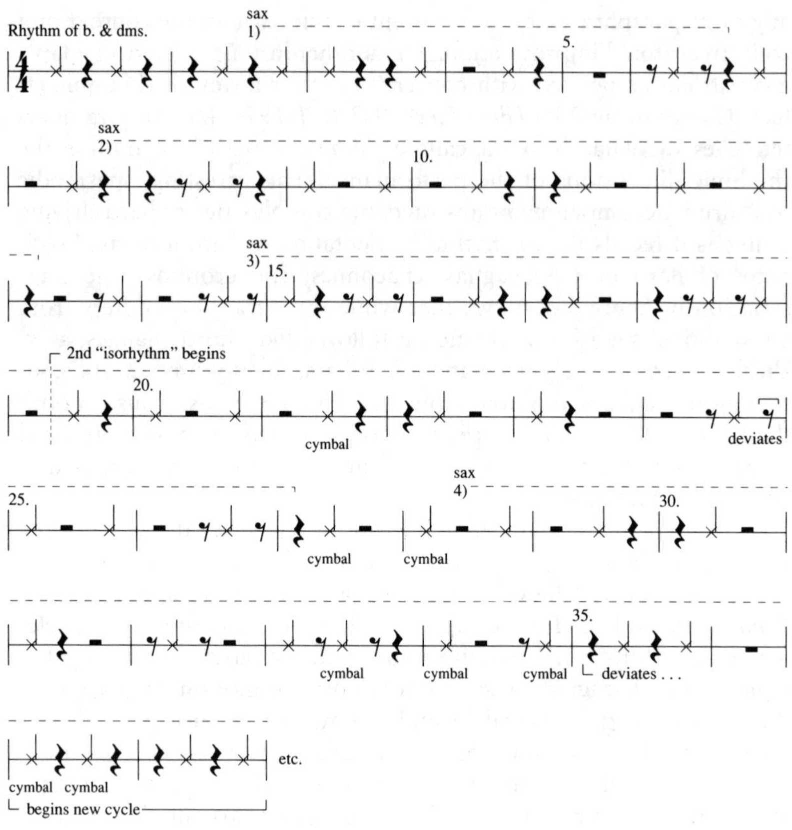

Figure 5.3. Author's transcription of the gravallic basic in *Composition 23G*.

Yet what the listener notices above all is the way in which Braxton's ensemble once again caricatures the march's most common stylistic features. On the surface, for example, instrumentation would seem quite conventional: soprano saxophone, trombone, bass, and drums have clear precedents in jazz as well as in field and concert marches. In the notated A sections, however, Braxton arranges the instrumentalists to exploit the extremes of their ranges as they articulate in octaves a rapid, rhythmically intricate, nine-bar theme. Voicing a comedy of clumsy, circus-music textures as they thread a complex, virtuosic line, the musicians parody orchestrations and phrasing that appear in popular marches. The theme itself is a caricature of sorts. Composed in 3/4—a departure from the 2/4 and 6/8 time signatures of most marches—it is phrased in two-beat groupings to create a metrical ambiguity hovering between duple and triple meter.

Other forms of parody appear in the improvised sections (B, C, D). Particularly captivating is the way in which the ensemble elaborates on the pervasive triplet motive as a call/response. Removed from its conventional formal and stylistic context, this common march figuration (♩♩♩ ♩ ♩♩♩ ♩) assumes the role of a vamp as it sets the basis for solo improvisations. Melodically and rhythmically recast during the course of the performance, the figure makes a series of new appearances, much in the same way that cubistic recontextualizations in visual art redefine the meaning of everyday images and objects. Additional figures, from the trombone's $\hat{5}-\hat{1}$ repetitions to a snare-drum roll preceding the recapitulation of the double A-theme, contribute to this process of recontextualization. Such juxtapositions have the effect of pastiche in what seems otherwise like a straightforward application of the march.

Existing outside the small-group repertory but operating along similar lines to the march alternatives is Braxton's *Composition 57* for big band or "creative orchestra." As it appears on the album *Creative Music Orchestra 1976* (1/3), the piece begins by re-creating a fairly literal version of the Sousa march style out of which jazz, through ragtime, grew: lead brass melodies and reed countermelodies, against an inspired, lower brass/reed duple rhythm. In each of the succeeding sections, however, Braxton once again abstracts and recontextualizes march figures to support a series of free improvisations. During the first solo, for example, a brass vamp accompanies an improvisation by trumpeter Leo Smith. At first, the vamp's tritone relation creates a sense of anticipation as the listener awaits harmonic resolution. Remaining unresolved, the vamp eventually cuts loose from its tonal bearings, becoming a free-floating slice of harmonic grammar in a mangled "oom pah" rhythm—a bewitching counterpoint to Smith's atonal coloristic sweeps. Similarly, in a subsequent section, Braxton performs a clarinet solo against a decontextualized brass rhythmic figure stemming from the original theme. The final theme reestablishes the march character to the point of exaggeration as it runs through an array of formulaic conventions.

Making sense of Braxton's recasting of the march leads one into the realm of speculation. His mixed emotions about the army experience may suggest an antimilitarist sentiment, yet such one-to-one correspondences seem too simplistic for a viable interpretation. Clearly Braxton was fond of march music, as he has noted on numerous oc-

Anthony Braxton at a New York studio rehearsal for the album *Creative Orchestra Music 1976*. Photo courtesy Bill Smith.

casions, and its rhythmically inspired, dance-beat character has made it amenable to African-American approaches over the years.[44] Yet the ironic nature of Braxton's march applications implies that such allusions meant more than a playful tribute. Subtly mocking through black modernist innovation the bravado of literal march rhythm, Braxton seems to be making fun of the music's most self-serious features. By casting displaced march elements in rhythmically and timbrally adventurous improvisational settings, Braxton gives voice to the presence and power of black musicality at the expense of a deformed master text. Significantly, if paradoxically, Braxton's recasting also expresses an ecumenical message consistent with a global, all-embracing populist vision. By refashioning the conventions of the march in the context of an experimental language, he calls attention to the radical potential of the everyday, much in the same way that the early modernist Charles Ives recast the ordinary into the supra-real. Whereas Ives championed the Euro-American voice, Braxton undermines its authority as he appropriates the music's spirited sense of freedom to articulate a multicultural ideal.

44. Olly Wilson, "The Association of Movement and Music as a Manifestation of a Black Conceptual Approach to Music-Making," *Report of the Twelfth Congress, Berkeley 1977* (Basel: Barenreiter/American Musicological Society, 1981), 98–105.

In yet another set of alternatives to song form, Braxton weakens rhythmic grounding to encourage free, nonhierarchic improvisations. By slowing tempo and reducing sense of pulse, he creates a sonic territory that encourages timbral and multi-instrumental experiment. Accordingly, timbre replaces rhythm as the chief defining element, generating a field of fluctuating tone colors that express, like rhythm, similar qualities of mutability and indirection.

In *Composition 23A* (*New York Fall 1974* 2/3), for example, a slow monophonic line punctuated by frequent sustains and silences establishes a flat, almost static surface, which sets the basis for timbral interplay. Free from intricate rhythmic constraints, the theme exploits a vivid range of unconventional timbres that interact as they maintain distinct coloristic space. At the midrange, harmon-muted trumpet and scratch-bowed violin appear as a timbrally related set of subtly distorted coloration; underneath, a haunting, acoustically complex voicing of contrabass clarinet and pizzicato bass resonate sympathetically. Into this web of coloration, sustained cymbal rolls enter and retreat as if to offset texture as they also provide a consistent surface anchoring. Melodically, the theme highlights timbral complexities. Not only does it move deliberately with plenty of sustains; it also accentuates tonal ambiguities that, by drawing the listener, give notice to textural invention. On one level, the melody stresses accessibility. Emphasizing perfect intervals, octave movement, and an initial A♮ centering, the theme is immediately familiar, attractive, nearly folklike. Quickly, however, these certainties slip away as Braxton begins to decenter tonal fixity. Complexity of line in turn heightens attention to intricacies of musical character, intensifying the listener's awareness of coloristic experiment.

In the improvisation, these delicate tone paintings are plotted and recast into an evolving field of fluctuating color. Soon homophony unravels into a polyphonic fray as musicians move independently, displaying some of the individual character of their instrumental voices. Brief stabs of buzz-lipped, harmon-muted color engage an eerie flutter of abrupt violin attacks; a conversant bass line that shifts from pizzicato to coarsely scraped arco accompanies Braxton's absurdist rhetoric at the extreme depths of instrumental sound. Texturally, dynamically, and stylistically, Braxton's voice is the centerpiece, the gruff, curmudgeonly presence to whom the others answer. As he runs the gamut of attacks, gestures, and timbral intricacies, his accompanists provide a sympathetic backdrop, which together appears as an enchanting display of shifting sound.

A final type of small-group alternative elaborates on the notated opening melodies to the point where improvisations are relegated to a perfunctory statement. Transcending the function of an initial theme or head, these extended sections transform the openings into separate sections or what might be called "head movements." The head movements appear across the repertory, reflecting Braxton's efforts to engage in composition while working in the commercial context of his touring groups. The previous discussion of *Composition 6J* (*Complete Braxton 1971* 1/2) in chapter 3 presented an early example of the head movement, performed with members of Circle. Within a couple of years, Braxton had produced two more, *Composition 23E* (*Five Pieces,* 2/1) and *23O* (*Four Compositions 1973* 2/2), the first stylistically akin to the slow-pulse melodies in *23A,* the latter a "pointillistic" work that comes close to imitating the rhythmic intricacy often associated with postwar serial composition. Particularly noteworthy in this context is *Composition 40G* (*Six Compositions 1982* 2/2), which consists of an extended written section that frames a fifty-second improvisation. Here, Braxton employs the head movement to experiment with an additive compositional procedure, inspired by set theory and serial composition. Figure 5.4 shows how he isolates brief motives and rearranges them in new orders, sometimes including smaller motives within the larger pitch groups. The bracketed sets (coded editorially with letters of the alphabet) identify the patchwork compositional procedure that Braxton employed.

IV

At a time when premier European innovators such as Peter Brötzmann, Han Bennink, Willem Breuker, and Alexander Schlippenbach were developing international reputations for their radical and uncompromising elaborations on 1960s "free" practices, Braxton occasionally redirected his constructivist concerns to lead ensembles in similarly open, collective explorations. These performances looked back to the essentially egalitarian approaches of the AACM as they furthered European attempts to excoriate from improvisation the stereotypes and performance remnants of traditional jazz practice. Yet Braxton's efforts to create, at the least, a loose set of constraints betrayed a proclivity for structured, preperformance planning. It also reflected the more formal orientation of American players, who, in their freest exercises, often showed strong roots in the tradition of show tunes, harmonic changes, and four-beat swing.

From Braxton's perspective, the European concern for "freedom" was something of a misconception since, in the end, all improvisations

Figure 5.4. Braxton's manuscript of *Composition 40G*. Courtesy Anthony Braxton.

operate according to limits and constraints, whether or not these constraints are predetermined or even consciously recognized.[45] Even in 1960s free jazz, celebrated for its anarchic transcendence of rule and law, improvisers continually imposed, as a matter of course, formulaic patterns and guides that dictated the formal progression of events. Indeed, constraints are a *direct consequence* of rational choice, of intelligent, conscious beings involved in spontaneous creative acts, whether through language, art, or music. For the European players who seemed to embrace freedom as a political—and ironically, anti-American—expression, the existence of unconscious constraints would be less relevant than their ideological intent as artists. Perhaps most significant about the distinction between Braxton and many of his European colleagues (with whom he otherwise shared many likenesses) is that for Braxton structures had become a fundamental element in defining his musical identity.

Accordingly, when Braxton planned his collaboration with Derek Bailey for performances in London's Wigmore Hall (1974) they were forced to compromise their respective commitments to structure and freedom. Beyond the preplanned scheme of stylistic "areas"—"staccato sounds," "sustained sounds," "repeated motifs," etc.—performance practice was left open.[46] On the recording, the musicians build from these areas as they articulate formal sections and subsections by periodically changing motives, rhythm, or performance procedure. In particular, Braxton and Bailey gradually shift types of collaborative relations. Recalling the approaches identified in Circle's improvisations, they move from hierarchy to nonhierarchy, interaction to opposition, imitation to accompaniment (cf. chapter 4). And Braxton further defines sectional divisions by changing instruments—flute, soprano clarinet, clarinet, contrabass clarinet, sopranino saxophone, alto saxophone—at strategic, formally significant moments.

In *Composition 21* (1971, *Together Alone* 1/1), Braxton and his former AACM colleague, Joseph Jarman, extrapolate from the AACM's approaches to improvisation to create what appears superficially like a formless collage of musical invention. Flooding the sonic canvas

45. As he remarks in an interview with Philippe Carles, "I do not play free jazz! It does not interest me to be 'free.' I try to find new solutions in contemporary music. I play solo and I want to work with an orchestra for the same reasons, because these things exist and because I have wanted to be able to work in all these different contexts." Carles, "Braxton: Le Jazz est une Musique Dangereuse," *Jazz Magazine* (France) (November 1972), 14. Translation by author.

46. See Martin Davidson's notes to *Live at Wigmore* (Inner City double re-release, IC 10401).

with a rich complex of percussion, noise effects, and instrumental imitations of electronic music, the musicians exceed even the loose, constraining boundaries of the Chicago style, verging on structurally "free" improvisation. Yet the swirling dynamic textures seem to provide in themselves a contour of sorts, glorifying a pan-African propensity for coloristic and rhythmic invention—what Morton Marks has described in the context of ritual action as "making noise."[47] Such a linkage carries special relevance in the context of this album, where a puckish revision of the title of a jazz standard (Howard Dietz and Arthur Schwartz's *Alone Together* as *Together Alone*) appears against the background of an Afrocentric visual depiction of black "vital force."[48] As a visual commentary, the artwork refers to a similar musical background, celebrating in the voice of black modernism the strength and resonance of the African legacy.

In this context, "making noise" seems an entirely suitable descriptor, conjuring up images of ring shouts, drumming, and other emotionally transfixing "flash[es] of the spirit."[49] The clamor of colors and percussion might actually suggest the work of several musicians, had not the credits indicated otherwise. Density does not, however, necessarily denote chaos; Braxton and Jarman sought (and realized) a rich texture of recognizable instrumental tones and electrically generated sounds that maintain a tension between familiarity and artifice. Unlike many of the previous works, which highlighted a single dimension of complexity (timbre, rhythm), *Composition 21* seems to explore virtually all dimensions at once, casting a sonic challenge to Western binary exclusions. Melodies are interposed one upon another and frequently against a sonic array, constructing a dense and propulsive rhythmic fabric; multi-instrumental explorations that present the range of woodwinds, from flute to soprano saxophone to alto saxophone to contrabass clarinet, create splashes of coloration and rich, sustained timbral complexities. Frequent "plastic" sounds of tape machines winding and rewinding and the "natural" color of tap-water

47. Marks, "Uncovering Ritual Structures in Afro-American Music," in *Religious Movements in Contemporary America,* ed. Irving Zaretsky and Mark P. Leone (Princeton: Princeton University Press, 1974), 60–134.

48. The cover art by Turtel Onli, a Chicago artist, features a nationalist color scheme (red/green/yellow) representing a human head with an enlarged cranium. The head shape is characteristic of West African depictions of intellect ("vital force"). Freida High Tesfagiorgis has noted in conversation that Onli's style is reminiscent of the pointillistic dot effect of Omarlama, an influential South Side artist during the 1960s.

49. Robert Farris Thompson, *Flash of the Spirit* (New York: Random House, 1983; Vintage, 1984).

running provide an exhilarating background to the similarly impersonal and personal (recorded and live) instrumental mix. At moments Braxton doubles the irony of the produced and reproduced, the real and unreal. Performing on a patently real acoustic instrument, the contrabass clarinet, he imitates the imitative colors of plastic, electronically generated sounds. Perhaps the only weak moment in this otherwise admirable performance is the ending: a fade-out during a period of transition. Yet this lack of completion may be appropriate in a recording that celebrates the mutability of African-American practices through a series of formal ironies.[50]

In another "open" performance, *Composition* 6C (1976, *Montreux-Berlin Concerts* 2/2), Braxton employs quotation and allusion in order to construct a humorous display of punning references to the American cultural landscape. Much of the prepared stylistic information in 6C refers again to the march, providing the basis for signifying improvisational play. Opening the work is a briskly bowed $\hat{1}-\hat{5}-\hat{1}$ ostinato that orients and ultimately defines rhythmic character, exaggerating the rigidity of an "oom pah" bass line. Cymbal playing, whistle blowing (both police and slide types), four-note ruffs, and bass-drum sock reinforce march imagery in a cacophonous reference to bands on the field. These elements accompany the main theme, a Weillesque melody performed by Braxton and trombonist George Lewis. The march elements here and during the ensuing improvisation take on a kind of twisted humor that voices cynicism as much as rhythmically dynamic joy. Both emotional dimensions develop from the subsequent spoofing of marches. For example, many of Braxton's improvised lines caricature march style and practice, such as the buffoonish contrabass clarinet motive appearing shortly after the theme, which imitates trombone countermelodies as it suggests the bassoon accompanimental figures of early animated films. Later, he salutes with mock patriotism the militaristic grandeur of college football by quoting *Fight On!,* the school song of the University of Southern California.[51] George Lewis also adds to the pastiche of march music with muted accompanimental figures, notably a series of $\hat{1}-\hat{5}-\hat{1}$ glissandos that pay tribute to a New Orleans past as they play on its conservative appeal. In the final section before the return of the theme, the ensemble cuts through

50. On another track, Jarman's *Morning (Including Circles),* simultaneity intensifies as Braxton and Jarman shout, out of phase, a collage of poetic and political references.

51. The source of this quotation was brought to my attention by Richard Crawford and H. Robert Reynolds.

the jocularity with an intense version of the stop-time strain of *Tiger Rag*. Voicing the "truth" of black rhythmic power, the performance at this point commands the fire and intensity characteristic of early territory bands.

More typically appearing in Braxton's "free" repertory are works that follow a preconceived plan as the basis for an extended ensemble improvisation. Braxton recalls that he began mapping out performance frames in the early 1970s after employing a similar method for his saxophone improvisations. By 1974, these had taken the form of compositional "schematics," detailed outlines of the structure that a performance would take. Central to the structure were contrasts between improvisation and notation. Yet Braxton also supplied other oppositions in performance practice and compositional style to flesh out an aurally recognizable, formal complex. Braxton attributes these efforts to his studies of concert music. Yet they may have just as easily stemmed from jazz, whose composers, arrangers, and artists have shared similar concerns about matters of formal articulation.

The Town Hall performance of *Composition 6P* (1972) marks a turn toward schematic structures, offering an example of how Braxton's "free" ensembles would sometimes work from predetermined performance constraints. For the concert, he developed a skeletal plan that, while not yet a full-fledged "schematic," operates as a kind of passageway through notated schemes (or head arrangements) and improvised sections of ensemble and solo playing. The recording suggests that Braxton aimed to articulate the details of this form by designating recurring shifts in register and style. Indeed, much of the success of the performance relates directly to the way in which the ensemble regulates levels of instrumental tension. The seemingly perfunctory cymbal/bass introduction, for example, does more than set the mood for the ensuing performance; it also establishes, through its pitch/nonpitch contrast, a defining stylistic opposition that characterizes the overall architecture. Oppositions of percussion/melody, noise/pitch, stasis/flow, and high register/low register determine subsequent sequences, as the performance moves on to explore a series of musical dichotomies. After a brief, ironic theme—double repetitions of a single pitch alternating with moments of silence—a section of halting, sporadic quartet playing gives way to a dense clatter of explosive, extended phrases during which Braxton, playing sopranino saxophone, takes the lead. Subsequent instrumental movement from a section of bass/drums to a pennywhistle/soprano saxophone/soprano voice create registral and coloristic shifts from low to high; later, new groupings of flute/voice/cymbal, moving to contrabass clarinet/bass/

drums, reverse registral and timbral movement from high to low. Other juxtapositions highlight melodic/percussive and pitch/noise contrasts. Midway through the improvisation, a sopranino saxophone/orchestra bell coupling evolves into a section emphasizing percussive sounds; near the end, (pitched) clarinet and bass clarinet improvisations frame a (nonpitched) drum solo. From a broad, formal perspective, moreover, the disparate array of textures establishes a large-scale contrast to the subsequent melodic resolution. This latter section—now the compositional centerpiece—begins with a slow, plaintive $\hat{1}$–$\hat{5}$ alternation. Voiced in the extreme lower registers of bass and contrabass clarinet, it sets the mood and tonal frame for Jeanne Lee's haunting lyric. Terse and unencumbered by melodic intricacy or ensemble density, the vocal passage provides a respite from the previous improvisational complexities. At the same time, the tonal ambiguities of the line, coupled with Braxton's poignant text, draw the listener into a sonic-lyrical portrait of social crisis and spiritual collapse:

> The real became us too
> everything we felt when living
> and fallen memories
> knowing that we had no voice
> as life receives a gift unknown behind a day
> the truth of our past.
>
> Actualities in finding nothing
> holding to prefabricated time slots
> waiting for contemporary mind cards
> we lost our dream.
>
> The real became us too
> offerings that went untouched
> destined to belong
> knowing that we had no voice
> watching as the world collides
> after all we've said and done there.

V

Braxton's experiments with the opposition of control vs. freedom also produced a class of works in which notations of differing regulatory specificity appear in a single composition. In these pieces, notations not only orient conventionally written sections; they also constrain improvisations and thus further obscure clear distinctions between composition and spontaneous expression.

Composition 37 for four saxophones (sopranino, alto, tenor, baritone) is a full-fledged "schematic" work composed in September 1974 for Braxton's debut album on Arista (*New York Fall 1974* 2/2). In his original notes to the score, Braxton explained that the work alternates between conventional staff notations (N) of a variable, four-note chordal "theme" and areas of guided improvisation (I). These, in turn, correspond to four overarching "zones," A–D, each of which is identified by a distinct stylistic character (figure 5.5).[52] In Zone A, the

A	B	C	D
N I N′	I′ N″	I″	N‴

Figure 5.5. Schematic outline of *Composition 37.*

chordal theme (N) takes the form of a rhythmic repetition, possibly an ensemble version of the saxophone "staccato language";[53] in Zone B, it utilizes a "revolving tonal center" (sustained inversions of the basic chord); in Zone D, it undergoes "weight shifts," chordal repetitions that continually and unpredictably change harmonic voicing. These latter orchestrations recall the third of Schoenberg's *Five Pieces for Orchestra,* opus 16 (1912), cast here as a rhythmically dynamic constellation. The improvisations, on the other hand, rely on "cell structures," a series of visual guides that specify tone color, rhythm, phrasing, and other "sound approaches."[54] In zones A and B, the improvisations are regulated by a "medium slow pulse factor"; in Zone C, they respond to stylistic controls that quicken the rate of interaction. Figure 5.6 shows that the actual structures are, quite simply, groupings of numbers encased in circles that correspond to the accompanying list of performance practices.[55] More than a mere stylistic pretension, the cells are as much symbols of Braxton's devotion to structure and "scientific rigor" as they are practical, prescriptive notations. In performance, they serve a dual role of disciplining improvisation while also allowing musicians to exercise their own musical choices. On a conceptual level, the cell structures are also important because they identify a new interface at a point when Braxton began

52. The original notes appeared with the composition. Braxton subsequently revised and published them in his *Composition Notes,* Book C.

53. When the repetition returns as N′, it accompanies a baritone saxophone solo.

54. *Composition Notes,* Book C, 34.

55. The positioning of the circles corresponds to the relative ranges of the instruments. Braxton first employed this notation in *Composition 9* for four shovels.

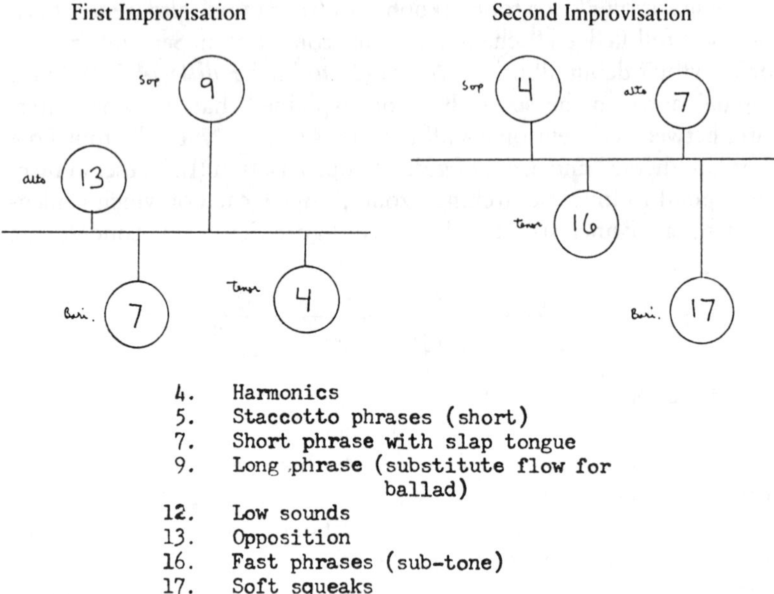

Figure 5.6. Cell structures in Zone C and performance-score instructions, *Composition 37*. Courtesy Anthony Braxton.

to merge his visual artistic summaries (formula titles, diagrams) with the compositions themselves.

In *Composition 76* for three multi-instrumentalists, Braxton employs an elaborate preplanned scheme to coordinate the "infrastructure" of an extended, multileveled performance. In his notes to the work, which accompany its commercial release as *For Trio* (1977), he explains that a given performance is regulated by a set of "coordinates" that chart the musicians' "routes" through an interplay of conventional and invented notations. The constraints serve here to move beyond song-form models while still preserving distinctions between improvisation and notation—or what Braxton calls "spontaneous" and "controlled" coordinates.[56] A close look at the compositional details suggests, in fact, that such simple dichotomies have ultimately collapsed, subverting logic through a network of creative possibilities. The excerpt in figure 5.7 shows that the musicians (identified by the systems, marked "¢") follow prescribed routes that present a series of performance choices. Moving from left to right, they encounter con-

56. Braxton, liner notes to *For Trio*.

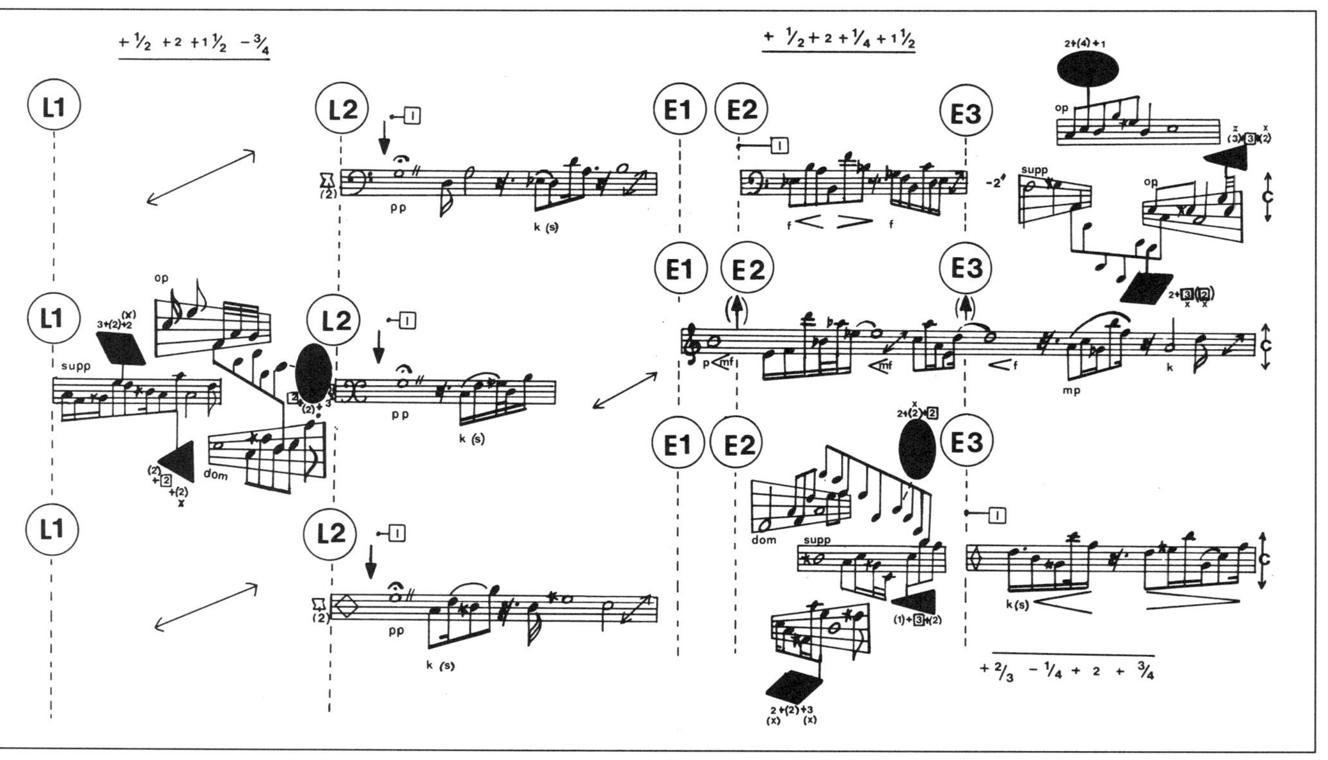

Figure 5.7. A double-page spread from the score of *Composition 76*. Courtesy Anthony Braxton.

ventional notations ("controlled coordinates"), which, where indicated, may be read backward or inverted; staffless noteheads that outline a general contour; and geometric "modulars" ("spontaneous coordinates") that correspond to a range of specified improvisational constraints, many of which depend on the activities of the other artists.[57] Working their way through the score, musicians frequently perform independently: they may skip parts, play fast or slow, read forward or back. At times they depart from their specified brass and woodwind instruments to draw from an assortment of percussion or to vocalize according to a predetermined scheme. At cue points, moreover, they converge to attend to an assigned collective task, only to resume on their independent, parallel investigations. Never does the listener know for sure the grammatical rules under which the musicians operate; and Braxton ensures obscurity by permitting new routes and new page orders with each performance. (The double versions appearing on the album—the first with Henry Threadgill and Douglas Ewart, the second with Joseph Jarman and Roscoe Mitchell—testify to the range of performance possibilities.) Through rigorous attention to the details of performance practice and compositional structure, Braxton abstracts and enlarges the freedom of jazz in a work whose codes remain impenetrable to even the most conscientious observer.[58]

VI

Appearing occasionally across the range of Braxton's art are works that rely principally or exclusively on conventional staff notations. In some, improvisations function only as minor highlights that enrich the character of an otherwise rigorously controlled performance; in others, all parameters are notated, thus disrupting the vital tension of composition and improvisation at the heart of Braxton's work. Yet what is lost in spontaneity is often gained in aesthetic explication, for here Braxton gives a precise accounting of the stylistic convergences occupying his musical imagination. Analysis shows that the stylistic and procedural diversity of Braxton's notated works reflects the expanses of his imagination, while the intricacies of jazz/concert-music interaction reveal how thoroughly the two realms had become internalized.

57. In differing circumstances, performers imitate, oppose, accompany, etc.

58. Similar efforts to "structure the whole of a given [extended] performance" appear in subsequent extended works, notably *Composition 98*. See notes to the recording (Hat Art 1984). Variations in page order first appeared in *Composition 10* (1969). Cf. chapter 3.

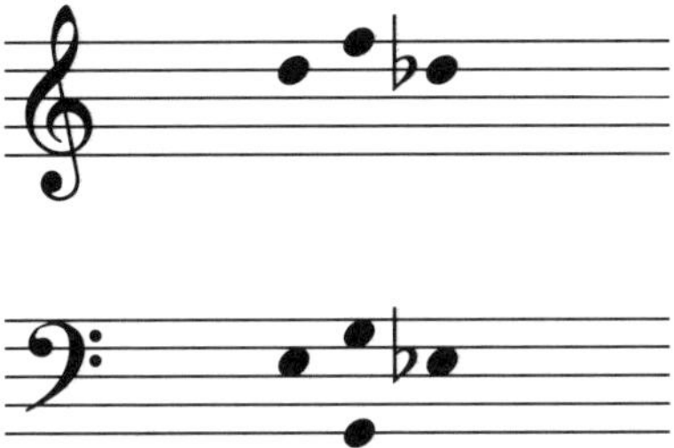

Figure 5.8. Author's transcription of the opening brass/woodwind cluster in *Composition 51.*

Such subtlety of integration appears above all in *Composition 51,* the lead track to Braxton's award-winning album, *Creative Orchestra Music 1976.* Positioned for high visibility, the performance highlights practices common to big-band jazz: themes in bop rhythm, engaging orchestrations, energetic solos, and brass/saxophone interaction, all of which appears against a propulsive rhythm-section accompaniment. In Braxton's compositional technique, however, one can observe an interplay of jazz and modernist elements that is traceable even to the details of note-to-note construction. The initial gesture, for example, reflects Braxton's principal influences in an elaborate presentation of timbral arrangement. Appearing in figure 5.8 as a block chordal cluster in multi-octave expansion (D♭ to G, omitting F♯), the gesture makes overt reference to the legacy of atonal composition and particularly to the intricate, texturally complex voicings of *Rothko Chapel, For Frank O'Hara,* and other works by Morton Feldman. With this pitch material, however, Braxton constructs voicing consistent with tonal harmony,[59] outlining relations that call to mind the coloristic orchestrations of Duke Ellington and Charles Mingus. Subsequent passages reflect similar stylistic integrations. The reed responses to the brass clusters, for example, recall the bop-inspired intricacy of 1950s "stage-band" charts as they mimic the abstract, nondevelopmental character of Braxton's own solos. Performed against an engaging and propulsive 4/4 rhythm-section accompaniment, these passages seem to move rapidly to nowhere; they distill the excitement of African-American rhythm as if to comment on the sober artistry of reified bop phrasing. Furthermore, in a second part of the opening section and again after a brief midsection of inspired solos, call/response patterns appear as

59. The outer-voice frame, G–F, in the appropriate harmonic setting, could pass as a highly decorated G^7 chord (omitting the third).

high brass and saxophones engage in a "controlled" conversation against a spasmodic, lower brass, gravallic basic. Interestingly, call/response intricacy at this point and particularly during the closing written portions becomes so complex that the jazz character collapses into a dynamic, atonal cacophony.

In *Composition 34* (1981, *Six Compositions Quartet* 1/3), a conventionally notated work for small group, Braxton once again gives a nod to serialism as he turns toward the magnified tonality of "minimalist" procedures he had first encountered in New York. Stylistically, the work recalls the methods of Philip Glass, Steve Reich, and Terry Riley in their application of limited pitch material and motives played in fast, repetitive sequences. Braxton's starting point is a six-note core motive that generates eleven transpositions according to the same melodic contour. (Notations of the motive and its transpositions appear in the liner notes.) On the recording, these appear singly, in layers, and as accompaniments to melodies and brief breaks. Yet whereas Glass and Reich would, in their early works, seek to obscure or at least subdue cadential preparation, Braxton prepares cadences by varying texture, shifting motives, inserting drum breaks, and employing other markers associated with conventional harmonic music. Similarly, while the appearance of eleven chromatic transpositions of the core motive (or "row") recall serial precompositional procedures, their application in the context of the work enhances rather than distorts tonal centering. In *Composition 23C* (*New York Fall 1974* 1/2), moreover, Braxton again creates a series of twelve motivic units, here arranged in sequence. The basic rule that governs the performance is that before the statement of any motive, all preceding motives must be restated in sequence. Thus, motive 1 is played and then repeated before motive 2; motives 1 and 2 are played again before introducing motive 3; motives 1, 2, and 3 are repeated before motive 4, and so on. This procedure takes place without pause between the end of one melody and the start of the next. As a result, melodic/tonal motion is continually interrupted, especially as the performance moves forward into motives 6–11, where lengthier phrases depart from the initial tonality and motivic contours. Significantly, this procedure is identical to one first employed by Philip Glass in his *Music in Fifths* (1969). In Glass's work, however, the melodic rhythm remains consistent; in Braxton's the melodic rhythm varies in order to articulate cadences.

Other composed works from the period show Braxton experimenting with still other modernist devices and forums. *Composition 95* (1980, *For Two Pianos*) combines minimal repetition patterns with a style firmly based in the atonal sound world that inspired his initial piano studies. *Composition 23K* (*Donna Lee* 2/2) and *Composition 20* (*Together Alone* 2/2) recall the languid, melodic incantations and shimmering timbral sound fields of the "head movements," building tension through oppositions of lyricism and tonal ambiguity. In *Composition 30–33,* moreover, a suite of four solo works for piano, Braxton adapts a procedure previously employed by Karlheinz Stockhausen in *Solo* (1965–1966): the performer constructs prior to performance a work from a pool of composed motives and phrases. By "phrase sequencing" the sections and phrases of one composition or a group of compositions and putting them in a new order, Braxton maintains the improvisational freedom inherent in jazz. In his notes to Frederick Rzewski's recording of the work, he compares the procedure to "parts of a puzzle that can be shaped as the performer desires."[60] This puzzle metaphor is significant, for it reveals the degree to which he had begun by the early 1970s to objectify compositional structures, to make them fit his constructivist understanding of musical form. Schematic structures, constraints for free improvisation, alternative methods of improvisational support—all betray a systematic mind at work, exploring ways of balancing structural oppositions against the multiplicity of dichotomies that inform his art. Such systematic concerns would later generate massive, multipart pieces such as *Composition 82* (1978) for four orchestras, which manages a complex array of procedures, media, and sectionalization.[61] Yet even more notable is the way that system would carry over to the macro level, influencing Braxton's perception of linkages and interconnections within his repertory as a whole.

VII

Paving the way toward a multiwork system was *Composition 25* for creative orchestra, featured at the Festival de Chatellerault in March 1972, and later released by Burkhard Hennen on Moers as *Creative Orchestra Music.*[62] Formally, the work consists of twelve discrete "units" (A–L), which may be categorized according to three performance approaches. Some units highlight an introductory written

60. Rzewski, *No Place to Go but Around* (1976). For the recording, Rzewski created a "mix" of four works for solo piano, all identified by the label "P-JOK."

61. Braxton has noted that the work was inspired by the grand orchestrations of Ives, Stockhausen (*Gruppen, Carré*), and Xenakis (*Polytope*). See notes to *For Four Orchestras.*

62. Braxton credits Kunle Mwanga (George Conley) for arranging this performance at a crucial point in his career. *Composition Notes,* Book B, 160.

Figure 5.9. Outline of ensemble activity in *Composition 25.*[a]

Unit A. ("Cloud Type Environment.")[b]
Pitchless textures predominate. Performers highlight breath sounds (blowing air through wind instruments) and percussive tapping of saxophone keys.

Unit B. Slow unison melody (flute/oboe) over breath sounds. Leads to collective improvisation (trumpet, flute, oboe), with breath/key-tapping accompaniment. Eventually shifts instrumentation (soprano saxophone, piano, trumpet, with occasional tenor sax and tuba interjections).

Unit C. Extended full ensemble theme, with set drumming. Fiery tenor saxophone solo with rhythm-section accompaniment; unaccompanied drum and piano solos.

Unit D. ("Giant Moving Shadows.") Slow, notated theme in octaves (tuba, contrabass clarinet, bass). Instruments open to pulseless collective improvisation with trumpet playing plaintively above. Contrabass clarinet (flutter tongued) overtakes trumpet, moves gradually to solo with extremely quiet instrumental background.

Unit E. ("Multiple Universe of Sound.") Anchoring theme integrating sustained pitches and staccato repetitions, moving as *klangfarbenmelodie* around performance ensemble. Gradually evolves into high-pitched sustains (balloons) with soprano saxophone/flute/percussion interjections. Soprano sax gradually increases presence and then initiates collective improvisation (soprano sax/flute/bass/tenor sax; soprano to clarinet). Balloon sustains appear intermittently. Braxton switches to alto, duo with piano against varying instrumental background. Unaccompanied bass solo; walking line links to Unit F.

Unit F. (Soloists are "angry at something.") Bop-oriented woodwind/brass theme against walking bass/rhythm section. Extended alto sax solo against rhythm section (Braxton showcased). Piano, trumpet against rhythm section follow; unaccompanied drum solo. Percussion (bells/chimes) links to Unit G^1.

Unit G^1. ("Dancing stars . . . like a Christmas tree in music.") Extended period of percussion colors (bells, chimes). Subsequently serves as accompaniment for series of solos (oboe, muted trumpet, flute [briefly]), and collective improvisation: soprano sax, flutes, trumpet.

Unit G^2. ("A dark-beamed like structure that moves to swallow up the space of the music.") Extended unison theme, characteristically slow, plaintive (low brass, arco bass, soprano sax, piano) against bells/chimes. "Meditation music" that lacks direction and that "re-directs the very center of its operating space."

Unit H. ("As honest as possible.") Extended unaccompanied tenor sax solo.

Unit I. ("As honest as possible.") Unaccompanied tuba solo. Prefigures ascending lines of Unit J.

Unit J. ("Lyrical line[s] that seem to both swim and dance inside this strange [sonic] universe.") Orchestral sustains evolving into a series of slow, staggered ascents in which instrumentalists move chromatically to construct a complex, weblike texture. Accompanies interactive solo; soprano sax and trumpet solos follow.

Unit K. Percussion duet (two set drummers with additional percussion).

Unit L. ("Sound mass block.") Brief (ten-second), cacophonous, full ensemble climax.

[a] Instrumentation and a list of performers appear in Appendix B.
[b] The metaphorical descriptions are taken from Braxton's discussion of *Composition 25,* published in *Composition Notes,* book B.

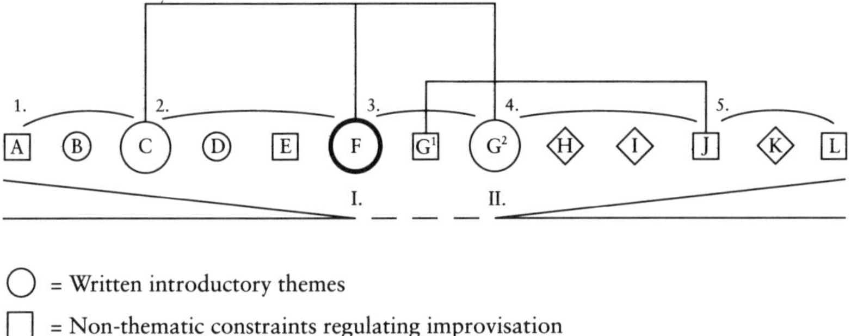

Figure 5.10. Reduction of formal sequences in *Composition 25*. ○ = written introductory themes; □ = nonthematic constraints regulating improvisation; ◇ = unconstrained space for solo/duo improvisation. Beams and slur markings show progression of events, highlighting structurally significant units. Roman numerals suggest overarching sectionalization and development.

theme that sets the basis for collective or solo improvisation (B, C, D, F, G^2); others assign nonthematic constraints that regulate ensemble interaction (A, E, G^1, L); still others provide an unconstrained space for extemporaneous solo or duo invention (H, I, K).[63] Figure 5.9 maps out the pattern of change from unit to unit, highlighting some of the most significant details appearing in the Moers recording. Figure 5.10, moreover, provides an interpretation of the formal consequences of this activity. The reduction shows that the initial units function as a prelude to Unit C, where a jazz-styled theme centers the work as it leads the way into three extended solos. Units D and E introduce new stylistic settings, timbral groupings, and performer relationships; especially noteworthy is Unit E, which moves away from conventional improvisational platforms as a "staccato long sound" provides the basis for performance. (At this point, the original score calls for an improvisation with 225 balloons.)[64] Unit F marks a compositional climax, during which a bop-styled theme accompanies Braxton's rousing, extended alto solo. Subsequent activity appears more exploratory than stylistically directional. The bell accompaniment of Unit G^1, for example, halts sense of development, creating what Braxton calls a "meditation music . . . a world that . . . seems to be changing but

63. The diagram divides Braxton's Unit G into two parts, since each appears to function as a separate area.

64. Balloon sounds also appear in *Composition* 6G (1969, *B-X°/N-0-1-47A* 2/1). Cf. chapter 3.

somehow remains the same."[65] The slow, monophonic theme that appears as Unit G^2 creates much the same effect. This initiates further improvisational explorations, including a series of engaging solos in Unit J, which appear over a dramatic field of overlapping, chromatically ascending instrumental voices. The final moments restore direction and provide closure. Unit K abstracts the jazz drum break that typically anticipates the return of the head; Unit L completes the structure with a vivid climax that recalls in style the most dynamic moments in Coltrane's *Ascension* (1965).

The architectural character and compatibility of units would suggest that *Composition 25* differs little from the multisectional, schematic compositions. Indeed, the performance is identified as a single work, and Braxton has taken pains to organize the units into a structurally coherent performance. Yet unlike the schematic works, the structure of *Composition 25* is not permanently fixed; units may be rearranged, or in some cases—for example, at the Théâtre de la Cité Internationale in May 1973—a single unit may serve as the basis for an entire performance.[66] Clearly, Braxton had perceived *Composition 25* as a collection of discrete subworks relating to a mutable, structurally variable "whole," even if some units appeared as nothing more than a time space for group improvisation.

Braxton's conception of performance as a systematic network of interconnected musical units would even affect the way he organized (and understood) the structure of his day-to-day quartet concerts. He explains that by the mid-1970s (and perhaps not long after Chatellerault) his quartet pieces were no longer a mere set of tunes or even "parts [of] a designated musical suite, [but rather] structural system-types to be utilized in an overall . . . inter-locking multi-system." Once a collection of independent platforms for improvisation, the quartet works had become a stock of materials, "each . . . designed to establish a particular focus" (i.e., to explore a specific performance procedure). Like the languages in the works for unaccompanied saxophone or the elements in *Composition 30–33*, the pieces themselves acquired meaning only when "coordinated" into a multisectional performance. Accordingly, the idea of a "coordinate music" took on broader meaning, describing the intercompositional system of small-group performance.[67]

65. Braxton, *Composition Notes*, Book B, 186.

66. Unit G served as the material base of *Lasya-4*. Alex Dutilh, "Pas D'entrechats pour Braxton," *Jazz Hot* (June 1973), 22.

67. Braxton, liner notes, *Performance 9/1/1979*. In his comments, Braxton reveals

A published version of Braxton's schematicized coordinate music appears as *Performance 9/1/1979,* a live concert recorded at the Willisau (Switzerland) Jazz Festival. Figure 5.11 reproduces the schematic of the concert, designating each work with a picture title and furnishing additional information about solo orders, language types, and time lengths. Commenting on the schematic, Braxton explained that after the written portions of compositions 1, 3, and 6, the musicians perform "soloist-rhythm" improvisations, while the second, fourth, and fifth works lead to "collage," "open," or "language" interaction. During language interactions, improvisers work from "line notation" (line drawings specifying pitch contour; cf. chapter 3), whereas in open improvisation, they "play in opposition. If one is going faster, the other might go slower; if one plays high, the other may play lower." Collage improvisations, on the other hand, operate with "a conscious decision to avoid connections. We are talking about total individualism in space."[68] Near the end of each section of improvisation, moreover, the quartet employs a variety of "linkage dynamics" that prefigure the melody of the next composition and enable the musicians to play without pausing between works. The variation in procedures relates ultimately to what Braxton calls the "master progression system" (MPS), which indicates fluctuations of emotional intensity. During nonhierarchical, interactive improvisations, the intensity remains low; during hierarchical, soloist-rhythm improvisations, the intensity increases, reaching a climax when Braxton solos in the third piece.[69]

The multicompositional structures are significant to Braxton's own creative development because they reflect a dramatic reconceptualization of the formal character of jazz performance. The procedures suggest that Braxton had come to terms with jazz by molding it in his own image; removed from preexisting contexts, it had now taken on the character of an experimental system. Significantly, this refashioning of jazz took place as Braxton had begun to reconsider the entirety of his art. A formerly disparate and highly varied collection of methods

---

the scientific origin of "coordinate," or, as he sometimes writes, "coordinant": "I have come to speak of my quartet music as a 'coordinant music' because this term serves to accent the position of science in my music, as well as the position of methodological dynamics in shaping the 'particular' of a given performance."

68. Notes to *Performance 9/1/1979.* This oppositional procedure has appeared consistently throughout Braxton's repertory, reaching back to the noninteractive approach of *Composition 6E,* which opens *Three Compositions of New Jazz;* cf. chapter 3.

69. The schematic indicates that the bass solo appears before the return of the head. On the recording it appears after.

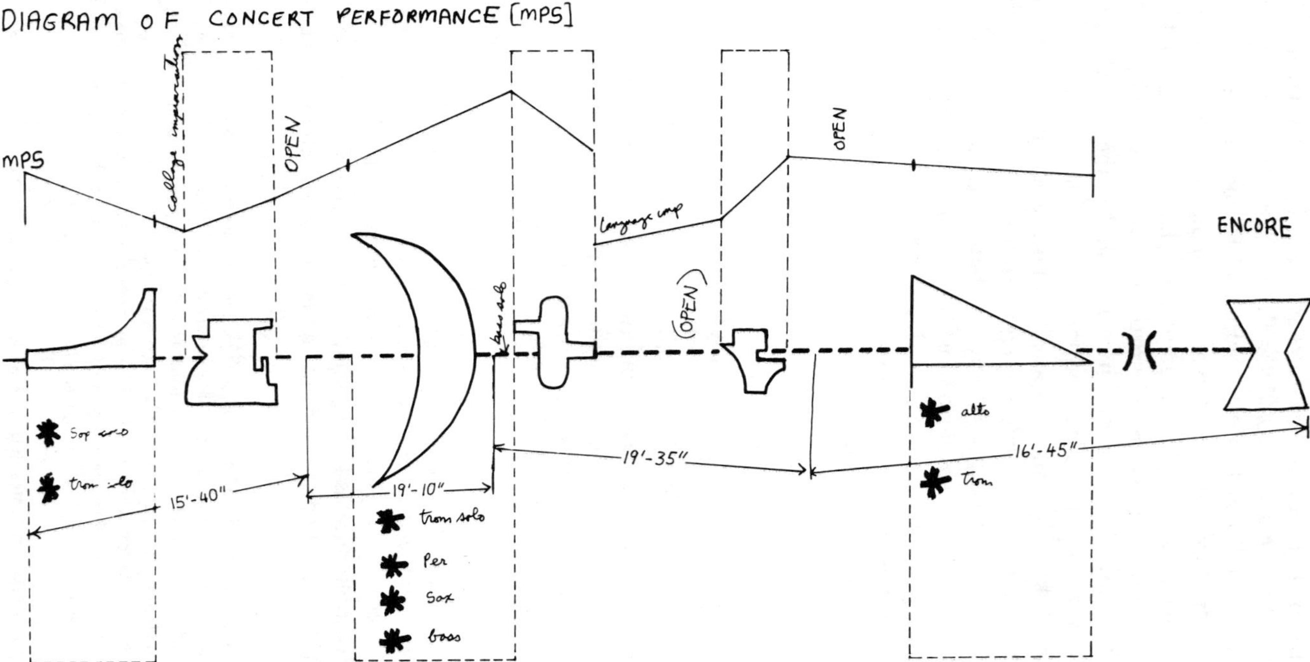

Figure 5.11. Braxton's schematic of *Performance 9/1/1979*. From the jacket notes of Braxton's 2-LP set *Hat Hut 2R19*. Courtesy Hat Hut Records, Werner X. Uehlinger, president. *Performance* is now available on compact disc as *Anthony Braxton, Performance* (*Quartet*) 1979) (hatART CD 6044).

and styles was now thought to express a unifying creative impulse that had generated overarching formal linkages. Predictably, the key link in this unification would be found to exist at Braxton's creative center: the music for unaccompanied saxophone. In a *Down Beat* interview from February 1974, Braxton explained that he now conceived of "saxophone music [as] nothing more than language systems, . . . systems which [allow me to] enter new areas."[70] After performing solo improvisations for seven years, Braxton had come to view what was once a stock of independent motives and phrases as an interrelated complex of elements. By creating syntactical relationships between saxophone motives in each of his improvisations, he believed he had departed from the mix-and-match technique of the past and was now moving toward procedures that resembled the workings of language.[71]

Braxton's concept of a "language music" is, of course, more figurative than it is linguistically accurate. The elements in this elaborate structure were, in the end, the same collection of materials he had always employed in his improvisations, and the divisions within the performance, for that matter, seemed little different from the divisions appearing in any jazz performance. The concept is important, nevertheless, because it shows that Braxton had now begun to recognize internal coherences that implied similar linkages in his entire repertory. When he began a systematic study of his complete works in 1977, he found precisely that: the saxophone vocabulary could be traced through the range of his musical expression. Every saxophone element, Braxton now believed, "appeared on more than one level, in more than one composition."[72] This recognition of an interactive system led to the intentional use of "languages" in order to codify a method he had developed unconsciously, "to integrate language music [musical materials] throughout my system."[73] In *Composition 82* (for four orchestras), in *Composition 95* (for two pianos), and in many of the quartet pieces composed in the mid-to-late 1970s and 1980s, Braxton consciously fused old languages or variations of old languages with new material.[74] Ultimately this preoccupation with system even

70. Townley, "Anthony Braxton," *Down Beat* (February 14, 1974), 12.

71. This procedure is reminiscent of Cage's system of piano music, outlined in *Variations II,* which Thomas De Lio calls "one large comprehensive system which itself represents the total accumulation of its many constituent realizations." De Lio, "John Cage's Variation II: The Morphology of a Global Structure," *Perspectives of New Music* (Spring/Summer 1981), 369.

72. Interview with Anthony Braxton (August 23, 1983).

73. Interview with Anthony Braxton (September 6, 1982).

74. While Braxton recognized—and indeed, discovered—the interrelationship of

affected the way he perceived the work of others. "Any composition," he came to believe, "whether it's mine or Schoenberg's or anybody else's, can be broken down into this. This explains the 'how,' the method."[75] Speculations about the deep-structural unity of compositional procedure would inspire a search for the "common tendencies" that, he believes, unite the music of humanity. In the 1980s, he would engage these prototypes—a modernist version of Curt Sachs's "tumbling strains"—to construct "composite scales" for a global music, synthetic prototypes from which all the world's sound systems were thought to have been derived.[76]

Braxton's belief in a grand systemic basis for creativity suggested a radical blurring of conventional conceptions of category and boundary. Grasping the deconstructive implications of structuralist thought, which privileged unconscious languaged-based systems over the local realities of a knowing subject, Braxton now believed that style, genre, and even a composer's identity could be reduced to a systematic sameness regulated by the notion of musical "language." This reworking of conventional categories of delineation would ultimately even mask distinctions between media, influencing the design and function of his picture titles. What were once isolated challenges to titular convention had taken on a new significance, becoming analogues of musical expression. The "dimensional drawings," as he calls his titles from the mid-1970s, exalted media interface by creating a synesthetic mix of spatial and sonic reference.[77] These drawings were Braxton's blueprints of sonic design, abstract interpretations of compositional form. While in most instances the associations seemed figurative, some titles, Braxton explains, made specific reference to compositional structure. Such might be the case with titles that suggest spatial conceptions of sound, appearing in two or three dimensions

parts, and has detailed his new way of creating "languages," when asked "What is language music," he inevitably replied "saxophone music." He has not, to my knowledge, made a distinction between language music as saxophone music and language music as the material appearing in all of his works, since he uses the same term to describe both. This confusion is heightened by his terminology "language notation" and "line notation," both of which are employed to describe notations in the saxophone music.

75. Interview with Anthony Braxton (February 17, 1983).

76. Sachs, *The Wellsprings of Music,* ed. Jaap Kunst (The Hague: M. Nijhoff, 1962), 51–59.

77. Between the formula titles and dimensional drawings, Braxton had also invented another kind of picture title, what he has called "alternative coding." These titles, identifying works from the early 1970s, were more or less akin to the formulas, except that they also carried "spiritual" meaning.

(e.g., *Composition 40G* and *Composition 40K*). In other cases, titles seem to have developed from formally unrelated sources. For example, the dimensional drawing of *Composition 69E* may have been based on the superimposition of line notations ("dimensional notations"), as the composite in figure 5.12 illustrates. On the other hand, the aggregates of abstract design accompanying *Composition 76, Composition 48,* and *Composition 50* suggest astronomical maps, computer graphics of molecules, and the geometric splendor of Calder mobiles. Later titles replace abstraction with representations of imaginary worlds and images of the everyday. *Composition 105A,* which decorates the jacket of *Four Compositions (Quartet) 1983,* contains cartoonlike drawings of a man, a human head, and a hand, whereas *Composition 123* depicts a theosophical tale. The picture title of *Composition 95* refers to a timely issue, nuclear power. (Picture titles appear in Appendix A.)[78]

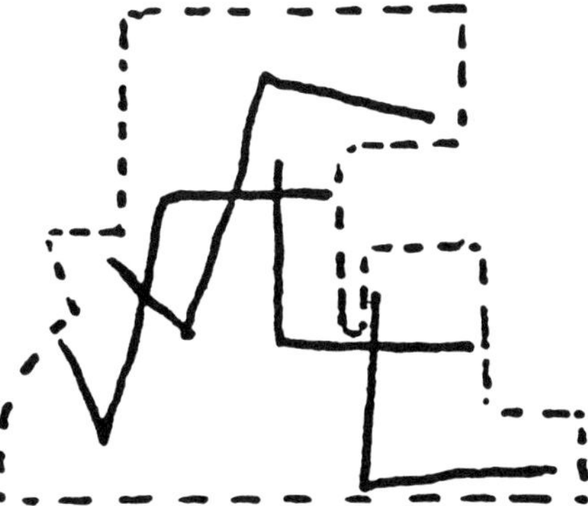

Figure 5.12. Relationship between superimposed line notations and the form of picture title (*Composition 69E*).

If the dimensional drawings were originally spatial conceptions of sound, by the mid-1970s they had become artworks in their own right, a kind of creative commentary on Braxton's work as a musician. The elaborate designs filled with vivid colors had transcended their earlier function as compositional titles, suggesting a kind of art about art, Braxton's secondary mode of creative expression. As references to music and musical structure, whether as blueprints of form or as

78. Braxton's representational titles began to appear in the mid-1980s, after he had retreated from jazz and focused attention on solitary work at home. As such, his children's artistic play—if not the realities of family life—may have inspired the application of everyday and domestic images.

spatial metaphors of his compositions, they helped further to erase the socially constructed boundaries that separated art from music, sight from sound. By implication, then, the titles' revisionist character posed a challenge to the many other dichotomies—black/white, low culture/high culture, jazz/concert music—that Braxton had sought to overturn.

In sum, Braxton's intermediated creative system remains a versatile, protean complex, a grand artistic scheme that responds and adjusts to the composer's changing interests and expressions. The system helps to supply coherence to an artist who tends to move in and out of methods rather than committing himself to one overarching procedure. "Due to my nature," Braxton explains, "I have tried to construct separate lines of development because variety is what interests me. It lets me search and grow, and to be the best 'me' that I can be."[79] The language system, schematics, and their corresponding titles offer Braxton a way of unifying the whole of an eclectic repertoire and a diversity of creative urges into a common order that collectively resists the jazz category into which he had become, by the mid-1970s, increasingly fitted. Significantly, the basis for this unification stemmed from science. As Braxton remarked in 1974, "Like a scientist I remove myself from the music and plot conceptually. If the conception is substantial it will lead into other things."[80] The language complex had become the precompositional "laboratory work" for the creation of a stylistically free, "scientific" music. By developing a personal system and a vocabulary to identify its workings, Braxton could bypass aesthetic limitations and stylistic conventions. Science, math, and system would assume the status of "objective" categories that transcended conventional social limitations as they aligned him with an elite group of composers—Cowell, Varèse, Partch, Cage, Babbitt—with similarly empirical orientations. Yet while Braxton's systematic interests most certainly drew influence from modernism, they had already surfaced well prior to his first encounters with the concert repertory and accordingly may indicate roots in his Chicago past. For in the end his assemblage of references to "cell structures" and Lord Kelvin, "weight shifts" and "system types," recalls the playfulness with which he approached science and technology as a boy. Furthermore, his visual abstractions of sound, whether they be titles or compositional schematics, are, if nothing more, elaborations on the wiring diagrams (or electrical "schematics," as they are called in the business) that he read

79. Interview with Anthony Braxton (September 19, 1983).

80. Townley, "Anthony Braxton," *Down Beat,* 12–13.

as a teenager attending Chicago Vocational High School. Just as Braxton the electrician employed wiring schematics to study radios and televisions, Braxton the composer relied on musical schematics for composing works and schematics titles to spatialize musical form. Together they reflect an experimental sensibility rooted in a personal vernacular that transcended the limits of formalized practice in either tradition, whether in concert music or in jazz.

VIII

If the structure of the language system reflects an ultra-rational sensibility gauged by the impact of structuralism and scientific thought, the content of the system betrays a prophetic ethos grounded in a parallel network of mystical and religious symbolism. For the language-music system, in its incarnations from the late 1970s, refers to more than a complex of sounds; it is the framework for a personal, idiosyncratic theosophy in which music assumes the primary position of power. After years of consideration of occult and mystical doctrine, Braxton became convinced that his music, and indeed all "creative music," operates according to "universal laws" that anticipate and often influence the path of human development. Linking a global conception of musical structure with the universal beliefs of the occult, Braxton advanced a view in which music became an active force and, in the proper hands, a tool for progressive social and cultural change. "There are forces," Braxton contends, "and [music] activates these forces—whether we know it or not."[81] Working toward that end, he began in the late 1970s to devise compositions and compositional procedures that would serve as sonic mechanisms for social change. Many of the compositions from the 1980s would be Braxton's political devices, instruments that could be put to use toward global transformation. The structural particulars of the language-music complex, then, transcended the system as such. "System" referred in the main to what Braxton called the "functional" role of sacred-sonic complexes, bridging the gap between utopian theory and social praxis.

Previous discussions have noted that Braxton's interest in mysticism and the occult dates back to the 1960s, when he first began to read contemporary theosophical studies. As a participant in free jazz and a member of the AACM, he encountered and eventually embraced spiritualist philosophies that related closely to nationalist interpretations of the African and Egyptian religious background. These views were

81. Interview with Anthony Braxton (September 6, 1982).

certainly fueled by the wide-scale appeal of alternative belief systems, which, in the form of astrology, numerology, and Eastern religions, became emblems of the counterculture's antirational, antitechnological social platform. Yet even as the public appeal of the exotic began to wane, Braxton grew increasingly interested in traditional orthodoxies and new-age elaborations. After a brief membership in the Church of Scientology and associations with "spiritualist" musicians in experimentalism and jazz (Coleman, Rzewski, Corea), he vigorously pursued information about mysticism and the occult.[82] Turning to his models in concert music, Braxton explored the mystical beliefs of Schoenberg, Webern, Varèse, and Cage, and, judging from certain comparisons, seemed to take to heart the romantic visions of Karlheinz Stockhausen.[83] Particularly influential on his perception of a cosmic-terrestial interface were the more esoteric mystical writings of Corinne Heline, Lawrence Blair, and Alice Bailey. For example, Bailey's claim that "the force centres found in men's bodies [correspond] to the force centres and currents of the solar system" suggests similarities to Braxton's own cosmology, whereas Blair's outline of the Egyptian application of magical formulas to control natural forces may have influenced his hopes to direct "universal laws" with corresponding sounds.[84] As a counterbalance to these worldly, pluralistic theories of significance, moreover—and fleshing out the range of Brax-

82. Sources included traditional texts such as the Kabbala and *Oahpse, The Egyptian Book of the Dead* and other studies edited by E. A. Wallace Budge, and Daisetz Suzuki's writings on Zen. Significantly, the "information approaches" ascribed to the human figure in the booklet to *For Four Orchestras* (1978) are traceable to the Kabbalist metaphor of the Ten Sefiroth, in which the emanations of God associate with areas of the human body.

83. Comparisons between Stockhausen's and Braxton's views of musical-spiritual linkages are often striking. In his conversations with Jonathan Cott, for example, Stockhausen employed a mystical language to describe sonic power: "Sounds can do anything. They can kill. . . . With sounds you can concentrate on any part of the body and calm it down, excite it, even hurt it in the extreme. [They] can lift the spirit of a person up into the supernatural regions so that he leaves his body. . . . We must know all that waves do to us . . . sound waves [and the] cosmic rays constantly bombarding and penetrating our bodies." Cott, *Stockhausen: Conversations with the Composer* (New York: Simon and Schuster, 1973), 81–82. Braxton has commented: "Music . . . can make a person feel wonderful or develop an illness. You can also blow up a building with it. . . . So music can be very dangerous, and too many people don't really know what they are dealing with." Interview with Anthony Braxton (September 6, 1982).

84. Bailey, *A Treatise on Cosmic Fire* (London: Lucis Press, Ltd., 1925), xiii; Blair, *Rhythms of Vision: The Changing Patterns of Beliefs* (London: Croom Helm, 1975), 5. See also Bailey, *The Rays and the Initiations* (1960). Braxton has elaborated on the importance of these particular texts in our discussions.

ton's influences—were the nationalist theories of Africa as cultural wellspring. Occupying a central position in Braxton's thinking were the perspectives of Yosef ben-Jochannan, a Harlem-based historian, whose books, *African Origins of Major "Western" Religions* (1970) and *Africa: The Mother of Civilization* (1971), sought to revise conventional European history by placing an ancient black-Egyptian civilization at the center of world culture. The essentialist compatibility of occult theory and nationalist classicism, in which each identified an immutable, core reality transcending "common sense"—one cosmic, the other grounded in black racialism—set the framework for Braxton's own theory of the *Tri-Axium* (*sic*). Begun casually in the mid-1970s, this project would eventually grow into an all-consuming passion, ultimately appearing as a three-volume set, published privately as *The Tri-Axium Writings* (1985).

Placing black music at the center of a proposed ecumenical world transformation, Braxton's *Tri-Axium* exalts African-American sensibilities in the tradition of Baraka's *Blues People* as it revises exclusionist tactics of the more vulgar forms of cultural nationalism. He shows an obvious sympathy for theories that centralize black expressions in the American context, while also seeking to create distance from separatist agendas. The potential for contradiction and ambiguity inspires frequent qualification as Braxton comments on his commentary in order, it would seem, to avoid the misunderstandings that plagued his public past. However, such qualifications also identify the double-sided, oppositional character of the *Tri-Axium,* which is built upon a delicate balance of ecumenicalism and Afrocentricity. As the text celebrates blackness, it calls racial categories into question; as it valorizes African-American performance practices and aesthetics, it blurs cultural distinctions into a world system in which a marginalized Western tradition occupies a central role. Braxton even enhances ambiguity by encouraging a dialogic of reception: the text is meant, like some of his *aleatoric* compositions, to lend itself to "multidimensional" readings by providing the reader with several ways to proceed and requesting public response to shape a multileveled plan of social action.[85] Mutability and indirection that span the expanse of Braxton's creativity determine the very structure and mechanics of the narrative.

As a challenge to the authority of jazz journalism, however, the *Tri-Axium* is specific and straightforward. The model itself is intended to correct critical misrepresentation of the black aesthetic by revealing

85. What Braxton means by "multidimensional" is unclear, yet the confusion remains consistent with the ambiguity of intention.

the inadequacy of Euro-Western measures of value. In this way, Braxton seeks to renew the debate about critical interpretations that accompanied the musical challenges of black vanguardism in the 1960s. It specifically calls to mind Baraka's seminal essay "Jazz and the White Critic" (1963), a compelling and insightful if somewhat caustic critique of the biases and subjectivities of the dominant class of writers.[86] Yet while Braxton responds fitfully to particular critical misrepresentations, he has constructed the *Tri-Axium* more as a corrective than as an attack. Indeed, the term "Tri-Axium" itself, which evokes Western religious symbols of the Trinity and axiomatic rules of law, expresses a Christian sense of tolerance as it presents an outline for an alternative creativity and social order.

Expressing the activist potentials of nationalism and the occult as well as the ambiguities of postmodern expression, Braxton's text treads a narrow line between ideological prescription and experimental writing. The *Tri-Axium* is as much an extension of his creative system as it is an outline for social change, blurring the separation of aesthetics and politics. Organized into three books, the argument follows a simple logic. The table of contents maps out a plan that takes the reader from general discussions of an "underlying philosophical basis" to specific considerations of creativity in world cultures. Sections on the impact of mass culture ("spectacle diversion syndrome"), music and politics, and the role of whites and women as creative activists elaborate on initial considerations. Each section is, in turn, subdivided into a trinity of subordinate parts that move from general discussions (1) to elaborations (2) to a concluding series of didactic "questions and answers" (3). Proceeding into the text, however, logic becomes obscured as the reader encounters a literary realm that rivals the idiosyncrasies of Braxton's musical system. Most striking and most challenging is the language itself, which presents a highly technical neology of mystical and scientific writing in the style of the most formal philosophical discourse. In order to service the reader, Braxton provides an elaborate glossary of terms, which aid understanding yet occasionally introduce tautologies that might be overcome only through painstaking textual dissection. In the name of precision, moreover, Braxton relies on reiteration and redundancy, which, while often serving the point, sometimes cloud the broader picture. Particularly fascinating is Braxton's application of schematic diagrams to abstract concepts and ideas (figure 5.13). Typically appearing at the conclusion of an argument, they condense the essentials

86. Baraka (LeRoi Jones), *Black Music* (New York: William Morrow, 1967).

RT. OP. - - - - - - SOC. RT.

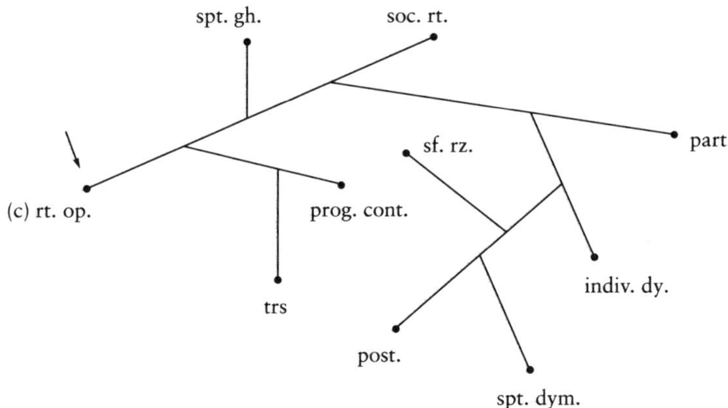

(c) rt. op.	Concept of reality option(s)	Rt. op.	Reality options(s)
Indiv. dy.	Individual dynamics	Sf. rz.	Self-realization
Part.	Participation	Soc. rt.	Social reality
Post.	Postulation	Spt. dym.	Spiritual dynamics
Prog. cont.	Progressional continuance	Spt. gh.	Spiritual growth
		Trs	Transition

Figure 5.13 Schematic diagram from Braxton, *The tri-Axium Writings*. Courtesy Anthony Braxton.

through a hierarchical scheme of abbreviated codes. The sections of texts are themselves coded according to another scheme that refers to the cosmic potential of color and number. Together, these elements challenge distinctions between creativity and science, literature and scholarship, art and politics, in a vanguardist display that recalls similarly unconventional literary exercises reaching across the experimental legacy from Ives and Cowell to Partch and Cage.[87]

"Tri-Axium" itself refers to the three-part rule of law encompassing perspectives of past, present, and future. As a position, it outlines a prescription for the future based on laws that have ruled the past and present. In order to identify these laws, one must look beyond the cloud of "misinformation" that dominates Western society (and, in turn, world culture) to seek "what seems to be really true" (vii) about the nature of human existence. According to Braxton, life's meanings

87. Ives, *Essays before a Sonata* (New York: W. W. Norton, 1947, 1961); Cowell, *New Musical Resources* (1930, 1969); Partch, *Genesis of a Music* (Madison: University of Wisconsin Press, 1949; Da Capo, 1974); Cage, *Silence* (Middletown: Wesleyan University Press, 1961).

can be reduced to the "principle information" (information regarding essential principles) that links human expression with an eternal, unchanging, cosmic logic. "Creative musicians" are those who, regardless of class, race, culture, and gender, share an affinity for the spiritual and axiomatic character of humanly created sound, who can "actualize" its power, and through performance, initiate greater spiritual awareness within the world community. While seemingly undeveloped in the West, creative musicians are, according to Braxton, all around us: they are the healers and shamans of traditional world cultures and the creative priests of the African-American legacy who have long recognized the sacred potential of musical expression. The limited evidence of this potential among white Westerners does not, however, exclude concert music from assuming a prophetic role. In fact, Braxton believes that the Western art tradition will help to lead the cultural transformation once its spiritual affinity is restored.

Such ambiguities toward the importance of Western high culture pervade Braxton's books. For example, he interprets concert music in Spenglerian fashion as an embodiment of European cultural decline, identified in an aggressive intellectualism that has, as a result of musical notation, precluded performer interaction and undermined a prior spiritualism: serialism represents the epitomy of existential crisis and collapse.[88] Yet that same intellectualism, when put to use by creative artists, becomes the transformational tool of a new age: the "restructuralism" of Webern, Cage, and Glass signals an upward turn in cultural development as these artists re-identify the spiritual center of art. Furthermore, by privileging absolute notions of "great music" and "great musical masters" from Bach to Beethoven, Braxton grants Europe the stature of a "dynasty" that would logically position lesser-developed cultures at lower ranks of value. This view contradicts a frequent insistence on the equal value of all cultures, at all points, in all circumstances.

But the central ambiguity of Braxton's *Tri-Axium* relates to the status and role of the black artist and, indeed, of "blackness" as a viable category. His explication of the cosmic sameness of humanity would suggest a transcendence of racial constructs, and Braxton's multicultural, multiracial image of the creative musician seems to support

88. It is noteworthy that Braxton's indictment of notation is consistent with the challenges to representation put forth by Charles Seeger and, most recently, postmodern anthropology. See, for example, Seeger, "Speech, Music, and Speech about Music," *Studies in Musicology, 1935–1975* (Berkeley: University of California Press, 1977); James Clifford and George Marcus, eds., *Writing Culture* (Berkeley: University of California Press, 1986).

such a view. Complicating the picture, however, is the special place reserved for black culture and musicians. By referring to the theories of ben-Jochannan and by citing the influences of Egypt on the West, he reveals—whether or not these assertions are correct—a sympathy for a nationalist "Trans-African" classicism, even as he contends that African and African-American experiences are fundamentally different. Furthermore, African Americans acquire a privileged stature as survivors of slavery, an experience that has reinforced the creative essentials of community, ritual, and spiritualism, as well as their musical analogues, collective improvisation and rhythm. As such, the racial offspring of Armstrong, Parker, and Coltrane, together with whites responsive to the same musical spirit, will now lead the way in reshaping the character of world culture as "Trans-African creativity [becomes] a tool for humanizing the Western aesthetic" (111). Such assertions about the black past may have developed from the surfeit of supporting evidence. Many scholars have come to recognize the effects of oppression on the survival of the sacred world and the development of a collectivist African-American musicality. Yet by centralizing the black experience over other legitimate expressions, Braxton establishes a hierarchy of value that subverts his own egalitarian ideals.

Taken as an empirical investigation, then, *The Tri-Axium Writings* would face as many challenges as it might gain committed advocates. As a highly developed form of experimental and nearly poetic expression, however, it presents yet another dimension to Braxton's intermediated artistic system, which in its fullest form spans across the musical, the visual, the literary. By blurring media, Braxton's creativity intellectualizes black artistic questioning of conventional Western categories to create a fusion of postmodern and Afro-centered, signifying oppositions. The fixed and the specific step to the side of a grand scheme of flexible indirection that is as totalizing and all-encompassing as it is historically constituted and in process. In Braxton's artistic world, the globally colorless and the local, racially bound share common positions; forces of the ancient past extend their rule into the here-and-now; expressions of rationality become tools of the mystical; icons of white authority assume positions of status in a trans-African continuum.[89] When centrality exists in Braxton's art-

89. Notably, Braxton's claim, taken from commentators such as J. L. Rogers, that Beethoven and Haydn were "black Germans." See Dominique-René de Lerma, "Beethoven as a Black Composer," *Black Music Research Journal* 10:1 (Spring 1990): 118–22.

istry, it resonates from a personal past that gives voice to the purity of a black vernacularism. Yet qualifications of racial integrity and the recognition of a "black aesthetic" in both world vernaculars and the premodern European past make black-centered vernacularism seem illusory, a grand mythology to which Braxton holds on even as he acknowledges the complexities of identifying African-American cultural distinctiveness.

The convergence of postmodernism and black-centered mutability in the *Tri-Axium* relates also to the multiple dualities that continually appear across the range of Braxton's artistry. Conventional musical distinctions between composition and improvisation, structure and spontaneity, virtuosity and amateurism, concert music and jazz, collapse into an assortment of deconstructed binary relations that challenge established, Enlightenment-based truths. Braxton's musical self seems to be based upon a slippery set of oppositions, eluding fixity, subverting causality. His identity is in fact an array of shifting images as his art subjects conventional notions of artistry to ethical critique. Accordingly, Braxton assumes the position of the vanguard artist as he carries on the very real legacy of African-American creative opposition.

As an index of expressive meaning, moreover, Braxton's aesthetic of exclusion/illusion unlocks a series of contrasting significances that would not otherwise be identified through "objective" interpretation. His works are at once playful and serious, mocking and arcane; against the background of the *Tri-Axium,* they become sources of power and expressions of the spirit, realizations of what Braxton sees as the sacred potential of world creativity. The punning stylistic allusions to marches and New Orleans jazz carry an added significance as signs of a sacred collective communication, just as the references to Ayler and Stockhausen, Parker and Desmond, acknowledge the cosmic potential of modernism and improvised sound. In fact, the realm of the sacred may well be the fundamental certainty in Braxton's art, a certainty reflecting traditional African-American associations between sound and the spirit. Its influence has ultimately recast the meaning of the schematic titles, which would transcend their originally "rational" function. More than poetic maps of form, they grew into icons of mystical power, whose colors and numbers refer to occult systems and whose geometric shapes identify the sacred significances of modernism. Braxton's system as a whole identifies not only structuralist proclivities but the systematic character of mystical thought, which typically observes a micro/macro connection between the particular and the general. Yet as a "certainty" based in mysticism, even

Braxton's spiritualism seems inherently unstable. And he seeks to keep it that way by shrouding the specifics of music's occult potential in a complex of mystical meaning. For, in the end, the art of illusion is Braxton's true center, an ever-changing self whose definition remains elusive much in the same way that the vital force of his musicianship, the phraseology of the improvised line, resists the grasp of analyst and critic.

6 Black Experimentalism as Spectacle

Tentative, unstable, seemingly betwixt and between, jazz in the early 1970s stood at the crossroads, the space of multiple direction that has identified the character of the blues since Robert Johnson.[1] Yet whereas in downhome blues the crossroads symbolized a confrontation with choice, of an either/or, the jazz crossroads offered varieties of indirection, of negation, of neither/nor. Like a mouse on a playwheel, jazz appeared to be circling endlessly, its diversity of paths offering occasional flashes of brilliance that ultimately traced steps to creative dead ends. Epitomizing this condition of flux was Miles Davis, whose nod to the rarefied sound of free jazz and ventures into rock- and funk-based fusion befuddled former admirers. His blur of sounds and styles that preserved at its core the current dance rhythms of a dance-beat people[2] would be dismissed as an act of creative sabotage by those who had once counted on him for mainstream advancement. In fact, Davis *did* have his finger on the music's pulse, as Gary Tomlinson so skillfully argues in "Cultural Dialogics and Jazz."[3] His vast range of stylistic allusions and words of praise for everyone except the stars of jazz—Karlheinz Stockhausen, James Brown, Krzysztof Penderecki, Jimi Hendrix—gave voice to the condition of sociocultural fracture that countered commonsense beliefs in the immutability of genre and style. For this, Davis would be ritualistically sacrificed by the critical and artistic mass, whose violence may explain more about his six-year silence than the hyperbole about creative, physical, and psychological collapse.[4]

1. Houston A. Baker, Jr., *Blues, Ideology, and Afro-American Literature: A Vernacular Theory* (Chicago: University of Chicago Press, 1984).

2. Albert Murray, *Stomping the Blues* (New York: Da Capo, 1976).

3. Tomlinson, "Cultural Dialogics and Jazz: A White Scholar Signifies," *Black Music Research Journal* 11:2 (Fall 1991): 229–64.

4. For reference to Stockhausen et al., see Jack Chambers, *Milestones 2: The Music and Times of Miles Davis since 1960* (Toronto: University of Toronto Press, 1983), 136, 281. Davis's illnesses and complications related to an inherited malady, sickle-cell anemia. Too often, commentators preferred to refer to his early addiction to heroin. Rhythmically, Davis had let the cat out of James Brown's [Papa's got a] "brand new bag," the

In fairness, the critiques of Davis appeared to displace concerns of a more general nature: most observers seemed personally offended not so much by his irreverent parodies as by what they implied about the fate of jazz. If Davis, the consummate trendsetter, the strategist of two, if not three, major styles, could find nothing new to say, how would the music proceed? Aging mainstreamers and young players seduced by rock and pop certainly could not be counted on; nor would the anarchic expressions of loft-based free jazz reestablish a steady course, particularly after the death of its mainstream mediator, John Coltrane. As noted in chapter 4, worrisome comment appeared frequently during the early part of the 1970s as writers cast their votes, pro and con, about the life expectancy of jazz. Titles alone voiced a yearning for stylistic specificity. "Is Jazz Coming Back?" queried Joel Vance, who read the surfeit of releases and reissues as an indication of decline. "Only time will tell," Ian Kendall seemed to reply in his nostalgic look at the successes of the past. And while William Anderson appeared fatalistic as he offered a final "reprise for jazz," others tried to make sense of the aesthetic potpourri by tackling head-on the ontological question, "What Is Jazz?"[5]

In the midst of this soul-searching and public rankling, the institu-

---

latter a reconceptualization as profound as Coltrane's *Ascension* (1965). Davis's revitalization of black vernacular rhythmic impulses, together with his disregard for the historical significance of standard discographical information (replacing personnel information on *On the Corner* with Corky McCoy's cartoon celebration of black street life), represented a powerful expression of resistance against the classicizing, fact-keeping sensibilities of official jazz culture.

5. Vance, "Is Jazz Coming Back?" *Stereo Review* (September 1972), 28–29; Kendall, "Only Time Will Tell," *Jazz and Blues* (October 1972), 14–15; Anderson, "A Reprise for Jazz?" *Stereo Review* (July 1974), 6; "What Is Jazz? Advent of Rock Puts New Sound in Old Groove," *Variety* (December 4, 1974), 56. See also Gilbert Easter, "So, What Is Jazz? A Mainstream View of the Avant-Garde," *Jazz and Blues* (June 1972), 25; Leonard Feather, "The Jazz Gap," *Down Beat* (March 2, 1972), 1; Ralph J. Gleason, "Perspectives: Nothing New under the Sun?" *Rolling Stone* (March 16, 1972), 30. In 1970 (1): 34–41, *American Music Digest* presented excerpts of several recently published essays referring directly to the sense of loss after Coltrane's death. The essay featured a photo of the late spirit of jazz (lifted from his "sacred" album, *Love Supreme*) positioned catty-cornered to a sketch of a tombstone with the epitaph, "Jazz, Down-and-Out?" In 1974, moreover, the year that Braxton appeared on the American scene, musicians and reviewers were still remarking about a creative decline, usually at the expense of free jazz. See, for example, Jon Hendricks, "Perspective," *Down Beat* (January 17, 1974), 30; Jim Schaffer, "Buddy [Rich] Raps About . . . ," *Down Beat* (April 11, 1974), 12–14, 32–33, 39; Bob Ness, "Have You Dug . . . Larry Coryell," *Down Beat* (May 9, 1974), 16, 34; Karl Macek, "Jazz, Hindsight or Foresight," *Music Journal* (September 1974), 48.

tions of official culture worked against the odds to reestablish a sense of coherence of genre and style. The key lay in identifying a figure of consensus, an artist who might consolidate the various streams of innovation and give new legitimacy to the popular cyclic theories of musical change and consolidation. While some observers turned to the legacy of Davis's influence—Keith Jarrett, Herbie Hancock, Chick Corea, Wayne Shorter—others ultimately placed their bets on one of the most unlikely candidates, Anthony Braxton. Returning from Europe in 1974 to join forces with Clive Davis's newly fashioned label, Arista Records, Braxton would, in the course of a year, be transformed from an obscure jazz vanguardist to the designer of a refurbished mainstream—a star who would recast the uncertainties of the past into a formula for new creative direction. No doubt Braxton's appeal related, in good measure, to his remarkable skills as an improviser and composer. Yet what really seemed to set him apart from the others was an ability to reflect creatively the uncertainties that typified the postmodern moment. From the expanses of his philosophical system to the details of his saxophone style, Braxton gave voice to the puzzling pastiche of 1970s style and culture. Significantly, he did this while also sidestepping his associations with 1960s vanguardism, frequently by calling into question the legitimacy of total musical "freedom." As a tradition-centered synthesist, he would, according to the critical view, make sense of the anarchy of the recent past by redefining it aesthetically in the context of the mainstream. In order to enhance the image of stylistic coherence, moreover, publicists attenuated the radicalism of Braxton's signifying art by shifting attention to more superficial matters. By centralizing the most diverting characteristics of Braxton's personality and creativity, they would shape a public image that on the surface celebrated pluralistic excess while maintaining a conventional center that reinforced traditional ideas about jazz. The idiosyncrasies of the caricature would, in turn, help to sell a hyperbolic story of "controversy" that supported promotional goals while matching claims of his larger-than-life importance.

Since the establishment of the modern discipline of cultural criticism, students of mass culture have recognized that public images regulate, if not determine, artistic meaning: the manufacture of media symbols sets the limits of public response as it reinforces the ideologies from which they arise. Despite their private, real-life personalities, public figures appear in the context of the mass media as little more than images—"signs"—whose meanings can be "read" as the critic reads a text. From this perspective, interpretation of value becomes less an isolated study of form than an analysis of the way in which pop

Anthony Braxton performing on alto saxophone at the Rising Sun, Montreal, in the mid- to late 1970s. Photo courtesy Bill Smith.

icons embody a diversity of culturally symbolic meanings. The most popular and enduring stars—Frank Sinatra, Elvis Presley, Bruce Springsteen—resonate with the impulses most central to a culture, collapsing into a single image an assemblage of views and associations.

In jazz, however, such realizations have, for the most part, escaped serious critical notice, possibly because of writers' assumptions about—and equally likely, identifications with—its marginality and aesthetic "purity." Whether originating on the plantation or field, in the ghetto or after-hours club, jazz seems to have "survived" as a cloistered Other whose primitive soul transcends the trivialities of modern mass culture. This myth has endured tenaciously and despite a historical association between artist and media since Paul Whiteman first assumed the throne as "King of Jazz." To be sure, mediated images have helped to popularize many leading artists: Benny Goodman, the severe jazz egghead; Artie Shaw, the rags-to-riches Hollywood charmer; Charlie Parker, the bestial musical savant. With the expansion of corporate control over cultural production, these images grew subtler as their importance increased. Engaging images not only vitalized the careers of postwar artists (Dave Brubeck, Ornette Coleman, John Coltrane), but their styles as well. Cool became the double-edged sign of forbidden fruits (narcotics, sex) and hip sophistication; soul jazz, the proto-nationalist challenge to white control; free jazz, the sound of primitive, black rage.[6] In the 1970s, moreover, when the integrity of style seemed all but shot, images began to lose the artistic underpinning on which they had been formerly based. As a result, publicists representing Braxton relied exceedingly on image over artistry as they crafted a star whose musical expression played a crucial, albeit secondary, supporting role. Echoing Braxton's own postmodern intermediations, the jazz community constructed a multimediated spectacle that celebrated confusion and fracture couched in the conventionality of a mainstream stylist. Braxton became a homology of discrete im-

6. The equation of drugs and jazz musicians appeared commonly in the press during the 1950s. Examples include "Dope Menace Keeps Growing," *Down Beat* (November 17, 1950), 10; L. Hallock, "Dope: The Shameful U.S. Jazz Record," *Melody Maker* (December 20, 1952), 3; S. Race, "Clean up the Profession," *Melody Maker* (September 17, 1955), 7. In a later report, moreover, references to drugs (Buddy Rich) and violence (Miles Davis) supported a coy, reproving headline, "Days in the Lives of Our Jazz Superstars," *Down Beat* (April 16, 1970), 11. The headline appears below a photograph of Louis Armstrong (supporting the prior article), whose use of marijuana was well known. Furthermore, evocations of black power and the noble savage frequently informed free-jazz reports, such as A. B. Spellman, "Revolution in Sound: Black Genius Creates a New Music in Western World," *Ebony* (August 1969), 84–89. How *Ebony*'s black readership received this is open to question.

ages, a centered artist made up of the decentered pastiche of the postmodern. As such, he embodied the fetishized character of the image itself: by playing out the role of the new star in an assemblage of current and historical stereotypes, Braxton, as David Harvey writes, activated the "aura of authority and power" to give official culture a means of "reestablish[ing] the . . . authority of its institutions."[7]

Braxton's ambitious efforts to draw public notice to the range of his art exacerbated the growth of spectacle and confusion about the true character of his work. On the surface, he seemed quite effectively to be contributing to his own parody by publicizing the most exotic qualities of his art and aesthetics. Yet beneath the literal comment, his actions suggested a kind of signifying subversion. By assuming the role of the eccentric, of jazz-music's cerebral comic or clown, Braxton sought to undermine the interpretive power and, as a result, the legitimacy of official media. Like other "controversial" black artists—Little Richard, "Screaming" Jay Hawkins, Jimi Hendrix, Public Enemy's Flavor Flav—Braxton, in the words of Hal Foster, "opted to play the fool, often in a canny way." That role, as Foster explains, can have a riotous effect: "If artful, the court jester is rewarded by the king; and if very artful, he may even conspire against him."[8] By fulfilling the contradictory (yet equally alienated) images of the primitive and intellectual while assuming simultaneously the role of stylistic leader, Braxton helped the community to sell an exciting yet nonetheless aesthetically secure vision of the music in magazines, over the air, and on record. At the same time, by constantly shifting the particularities of his image, he could dance around critics' defining efforts while parodying the supposed integrity of jazz as a historical genre. As soon as he retreated musically from this formula, the "noise" of his purportedly mainstream artistry revealed itself, leading to the collapse of the image as well as the version of jazz it supported.

I

The falsity of the press characterizations appears most blatant in coverage prior to Braxton's ascension within the popular ranks. While known among writers in the 1970s for his radical deconstructions of jazz practice, Braxton was hardly at the center of controversy; aside from passing comment in "Blindfold Tests" and polls for minor tal-

7. David Harvey, *The Condition of Postmodernity* (Oxford: Basil Blackwell, 1989), 287–88.

8. Foster, *Recodings: Art, Spectacle, Cultural Politics* (Seattle: Bay Press, 1985), 52.

ents, he received, at best, occasional notice, and almost always with reference to his respectable associations with the AACM and Chick Corea. Occasionally, however, the peculiarities of Braxton's creative complex would confound writers, revealing their potential as sources of spectacle. In a review of Braxton's 1972 performance at Town Hall, for example, John S. Wilson balanced references to Braxton's most visible achievements with glib comment about his unorthodox style and procedures. As "a prominent member of Chicago's jazz avant-garde," Braxton gained credibility as he would for his "very capable [skills as a] jazz alto saxophonist in the context of Chick Corea's group, Circle." Yet as he reinforced the image of the saxophone master, Wilson also underscored Braxton's ties with the "unmusical" practices taking place in New York's lofts. Equally troubling for Wilson were the titles in the program, which reinforced the rarefied character of the performance. To him, the titular "diagrams consisting of letters and numbers . . . were as obscure as the music produced."[9] Barry McRae, on the other hand, sought to limit Braxton's associations with the most anarchic forms of free jazz by more actively stressing images of continuity and order. After positioning Braxton against the background of Chicago innovators since Earl Hines, McRae discussed a recent release, Circle's *Paris Concert,* with specific reference to Braxton's performance on *Duet.* The improvisation, McRae argued, was "very typical of [the style of] the present Chicago jazz scene,"a questionable assertion that nonetheless reinforced continuities with Braxton's Chicago past.[10] Images of continuity could even appear in the mechanics of the analysis itself. Searching for a method to a seemingly musical madness, McRae explained in a Braxtonesque literary style how "motivic particles assembled at random [assumed] a logical progression." According to Barry Tepperman, however, Braxton, despite his roots, had transcended categorization. As "the most intensely eloquent alto voice to emerge from the Chicago pressure-cooker of new jazz," he embodied the music's new direction. "Each generation in the music produces only one genius of this magnitude," Tepperman explained, and "Anthony Braxton is such a genius."[11]

9. Wilson, "Braxton Performs on Alto Saxophone," *New York Times* (May 24, 1972), 1:55. Wilson's comment about "the ridiculousness of gasping shrieks and squeals" seemed remarkably genteel after more than a decade of free activity. Furthermore, it would appear that he was unfamiliar with previously published examples of Braxton's titles on album jackets.

10. McRae, "Avant Courier," *Jazz Journal* (London) (December 1972), 20–21.

11. Tepperman, "Heard and Seen: Anthony Braxton," *Coda* (September/October

The images appearing in these brief reports identify the underlying themes that would later work to establish Braxton's reputation. As a saxophonist with undeniable roots in cultural nationalism and free jazz, Braxton played the character of the unpredictable black radical, whose art echoed 1960s challenges of "primitive" rage. As the inventor of arcane titles and "highly formal . . . chamber performance[s],"[12] however, he assumed the contrasting role of the austere, intellectual Other. At his most spectacular, Braxton would combine images of the clinician and tribal priest, becoming its composite: the mad scientist of jazz.[13] As a counterpoint to these sensational images, moreover, publicists promoted the paradoxical claim that Braxton's art held the potential to recenter the growth of jazz. By treating his theosophy and aesthetics as (black) comedy, they trivialized oppositional elements in order to advance the familiar theme of progress; titles and theories were merely playful antics that cloaked a form of rough-and-ready jazz. The intimidating presence of the creative music system would, then, be passed off as romantic excess even as it supplied an essential journalistic hook to draw listeners back to jazz.

A key article published in February 1974 served to flesh out the dimensions of Braxton's image as it revealed further his potential as the new jazz star. In a two-page interview appearing in *Down Beat,* Ray Townley ably worked the exotic extremes of Braxton's creativity in a masterful juxtaposition of oppositional imagery. In the lead paragraph, Townley set the basis for his essay by establishing the sensationalistic critical formula of a racialist/intellectual homology. Evoking an image of Braxton's stage appearance, Townley described an artist "walk[ing] onto the dimly lit stage, his fuzzy hair evincing the strands of the absent-minded professor." By melding "black" references (ambience, hair type) to the stereotype of the academic nerd, Townley constructed a figurative composite of two familiar American outcasts. Moving on, he continued to work this peculiar mix in a series of dramatic juxtapositions: the primitive artist with "prominent forehead" engaged in serious, "thoughtful contemplation"; the alienated, black "intellectual . . . alone on stage, [who] lifts the horn to his lips as *natu-*

1973), 43–44. Tepperman reviewed Braxton's performance at Toronto's St. Clair Music Library on June 16, 1973.

12. McRae, "Avant Courier," *Jazz Journal.*

13. Kevin Lynch writes: "If a mad scientist ever drank a potion he had concocted to formulate a 'jazz musician,' he would undoubtedly transform into Anthony Braxton." "Record Reviews: Anthony Braxton, Solo Live at Moers Festival," *Coda* (February 1978), 18.

rally [emphasis added] as he would take a drag from his [marijuana-filled?] oom-pah [*sic*] pipe." In subsequent paragraphs, moreover, Townley elaborated on these images, which, as oppositions, served to reinforce the surface theme of musical diversity. Quoting liberally, he described Braxton's account of the "mathematical . . . language system," his work as a musical "scientist," his compositional methods involving "weight shifts," his opinions of various modernist composers. Diverse images of exotica were then counterpoised to his potential as a jazz innovator. At once, Braxton emerged as the creator of arcane solo works that could be likened to the masterpieces of Bach; the down-to-earth jazz improviser, who, according to an unnamed critic, would replicate the command of Coltrane in the 1970s. Ultimately, Townley took the images of diversity to a comical extreme by assembling an outlandish pastiche of Braxton's eclectic interests. Parade music, serialism, and his work for one hundred tubas appeared against "pet metaphysical theories" and references to the "notorious" picture titles, as Townley fashioned an image of a playful, if eccentric, intellectual clown. In a final paragraph, he gathered these images into a lavish display, boiled down to this exotic equation:

> Anthony Braxton's world revolves around three systematic and calculating realms: mathematics, music, and chess. When he not [*sic*] computing or conceptualizing his music, he's sitting alone, across from a chessboard, pondering his next move. He could just as well be shifting weights or cataloging sounds. Or standing alone on a dimly lit stage, manipulating his saxophone keys.[14]

As if to counter *Down Beat*'s parody, *Coda,* a modest Toronto-based magazine oriented to free jazz, devoted the bulk of its April 1974 issue to a celebration of Braxton's art. The issue was largely the work of *Coda*'s art director, Bill Smith, whose featured centerpiece, an 8,000-word interview, represented a personal triumph: "the most important document that I have been personally responsible for."[15] Smith's enthusiasm clearly stemmed from his unbridled admiration for the artist. According to Smith, Braxton was not just another stylist, but "the new high priest" whose lavish experimentalism would chart the course to the next musical era. Echoing the predictions of Townley's unnamed critic, Smith declared Braxton to be the music's creative savior or perhaps even something more: through his art, "jazz music has reached yet another high plain, a level that lifts it above all else."[16]

14. Townley, "Anthony Braxton," *Down Beat* (February 1974), 12–13.
15. Smith, "Anthony Braxton: Saxophone Improvisations Series F; Town Hall 1972; Trio; The Complete Braxton," *Coda* (April 1974), 15–16.
16. Smith, "Anthony Braxton" [record review], *Coda,* 15–16.

In the closing paragraph of his review of Braxton's recent releases, Smith presented this litany to the jazz masses:

> He is here, playing, just waiting for you to listen. He knows already what he is, and presents these opportunities for you to discover who you are. It does not matter if your likes are Johnny Hodges, Lester Young, Bird, Ornette or Trane, for Anthony Braxton is the present account of that lineage. He is THE one. So take it now, don't wait like you did with all the others, for ten years to pass. His music is pure and accessible, it's real and if it does not reach your ears/head/heart then it is you who will be the poorer.[17]

Casting Braxton as both radical iconoclast and the progeny of past greats, Smith created a portrait of the artist in terms that would appeal to mainstream sensibilities as it gave new legitimacy to the beleaguered free movement. Free jazz, in its revised form, would divest itself from an earlier vanguardist agenda in order to reestablish the progressivist impulses of modernism and the swing/bop/hard-bop continuity. The oppositional strategies of the "language system" and, indeed, Braxton's own proclamations of resistance—"I'm not a jazz musician"—represented, according to Smith, not so much a departure as a new, improved version of the original.[18] To support this essentialist proposition, Smith presented a detailed account of Braxton's roots in black music, his eclectic jazz and pop background, and his favorite jazz musicians and saxophonists. In an extended discussion of Braxton's music and aesthetics, moreover, Smith challenged Townley's comedic sketch by underscoring the complexity and sophistication of his views of the arts. The accompanying discography helped further to establish Braxton's credibility as a jazz-centered performer, even while the peculiar details of his oppositional art conveyed, at least for some, the impression of a black iconoclast masquerading as an intellectual.

Other essays from the period expressed similar enthusiasm for Braxton's recasting of jazz against the background of an assimilated free style. In a five-star (excellent) rating of *Four Compositions 1973,* Ray Townley noted that "Braxton has entered a new, and more harmonious phase" marked by "uncommon popular accessibility." As both saxophonist and a clarinetist, he had become "a leading exponent . . . [to] be reckoned with."[19] Similarly, Will Smith recognized in the *Town Hall* recording "a tremendous breakthrough" in Braxton's art, for which he was awarded additional kudos. "Gone are the occa-

17. Ibid.

18. Smith, "Anthony Braxton Interview," *Coda,* 2.

19. Townley, "Anthony Braxton: Four Compositions (1973)," *Down Beat* (April 11, 1974), 22.

sional flights of aimlessness" attributable to "his involvement with the European 'new music' syndrome." Braxton had, in musical terms, come home, "saying things uniquely, directly, and with emotional purity."[20] Coming home stylistically did not, then, hinder innovation; indeed, Braxton had captured the attention of North American writers precisely because he had managed to strike a balance between freedom and control, thus maintaining the formally conservative nature of pre-1960s jazz. While posing "a challenge [for the listener] to reconsider all one's tacit assumptions about music," he remained "a major soloist" who had unified jazz from Armstrong to Ayler.[21] Put simply by *Melody Maker*'s Steve Lake, "Braxton's an iconoclast, absolutely, but with a love for jazz's tradition and heritage. That's what makes him the giant he is."[22]

From the indications on record, it certainly appeared as if Braxton had, from a conservative perspective, "gotten serious" about art and finally learned to play jazz the way it's supposed to be played. The bulk of favorable comment focused on Braxton's small-group recordings, which featured a jazz-oriented (solo/rhythm accompaniment) performance style and the talents of a revolving core of jazz artists. The likes of Dave Holland, Barry Altschul, Jerome Cooper, and Kenny Wheeler seemed to have reestablished jazz at the center of Braxton's art, a "breakthrough" about which a fraternity of writers, whose tastes had been shaped in bop and postbop, were delighted. From Braxton's perspective, however, the music for quartet and quintet was hardly a center, but merely a means by which he could support his newlywed wife, Nickie, and later a family. While he enjoyed the music, he has explained in interviews that he would have preferred to commit his time to composition and music for concert ensembles. This distinction is important, for it reveals a fundamental way in which Braxton's aesthetic would be translated. With the quartet music as the centerpiece, all else—the solo improvisations, concert music, picture titles, theories—could be interpreted as superficial background. Braxton's mediated images had now assumed a hierarchy, with continuity and accessibility positioned front and center and appearances challenging this construct relegated to the rear. By foregrounding accessibility

20. Smith, "Anthony Braxton: Town Hall 1972" and "Saxophone Improvisations Series F," *Down Beat* (June 20, 1974), 18. Townley awarded five stars to the former, three and a half to the latter.

21. Barry Tepperman, "Heard and Seen: Anthony Braxton," *Coda* (November 1974), 37–38; Barry McRae, "Lookout Form," *Jazz Journal/Jazz and Blues* (August 1974), 19.

22. Lake, "Jazz Records: Anthony Braxton," *Melody Maker* (July 27, 1974), 49.

against a dressed-up spectacle of "controversy," mainstream institutions would supply the means for selling Braxton to the public when he literally came home to head Arista's lineup, "The Art Form of Contemporary Jazz."

II

Founded in 1974 by Clive Davis, former president of Columbia Records, Arista was cast in the image of cultural diversity as if to celebrate the fragmentation and stasis of the times. Maintaining his past strategy at Columbia, Davis sought to develop broad stylistic representation as other labels—including Columbia, which had dismissed him in 1973—were making moves toward consolidation.[23] Arista would gather under its wing an impressive roster of artists who had each forged highly individual expressions. Together they would, in Davis's words, make Arista and its Columbia Pictures parent "the hallmark of originality"[24] For Davis, "originality" seemed to define glamour as much as the aura of integrity as he worked to create a circle of performers that might match the prestige of Janis Joplin, Sly Stone, Bruce Springsteen, and other Columbia celebrities. Former pop icons such as Eric Andersen and Dionne Warwick (and later, Aretha Franklin) were resurrected to appear alongside the budding stars Barry Manilow and Melissa Manchester; established rock groups—the Kinks, the Grateful Dead—stood in contrast to new FM-oriented bands, including the Outlaws and the more experimental innovators, Patti Smith, Lou Reed, and Graham Parker. Deeply sensitized to the importance of image, moreover, Davis sought to add to this list a jazz component that might enhance Arista's appearance of sophistication while reminding listeners of his past successes as a promoter of black music, notably his publicized backing of Miles Davis's venture into fusion.[25] Hiring

23. While Davis was officially dismissed for misuse of company funds, Richard A. Peterson and David G. Berger imply a link with his business approach. See "Cycles in Symbol Production: The Case of Popular Music," *American Sociological Review* 40 (1975), rep. in *On Record, Rock, Pop, and the Written Word,* ed. Simon Frith and Andrew Goodwin (New York: Pantheon, 1990). The ability to maintain a diverse lineup during a phase of retrenchment suggests a break from an earlier cycle in which major corporate control of the market typically reflected stylistic homogeneity. For the Columbia view, see Chet Flippo, "Arista's Clive Davis: From out of the Middle," *Rolling Stone* (December 18, 1975), 24.

24. Ted Fox, *In the Groove: The People behind the Music* (New York: St. Martin's Press, 1986), 221. Arista grew out of Columbia Pictures' faltering Bell Records. See Flippo, "Arista's Clive Davis," *Rolling Stone.*

25. Chris Albertson, "Avant-Garde Jazz Finds an Unexpected Outlet on the Arista

Steve Backer to manage the jazz series, he secured for the label a respected producer and promoter who had most recently refurbished ABC's Impulse jazz line. Granted an unusual degree of autonomy for a producer of jazz, Backer constructed a lineup that matched the diversity of Arista's image: "I'm going to deal with the entire spectrum of modern jazz," he explained, "from bop to avant-garde, including all the current fusions."[26] In fact, one suspects that Backer's chief role was that of the promoter and publicist: he would be charged with finding performers who, with limited investment, would help to distinguish Arista from main-line labels while reinforcing Davis's own "controversial" image.[27] Such reasoning might explain why he chose Braxton as his challenger for the title as leader of the jazz world.

Recognizing the inaccessibility of some of Braxton's early recordings, Backer devised a plan that would nurture his star potential by easing his way into the commercial market. He advised Braxton to prepare short, accessible works for his first albums, highlighting his quartet music. He also stipulated conditions that would encourage radio stations to play the recordings on the air. In an interview with Michael Ullman, Backer described the formula that would situate mainstream jazz at the heart of Braxton's developing reputation:

> There are things that not every artist is aware of. For instance, when you record for a major label and play one twenty-minute piece on each side, there is nothing that will be played on the radio. Even the sequencing can turn off a lot of radio people. If you start with more difficult material, the guy who listens to the albums at a station will never listen to the whole album to find the more accessible cut. [So we asked Braxton to] deal with time and meter

---

Label," *Stereo Review* (August 1975), 90–91. According to Cynthia Kirk, Manchester and Manilow were holdovers from Bell Records. See Kirk, "Ariola to Buy Arista from Columbia," *Variety* (August 1, 1979), 65, 71; Clive Davis with James Willwerth, *Clive: Inside the Record Business* (New York: Ballantine, 1974); for a different perspective, see also Nelson George, *The Death of Rhythm & Blues* (New York: E. P. Dutton, 1988), 141–42.

26. "Backer Pacts with Davis," *Down Beat* (November 21, 1974), 8.

27. The reference to Davis as "controversial" appeared in Flippo, "Arista's Clive Davis," *Rolling Stone*. New artists would include the Brecker Brothers, John Scofield, John Klemmer, and Michael Gregory Jackson. Much of the initial material by the likes of Cecil Taylor, Gato Barbieri, Marion Brown, and Albert Ayler had appeared before on Alan Bates's English label, Black Lion/Freedom. See Albertson, *Stereo Review* (August 1975); Fred Bouchard, "Steve Backer Maneuvers in the Front Line," *Down Beat* (March 1980), 31–32, 65; Steve Lake, "I Made More Money at Chess than at Music," *Melody Maker* (October 11, 1975), 48; Michael Ullman, "Steve Backer," in *Jazz Lives: Portraits in Words and Pictures* (Washington, D.C.: New Republic Books, 1980; Perigee, 1982), 215–22.

[on the first albums]. Then we were able to make more people in the jazz community embrace his music. And then we went to the big band album that dealt with time also. . . . From there Braxton went into various stretched-out, open-ended free improvisational approaches.[28]

An examination of Braxton's first releases shows that Backer's production guidelines were followed precisely. On the first album, *New York Fall 1974,* Backer, together with producer Michael Cuscuna, positioned six seven-minute compositions—a duration suited for airplay—to highlight his most accessible compositions. On side one, they featured two bop-oriented works, compositions *23B* and *23D,* which highlighted Braxton's skills as an improviser. The lead track, *Composition 23B,* is as rhythmically intense as it is dramatic: good bait for a radio station's music programmer. Positioned in the middle is *Composition 23C,* the "minimalist" work based on a rich and varied melodic palette. On side two, the producers placed works that require greater effort for the listener to comprehend: *Composition 38A* for clarinet and synthesizer (performed with Richard Teitelbaum) and *Composition 23A,* an alternative form, scored for trumpet, violin, contrabass clarinet, and bass. While perhaps a challenge to the standard jazz format, these works, which highlighted a pleasant assortment of rich sound-colors and inventive textures, most likely appealed to pop-oriented listeners accustomed to the static sound fields of fusion, rock jams, and "new age" music. And because the tracks are relatively short, they could be tolerated by those who disliked them. The most accessible work on the side, *Composition 37* for saxophone quartet, is predictably the longest, lasting more than eight minutes. It, together with the others, appeared in a jacket graced with a handsome picture of Braxton as jazz professor, smoking his pipe. On the back, picture titles adorned a whimsical, translucent image of the artist, cast saintlike, skirting along a wooded terrain. Later albums demonstrated similar promotional care: *Five Pieces 1975* is stylistically similar to his first album, employing as a lead track the jazz standard *You Stepped out of a Dream. Duets 1976* with Muhal Richard Abrams, which includes compositions in a free style, highlights the more accessible works, such as Eric Dolphy's *Miss Ann,* which leads the first side, and Scott Joplin's *Maple Leaf Rag,* featured on the second.

Arista's style controls and packaging worked. By gearing the albums for radio and by eliminating performances that listeners might find repellent, the label set the stage for the rise of its new jazz star.

28. Ullman, "Steve Backer," *Jazz Lives,* 220. The book also includes an essay on Braxton.

Supported by massive distribution and a half-page ad celebrating "Braxton. A new name half the world already knows," *New York Fall 1974* moved quickly up the jazz charts. According to national playlists published in *Radio Free Jazz,* Braxton's early Arista recordings (1975–1977) ranked in the "top-ten" category five times.[29] These rankings were fueled by the profound increase in press reports—most of which were exceedingly positive—appearing in North American and British magazines.[30] As critics showered Braxton with praise, his record sales climbed, reaching 20,000—an impressive figure for a jazz-oriented artist.[31] At that moment Arista released *Creative Orchestra Music 1976,* which in 1977 won *Down Beat*'s critics' award for best album. After subsequent releases further reinforced Braxton's jazz affiliation, Backer permitted him to expand his offerings with albums—recorded, Braxton contends, mostly at his own expense—from his concert-music repertory.

III

The promotional achievements of Arista's marketing team inspired a closer look at the details of Braxton's personality and opinions. Aesthetics and tastes that had previously received only passing notice now appeared in full view, to be scrutinized by the jazz public. Two of the most conspicuous commentaries from the Arista period appeared as liner notes to Braxton's initial releases, *New York Fall 1974* and *Five Pieces 1975*. In the first, Bill Smith took advantage of the forum to advance *Coda*'s brand of advocacy journalism. In a pledge of "privilege to be witnessing" the drama of Braxton's music, he underscored the continuity theme that had appeared in previous essays. Situating the artist against the background of the AACM and the likes of Parker and Coleman, Smith repeated for a mass audience his claim that Braxton "[had] supplied the continuation of the [jazz] lineage." As he encompassed the totality of bop and postbop, Braxton realized continuity in its all-consuming completeness; he was, Smith reasserted, "the most complete musician in this period of American music."

Robert Palmer, on the other hand, applauded Braxton's work without making claims about its ultimate importance. He seemed most

29. See the airplay lists published in *Radio Free Jazz* from May 1975; January, July, and August 1976; and August 1977. The ad appeared in the same magazine in April 1975.

30. A count of major articles, reviews, and features from 1967 to 1973 totaled around eleven; the total for 1975 to 1977 alone exceeded fifty-six.

31. Ullman, *Jazz Lives,* 219.

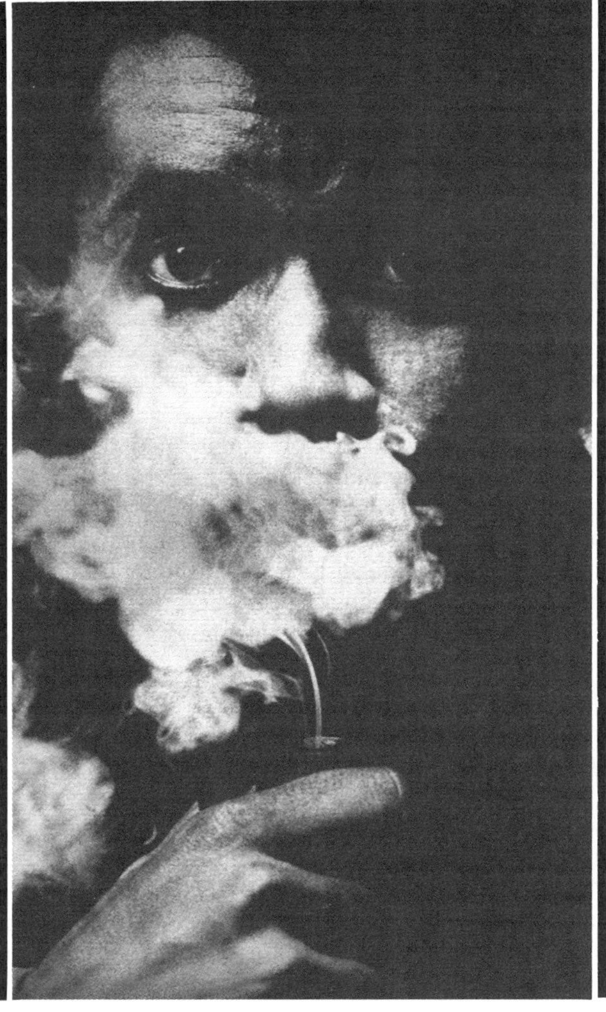

Front cover of the album *Five Pieces 1975*. Courtesy Giuseppe Pino and Arista Records.

concerned with disarming a controversy that had already begun to get out of hand. Mapping out the extremes of the insiders' debate, he began his notes to *Five Pieces 1975* with this:

> I would like to propose now, at the beginning of this discussion, that we set aside entirely the question of the ultimate worth of Anthony Braxton's music.

There are those who insist that Braxton is the new Bird, Coltrane, and Ornette, the three-in-one who is singlehandedly taking the Next Step in jazz. There are others who remain unconvinced. History will decide, and while it is doing so, we should appreciate Braxton's music for its own immediate value.

Attempting to temper the disputes that had animated the jazz community, Palmer proceeded to show that much of the controversy attributed to Braxton related to misunderstandings about his unusual image. Moving from the difficulties of his rhetoric to the unorthodoxy of his appearance—which mixed contrasting references to the fashions of the street ("mutton chops") and suburb (cardigan sweaters)—Palmer sought to demystify the images "that his detractors love to pounce on," to separate matters of style from the substance of an art that he considered important and accessible.[32] Assuming a casual, informal tone, Palmer described the empirical character of the schematic titles as nothing more than "diagram[s] suggesting the kinds of (improvised) things that can happen in [a composition]." Turning to Braxton's interest in concert music, he showed that what had been mistaken for pretense actually developed from a sound knowledge of the modern repertory. Nor did Braxton's concert-music proclivities negate an ability to match the best at playing straight-ahead jazz, a feat that Palmer himself witnessed in an informal session. Yet the recording at hand provided the ultimate proof, as he noted with insistence: "The music is original, thoughtfully conceived, brilliantly executed, and not at all difficult. In fact, compared to a number of works of so-called experimental jazz it is downright old-fashioned."

As a reply to Smith's enthusiasm, Palmer's essay represented an impressive exercise in critical analysis. As an attempt to balance perspective, however, it ultimately had little effect. For what seemed especially to annoy Braxton's "detractors" was the attention that this showy Arista artist had been getting. Now the newly established king of jazz, Braxton gained status at the expense of many equally able, if less adventurous, performers. Worse, his presence might not only redefine the style but perhaps even change the character of the community as a whole. No doubt some observers feared Michael Ullman's speculation that "there are countless teenagers who are cultivating a wide-eyed look, affecting cardigan sweaters, and learning to stutter on the alto sax in order to be like Anthony Braxton."[33] Concerns about the integ-

32. Bob Blumenthal suggests that Braxton's cardigans challenge the "exotic garb of guru-types in a musical world which celebrates styles of non-conformity." "Reedman Anthony Braxton Plays by His Own Rules," *Rolling Stone* (June 2, 1977), 30–31. In the context of jazz, Braxton seemed to be the nonconformist.

33. Ullman, *Jazz Lives,* 214.

rity of the genre and its subculture seemed especially to motivate those few who spoke out against him. In a review of a quartet performance at New York's Bottom Line, for example, Scott Albin seemed most upset about Braxton being "overrated and overpublicized"; similarly, John Storm Roberts appeared to object more to what Braxton represented than what he actually played, castigating him for his "decadent . . . flirt[ations] with Europe" and insisting that he "stop Messiaen about."[34] Furthermore, many of the passing comments that appeared from 1975 to 1979 suggest that much of the confusion stemmed from the observers' vague awareness about what constituted Braxton's music. As in the tale of the blind men and the elephant, journalists and musicians seemed to be pointing in different directions when they remarked about the particulars of the artist's highly elaborate musical complex. As Whitney Balliett referred whimsically to Braxton's "ingenuously egoistic mode: by himself," Chris Albertson argued that *Five Pieces* had avoided the "pretentiousness" of those "high on gimmickry and low on talent";[35] as Art Farmer, in a "Blindfold Test," ridiculed the "musical masturbation" and "abstraction" of *84° Kelvin* (*Montreux/Berlin* 2/1) ("[it] sounds like the soundtrack for a Mr. Magoo short subject"), Robert Palmer suggested that *Creative Orchestra Music 1976* would attract "a wide audience" and ultimately "convince the skeptics";[36] as Gary Giddins criticized the "cute and constipated" indulgences of *Composition 23C* (*New York Fall* 1/2), Michael Zipkin offered high praise for Braxton's performances with Max Roach, which, he argued, "may come as a swinging velvet hammer to his detractors, wont to label him academic, intellectual, dry, etc."[37]

Objections to Braxton's dramatic image and confusion about the true character of a multifaceted art might help partially to explain why the vast majority of writers, while showing enthusiastic support for his

34. Albin, "Caught: Anthony Braxton Quartet," *Down Beat* (March 25, 1976), 41, 48; Roberts, "Anthony Braxton," *Melody Maker* (February 7, 1976), 47.

35. Balliett, "Jazz: New York Notes," *New Yorker* (April 4, 1977), 84–86. Balliett was referring to his work as an unaccompanied saxophonist. Albertson, "Anthony Braxton: Improvisations as Liberated and Fresh as Louis Armstrong's," *Stereo Review* (February 1976), 76. Albertson wrote that "Braxton is not, in fact, a musical revolutionary; what he does is rather tame compared to the output of most of his contemporaries in the field of the so-called 'new music.'"

36. Leonard Feather, "Blindfold Test," *Down Beat* (September 8, 1977), 43; Palmer, "Creative Orchestra Music 1976," *Rolling Stone* (August 12, 1976), 59. The Kelvin work is not identified in Braxton's catalog.

37. Giddins, "Anthony Braxton as Idea Man," *Village Voice* (April 28, 1975), 112; Zipkin, "Record Reviews: Max Roach/Anthony Braxton," *Down Beat* (September 6, 1979), 28.

highly visible efforts on Arista, continued to refer to a mounting "controversy." As "detractors" called into question Braxton's obscure, conspicuous experiments, supporters praised the accessibility of works most commonly available to the American jazz public. Yet such a theory does not explain why, despite high marks in polls and scores of positive reviews, many still felt compelled to "convince the skeptics."[38] Indeed, confusion alone cannot explain the magnitude of the controversy, whose presence stood in contradiction to the overwhelming praise. It would seem more likely that "controversy," in the end, could be attributed directly to the commentary of the journalists themselves. As part of the spectacle, commentators fueled Braxton's undeniably controversial image by exaggerating the magnitude of the debate about his music. Expressing an irony perhaps fitting for such an elusive artist, the *reports* of "controversy" identified the true controversy, one that had been built upon false claims about a "not at all difficult" music. These claims would ultimately shape perceptions of Braxton's art, regardless of style and content, as image and spectacle overwhelmed the reality of form.

IV

In his famous essay about the revolutionary potential of mass media and culture, Walter Benjamin identified the source of hierarchical erosion in the elimination of classical art's ritualistic "aura."[39] As an allusion to the sacred, aura defined the mystification of traditional high culture, which, through the processes of mass mediation and mechanical reproduction, had begun to lose its exclusivity, its integrity, and, ultimately, its position of aesthetic superiority. Extrapolating on Benjamin's prophetic analysis—while often siding with the negative conclusions that Adorno had reached—social theorists have argued more recently that aesthetic aura has not been entirely eliminated but rather eclipsed by the potency of the mass-cultural image.[40] Empowered by the status of corporate capital and high visibility, public im-

38. From 1975 to 1979, Braxton ranked between third and fifth in *Down Beat*'s critics' polls for alto saxophone. In 1977, he also ranked second in the "composer" category. In 1976 and 1977, he placed sixth and fourth respectively in the voting for readers' "Jazz Man of the Year."

39. Benjamin, "The Work of Art in the Age of Mechanical Reproduction" (1936), in *Illuminations,* trans. Harry Zohn (New York: Schocken, 1969).

40. Adorno's response appeared as "On the Fetish Character of Music and the Regression of Listening," in *The Essential Frankfurt School Reader,* ed. Andrew Arato and Eike Gebhardt (New York: Urizen, 1978; Continuum, 1982).

ages of art have acquired a new simulated aura through the "irreality" of the mass-mediated spectacle. The "loss of the real" that critics lament relates to the dominance of commercially generated images, to what Henri Lefebvre calls, in his oft-quoted phrase, an "emptiness filled with signs."[41] In the postmodern era, conventional notions of artistic value have been replaced with "image value," a determination of worth as a commodified sign.[42] Rather than emancipatory, the fractious challenge to traditional hierarchies reveals, in its turn, a hegemonic potential. Despite the loss of unity that invigorated vanguardist and popular arts, "spectacle" describes, according to Guy Debord, "the diplomatic representation of hierarchic society to itself." It is a "laudatory monologue, . . . [an] uninterrupted discourse [of] the existing order."[43]

As the celebrated star of jazz, Anthony Braxton seemed to embody a range of images associated with stability. More than a "three-in-one," he occupied a complex of signs that signified artistic innovation. At the core of the complex, however, there existed only, in Lefebvre's term, "emptiness"; peeling away the images of Braxton's mediated projection, one was left with the peelings themselves. For Braxton's true public self consisted of an assemblage of selves that echoed the mutability of his private musical world.

Comparisons between new artists and innovators of the past have been a staple in jazz writing since the genre was first established in the 1930s. As in most Western arts, in jazz, authority stems from associations with the pantheon, even as artists continually seek to find their own personal voice. Such comparison is perhaps inevitable in any coherent legacy, and particularly in an oral one like jazz, where the musician's artistry is closely linked with that of innovators of the past. In Braxton's case, however, comparisons appeared with such regularity that associations became ambiguous and confused. Hoisted to the center of attention, Braxton inspired an array of comparisons, creating a vivid pastiche of the jazz past. In Braxton, Barry Tepperman heard likenesses to Coltrane, Coleman, Marsh, and Parker, a composite to which John Litweiler added Mitchell and Tristano, Gary Giddins added Konitz, and Chip Stern added Dolphy.[44] Chris Albertson heard

41. Baudrillard, *Simulacres et Simulation* (Paris: Editions Galilée, 1981), 69–76, quoted in Hal Foster, *Recodings: Art, Spectacle, Cultural Politics* (Seattle: Bay Press, 1985), 76; Lefebvre, *Everyday Life in the Modern World* (London: Allan Lane, 1971).

42. Foster, *Recodings,* 92.

43. Debord, *Society of the Spectacle* (Paris: Editions Buchet-Chastel, 1967; Detroit: Black and Red, 1983), numbered paragraphs 23, 24.

44. Tepperman, "Record Reviews: Anthony Braxton New York Fall, 1974," *Coda*

some of the same, while insisting that Braxton had surpassed the innovations of Ayler and Shepp, having created, as his title indicates, "Improvisations as Liberated and Fresh as Louis Armstrong's."[45] For Art Lange, Braxton's duets with Abrams recalled the swing era's Venuti and Lang, while his clarinet playing brought to mind Pee Wee Russell.[46] Whitney Balliett, on the other hand, heard in 1975 an all-encompassing composite: "the best of Coleman and Eric Dolphy and Miles Davis and Benny Carter and Paul Desmond"; by 1977, the composite had lined up behind Carter's influence, now that Braxton had assumed "the same Victorian tone . . . the same high-collared intensity" of the swing composer and multi-instrumentalist.[47] After the release of *Creative Orchestra Music 1976*, moreover, comparisons to big-band composers began to rival the search for Braxton's soloistic precedents. Apart from passing references to Gil Evans and Fletcher Henderson,[48] most writers evoked the name of Ellington as they described Braxton's lush orchestrations. Evocations of "the Duke" also encouraged comparison between Braxton and Harry Carney, Ellington's baritone saxophonist and occasional bass clarinetist.[49] As the artist for whom "the conventional critical system of comparisons just doesn't apply," Braxton seemingly had adopted multiple personalities, becoming what Peter Occhiogrosso called "a sort of archetype" of the tradition-centered contemporary jazz musician.[50]

The conception of Braxton-as-aggregate identifies the "irreality" of his public appearance. By acquiring associations with the legacy of innovators, he became an emblem of its history, its mystique, its larger-than-life presence. The grandeur of the jazz legacy, in turn, encouraged

(June–July 1975), 24–25; Tepperman, "Perspectives on Anthony Braxton," *Jazz Forum* (January 1977), 34–37; Litweiler, "Record Reviews," *Down Beat* (June 5, 1975), 18; Giddins, "Anthony Braxton as Idea Man," *Village Voice;* Giddins, "Anthony Braxton Marches as to Jazz," *Village Voice* (August 30, 1976), 67; Stern, "Kelvin 7666 = Blip Bleep," *Village Voice* (June 11, 1979).

45. Albertson, "Improvisations," *Stereo Review.*

46. Lange, "Record Reviews: Trio and Duet, Duets 1976," *Coda* (February 1978), 18–19.

47. Balliett, "Jazz," *New Yorker* (November 3, 1975); "Jazz: New York Notes," *New Yorker* (April 4, 1977), 84–86.

48. Steve Lake, "I Made More Money," *Melody Maker,* 48; Charles Mitchell, "Record Reviews: Anthony Braxton," *Down Beat* (October 7, 1976), 20; Balliett, "Jazz," *New Yorker* (April 4, 1977).

49. Steve Lake, "Braxton: Curiouser and Curiouser," *Melody Maker* (May 29, 1976), 30.

50. Occhiogrosso, "Anthony Braxton Explains Himself," *Down Beat* (August 12, 1976), 15.

the making of exaggerated claims about his stature and influence. Tossing aside Palmer's caveat, journalists translated the spectacle of historical references into hyperbolic signs of innovation and invention. Braxton, the "genius" and "Renaissance man," who must either "play or die," would be "hailed . . . through no fault of his own," Balliett observed, "as the new messiah."[51] Clusters of accolade, while perhaps meaningful at one level, assumed grand proportions as they piled up one upon the other. If Braxton were "one of the most singular and vibrant musical personalities" of the era, or even, as David Less had suggested, "the premier reedman of the 1970s,"[52] the intensity and repetition of such claims led to the construction of something more. Magnified and exaggerated, Braxton's image grew from one of importance into that of the immortal titan, a jazz version of the mythic romantic artist. He became a creative voice who, from the evidence of a single concert, held promise of recasting the entire history of jazz; he was the performer who alone "could bring about a more thoroughgoing reorganization of the Afro-American art improvisational aesthetic than did Parker, or Coleman, or Coltrane in their times."[53]

As writers reinforced Braxton's associations with the legacy, they also accentuated his radicalism in order to distinguish him from the mundane matters of conventional practice. Difference in the form of transcendence ironically served to underscore his importance to what they felt to be a consistent and coherent tradition. At once, Braxton could be the same as and different from (and thus, superior to) the very best in jazz. Drawing comparison to Coleman, he shared likenesses to Desmond; standing beside Coltrane, he seemed similar to Schoenberg. If Gary Giddins found him "academic" and "intellectualized," John S. Wilson had now heard something "much more readily accessible," particularly when compared to the work of Braxton's former colleagues in the AACM.[54] Sometimes opposing references appeared in the very same report. Conrad Silvert, for example, stated

51. Tepperman, "Heard and Seen," *Coda* (September/October 1973), 43–44; Tepperman, "Record Reviews: Anthony Braxton and Derek Bailey," *Coda* (January–February 1976), 23–24; Peter Rothbart, "Play or Die: Anthony Braxton Interview," *Down Beat* (February 1982), 20–23; Balliett, "Jazz," *New Yorker* (November 3, 1975).

52. Bryan Hunt, "Anthony Braxton: A Space, Toronto," *Coda* (January–February 1976), 33; Less, "Richard Teitelbaum: Record Review," *Down Beat* (October 20, 1977), 29.

53. Hunt, *Coda* (January–February 1976); Tepperman, "Record Reviews, Anthony Braxton New York Fall 1974," *Coda.*

54. Giddins, "Anthony Braxton as Idea Man," *Village Voice;* Wilson, "Braxton Is Nimble as Jazz Musician," *New York Times* (October 9, 1975).

emphatically that Braxton was "one of the very best on the instrument since Parker." Yet on second thought—and apparently with no sense of contradiction—he ultimately stood "closer to Stravinsky and Bartók."[55] For Mikal Gilmore, the saxophonist seemed remarkably "unpretentious" even as he could be "unearthly intimidating," while Occhiogrosso argued that despite "what one reads about Braxton's iconoclastic attitude . . . he appears essentially a traditionalist."[56] Furthermore, the dramatic reach of Braxton's eclecticism accentuated the ambiguity of his character. Diverting references to his interests in voodoo and hieroglyphics, his following in the Soviet Union, and his theories of a "world music juncture" of Japan, Africa, and India suggested that his "jazz" encompassed the totality of known expression. Ranging across the world musical order, Braxton eventually called into question even the constructs of language and race, all the while "acknowledg[ing] the past" and his place, as his album title indicated, *In the Tradition*.[57]

Both the insider and outsider, iconoclast and conservator, voice of darkness and light of reason, Braxton materialized, as the 1970s jazz star, the collapse of certainty that characterizes the postmodern. Like his art and the culture in which it existed, Braxton's image slipped through the cracks of conventional categories and identification. Yet the reality of ambiguity could be smoothed over by contradicting the contradiction, by adapting Braxton to advance the theme of cohesion and order. For as both Dick Hebdige and Stuart Hall have observed, officiators of media "not only record resistance, they 'situate it within the dominant framework of meanings' "—in this case, in the theme of mainstream survival.[58] As the controversial radical working in the

55. Silvert, "Talent in Action: Anthony Braxton," *Billboard* (November 1, 1975), 38.

56. Gilmore, "Anthony Braxton," *Down Beat* (February 10, 1977), 20; Occhiogrosso, "Anthony Braxton Explains Himself," *Down Beat,* 16. For Giddins, Braxton was both the one who "plays jazz as though he were a chemist studying it through a microscope" and the representative of a "neoclassical turn to classic forms . . . in a conservative period of retrenchment." Giddins, "Anthony Braxton Marches as to Jazz," *Village Voice*.

57. Bob Henschen, "Anthony Braxton: Alternative Creativity in this Time Zone," *Down Beat* (February 22, 1979), 18–20; Nathan Leytes, "Braxton, Ganelin Trio Tops in Critics Poll," *Jazz Forum* (February 1974), 14; Mark Weber, "Around the World: Ann Arbor," *Coda* (May–June 1977), 26–29; Smith, "Anthony Braxton Interview," *Coda*.

58. Hebdige, *Subculture: The Meaning of Style* (New York: Methuen, 1979), 94. Hebdige quotes from Stuart Hall's "Culture, the Media, and the 'Ideological Effect,'" in J. Curran et al., eds., *Mass Communication and Society* (London: Edward Arnold, in association with the Open University Press, 1977).

name of the jazz tradition, Braxton would create madness to restore order, as art "cohere[d] in contradiction" to its own message.[59] To celebrate Braxton, then, official culture "made sense" of his challenge, his *noise,* by revising it to fit the themes of a mythology to which it was categorically opposed.

Most central to the image would be fittingly the most ironic: the reference to controversy, which ultimately took on a life of its own, as a figuration that oriented both critical and readerly perception. According to the standard formula, no middle ground existed in the interpretation of the new jazz master: "People seem to love Braxton ardently or shun him completely."[60] As such, he endured life at the center of a perpetual "storm of controversy," the victim of what might be likened to a critical lynching by an always anonymous group of "detractors."[61] As a critical formula, "controversy" provided the dominant hook, a tool of public enticement that kept Braxton a safe distance from the conventions of the everyday even as it contradicted revelations about his "downright old-fashioned" music. Indeed, insistence about Braxton's "accessibility" served as a contradictory, secondary theme that provided coherence to the spectacle in headlines announcing that Braxton would finally "explain himself." In this way, Braxton could subject himself to the "acidic critical comments from his own community," while remaining a fixture in that same community. As the radical spy playing conventional jazz, he advanced the ebb-and-flow model of progress while his champions condemned "those detractors who choose to evaluate his work in their own backyards."[62]

V

In her fascinating book *Gone Primitive,* Marianna Torgovnick argues that the idea of the primitive, once a discrete, autonomous concept, has existed in the twentieth century as a composite of the modern and Other. A powerful trope, it conforms to social need; malleable, it can be crossed to create a "never-never land of false homologies."[63] In the previously cited characterizations of Braxton, two images seemed

59. Hebdige, *Subculture,* 85.

60. Litweiler, "Record Reviews," *Down Beat* (June 5, 1975), 18.

61. Lange, "Record Reviews: For Four Orchestras," *Down Beat* (June 7, 1979), 18.

62. Hunt, "A Space, Toronto," *Coda;* Charles Mitchell, "Record Reviews," *Down Beat* (October 7, 1976), 20.

63. Torgovnick, *Gone Primitive: Savage Intellects, Modern Lives* (Chicago: University of Chicago Press, 1990), 10.

to stand out: the noble black primitive and the natural intellectual or genius. At once Braxton embodied two highly disparate and contrasting personas that could attract and repel (and, as a result, attract again) young jazz audiences. What made this characterization so engaging were the extremes of the imagic contradiction; popular constructions of resistance succeed when they maintain familiarity as they create foreignness and a sense of distance. As a result, they become, as Dick Hebdige writes, "both more and less exotic than they actually are. They are seen to contain both dangerous aliens and boisterous kids, wild animals and wayward pets."[64]

Close scrutiny of the primitive/intellectual homology suggests that the images do not simply exist side by side but share much in common. In the form of the "natural man" (Tarzan) and the ivory-tower scientist (Einstein), for example, they both exercise control over their environments by taking command of mysterious "natural" forces—the jungle; matter invisible to the naked eye. As the noble savage and laboratory researcher, they operate in the realm of mystery and arcane knowledge, becoming, in the popular, *Star Wars*'s Yoda and Mr. Wizard. At the other extreme, the primitive and the intellectual activate negative imagery, representing the dangerous, unpredictable Other. Here, they demonstrate herculean power that threatens to explode out of bounds. They are the Indian savage and Robert Louis Stevenson's Mr. Hyde; the Zulu "head hunter" and Dr. Frankenstein. And at their most spectacular, they translate into the comic: Dr. Who meets the Terminator 2.

In jazz, the construction of the primitive/intellectual homology coincided with a reconsideration of the character of the black artist in postwar America. Contrasting images of respectability and degeneracy, of noble romanticism and black bestiality, came to dominate perceptions as white observers measured the mixed signals epitomizing the jazz artist. Was jazz the classical art of the new "New Negro" or the voice of a subculture built on the illicit and licentious? Was jazz Dave Brubeck or Thelonious Monk? Nat Cole or Billie Holiday? In many cases it seemed to be all of these as leading exponents assumed images that tempered the trivialized characterizations of the past.[65]

64. Hebdige, *Subculture,* 97.

65. Primitive imagery appeared commonly in the early characterizations of jazz and the jazz musician, as evidenced in the texts of Robert Goffin, Hugues Panassié, and Rudi Blesh. Observations of the music against the background of Africa betrayed a questionable association that still characterizes many recent jazz texts. In Blesh's *Shining Trumpets* (1946/1958), for example, the introductory chapter on "black music" argues that "Jazz . . . began not merely as one more form of Negro folk music in America but as a

At the extreme, hokum figures gave way to the likes of John Lewis and Gunther Schuller, as Ellington acquired a new respectability that would ultimately encourage comparisons with European masters.[66] More often, musicians struck a balance between the intellectual artist and the exotic Other, seemingly based on the casting of Charlie Parker as the drug-crazed creative genius victimized by the urban jungle.[67] Likenesses of Parker, the intellectual pagan, appeared in the portraits of Rollins, Coleman, Blakey, Mingus, Weston, Coltrane, and other artists from the 1950s and 1960s who embodied the image of the progressive nourished by natural inspiration from "mother Africa."

Braxton's interests and background seemed ready made for advancing a particularly dramatic version of the primitive/intellectual homology. Balancing interests in the rational and occult, he could perform the roles of the musical scientist and the tribal mystic who kept secret his creative intentions in a set of visual-literary codes. Furthermore, by tempering the cacophony of free while asserting the political potential of music in a semireligious rhetoric, he became the jazz version of the street preacher, evoking images of Reverend Martin Luther King, Jr., John Coltrane, and Malcolm X. Indeed, Braxton represented the supreme anomaly: while possessing the "calculating mind" of an "intellectual," he reinforced traditional images of jazz through his blackness. Despite objections to the contrary, he remained committed to jazz, for after all, he "look[ed] like a jazz musician."[68] To be sure, Braxton would never be treated entirely as a legitimate intellectual no matter how much he might have hoped for and deserved that attribution. While writers would provide space for him to elaborate on his ideas, his references to mathematics and science inevitably sounded peculiar, if not comical and absurd, when read in the context of popular magazines and against the background of his spec-

fusion of all the Negro musics already present here. These . . . all stemmed back more or less completely to an African spirit and technique. Negro creative power, suddenly freed as the Negroes themselves were freed from slavery . . . poured these rich and varied ingredients into his own musical melting pot and added his undying memories of life on the Dark Continent and the wild and tumultuous echoes of dancing, shouting, and chanting" (p. 3).

66. Ellington's revival is frequently attributed to the 1956 performance at Newport. Yet the social context of this revival—the ascendency of a new "New Negro" at the time of integration and the "decadence" of rock 'n' roll—is typically missed.

67. Ralph Ellison, "On Bird, Bird-watching, and Jazz," in *Shadow and Act* (New York: Vintage, 1964, 1972), 221–32.

68. Townley, "Jarman/Braxton: Together Alone," *Down Beat* (January 16,1975), 22, 24; Rafi Zabor, "Funny, You Look Like a Jazz Musician," *Village Voice* (July 2, 1979), 72–73.

tacular image. As Braxton continued to "explain himself," writers incessantly contradicted reason with parody, incorporating rational comment with irrational allusions to Braxton's theosophy, picture titles, and beliefs in the limitations of language. Clearly, Braxton's intellectualism would be carried only as far as it reinforced mainstream suppositions. Beyond that, it served mainly as spectacle, his "scientific detachment," his "logarithmic loquaciousness," and his "arithmetical way of phrasing" exposing what most thought him to be: "the Buckminster Fuller of jazz."[69]

"Go[ing] back to Africa [to] jump to Mars," as Braxton put it in one of his more outlandish public statements, writers situated the artist at the helm of stylistic advancement by relying on images that seemed to confound the very idea of continuity and tradition.[70] Yet the stereotypes—the primitive as tribal priest, the intellectual as astronomical explorer—served, like the controversy itself, to enhance the theme of tradition and aesthetic hierarchy. Having ascended from the "jungle" of black Chicago and the "fairly militant" AACM,[71] Braxton tempered the savage roots of free jazz as he relied on them for new direction. Evoking images of primitive mysticism and science, he took control of the crucible of black power—"create, destroy, create"—for a legitimate end: to advance jazz as high art.[72] In the archetypal "downhome" of ancient Africa, moreover, Braxton found his true roots in a past that ultimately linked with the other Otherness of the future. As a kind of postmodern noble savage, he resisted primitive desires "to kill someone in the audience" and, restraining the "decadent" character of the black beast, he operated naturally and free, "play[ing] by his own rules" in the timeless space that integrated past and future.[73] Indeed, freedom became central to Braxton's image despite his commitment to structure as a performing musician. Advancing a radical, "alternative creativity," free from the laws of jazz, of language, of swing, he readjusted rhythmic procedures according to a mystical "vibrational" structure.[74] Braxton's recasting of rhythmical

69. Respectively: Giddins, "Riffs: Anthony Braxton Marches as to Jazz," *Village Voice;* Stern, "Kelvin 7666 = Blip Bleep," *Village Voice;* Balliett, "Jazz," *New Yorker* (November 3, 1975); Stern, "Kelvin 7666."

70. Townley, "Anthony Braxton," *Down Beat* (February 14, 1974), 13.

71. Steve Lake, "I Made More Money at Chess," *Melody Maker,* 48.

72. Howard Mandel, "Caught: Anthony Braxton/Muhal Richard Abrams," *Down Beat* (August 11, 1977), 41, 43.

73. Eugene Chadbourne, "Anthony Braxton, University Theatre, University of Toronto," *Coda* (January/February 1976), 45; Blumenthal, "Reedman Anthony Braxton Plays by His Own Rules," *Rolling Stone* (June 2, 1977): 30–31.

74. Occhiogrosso, "Braxton Explains Himself," *Down Beat.*

freedom suggested a rethinking of a fundamental impulse of African-American music: freeing swing from present conformities by infusing it with the integrity of the past and the innocence of the future, he would reinvigorate its lifeblood with the secrets of the ancients and outer space. Existing at the ultimate point of freedom, Braxton, like the prototypical primitive artist, "express[ed his] feelings [directly], free from the intrusive overlay of learned behavior."[75] As a scientist, moreover, he had transcended the limitations of time and space, incorporating the mythic past into forward-looking projections to the point where culture and history stood still.[76] *Newsweek*'s characterization of Braxton, the "free spirit," as the modern version of the antediluvian noisemaker captures the mass of stereotypes of "the most innovative force in the world of jazz":

> Braxton is a virtuoso on the saxophone, and the instrument has never been subject to such assault. He squeezes out bizarre sounds and clashing, hitherto unheard tone colors. He plays like a man possessed, in a paroxysm of animalistic grunts, honks, rasps, and hollers. He rends the fabric of conventional musical language as he reaches into himself—and back into pre-history—for some primordial means of communication.[77]

Here, the controversy at its most spectacular assumed mythic and coyly racist proportions. And after having been subjected to depictions as a cerebral zombie, as jazz music's mystical black beast, Braxton could hardly have expected to gain respectability as a concert artist, no matter how many interviews he granted. As attention mounted, the spectacle grew proportionately, to the point where Braxton, as jazz

75. Sally Price, *Primitive Art in Civilized Places* (Chicago: University of Chicago Press, 1989).

76. Johannes Fabian, *Time and the Other: How Anthropology Makes Its Object* (New York: Columbia University Press, 1983).

77. H. Saal, "Two Free Spirits," *Newsweek* (August 8, 1977), 52–53. Precedents for such visions inform much of the historical jazz commentary. In *All about Jazz,* for example, the British writer Stanley Nelson equates rhythm with intoxication, primitivism, progress, and the black race: "The Negro undoubtedly has a phenomenal sense of rhythm. In Central Africa are still to be found savages in the last stage of barbarism, but the primitive music of the tom-tom and the reed-pipe will mould these creatures to the plasticity of clay. . . . Right from his origin in the African jungle, through his slavery to his present more or less emancipated condition, the Negro has retained this innate sense of worship of rhythm. Beverley Nichols has described the Negroes dancing in a Harlem cabaret as 'drunk with rhythm.' . . . Rhythm may therefore be said to be the elixir of life. Wherever we look we find it; without it, we cannot satisfactorily exist; because of it, we have widened the gulf between the human species and the lower orders to an enormous width. . . . For rhythm, while not postulating progress, is usually hand in hand with it." Nelson, *All about Jazz* (London: Heath Cranton Ltd., 1934), 13, 17.

music's court jester, subverted his own integrity by shifting jazz recordings to European labels and reserving his concert music for Arista. The release of *For Trio* (1977), *For Four Orchestras* (1978), and *For Two Pianos* (1980) finally factualized the fiction of Braxton's inaccessibility, undermining the formula on which his popularity was based. As critical attention declined, so did his following, which led Arista to withdraw its support, a move that effectively eliminated him from the American jazz picture.[78]

As the inadvertent comic of jazz, Braxton would seem on one level to be its pathetic victim: an artist consumed by institutional machinations as well as by his own ambitions. Yet on another, he appeared more savvy than the victim theory gives him credit for. In fact, at many points Braxton appeared to handle his image-making deftly, fueling controversy that would increase visibility while baiting and teasing with oblique expressions of oppositional "style."[79] Resisting associations with jazz, concert music, and even at moments the AACM, Braxton transgressed boundaries to remain limited by no single one. He assumed "the impossible position" that Benjamin attributed to the intellectual's place in the class structure, but stretched its impossibility in multiple directions.[80] Celebrated as a jazz star, Braxton retorted, "Jazz is only a very small part of what I do"; compared to Bach and Webern, Braxton insisted on the preeminence of the black aesthetic; compared to his Chicago cohorts, he branded the Art Ensemble's "Great Black Music" logo as "racist."[81] Perhaps best expressing Braxton's subversive tactics, moreover, were his explanations of his titles, which, from moment to moment, shifted to one of a multitude of meanings. Were they expressions of the absurd or "just titles"? A "cataloging system" or "outlines of structure"? Mystical codes or alternatives to language? According to Braxton, they were all of these, yet when pinned down he resisted, replying, "I could explain [them] to you, but you really don't want to know."[82] From the public view,

78. Braxton's dismissal may have also been influenced by the company's changing hands; it was sold to Ariola/Eurodisc, a subsidiary of Bertelsmann A.G., in 1979. See Cynthia Kirk, "Ariola to Buy Arista from Columbia," *Variety* (August 1, 1979), 65.

79. "The challenge to hegemony . . . is not issued directly. . . . Rather it is expressed obliquely in style." Hebidge, *Subculture,* 17.

80. Benjamin, "Author as Producer," in *The Essential Frankfurt School Reader,* 261.

81. Lake, "I Made More Money at Chess," *Melody Maker,* 48.

82. Postif, "Anthony Braxton," *Jazz Hot* (April 1971); Townley, "Anthony Braxton," *Down Beat* (February 14, 1974); Lake, "I Made More Money at Chess," *Melody*

the picture titles, like nearly all else in the creative system, seemed like not only one thing but another, calling to mind the child's candy-box hologram whose image changes with a subtle turn of the wrist. Braxton's public image, like his private creative world, effects a bricolage of ever-changing signs that signify on the controlling categories of official culture. By extending his art of illusion to the construction of spectacle, Braxton succeeded in "conspiring against the king" (recalling Foster's metaphor) as a way of preserving the integrity of a highly private realm of creative expression.

Maker; Palmer, notes to *Five Pieces 1975;* Leo Smith, notes to *The Complete Braxton 1971* (Arista reissue); Henschen, "Alternative Creativity in this Time Zone," *Down Beat;* Lake, "I Made More Money at Chess."

Epilogue: Jazz Recast

Two perspectives framed the decade of jazz in the 1980s. The first, written by Dan Morgenstern, looked forward as it reflected back on the character of invention since the death of John Coltrane. According to Morgenstern, jazz circa 1980 had yet to redefine its direction after the challenges of fusion and free. "The music has not ceased to change and develop," Morgenstern observed, "but it is changing and developing in many directions, with no single pied piper to call the tune." Recalling Leonard Meyer's perception of a "dynamic stasis," Morgenstern recognized a healthy, if somewhat calamitous, moment. There is "no energy crisis," he contended. Rather, he saw "unity in diversity."[1] Significantly, for Morgenstern the unifying glue was the draw of the jazz tradition. "Tradition" identified the spark of invention, whether deriving from small-group swing, bop, or free. By the end of the decade, however, diversity seemed to have given way to a new focus. While tradition still informed innovation, its interpretation had become more regulative, more prescriptive. Articulating the details of that prescription was Wynton Marsalis, the gifted trumpeter who had emerged from New Orleans, the archetypal "cradle of jazz." First appearing in profiles shortly after the publication of Morgenstern's comment, Marsalis rapidly gained the backing of the national media and jazz press. Hoisted to the throne—and onto the covers of *Time* and *Down Beat*—he became the new "pied piper" of a revitalized jazz tradition. In his wake many others would follow, including an interracial troupe of spunky, ambitious artists who could also *talk the talk* of modern jazz. As a cover story in the *New York Times Sunday Magazine* proclaimed, they were all "Young, Gifted and Cool."[2]

Note: These comments on the current state of "jazz" first appeared in slightly varied form as part of my paper "Jazz Neoclassicism and the Mask of Consensus," delivered at the annual conference of the Society for Ethnomusicology, Oakland, Calif., November 1990.

1. Morgenstern, "Jazz in the '70s: No Energy Crisis," *Down Beat* (January 1980), 19. Meyer's views are outlined in chapter 1.

2. Tom Piazza, "Young, Gifted and Cool," *New York Times Sunday Magazine* (May 20, 1990), 34–35, 64–69; Thomas Sancton, "The New Jazz Age: Horns of

The revitalization of jazz as a new traditionalism or "neoclassicism" has been welcomed by many observers at a time of great cultural ferment.[3] For some, it suggests that white America has now finally begun to recognize the achievements of black musicians, not simply as entertainers in the tradition of Sambo and Buckwheat, but as artists of real merit, and arguably of equal importance to the innovators of European high culture.[4] Having been honored by Congress and canonized by America's most august cultural institutions—the Smithsonian, New York's Lincoln Center—the leading musicians of jazz seem out of place in blatantly commercial, popular settings. As our newly appointed "classical artists," Marsalis, Terrence Blanchard, Donald Harrison, and Marcus Roberts convey a sense of authority and self-confidence that distinguishes them from the early "Negro musicians" who had once constituted the lower end of a race-conscious cultural hierarchy. Joined by former free players, notably David Murray, Henry Threadgill, and the musician-turned-critic, Stanley Crouch, these "young lions," as Gary Giddins calls them, deliver a powerful message.[5] They suggest that jazz is perhaps the lone certainty in an uncertain artistic era, a "true art" innovated by blacks. As it transcends difference it reaches the height of cultural achievement, becoming, once again, "America's classical art form."

Where the neoclassical model goes wrong, however, is in its presumption of telling the whole story of jazz. No need for charting the complexities of the past, it would seem, for neoclassicism, recast as a mode of interpretation, now supplies all the answers. Important countermovements fall by the wayside; notable challenges recede into a clutter of ancillary diversions. Clearly the representatives of the new traditionalism are motivated by the best intentions to preserve an im-

Plenty," *Time* (October 22, 1990), 64–71. Marsalis's appearances in *Down Beat* were numerous, notably Howard Mandel, "The Wynton Marsalis Interview" (July 1984), 16–19, 67; Stanley Crouch, "Wynton Marsalis: 1987" (November 1987), 16–19, 57. More recently, the magazine published as a cover story Marsalis's reflections about his love of Ellington's music. See Marsalis, "Ellington Sweets: Reflections on Duke's Amazing Artistry," *Down Beat* (June 1991), 16–20. A comment on the contents page encouraged a comparison of the two musicians: "The world of music exploded when a certain young trumpeter heard Duke Ellington in a certain way. Wynton Marsalis shares his reflections on a giant influence."

3. Giddins, "Wynton Marsalis and Other Neoclassical Lions," *Rhythm-a-ning, Jazz Tradition and Innovation in the '80's* (New York: Oxford University Press, 1985), 156–61.

4. Martin Williams, "How Long Has this Been Going On?" in *Jazz in Its Time* (New York: Oxford University Press, 1989), 45–46.

5. Giddins, *Rhythm-a-ning*, 156–61.

portant contribution to American culture. While seemingly allied with the most reactionary cultural politics, they more typically express progressive positions in an attempt to redefine popular assumptions about what constitutes black creativity. But their very actions, especially when presented in the language of the high-culture publicist, also fetishize an expression that has continually resisted official culture's definitions. On one level, the advocacy of a high, black musical culture may make perfect sense in its recognition of African-American artists' crowning achievements. Yet as an interpretation of culture, it ultimately obscures historical particulars as it oversimplifies the character of the arts at the moment. The reality of music in the United States—if we can speak of "realities" anymore—is surely something more ambiguous and conflicted than what classicism's advocates care to present.

When observed against the background of postwar representations, the neoclassical model recalls an earlier construct that defined jazz according to the conception of a "mainstream." As did mainstream in the 1950s, neoclassicism argues for a unilinear continuity that stretches from early New Orleans to the cold-war recasting of bop. Where the former left off, the latter continues, leapfrogging over twenty years of artistic "aberration" to foster in the 1980s and 1990s the "Swing Back to Tradition."[6] As it emerges in the thick of the postmodern moment, this revived mainstream appears on insecure ground. Re-creating the old in the context of the new, neoclassicism suggests a kind of wishful thinking about the present, cast in a nostalgia about the past. One cannot deny that the Jazz Tradition is with us today. To be sure, recent innovators have looked again at the creative potential of earlier achievements, and in more literal ways than the likes of Coleman, Ayler, and Shepp did before. When removed from the lens of classicist ideology, however, these revivals appear no more central than a number of other conflicting contemporary expressions. Indeed, one is hard put to recognize *any* clear focus in the current "convulsion of culture," as Arthur C. Danto calls it, a convulsion that challenges pluralist visions of a steadily evolving, improving consensus. "In effect," Danto writes in another instance, we live with "no mainstream as such at all, simply confluences of individual tributaries with no mainstream to flow into."[7]

6. Jon Pareles, "Jazz Swings Back to Tradition," *New York Times Sunday Magazine* (June 17, 1984), 22–23, 54.

7. Danto, "What Happened to Beauty," *Nation* (March 30, 1992), 418–21; Danto, "Women Artists, 1970–85: Women and Mainstream Art," *Nation* (December 25, 1989), 794–98.

What is so striking about the neoclassical perspective (even when articulated by the most trenchant critical observers) is that it appears with so little acknowledgment of the trends that surround it. It is as if jazz has survived as a protected gem of black creative wisdom, growing and changing yet miraculously unaffected by the overarching shifts in American life. Perhaps such views can be justified within the community, where musicians have traditionally sought to deflect outsiders' perspectives. In this respect, neoclassicism appears as the jazz answer to the historically static, Afrocentric versions of rap—X Clan, Brand Nubian—that celebrate a classical blackness as a response to official culture's distortions of African-American creativity. In the broader context of culture, however, neoclassicism suggests a variety of contradictory, often confused meanings. For its innovators, it is an expression of the *Black Codes* that identify African-American artistic greatness;[8] for its challengers in improvised, experimental music, it is often seen as a travesty of the flexibility that is said to characterize black aesthetics; for its staunchest supporters—whose definitions of "tradition" sometimes stretch across a surprisingly broad stylistic terrain[9]—it is a shard of high-cultural truth that provides some semblance of order in a disordered world. For the casual and often bemused listener, jazz neoclassicism offers any combination of these, conveying a curious and contradictory mix, a perversion of Baraka's "changing same."[10] Jazz becomes both canonical and fluid, objectified and elusive. In the popular, where the majority of listeners find it, neoclassicism voices a similar schizophrenia as a mass-mediated facsimile of African-American artistic integrity. Most troubling about the neoclassical movement is not so much the music as what the music in

8. Wynton Marsalis, *Black Codes (from the Underground)* (1985).

9. In his review of the Art Ensemble of Chicago's *Urban Bushmen,* for example, Stuart Nicolson distances the group from prior radicalism to advance an oxymoronic classical vanguard: "The AEC have continued to hold onto their hard-earned corner of the avant-garde into their third decade; their music simultaneously far-out or accessible—depending on which end of the telescope you view them from. Their ability to rationalize the freedom of the '60s with dynamics, form and structure, sprang from a realisation that the great energy of players such as Coltrane in his final period, Ayler and to a lesser extent Shepp, was ultimately destructive." Nicolson, "Urban Bushmen," the *Wire* (UK), special double issue (December/January 1989–1990), 54. Similarly, for Francis Davis (or for one of *Down Beat*'s editors), Anthony Davis shared a common ground with the neoclassicists as a "new music traditionalist." See Davis, "New Music Traditionalist," *Down Beat* (January 1982).

10. "The changing same" is Baraka's (LeRoi Jones's) notion of the interplay between personal, artistic innovation and the black musical tradition. "The Changing Same," *Black Music* (New York: William Morrow, 1967), 180–212.

mass culture represents. In the most visible contexts, "classic jazz" sacrifices integrity for the diverting image of high-culture cool. At best, performers seem like projections that convey only the *appearance* of the serious artist. And for the jaded listener, who sees neoclassicism as an exception to a cultural rule of "primitive" rappers and crack addicts, the likes of Ellington, Marsalis, and perhaps even the sentimental white answer, Harry Connick, are probably just a step away from the suffering bluesman, now dressed up in an Italian suit.

It is perhaps fittingly ironic that Braxton would represent the inverse of the prior formula: while expressing a commitment to the central impulses defining jazz —to conviction, to dues paying, to vision, to integrity—he would be cast off as a warped facsimile. In a world seeking certainties through a fictionalized reading of the past, Braxton's post-Arista artistry posed an interesting contradiction and one that would most likely appeal only to those recognizing its radical message. In this sense, Braxton's fall from a tentative grace may have been as inevitable as matters could be in the unpredictable circumstances of the 1980s. It certainly created serious hardships, forcing Braxton, until better fortunes arose, to manage a meager living for his family through occasional recordings, sporadic performances at clubs and American universities, and annual tours of Europe. (The 1985 European tour produced a celebration of Braxton's music, Graham Lock's *Forces in Motion.*)[11] In creative terms, however, Braxton's reassignment to the experimental category helped to focus his attention on projects relating directly to an "alternative creativity." From 1982 to 1992, he composed not only for small groups but increasingly for ensembles more typically associated with the concert tradition. His recordings with the Robert Schumann Quintet and performances with Pauline Oliveros continued involvements begun in the 1960s. A venture into the music of Richard Wagner inspired a major theatrical work, *Composition 102* (1982), performed by the Texas Chamber Orchestra, and an opera, *Composition 120* (*Trillium,* five movements, 1984). The bulk of his time was devoted to lectures on the continuing evolution of his musical system[12] and to two monumental literary projects: *The Tri-Axium Writings* (1985), described in chapter 5, and a five-volume series of

11. In 1986, he joined the faculty of Mills College. In 1990, he received tenure at Wesleyan University in Connecticut. Lock's *Forces in Motion* was published by Quartet Books, London, in 1988. It was reprinted for American circulation by Da Capo in the same year.

12. Notably, the "Cell Structure and Language Design" lectures presented at the California Institute of the Arts and elsewhere in the mid-1980s.

Photographic portrait of Anthony Braxton (1988). Courtesy Rolf Hans.

Composition Notes (1988), which detailed the rules and procedures guiding his works. As with the *Tri-Axium,* the latter collection reinforced Braxton's identification with the tradition of modern composers from Schoenberg to Stockhausen to Cage, who had also defined their creative activity "in their own terms."

Despite the lacuna of comment about Braxton in recent jazz chronicles—limited mainly to brief reviews of new releases and reissues—he is as much a part of these times as the neoclassicists who officially represent them. In fact, Braxton's pastiche of mutable artistry seems more literally reflective of a period when voices of "definition" rise and recede without apparent rhyme or reason. His importance has most certainly been recognized by those appearing in his wake: many in the school of experimental-jazz improvisers have acknowledged their debt to Braxton, and in the styles of John Zorn, Jane Ira Bloom, and the late John Carter one occasionally hears glimpses of that influence. Similarly, composers and ensembles from Anthony Davis and George Lewis to the World Saxophone Quartet have paid tribute to Braxton's leadership, either directly or in following his efforts to reconceptualize a jazz-inspired musical practice. One can even discern connections between Braxton and the innovation of hip-hop artists such as Public Enemy. While perhaps not sharing a direct line of influence, both have appropriated modernism in order to revive black methods of creative resistance.

Yet such talk of influence, while significant on one level, explains little about the most profound importance of Braxton as an artist. It may not even be appropriate to judge his efforts according to the paradigm of stylistic leadership, since so much of his work seeks to undermine prior associations and measures of value. What makes Braxton's artistry so special, after all, is its uniqueness, its commitment to difference. Braxton draws attention by speaking in the commanding voice of an African-American musician sensitized to the noise of the postmodern; he evokes through a breadth of experiment a sense of the confusion, the convulsion that informs our lives. In the midst of these expressive uncertainties, however, so does he also express a more conventional, nearly Afro-Christian sense of hope. At once foreboding and optimistic, he forever keeps a safe, punning distance from the confines of identification. As such, Braxton is perhaps one of the most resonant voices in this tentative, unstable era. His music is not a centering force, but, on the contrary, an emblem of the dynamism that undermines common definitions. As is jazz in the postmodern, Braxton's art is both jazz and not jazz. It communicates the music's vital forces as it dances around them; it complicates and contradicts as it responds to the impulses of the tradition. Jazz is, returning to Ellison, the musical embodiment of a "cruel contradiction [as] an art of individual assertion within and against the group. . . . Because jazz finds its very life in an endless improvisation upon traditional materials, the jazzman must lose his identity even as he finds it."[13] Passionately committed to the African-American tradition as he persistently steps outside it, Braxton doubles the loss as he identifies "blackness" as both itself and the other.

13. Ellison, *Shadow and Act* (New York: Vintage, 1964, 1972), 234.

Appendix A: Pictures Titles of Compositions Cited

Composition 1

Piano piece No. 1 (1968)

Composition 3

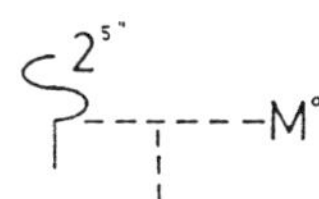

for eleven instruments (1968)

Composition 4

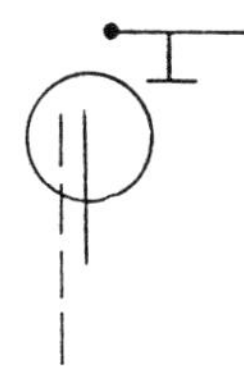

for five tubas (1968)

Composition 5

W C
12°
4

for piano (1968)

Composition 6A

67M
F-12

Composition 6C

C-M=B05
7

Composition 6E

(840)
REALIZE
44M
44M

Composition 6G

M
O
47A
B-X°

Composition 6I

R76

4

Composition 6J

J-572
(431)-1

Composition 6K

N508-10
(4G)

Composition 6L

JNK
4°

Composition 6N

S-37C-67B
|
F7

Composition 6P

W-12 ——— B-46
C28-12
⋮
4

Composition 7

D-J-30
N

for orchestra (1969)

Composition 8A

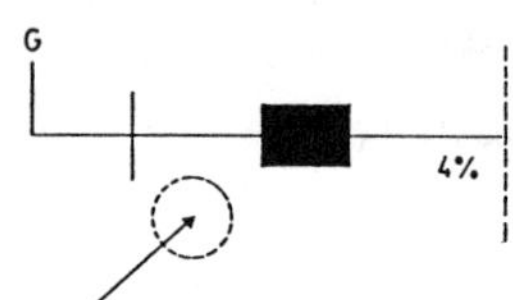

Composition 8B

Composition 8C

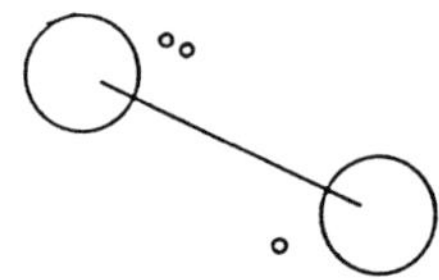

Composition 8I

BWC-12
N-48K

Relationship series.

Composition 8K

JD-C
IP-(LIL)
⋮
M

Composition 9

SH-G46
|
(337)

for four amplified shovels (1969)

Composition 10

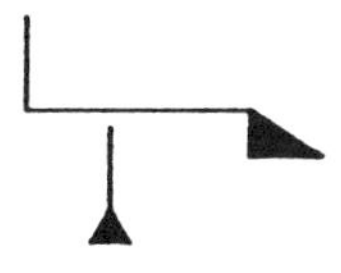

for solo piano (1969)

Composition 11

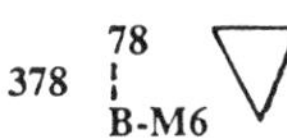

for creative orchestra (1969)

Composition 12

W-306
(427)

for woodwind quintet (1969)

Composition 14

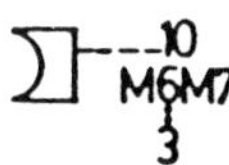

for solo instrumentalist (1970)

Composition 17

8KN-(B-12)
|
R[10]

for string quartet (1971)

Composition 20

SBN-A-12
66K

for two instruments (1971)

Composition 21

CK7(GN)
437

for recorded tape with or without instruments (1971)

Composition 23A

KA-47---
|
B-3F
|
6

Composition 23B

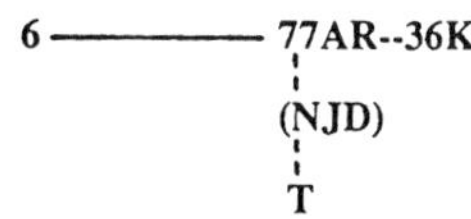

Composition 23C

MDO—3—
P-3Z
63D
12

Composition 23D

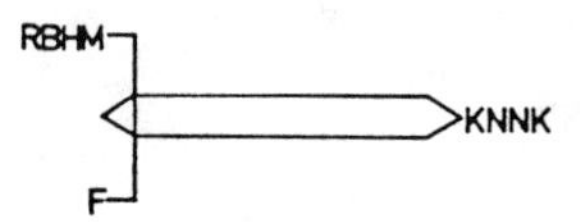

Composition 23E

489M
70-2--(TH-B)
M

Composition 23G

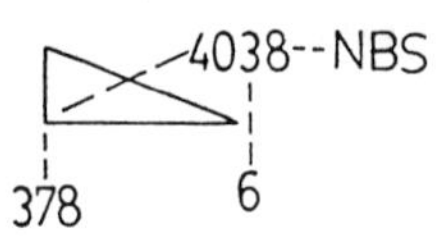

Composition 23K

60666C
66M

Composition 23M

MHB
7KX88
R|CZY
3779

Composition 23O

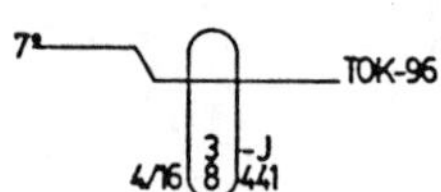

Composition 25

RBN---3°
K-12

for Creative Orchestra (1972)

Composition 26A

NR-12-C
(33M)

Composition 26B

JMK-80
CFN-7

Composition 26E

AOTH
MBA
H

Composition 26G

RZ04M(6)
AHW

Composition 26H

NNWZ
48 KB
N

Composition 26J

RFO-M°
F(32)

Composition 30

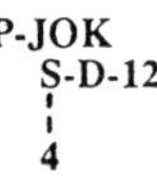

for piano (1973)

Composition 34

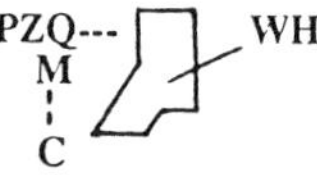

Composition 37

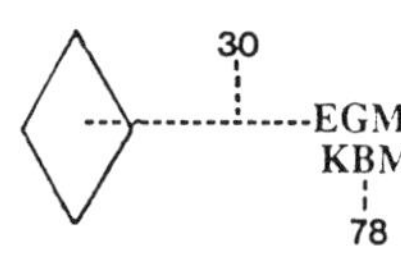

for saxophone quartet (1974)

Composition 38

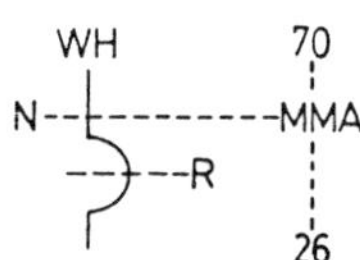

Composition 40F

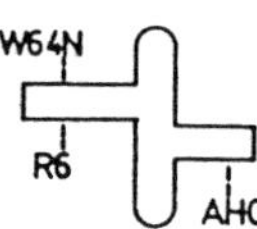

Composition 40G

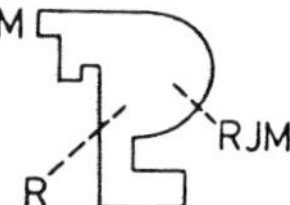

Composition 40I

F04(G)WN
OQO-26–

Composition 40K

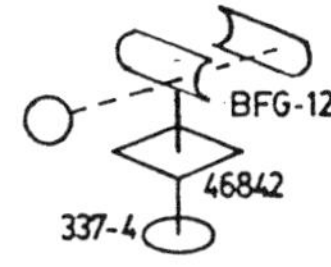

Composition 48

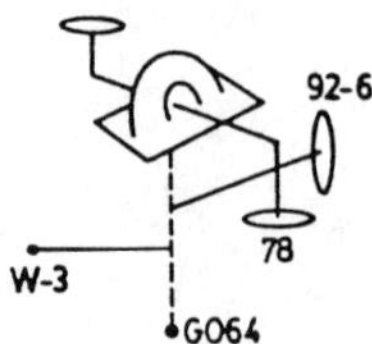

Composition 50

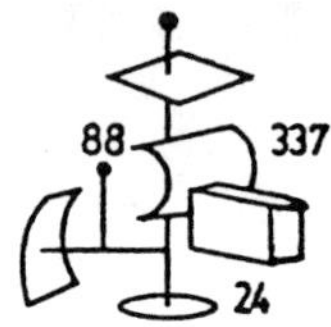

for two instrumentalists and two synthesizer players (1975)

Composition 51

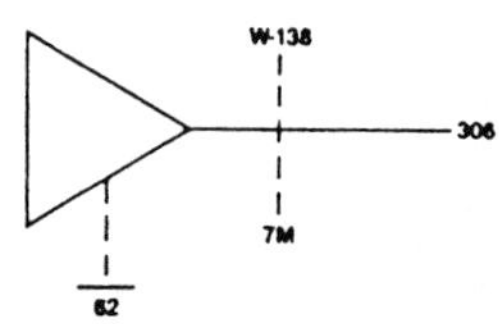

for creative orchestra (1976)

Composition 55

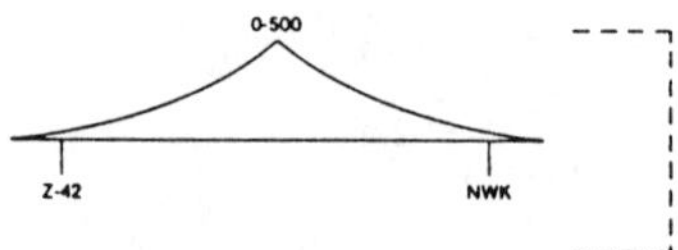

for creative orchestra (1976)

Composition 57

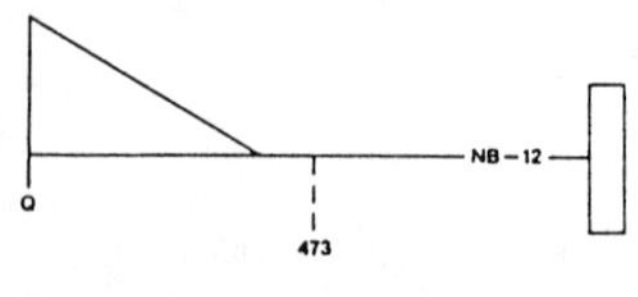

for creative orchestra (1976)

Composition 69C

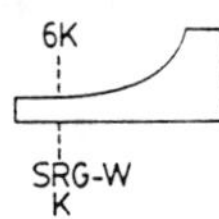

Composition 69E

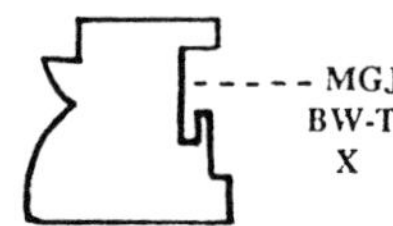

Composition 69F

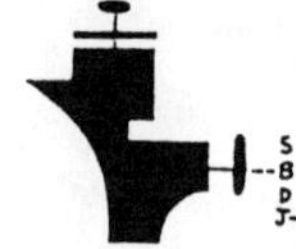

Composition 69G

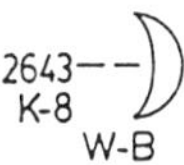

Composition 82

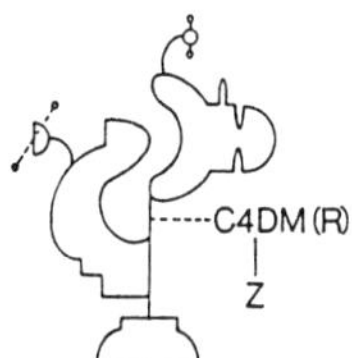

for four orchestras (1978)

Composition 69H

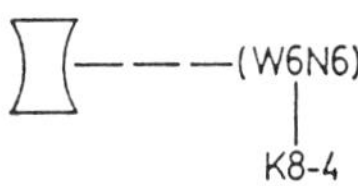

Composition 95

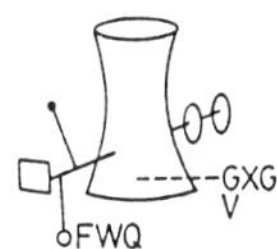

for two pianists (1980)

Composition 69M

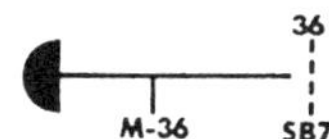

Composition 98

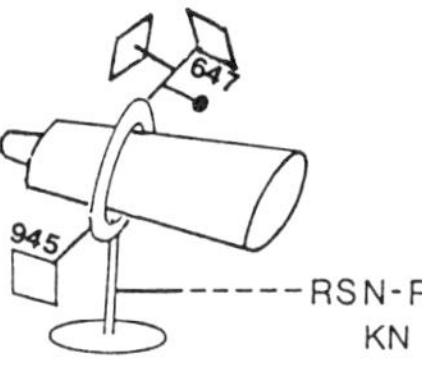

Composition 76

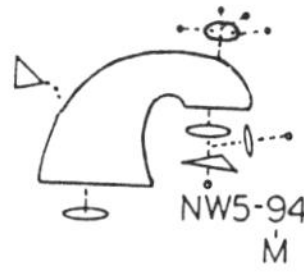

for three musicians (1977)

Composition 105

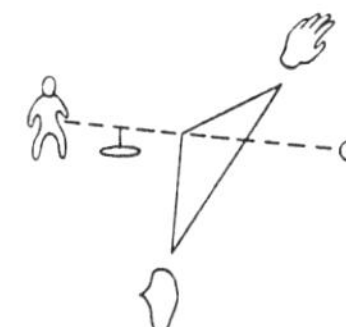

Composition 123

....SHALA ADDRESSES THE CONCERNS OF THE GUARDSMEN (AND REDIRECTS THEIR ENERGIES)

for solo flute, slides, and constructed environment (1985)

Appendix B: Recordings Cited/ Anthony Braxton on Record

Recordings Cited

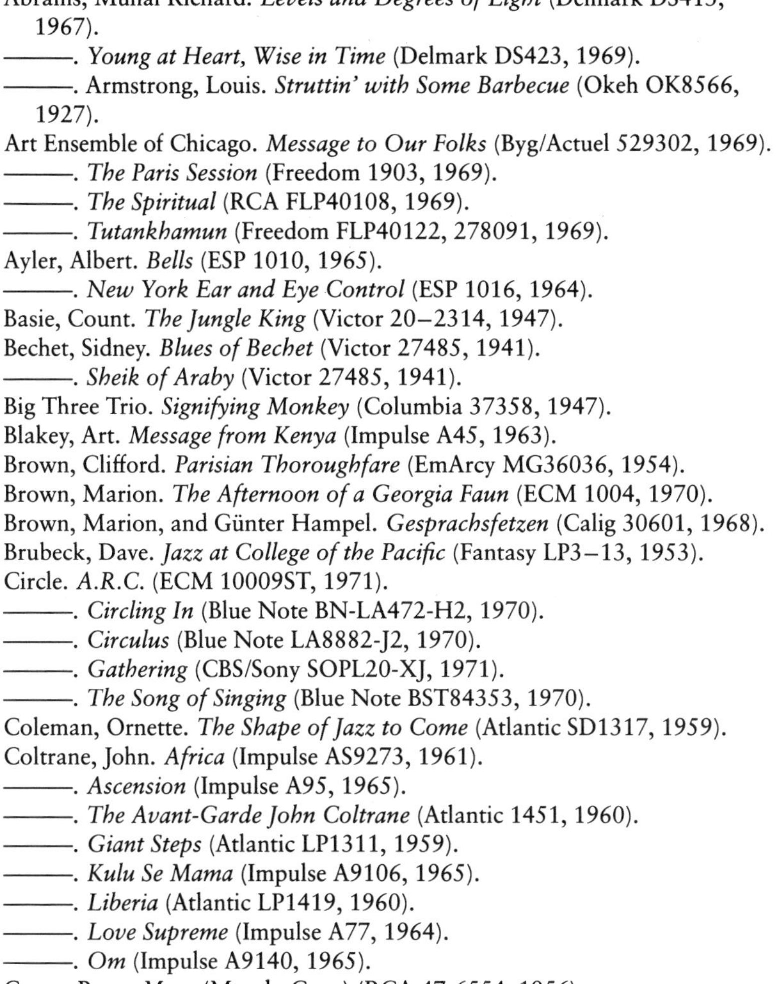

Abrams, Muhal Richard. *Levels and Degrees of Light* (Delmark DS413, 1967).

———. *Young at Heart, Wise in Time* (Delmark DS423, 1969).

———. Armstrong, Louis. *Struttin' with Some Barbecue* (Okeh OK8566, 1927).

Art Ensemble of Chicago. *Message to Our Folks* (Byg/Actuel 529302, 1969).

———. *The Paris Session* (Freedom 1903, 1969).

———. *The Spiritual* (RCA FLP40108, 1969).

———. *Tutankhamun* (Freedom FLP40122, 278091, 1969).

Ayler, Albert. *Bells* (ESP 1010, 1965).

———. *New York Ear and Eye Control* (ESP 1016, 1964).

Basie, Count. *The Jungle King* (Victor 20–2314, 1947).

Bechet, Sidney. *Blues of Bechet* (Victor 27485, 1941).

———. *Sheik of Araby* (Victor 27485, 1941).

Big Three Trio. *Signifying Monkey* (Columbia 37358, 1947).

Blakey, Art. *Message from Kenya* (Impulse A45, 1963).

Brown, Clifford. *Parisian Thoroughfare* (EmArcy MG36036, 1954).

Brown, Marion. *The Afternoon of a Georgia Faun* (ECM 1004, 1970).

Brown, Marion, and Günter Hampel. *Gesprachsfetzen* (Calig 30601, 1968).

Brubeck, Dave. *Jazz at College of the Pacific* (Fantasy LP3–13, 1953).

Circle. *A.R.C.* (ECM 10009ST, 1971).

———. *Circling In* (Blue Note BN-LA472-H2, 1970).

———. *Circulus* (Blue Note LA8882-J2, 1970).

———. *Gathering* (CBS/Sony SOPL20-XJ, 1971).

———. *The Song of Singing* (Blue Note BST84353, 1970).

Coleman, Ornette. *The Shape of Jazz to Come* (Atlantic SD1317, 1959).

Coltrane, John. *Africa* (Impulse AS9273, 1961).

———. *Ascension* (Impulse A95, 1965).

———. *The Avant-Garde John Coltrane* (Atlantic 1451, 1960).

———. *Giant Steps* (Atlantic LP1311, 1959).

———. *Kulu Se Mama* (Impulse A9106, 1965).

———. *Liberia* (Atlantic LP1419, 1960).

———. *Love Supreme* (Impulse A77, 1964).

———. *Om* (Impulse A9140, 1965).

Como, Perry. *More* (Mondo Cane) (RCA 47-6554, 1956).

Corea, Chick. *Now He Sings, Now He Sobs* (Solid State 18039, 1968).
———. *Tones for Joan's Bones* (Vortex 2004, 1966).
Dolphy, Eric. *God Bless the Child* (Prestige PRLP7304, 1961).
Donaldson, Lou. *Midnight Creeper* (Blue Note BST84280, 1968).
Ellington, Duke. *Deep South Suite* (Prima DC02, 1946).
———. *Liberian Suite* (Prestige 24075, 1947).
Haley, Bill. *Rock around the Clock* (Decca 29124, 1954).
Hampel, Günter. *The 8th of July 1969* (Birth NJ001, 1969).
Hawkins, Coleman. *Picasso* (Clef MGC647, 1948).
Hill, Andrew. *Black Fire* (Blue Note BLP4151, 1963).
Hines, Earl. *Jelly Jelly* (Blue Bird B11065, 1940).
Jamal, Ahmad. *Live at the Pershing* (Argo LP628/LP667, 1958).
Jarman, Joseph. *As If It Were the Seasons* (Delmark DS 417, 1968).
———. *Song For* (Delmark 410, 1967).
Kenton, Stan. *City of Glass* (Robert Graettinger, composer) (Capitol 63, 1951).
Little Richard. *Tutti Frutti* (Speciality 561, 1956; *The Specialty Sessions* [Specialty SPCD 8508, 1989]).
Lymon, Frankie. *Why Do Fools Fall in Love?* (Gee 1002, 1956).
McLean, Jackie. *Let Freedom Ring* (Blue Note BLP4106, 1962).
Marsalis, Wynton. *Black Codes from the Underground* (Columbia FC38641, 1985).
Miller, Mitch. *The Yellow Rose of Texas* (Columbia 13-33002, 1955).
Mingus, Charles. *Foggy Day* (Atlantic LP 1260, 1956.)
———. *Pithecanthropus Erectus* (Atlantic LP1237, 1956).
Mitchell, Roscoe. *The Little Suite* (Delmark DS408, 1966).
———. *Sound* (Delmark DS408, 1966).
———. *Congliptious* (Nessa N2, 1968).
Morton, Jelly Roll. *Sidewalk Blues* (Victor 40-0118, 1926).
New York Contemporary Five. *The Funeral* (Sonet SLP36, 1963).
Oliver, King. *Dippermouth Blues* (Gennett 5132, 1923).
Phillips, Barre. *Journale Violone* (Music Man 601, 1968).
Presley, Elvis. *Hound Dog* (RCA 47-6604, 1956).
Riddle, Nelson. *Lisbon Antiqua* (Capitol F3287, 1955).
Rollins, Sonny. *Airegin* (recorded with Miles Davis on the album *Cookin'*) (Fantasy OJC-128, 1954).
———. *Freedom Suite* (Riverside RLP12-258, 1958).
———. *It Can Happen to You (The Sound of Sonny)* (Riverside 241, 1957).
Roach, Max. *Percussion Bitter Suite* (Impulse AS-8, 1961).
———. *We Insist! Max Roach's Freedom Now Suite* (Sweden: Amigo AMLP 810; Candid 8002, 1960).
Rzewski, Frederick. *Stockhausen, Klavierstücke No. 10* (Heliodor Wergo 2549016, 1969).
Sanders, Pharoah. *Tauhid* (Impulse A9138, 1966).
Schuller, Gunther. *Abstraction* (Atlantic SD1365, 1960).
Shepp, Archie. *Both/And Club* (Impulse A9161, 1966).

Shorter, Wayne. *Juju* (Blue Note BLP1562, 1964).
———. *Nefertiti* (Blue Note BLP4182, 1967).
Silva, Alan. *From the Lunar Surface* (Byg 529312, 1969).
Silver, Horace. *Home Cookin'* (Blue Note BLP1562, 1957).
———. *Juicy Lucy* (Blue Note BLP4008, 1959).
———. *Opus de Funk* (Blue Note BLP5034, 1953).
Simone, Nina. *Mississippi Goddamn!* (Philips PHM200-135, 1963).
Sinatra, Frank. *Learnin' the Blues* (Capitol F3102, 1955).
Taylor, Cecil. *Chimampas* (Leo CD LR 153, 1991).
———. *Enter Evening*. Appears on *Unit Structures* (Blue Note BLP4237, 1966).
———. *Hard Driving Jazz*. (United Artists 5014, 1959; re-released as John Coltrane, *Coltrane Time* (United Artists 15001, 1962.)
———. *Unit Structures* (Blue Note BLP4237, 1966).
Tristano, Lenny. *Digression (Intuition II)* (EAPJ-491, 1949).
Weston, Randy. *Music from the New African Nations* (Colpix CP456, 1963).
———. *Uhuru Afrika* (Roulette R65001, 1960).

Anthony Braxton on Record

Abbreviations

acc	accordion
as	alto saxophone
a-tb	alto trombone
b	bass (double)
bcl	bass clarinet
b-d	bass drum
bfl	bass flute
b-g	bass guitar (electric)
bs	baritone saxophone
cbcl	contrabass clarinet
cl	clarinet
cym	cymbals
dms	drums

Note: The list that follows provides a synoptic overview of Anthony Braxton's music on record. While omitting picture titles and personnel for larger sessions, it includes all known commercial releases of Braxton's music. For more thorough discographic coverage, see Hugo De Craen and Eddy Janssens, *The Anthony Braxton Discography* (Brussels: New Think, 1982), and Hans Wachtmeister, *A Discography and Bibliography of Anthony Braxton* (Stocksund, Sweden: Blue Anchor Bookshop, 1982). Graham Lock's *Forces in Motion* (London: Quartet Books, 1988; Da Capo, 1988) provides additional titles not appearing in the discographies. While this list seeks to update Lock's, in some cases—particularly on obscure, recently identified sessions—the personnel listings and record numbers were not available at the time of publication.

fl flute
flghn flügelhorn
frhn French horn
g guitar(s)
hm harmonica
l-s "little instruments"
misc miscellaneous instruments
perc percussion
picc piccolo
picc-tp piccolo trumpet
pno piano
sis sopranino saxophone
ss soprano saxophone
synth synthesizer
tb trombone
tba tuba
tp trumpet
ts tenor saxophone
v voice
vib vibraphone
vl violin
vla viola
xylo xylophone

Anthony Braxton as Leader

Three Compositions of New Jazz (Delmark DS415, 1968).
Braxton (as, ss, cl, fl, l-s); Leo Smith (tp, mellophone, xylo, bottles, kazoo); Leroy Jenkins (vl, hm, b-d, cym, recorder, slide whistle).
For Alto (Delmark DS420/421, 1968).
Braxton (as).
Silence (Freedom FLP40123, 1969).
Braxton (as, ss, fl, cbcl, acc, l-s); Leroy Jenkins (vl, vla, hm, fl, acc, l-s); Leo Smith (tp, flghn, l-s).
B-X° /N-O-1-47A (Affinity AFF15, 1969).
Braxton (as, ss, fl, cl, cbcl, sound machine, misc); Leo Smith (tp, flghn, misc); Leroy Jenkins (vl, vla, fl, hm, organ); Steve McCall (perc).
This Time (Affinity AFF25, 1970).
Braxton (as, ss, fl, cl, cbcl, sound machine, chimes, v [poetry recitation]); Leo Smith (tp, flghn, horns, sirens, logs); Leroy Jenkins (vl, vla, fl, hm, hohner organ).
Recital Paris '71 (Futura GER23, 1971).
Braxton (as).
The Complete Braxton (Freedom FLP40112/113, 1971; Arista AF 1902, 1977).

Braxton (ss, as, fl, cbcl); Chick Corea (pno); Dave Holland (b, cello); Barry Altschul (perc).

Donna Lee (America 30 AM 6122, 1972).
Braxton (as, ss, fl, cbcl); Michael Smith (pno); Peter Warren (b); Oliver Johnson (dms).

Saxophone Improvisations Series F (Inner City IC1008, 1972).
Braxton (as).

Creative Orchestra Music (Ring 01024/5/6, 1972).
Braxton (as, ss, cl, fl, cbcl); Bob Taylor (ts); Hugh Levick (ts, ss); Jean Beauchard (as); Ambrose Jackson (tp); James Maceda (tp); Ray Stephen Oche (tp); Cesare Massarenti (tp); Gilbert Aloir (tba); Joachim Kuhn (pno); François Mechali (b); Pancho Blumenzweig (b); Oliver Johnson (perc); Sabu Toyozumi (perc).

Anthony Braxton, Günter Hampel, Jeanne Lee: Familie (Birth 008, 1972).
Braxton (as, ss, fl, cl, cbcl); Hampel (vib, ss, fl, bcl); Lee (v).

Town Hall 1972 (Trio PA3008/9, 1972).
Braxton (as, ss, fl, cl, cbcl, perc); John Stubblefield (ts, bcl, fl, perc); Jeanne Lee (v); Dave Holland (b); Barry Altschul (perc); Philip Wilson (dms).

Four Compositions 1973 (Denon NCP8504, 1973).
Braxton (as, ss, fl, cl, cbcl); Masahiko Sato (p); Keiki Midorikawa (b).

In the Tradition, vol. 1 (Inner City IC2015, 1974).
Braxton (as, cbcl); Niels-Henning Orsted Pedersen (b); Tete Montoliu (pno); Albert Heath (dms).

In the Tradition, vol. 2 (Inner City IC2045, 1974).
Same personnel as above.

Solo: Live at Moers Festival (Ring 01002, 1974).
Braxton (as).

Quartet Live at Moers Festival (Ring 01010/11, 1974).
Braxton (as, ss, cbcl, cl, fl); Kenny Wheeler (tp); Dave Holland (b); Barry Altschul (perc).

Duo, vols. 1 and 2 (with Derek Bailey) (Emanem 3313/14, 1974).
Braxton (as, ss, fl, cl, cbcl); Bailey (g).

Royal, vol. 1 (with Derek Bailey) (Incus 43, 1974).
Braxton (as, ss, fl, cl, cbcl); Bailey (g).

Trio and Duet (Sackville 3007, 1974).
Braxton (as, cl, cbcl, chimes, b-d); Leo Smith (tp, flghn, pocket tp, perc); Richard Teitelbaum (synth, perc); Dave Holland (b).

New York, Fall 1974 (Arista AL4032, 1974).
Braxton (as, fl, cbcl); Kenny Wheeler (tp, flghn); Leroy Jenkins (vl); Dave Holland (b); Jerome Cooper (dms).

Five Pieces 1975 (Arista AL4064, 1975).
Braxton (as, ss, cl, cbcl, fl); Kenny Wheeler (tp, flghn); Dave Holland (b); Barry Altschul (dms).

Montreux-Berlin Concerts (Arista AL5002, 1975, 1976).

Braxton (as, ss, cl, cbcl); Kenny Wheeler (tp); Dave Holland (b); Barry Altschul (perc).

Creative Orchestra Music 1976 (Arista AL4080, 1976).
Braxton (as, ss, cbcl, cl, fl); ensemble of twenty-one musicians.

NY City Jazz-2 (Polydor 81511-1IMS, 1976).
Braxton (as, cl, cbcl); George Lewis (tb); Michael Jackson (g); Fred Hopkins (b); Barry Altschul (dms); Phillip Wilson (perc).

Elements of Surprise (with George Lewis) (Moers MOMU01036, 1976).
Braxton (as, ss, cl); Lewis (tb).

Duets 1976 (with Muhal Richard Abrams) (Arista AL4101, 1976).
Braxton (as, ss, cl, cbcl); Muhal Richard Abrams (pno).

Dortmund (Quartet) 1976 (Hat Art CD6075, 1976).

For Trio (Arista AL4181, 1977).
Braxton (fl, ss, cbcl, cl, as, *taragata,* perc); Henry Threadgill (fl, bfl, cl, as, ts, bs, perc); Douglas Ewart (picc, fl, ss, bcl, cl, as, bassoon, perc, homemade aerophone). Version Two: substitute Roscoe Mitchell and Joseph Jarman for Threadgill and Ewart.

For Four Orchestras (Arista A3L8900, 1978).
Four orchestras (each with forty musicians) perform Braxton's *Composition 82.* Recorded with the help of students and staff of the Oberlin Conservatory.

Birth & Rebirth (with Max Roach) (Black Saint BSR0024, 1978).
Braxton (as, ss, cl, sis); Roach (dms).

Alto Saxophone Improvisations 1979 (Arista AL8602, 1978–79).
Braxton (as).

8KN-(B-12) IRIO (for string quartet) (with the Robert Schumann String Quartet) (Sound Aspects SAS009, 1979).
Braxton (as); Michael Geiser (vl); Chiharv Yuuki (vl); Jurgen Weber (vla); Wolfgang Mehlhorn (cello).

One in Two, Two in One (with Max Roach) (Hat Hut 2R06, 1979).
Braxton (as, ss, sis, cbcl, cl, fl); Roach (dms, gongs, tuned cym).

Performance 9/1/1979 (Hat Hut 2R19, 1979).
Braxton (as, ss, sis, cl, cbcl); Ray Anderson (tb, a-tb, perc); John Lindberg (b); Thurman Barker (perc).

Seven Compositions 1978 (Moers MOMU01066, 1979).
Same personnel as above.

Composition No. 95 for Two Pianos (Arista AL9559, 1980).
Frederic Rzewski and Ursula Oppens (pno, zither, melodica).

Composition 98 (Hat Art 1984, 1981).
Braxton (as, ts, ss, sis, c-melody sax); Hugh Ragin (tp, flghn, picc. tp); Ray Anderson (tb, a-tbn); Marilyn Crispell (pno).

Six Compositions: Quartet (Antilles AN1005, 1981).
Braxton (as, ts, ss, sis, cbcl); Anthony Davis (pno); Mark Helias (b); Ed Blackwell (dms).

Four Pieces (with Giorgio Gaslini) (Dischi Della Quercia Q28015, 1981).
Braxton (as, ss); Gaslini (pno).

Composition 96 (Leo 169, 1981).
Braxton, conductor.
Open Aspects '82 (Hat Art 1995/96, 1982).
Braxton (as, sis), Richard Teitelbaum (synthesizer, microcomputer).
Six Duets (1982) (with John Lindberg) (Cecma 1005, 1982).
Braxton (as, sis, cl); John Lindberg (b).
Four Compositions (Quartet) 1983 (Black Saint BSR0066, 1983).
Braxton (as, sis, cl); George Lewis (tb); John Lindberg (b); Gerry Hemingway (perc).
Composition 113 (Sound Aspects SAS003, 1983).
Braxton (sis).
Six Compositions (Quartet) 1984 (Black Saint BSR0086, 1984).
Braxton (as, ss, c-melody sax, cl, fl); Marilyn Crispell (pno); John Lindberg (b); Gerry Hemingway (perc).
Prague 1984 (Quartet Performance) (Sound Aspects SAS CD038, 1984).
Quartet (London) 1985 (Leo CD/LR 200/201, 1985).
Quartet (Birmingham) 1985 (Leo CD/LR 202/203, 1985).
Five Compositions (Quartet) 1986 (Black Saint BSR 0106, 1986).
Braxton (as, ss, sis, c-melody, sax, cl, fl); David Rosenboom (pno); Mark Dresser (b); Gerry Hemingway (dms).
The Country Concert (West Wind 001, ca. 1987).
Braxton (reeds); Marilyn Crispell (pno); Mark Dresser (b); Gerry Hemingway (dms).
Six Monk's [*sic*] *Compositions 1987* (Black Saint BSR0116, 1987).
Braxton (as), Mal Waldron (pno); Buell Neidlinger (b); Billy Osborne (dms).
Duets 1987 (with Gino Robair) (Rastascan Records BRD002, 1987).
The Aggregate (with Rova Saxophone Quartet) (Sound Aspects SAS023, 1988).
Braxton (as, ss, sis); Jon Raskin (cl, as, bs); Larry Ochs (sis, ts); Andrew Voight (sis, ss, as, fl); Bruce Ackley (cl, ss).
Compositions 99, 101, 197 & 139 (Hat Art CD6019, 1988).
Braxton (as, sis); Garrett List (tb); Marianne Schroeder (pno).
19 (Solo) Compositions, 1988 (New Albion NA023CD, 1988).
Solo (London) 1988 (Impetus IMPLP 18818, 1988).
Ensemble (Victoriaville) 1988 (Victor 07, 1988).
Kol Nidre (with Andrew Voight) (Sound Aspects SAS CD031, 1988).
Seven Compositions (Trio) 1989 (Hat Art CD6025, 1989).
Braxton (as, c-melody sax, cl, fl, ss, sis); Adelhard Roidinger (b); Tony Oxley (dms).
Eugene (1989) (with Northwest Creative Orchestra) (Black Saint 120137-2, 1989).
Duets Vancouver 1989 (with Marilyn Crispell) (Music and Arts CD611, 1989).
Eight (+3) Tristano Compositions 1989 for Warne Marsh (Hat Art CD6052, 1989).

Two Compositions (Ensemble) 1989/1991 (Hat Art CD6086, 1989/1991). Anthony Braxton, conductor.
Eight Duets (Hamburg) 1991 (with Peter Wilson) (Music and Arts, 1991).
Quartet (Willisau) 1991 (Hat Art, 1991).

Anthony Braxton as Sideman

Muhal Richard Abrams, *Levels and Degrees of Light* (Delmark DS413, 1967).
Braxton (as); Abrams (cl, pno); Maurice McIntyre (ts); Charles Clark (b); Emmanuel Cranshaw (vib); Thurman Barker (dms); Penelope Taylor (v).
Günter Hampel, *The 8th of July 1969* (Birth NJ001, 1969).
Braxton (as, ss, cbcl); Hampel (pno, vib, bcl); Willem Breuker (as, ts, ss, bcl); Arjen Ghorter (b, b-g); Steve McCall (dms); Jeanne Lee (v).
Instant Composers Pool (ICP 007/008, 1969).
Braxton (cbcl); Günter Hampel (vib); Willem Breuker (bcl); Arjen Ghorter (b); Steve McCall (dms); Jeanne Lee (v). (Braxton appears on *Gib Mir Noch ein Spiegelei Mit Schinken.*)
Jacques Coursil, *Black Suite* (BYG Actuel 49, 1969).
Braxton (cbcl); Coursil (tp); Arthur Jones (as); Burton Greene (pno); Beb Guerin (b); Claude Delcloo (perc).
Alan Silva, *Lunar Surface* (BYG Actuel 12, 1969).
Braxton (as, ss); Silva (vl); Bernard Vitet (tp, flghn); Grachan Moncur III (tb); Kenneth Terroade (ts); Archie Shepp (ss); Leroy Jenkins (vl, vla); Beb Guerin (b); Malachi Favors (b); Claude Delcloo (dms).
Archie Shepp—Philly Joe Jones (Fantasy 86018, 1969).
Braxton (as, ss); Shepp (ts, pno); Jones (dms); Leroy Jenkins (vl); Chicago Beau (v, hm, ss); Julio Finn (hm); Earl Freeman (b).
Creative Construction Company, vol. 1 (Muse MR5071, 1970).
Braxton (as, ss, cl, cbcl, fl, chimes); Leroy Jenkins (vl, vla, recorder, xylo, hm, bicycle horn); Leo Smith (tp, flghn, frhn, seal horn, perc); Muhal Richard Abrams (pno, cello, cl); Richard Davis (b); Steve McCall (perc).
Creative Construction Company, vol. 2 (Muse MR5097, 1970).
Same instrumentation as above.
Marion Brown, *Afternoon of a Georgia Faun* (ECM 1004, 1970).
Braxton (as, ss, fl, cl, cbcl, perc, "chinese musette"); Brown (as, perc, *zomari*); Bennie Maupin (ts, as, fl, bcl, bells, perc); Chick Corea (pno, bells, gong, perc); Andrew Cyrille (perc); Jack Gregg (b, perc); Jeanne Lee (v); Gayle Palmore (pno, perc, v).
Chick Corea, *Circulus* (Blue Note LA882-J2, 1970).
Braxton (as, ss, cl, cbcl); Corea (pno, prepared pno, vib, bass marimba, perc); Dave Holland (b, g, perc); Barry Altschul (dms, bass marimba, perc).
Chick Corea, *Circling In* (Blue Note LA472-H2, 1970).
Same personnel as above.

Chick Corea, *Live in New York City* (Oxford OX 3005, 1970).
Same personnel as above.
Circle, Live in Germany Concert (CBS/SONY SOPL 19 XJ, 1970).
Same personnel as above.
Circle: The Paris Concert (ECM 1018/19, 1971).
Same personnel as above.
Circle: Gathering (CBS/SONY SOPL-20-XJ, 1971).
Same personnel as above.
Celestial Communication Orchestra, *My Country* (Leo CDLR 302, 1971).
Dave Holland, *Conference of the Birds* (ECM 1027, 1972).
Braxton (as, ss, cl, fl); Holland (b); Sam Rivers (ts, ss, fl); Barry Altschul (perc, marimba).
Dave Brubeck, *All the Things You Are* (Atlantic SD 1684, 1974).
Braxton (as); Brubeck (pno); Jack Six (b); Roy Haynes (dms).
Leroy Jenkins, *For Players Only* (JCOA 1010, 1975).
Braxton (cbcl); Jenkins (vl); ensemble of sixteen musicians.
Günter Hampel, *Enfant Terrible* (Birth 0025, 1975).
Braxton (fl, as, ss, cl, cbcl); Hampel (fl, vib, bcl, pno); Mark Whitecage (fl, as, cl); Thomas Keyserling (fl); Perry Robinson (cl); Jeanne Lee (v); Jack Gregg (dms); Martin Bues (dms).
Globe Unity Orchestra, *Pearls* (FMP 0380, 1975).
Braxton (as); ensemble of fifteen musicians.
Globe Unity Orchestra, *Jahrmarkt Local Fair* (PO Torch PTR/JWD-2, 1975).
Braxton (as); ensemble of fourteen musicians.
Anthology of New American Music, vol. 3 (Folkways 33903, 1975).
Braxton (cl); Karl Hans Berger (vib); David Holloway (v); Jon Deak (b); Joan Kalish (vla); Marcia Heller (oboe); Garrett List (tb); Ursula Oppens (organ); Frederick Rzewski (pno); Mike Sahl (b-g); Kathy Seplow (vl).
Wildflowers, vol. 2. (Douglas NMDP7046, 1976).
Braxton (as, cl, cbcl); George Lewis (tb); Michael Jackson (g); Fred Hopkins (b); Barry Altschul (dms); Philip Wilson (perc). Pianist not listed.
Richard Teitelbaum, *Time Zones* (Arista AL1037, 1976).
Braxton (as, ss, cbcl); Teitelbaum (synth).
Company, vol. 2 (Incus 23, 1976).
Braxton (ss, as, fl, cl, cbcl); Evan Parker (ss, ts); Derek Bailey (g).
Roscoe Mitchell, *Nonaah* (Nessa N9/10, 1977).
The album includes a performance of *Off Five Dark Six* by Braxton (ss) and Mitchell (as).
Woody Shaw, *Iron Men* (Muse MR5160, 1977).
Braxton (cl, as); Shaw (tp, cornet); Muhal Richard Abrams (pno); Cecil McBee (b); Joe Chambers (dms).
Company, vols 5–7 (Incus 28, 29, 30; 1977).
Braxton (as, ss, cl, fl); Tristan Honsinger (cello); Leo Smith (tp, fl); Steve

Lacy (ss); Maarten Van Regteren Altena (b); Han Bennink (dms, vla, banjo); Derek Bailey (g); Evan Parker (ss).

Muhal Richard Abrams, *1-00A+19* (Black Saint BSR0017, 1977).
Braxton (as, fl, ss, cl, v); Abrams (pno, synth, v); Henry Threadgill (as, ts, fl, v); Leonard Jones (b); Steve McCall (perc, v).

Roscoe Mitchell, *Duets with Anthony Braxton* (Sackville 3016, 1977).
Braxton (as, ss, cl, cbcl, bs); Mitchell (fl, as, bs, ss, ts, cl).

Roscoe Mitchell, *L-R-G, The Maze, S II Examples* (Nessa N14/15, 1978).
Braxton (perc); Mitchell (perc); Henry Threadgill (perc); Thurman Barker (perc); Malachi Favors (perc); Joseph Jarman (perc); Famadou Don Moye (perc); Douglas Ewart (perc).

Three Motions with Soloists from Chicago, New York and Vienna (R.A.U. 1010, 1978).
Braxton (as); Walter Muhammad Mali (ss, dms); Clifford Thornton (tp); Paul Fickl (vl, pno, ts); Fritz Novotny (fl, cl); Walter Schieffer (perc); Heinz Jager (b).

Ran Blake, *Rapport* (Arista/Novus AN3006, 1978).
Braxton (as); Blake (pno).

Walter Thompson, *Four Compositions* (Dane 001, 1979).
Braxton, (sis, perc, cbcl); Thompson (as, perc).

Roscoe Mitchell, *Snurdy McGurdy and Her Dancin' Shoes* (Nessa N20, 1980).
Mitchell and his ensemble perform Braxton's *The March*.

Leo Smith Creative Orchestra, *Budding of a Rose* (Moers 02026, 1979).
Braxton, Douglas Ewart, Wallace McMillan, Dwight Andrews, Marty Ehrlich (all reeds); Leo Smith, Kenny Wheeler, Hugh Ragin, Mike Mossman, Rob Howard (all tp); George Lewis, Ray Anderson, Alfred Patterson (all tb); Pinguin Moschner (tba); Roscoe Mitchell (as); Bobby Naughton (vib); Marilyn Crispell (pno); Wes Brown (b); Pheeroan Aklaff (dms, perc).

Roscoe Mitchell Creative Orchestra, *Sketches from Bamboo* (Moers 02024, 1979).
Same personnel as above.

Paul Smoker, *QB* (Alvas Records AR101, 1984).

Richard Teitelbaum Group, *Concerto Grosso (1985)* (Hat Art CD6004, 1985).
Braxton (reeds, electronics); Teitelbaum (pno, synth, electronics); George Lewis (tb, electronics).

Richard Teitelbaum, *Concerto Grosso* (Hat Art CD6004, 1985).

Recordings of Braxton's Music by Other Leaders

Frederic Rzewski, *First Recordings* (Finnadar SR9011, 1976).
Rzewski (pno) performs a version of *P-JOK*.

Dave Holland, *Emerald Tears* (ECM 1109, 1977).
Dave Holland performs Braxton's *Composition 69Q*.

Vienna Art Orchestra, *From No Time to Rag Time* (Hat Art 1999/2000, 1982).
The orchestra performs an arrangement of Braxton's *Composition 6K* as well as works by other composers.
ROVA Saxophone Quartet, *Beat Kennel* (Black Saint 120–126, 1987).
The London Jazz Composers Orchestra, *Zurich Concerts* (Intakt 004/005, 1988).

Music Index
(a general index follows this index)

A. Compositions and Recordings by Anthony Braxton

Recordings

All the Things You Are, 196
Alto Saxophone Improvisations 1979, 136, 191
Braxton and Bailey: Live at Wigmore, 183n.14
B-X°/N-O-1-47A, 126–28, 141 n.6, 148, 221 n
Complete Braxton 1971, The, 55 n, 172, 185, 207, 266n.82
Creative Orchestra Music 1972, 182, 219
Creative Orchestra Music 1976, 200 n, 203, 217–18, 252, 255, 258
Donna Lee, 196, 219
Duets 1976, 251
Embraceable You, 196
Five Pieces 1975, 1 n, 196, 201, 207, 251–55, 266 n.82
For Alto, 134–36, 178
For Four Orchestras, 230 n, 266
For Trio, 214–16, 266
For Two Pianos, 218–19, 266
Four Compositions 1973, 1 n, 183 n.12, 196–97, 207, 247
Four Compositions (Quartet) 1983, 227
In the Street, 127–28
In the Tradition, 1 n, 183, 196, 260
Live at Moers Festival 1974 (Quartet album), 1 n, 196
Live at Moers Festival 1974 (Solo album), 136, 190–91
Montreux-Berlin Concerts, 210, 255
New York Fall 1974, 1 n, 205, 213, 218, 251–52, 255
Performance 9/1/1979, 197, 201 n, 222 n, 223–25
Recital Paris '71, 181, 184, 186, 189 n, 190
Saxophone Improvisations Series F, 185, 190–91
Seven Compositions 1978, 197, 201
Six Compositions Quartet 1982, 207, 218
Song Is You, The 196
This Time, 127–28, 130–31, 148, 181
Three Compositions of New Jazz, 127, 131, 147–48, 180, 223 n
Together Alone, 182, 208, 219
Town Hall 1972, 182 n.9, 196
Trio and Duet, 196
You Go to My Head, 196
You Stepped out of a Dream, 196, 251

Compositions

"Composition 1," 130–31
Composition 1, 120–21
Composition 3, 124
Composition 4, 177
Composition 5, 120, 122
Composition 6A, 173
Composition 6C, 210–11
Composition 6E, 131, 223 n
Composition 6G, 126, 221 n
Composition 6I, 174, 197
Composition 6J, 174–76, 207
Composition 6K, 176
Composition 6L, 176
Composition 6N, 196
Composition 6P, 211
Composition 7, 122
Composition 8A, 134–36, 181 n.4
Composition 8B, 135

Composition 8C, 134–35
Composition 8I, 191
Composition 8K, 137
Composition 9, 126–27, 213n
Composition 10, 122, 216n
Composition 11, 124
Composition 12, 122
Composition 14, 122
Composition 17, 161
Composition 20, 219
Composition 21, 208–10
Composition 23A, 205, 207, 251
Composition 23B, 197–200, 251
Composition 23C, 218, 251, 255
Composition 23D, 196, 251
Composition 23E, 207
Composition 23G, 201
Composition 23K, 219
Composition 23M, 196–97
Composition 23O, 207
Composition 25, 182, 219–22
Composition 26A, 190
Composition 26B, 191–94
Composition 26E, 190
Composition 26G, 190
Composition 26H, 190
Composition 26J, 190
Composition 30-33, 219
Composition 34, 218
Composition 37, 213–14, 251
Composition 38A, 251
Composition 40F, 197
Composition 40G, 207, 227
Composition 40K, 227
Composition 48, 227
Composition 50, 227
Composition 51, 217–18
Composition 57, 203
Composition 69E, 227
Composition 69G, 197
Composition 69H, 201
Composition 69M, 201
Composition 76, 214–16, 227
Composition 77B, 190
Composition 82, 219, 225
Composition 95, 218–19, 225, 227
Composition 97, 200n
Composition 98, 216n
Composition 102, 274
Composition 105A, 227
Composition 120 (Trillium), 274
Composition 123, 227

B. Compositions and Recordings Cited

Abrams, Muhal Richard: *The Bird Song,* 106; *Levels and Degrees of Light,* 90n.45, 105–6, 117; *My Thoughts Are My Future,* 106, 117, 135; *Young at Heart/Wise in Time,* 105–6
Armstrong, Louis: *Struttin' with Some Barbecue,* 138
Art Ensemble of Chicago: *A Jackson in Your House,* 144; *The Paris Session,* 144; *The Spiritual,* 144; *Tutankhamun,* 144; *Urban Bushmen,* 273n
Ashley, Robert: *In Memorium Kit Carson,* 160
Ayler, Albert: *Bells,* 72, *New York Ear and Eye Control,* 71n
Blakey, Art: *Message from Kenya,* 64n.96
Bowie, Lester: *Jazz Death?* 138
Brown, Clifford: *Parisian Thoroughfare,* 127
Brown, Marion: *Afternoon of a Georgia Faun,* 164n, 181
Brubeck, Dave: *All the Things You Are,* 1n; *At College of the Pacific,* 51
Bryant, Allan: *Pitch Out,* 160n
Cage, John: *Reunion,* 136n; *Variations I,* 23n; *Variations II,* 122, 225n
Circle: *A.R.C.,* 163; *Ballad II,* 164n, *Circling In,* 165, 168; *Circulus,* 163; *Duet,* 244; *Fragments,* 165; *Gathering,* 164; *Nefertiti,* 164n, 167; *Paris Concert,* 169, 200n, 244; *The Song of Singing,* 164n, 171n; *Starp,* 167–68, 191; *There Is No Greater Love,* 166–67; *Toy Room/Q&A,* 164n, 171–72
Coleman, Ornette: *Change of the Century,* 70n; *Forms and Sounds for Wind Quintet,* 109n; *Inventions of Symphonic Poems,* 109n; *Saints and*

Soldiers, 109n; *The Shape of Jazz to Come,* 52n, 72; *Skies of America,* 109n; *This Is Our Music,* 70n
Coltrane, John: *Africa,* 64n. 96; *Ascension,* 70n, 72, 222, 239n; *Avant-Garde John Coltrane,* 72n; *Giant Steps,* 52n; *Kulu Se Mama,* 72n; *Liberia,* 64n.96; *A Love Supreme,* 72n; *Om,* 72n
Como, Perry: *More,* 42n
Corea, Chick: *Is,* 165; *Now He Sings, Now He Sobs,* 149n.36, 164; *Tones for Joan's Bones,* 164
Coursil, Jacques: *Black Suite,* 181
Curran, Alvin: *Home-Made,* 160n
Dolphy, Eric: *Miss Ann,* 251
Donaldson, Lou: *Midnight Creeper,* 153
Ellington, Duke: *Deep South Suite,* 64n.96
Erickson, Robert: *Cardenitas,* 160n
Feldman, Morton: *For Frank O'Hara,* 217; *Rothko Chapel,* 217
Fight On!: 210
Glass, Philip: *Music in Fifths,* 218
Haley, Bill: *Rock around the Clock,* 42n
Hampel, Günter: *The 8th of July,* 145n.18, 147
Hill, Andrew: *Black Fire,* 64n.96
Hines, Earl: *Jelly Jelly,* 138
Home Cookin' (Horace Silver): 67
Jamal, Ahmad: *Live at the Pershing,* 51
Jarman, Joseph: *As If It Were the Seasons,* 89, 106; *Morning (Including Circles),* 210n; *Song For,* 81n; *Song for Christopher,* 106
Joplin, Scott: *Maple Leaf Rag,* 251
Juicy Lucy (Horace Silver): 67
Kenton, Stan: *City of Glass,* 52
Lincoln, Abbey: *Straight Ahead,* 65
Little Richard: *Tutti Frutti,* 44
Lucier, Alvin: *Chambers,* 160n
Lymon, Frankie: *Why Do Fools Fall in Love?* 46
McLean, Jackie: *Let Freedom Ring,* 64n.96
Marsalis, Wynton: *Black Codes,* 273
Martirano, Salvatore: *L's GA,* 155
Miller, Mitch: *The Yellow Rose of Texas,* 42n
Mingus, Charles: *Foggy Day,* 127; *Pithecanthropus Erectus,* 64n.96
Mitchell, Roscoe: *Congliptious,* 106, 132; *The Little Suite,* 106; *Sound,* 87, 106
Morton, Jelly Roll: *Sidewalk Blues,* 127
Music, Maestro Please (Arturo Toscanini): 10
Neuhaus, Max: *Public Supply,* 160
Newport Rebels: 85, 85n
New York Contemporary Five: *The Funeral,* 64n.96
Old Rugged Cross: 46
Oliver, King: *Dippermouth Blues,* 126
Oliveros, Pauline: *Psi Star Psi d Tau Equals One,* 160n.69; *Rosemoon,* 160n
Opus de Funk (Horace Silver): 67
Parker, Little Junior: *Mystery Train,* 44
Presley, Elvis: *Hound Dog,* 44
Ravel, Maurice: *Asie,* 105
Riddle, Nelson: *Lisbon, Antigua,* 42n
Riley, Terry: *In C,* 160
Roach, Max: *Garvey's Ghost,* 64n.96; *Man from South Africa,* 64n.96; *We Insist! Freedom Now Suite,* 65
Rollins, Sonny: *Airegin,* 64n.96; *Freedom Suite,* 64n.96
Rzewski, Frederick: *No Place to Go but Around,* 219n; *Street Music,* 127n, 158n.66
Schoenberg, Arnold: *Five Pieces for Orchestra,* 213; *Three Pieces for Piano,* 128n
Schuller, Gunther: *Jazz Abstractions,* 109
Shepp, Archie: *Three for a Quarter, One for a Dime,* 150
Shorter, Wayne: *Juju,* 64n.96; *Nefertiti,* 64n.96
Simone, Nina: *Mississippi Goddamn!* 64n.96
Sinatra, Frank: *Learnin' the Blues,* 42n
Stockhausen, Karlheinz: *Aus den Sieben Tagen,* 122; *Carré,* 219n; *Gruppen,* 219n; *Klavierstücke XI,* 122; *Solo,* 219; *Zeitmasse,* 110
Stravinsky, Igor: *L'histoire du soldat,* 110; *Rite of Spring,* 176
Sun Ra: *Angels and Demons at Play,* 83n

Taylor, Cecil: *Chimampas,* 110n; *Enter Evening,* 110; *Hard Driving Jazz,* 72; *Unit Structures,* 110n
They Picked Poor Robin Clean: 106
Three Pieces for Piano (Arnold Schoenberg): 73
Tiger Rag: 211
Tristano, Lennie: *Digression,* 176
Tusques, François: *Free Jazz,* 143
Webern, Anton von: *Five Songs,* 176
Weston, Randy: *Uhuru Afrika,* 64n.96; *Music from the New African Nations,* 64n.96
Wolff, Christian, *Sticks,* 160n
Xenakis, Iannis, *Polytope,* 219n

General Index

Abraham Lincoln Center (Chicago), 83, 85, 88n, 113, 116, 133
Abrams, Muhal Richard, 78, 112, 116; as AACM adminstrator, 86; on aesthetic spiritualism, 100–101, 104–7; compared with Coltrane and King, 81; influence on Braxton, 114–15, 131–32; influence on young members of AACM, 81–82; on intentions of AACM, 89; on "little instruments," 99; on musical approach of Experimental Band, 79, 87; musical background, 79n; recording with Braxton, 251
Adderley, Cannonball, 63n.92, 66; in Chicago, 79n.7, 143n
Adler, Guido, 13n
Adorno, Theodor, 8n, 10n, 256. *See also* Media, mass
Afam Gallery, 93
Affro Arts Theater, 94
Africa: and AACM, 99–101; identification with on South Side, 36, 95–99; and jazz, 64–65, 69; jazz titles referring to, 64n; in references to Braxton, 264
African Americans: creative responses to charges of inferiority, 118–19; economic optimism among, in 1950s, 33; impact of tradition on AACM, 83–84; linking vernacular and musical nationalism, 66–67; physicality in, 204n; rhetorical voice in creative expression, 118–19, 162, 194, 200; trickster images among popular musicians, 243; vernacular musical culture, 18–19, 235–36
African Lion, 96
African Look, 96
Afro-American Dance and Culture Club, 93
Afrocentricity: in the AACM, 99–104; and Beethoven, 97, 234, 235n; and Braxton's aesthetics, 4, 60, 141–42, 180, 188, 209–10, 229–31, 234–35; and Braxton's picture titles, 137–39; critique of, 98–99; description of, 4n; early modern theorists, 97–98; in free jazz, 63; in rap, 273; and Yosef ben-Jochannan, 231, 235
Albertson, Chris, 153, 255, 257
Albin, Scott, 255
Altschul, Barry, 248; with Circle, 163–65, 171–73, 176, 182
American Center (Paris), 143, 144, 182–83
Ammons, Gene, 63n.92
Amougies Festival (Belgium), 145
Andersen, Eric, 249
Anderson, Fred, 82, 83, 86n, 103
Anderson, Ray, 197
Anderson, William, 239
Anti-jazz. *See* Jazz, free
Antin, David, 129
Archway, 80
Arista Records: and Braxton, 1, 179, 186, 191, 213, 254; dismissing Braxton, 4, 188, 266; marketing Braxton, 3, 198, 249–52; roster of artists, 249, 250n; signing Braxton, 240, 248–49
Armstrong, Louis, 118, 200, 235, 248, 258
Army. *See* Braxton, Anthony
Arriagada, Jorge, 183
Art and Soul Workshop, 93
Art Ensemble of Chicago (AEC), 55, 87, 124, 128; and Great Black Music, 99, 266; opposition to critical categories, 104; in Paris, 144–45, 153. *See also* Mitchell, Roscoe, Art Ensemble

Asante, Molefi, 4n
Ashley, Robert, 60, 160n
Association for the Advancement of Creative Musicians (AACM), 25, 75, 128, 169, 178, 207, 252; Abrams's leadership of, 81–82; administration, 86; aesthetic spiritualism and, 89, 100–108; and Afrocentricity, 89, 99–104; antiformalism in, 103, 126n; appropriation of modernism, 112; and black nationalism, 89–92; Braxton's membership in, 112–20; and civil rights groups, 91–92; collectivist precedents in black tradition, 83–84; concert music interests of, 81; conflicts in, 81–82, 100; day jobs of members, 140n; decline of, 140–42; decline of jazz and effect on, 83; early hangouts, 82; early musical style of, 79; embraces free jazz, 86–87; Experimental Band, 79–83, 86–87, 100; formation of, 85–89; initial memberships, 86; local coverage of, 88; members from Wilson Junior College, 55; performance spaces, 88n; planning of, 83; precursors as rehearsal band, 77–79; references to, in French criticism, 142, 144; rejection of harmony in, 104–8; relation to other arts groups, 93–95; as stable organization, 87–89; women members, 88–89
Austin, Larry, 126, 161
Avant-Garde, 2n. *See also* Modernism
Ayler, Albert, 272; as Arista artist, 250n; his antagonism toward harmony, 108; and musical spiritualism, 71; named in Braxton's press coverage, 248, 258; in Paris, 143n; references to, in Braxton's music, 193, 236

Babbitt, Milton, 11n, 17, 228
Backer, Steve, 250–52
Bailey, Alice, 230
Bailey, Derek, 183, 208
Baker, David N., 82n, 102
Baker, Houston A., Jr., 18n, 19, 189, 238
Bakhtin, Mikhail, 41
Baldwin, James, 62, 95
Balliett, Whitney, 13n, 255, 258–59
Band, 151
Baraka, Imamu Amiri (LeRoi Jones), 19, 26n, 67–69, 94, 231–32, 273
Barker, Thurman, 86n, 116, 141n
Bartók, Bela, 110, 260
Basie, Count, 64, 84, 136
Bass, Fontella, 89
Bechet, Sidney, 59, 142n
Beethoven, Ludwig von, 60n; named in Afrocentric theory, 97, 234, 235n
Behrman, David, 25, 159, 161
Beirach, Richard, 156n.57
Benjamin, Walter, 256, 266
ben-Jochannan, Yosef, 231, 235
Bennink, Han, 207
Benson, George, 153
Berendt, Joachim-Ernst, 14n.30
Berger, David G. *See* Peterson, Richard A.
Berger, Morroe, 12n
Berio, Luciano, 154
Berklee School of Music (Boston), 52n, 78n
Berlin, Irving, 42
Berry, Chuck, 44, 45, 74
Berry, Fred, 78n, 82n
Betsy Ross Elementary School, 37
Bird. *See* Parker, Charlie
Black aesthetics: and AACM, 99–108, 112; and Africa, 93–99; Braxton's advancement of, 4, 60, 119–20, 137–42, 180, 188, 203–4; Chicago organizations supporting, 93–95; and Davis, Miles, 238n; as expression of cultural resistance, 19–21, 26; and indeterminacy, 125–26; and modernism, 26; and spiritualism in free jazz, 69–72
Black Arts for Community Action, 157
Blackburn, Darlene, 89, 96n
Black church: Braxton's participation in, 37–38, 50, 232, 275; influence on AACM, 102–3; influence on civil rights groups, 91; influence on musical community, 84; influence on South Side, 35–36
Black Codes, 273
Black Order of Revolutionary Enterprise, 156
Black press: in Chicago, 33; reporting on racial conflict, 31–32

Black protest: in AACM, 89–92; Braxton's participation in, 61–63; early postwar expressions of, 48–49; in jazz, 19–21, 63–72, 85; jazz critics' aversion to, 64; jazz titles referring to, 64n.96; and soul jazz, 66–67
Black Liberator, 92
Black Panthers, 141
Black Truth, 88, 92
Black World, 90
Blackyard (House of UMOJA), 93
Blair, Lawrence, 230
Blakey, Art, 51, 64, 65, 263
Blanchard, Terrence, 270
Blesh, Rudi, 262n
Blevins, Brian, 147
Blindfold Test. See *Down Beat*
Bloom, Jane Ira, 275
Blue Devils Orchestra, 106
Blue Gargoyle, 88n, 155n.53
Blue Heaven, 38
Blue Note (Chicago), 51, 51n.61
Blue Note (Paris), 143
Blues People, 231. *See also* Baraka, Imamu Amiri
Boulez, Pierre, 110, 142; Braxton's musical references to, 26; influence on Braxton, 137; named in Braxton's press coverage, 3; in New York, 155
Bowie, Lester, 112, 116n, 132, 142, 144
Brand Nubian, 273
Braxton, Anthony (aesthetics): 24–27; appropriations of modernism in, 119–20, 130–31; black assertions in, 4, 60, 119–20, 137–42, 180, 188, 203–4, 209–10, 229–31, 234–36, 266; creative music and, 74, 99–100, 115, 229, 234; criticism of Cage, 162; developing political linkages with, during army period, 58–63; early embrace of jazz classicism, 52, 73–74; free jazz as false principle, 185, 207–8; free jazz as liberation, 72–73; iconoclastic prophesies in, 115n; identity and, 188–89, 194; influence of Asian philosophy on, 114; interest in science and technology (in childhood) 39, (in high school) 47–48, 110, (as professional) 26, 180, 185, 228; oppositions and subverted binaries in, 26, 60, 63, 74–75, 114–16, 115n, 123, 128, 137–39, 141–42, 180, 188–89, 226, 228, 236, 266–67; parody and satire in, 122–23, 127, 130–31, 136, 236, 266–67, 275; reads Cage's *Silence,* 114; restructuralism, 74, 118, 134, 189, 234; saxophone music as center of, 189, 225; socialist themes in, 178–79; theosophical thought in, 169–71, 229–37. *See also* Afrocentricity; Creative music; *The Tri-Axium Writings*
Braxton, Anthony (biographical): in AACM, 88n.36, 100, 112–20, 140–41, 182; Abrams's influence on, 114–15; as Arista artist, 1, 3–4, 179, 186, 188, 191, 198, 213, 240; army experiences, 56–60; black church experience, 37–38, 50, 232, 275; chess playing, 47, 136, 186; Chicago neighborhood, 37–38; childhood friends, 39, 45; with Circle, 163–79; family members, 38–39; impact of city on childhood, 39; jazz and adolescent alienation, 49–52; limited alternatives to AACM membership, 115; living with Coleman, 154–55; march interests, 39, 56; meeting experimentalists, 161; in Musica Elettronica Viva, 157–63; in New York, 153–63; in the 1980s, 274–76; in Paris, 142–46, 180–86; participation in black protest, 61–63; as postmodern musician, 24–27, 236–37, 240, 242–43, 274–76; recollections of racial tensions in Chicago, 29–32, 47–50; rejection of jazz category, 247; rejection of racial separatism, 74–75, 157; response to cultural hierarchy, 60–61; and rock 'n' roll, 45–47; in Tokyo, 183–84
Braxton, Anthony (compositions and compositional procedures): as AACM member, 120–39; alternatives to song form, 200–207; cell structures, 213–14, 228, 274n; conceptual grafting, 134; coordinate music, 214–16, 222–23; early concert works, 120–24; early works for improvising ensembles, 124–27; gravallic basic, 201–2, 218; head

Braxton, Anthony (compositions) (*cont'd*) movements, 174–76, 207, 219; intermediations in, 235–36; Kelvin compositions, 176–77, 200n.41, 200–201, 255; language music, 120, 134, 188, 192, 213, 222–26, 228–29; march parodies, 201–3, 210–11; moment form in, 129–30; notational innovations, 122–23, 134, 177, 213–14, 223, 227; oppositions in, 211–12; parody in, 122–23, 201–3, 236; phrase sequencing, 219; picture titles, 47, 120 137–39, 180, 226–29, 266–67; precompositional procedures, 136–37; Project Is, 182; schematic works, 211–16, 219, 222, 228–29; serialist references, 197, 207, 218; structure and system in, 194, 222–29. *See also* names of principal influences, titles of individual compositions

Braxton, Anthony (improvisations and improvisational methods): AACM trio, 127–31, 142n, 144–48, 153; "free" improvisations in, 207–12; noninteraction in, 129–30, 223; opposition in, 198–200; parody and revision in, 130–31, 136, 166–68, 197; phrase structure studies, 117–18; preperformance procedures, 133; saxophone music (accompanied), 166–68, 194–200; saxophone music (unaccompanied), 25–26, 131–37, 189–94, 225–26; studying saxophone, 56, 114. *See also* names of principal influences, titles of individual compositions

Braxton, Anthony (musical learning): 50–52, 56, 60–61; AACM membership, 120–39; AACM's impact on musical confluences, 114–15; effects of race consciousness on, 61–63; introduction to concert music at Roosevelt, 60–61; reading music history, 114; studying concert music, 114; studying electronic music, 183; transcribing jazz improvisations, 114

Braxton, Anthony (in performance and performance practices): in AACM groups, 116; with Abrams, 117–18; "Forms" concert, 182; leading AACM groups (musicians and venues), 116; in Paris, 181–82. *See also* Braxton entries above, titles of individual compositions

Braxton, Anthony (representations of): advocacy journalism of, 246–47; conflicting reports on, 1–4, 255–61; controversy (as false construct), 240, 243–44, 252, 255–56, 261; criticisms of, 254–56; decline of appeal, 265–67; early idiosyncrasies supporting later image, 244–45; as figure of consensus, 240, 242–43, 248–49, 252–53, 258–61; as homology of Otherness, 242–47, 263–67; language system, 247; in Paris, 143–46, 180–86; picture titles, 246, 254, 260, 266–67; quartet music as marking stylistic center, 248–49; as savior of jazz, 239–40, 242–43, 247–49, 252–54, 258–61; stereotypical images of (as AACM artist), 244, 252, 259, (in cardigan), 254, (chess playing), 250n, (and Circle), 244, (as mystic), 245–46, 260, 264, (as nationalist), 263–64, (as preacher), 263, (as primitive), 180, 245, 263–67, (as professor), 245, (as scientist), 246, 264–65, (as serialist), 246; subversion of critical stereotypes, 243, 266–67. *See also* individual album titles

Braxton, Clarence, Jr. (Juno), 38, 45, 47

Braxton, Clarence Dunbar, Sr., 38

Braxton, Julia Samuels (Fouché), 38

Brecht, George, 126

Breuker, Willem, 145n, 207

Brimfield, Bill, 86n

Brooklyn Academy of Music, 159

Brötzmann, Peter, 207

Brown, Earle, 122, 159

Brown, Frederick, 155n.54

Brown, James, 71, 115n, 200, 238

Brown, Marion, 145n.18, 150, 250n

Brown, Richard "Ari," 54

Brown vs. Board of Education, 33

Brubeck, Dave, 1n, 242, 262; black musicians' resentment toward, 54; and civil rights movement, 63; as com-

mentator, 12, 17n; and jazz classicism, 51, 53, 74, 131
Bryant, Allan, 159–60
Budge, E. A. Wallace, 230n
Bürger, Peter, 2n, 112
Burkholder, J. Peter, 22n

Cage, John, 27, 110, 126, 234; antagonism toward harmony, 111; challenging authority of Western high culture, 60, 125–26; critical references to, 146, 150; and experimentalism, 5; and happenings, 87n; influence on Braxton, 122, 125, 129, 178, 225n, 228, 230, 275; as leader among experimentalists, 22, 125–26, 159; literary work, 233
Calumet Park, 50
Carisi, John, 52n
Carles, Philippe, 181
Carmichael, Stokely, 91
Carnegie Recital Hall, 182
Carney, Harry, 258
Carter, Benny, 258
Carter, John, 275
Carter, Michael, 39
Case, Brian, 141
Caux, Daniel, 144, 146
Cayton, Horace, 29n
C. & C.'s, 78, 80
Cherry, Don, 71, 110
Chess: Braxton's interest in, 47, 136, 186
Chess (record co.), 46
Chicago: black arts organizations in, 93–95; black newspapers in, 92–93; books about, 29n–30n, 37n, 47n; civil rights organizations in, 92–93; decline of jazz in, 80; Democratic National Convention in, 141; jazz clubs in, 79–80, 155; jazz in, 79–80; jazz performers in, 79n.7; race riots on West Side, 92n; radio announcers in, 51; radio programs, 93–94; record companies in, 46. *See also* South Side
Chicago Defender, 31, 33, 37, 45, 93
Chicago Freedom Movement, 92, 93, 140
Chicago Musical College (of Roosevelt University), 51
Chicago Transit Authority (music group), 115n
Chicago Vocational High School, 47–48, 229
Christian, Jodie, 78, 79n.7, 83, 87n
Cicero (Illinois), 31, 50
Cinema Le Vézelay, 182
Circle, 163–79, 180–81; group improvisational procedures, 170–72, 208; references to, 244
Circle Inn, 38
Civil rights movement: musicians' support of, 63–64, 85. *See also* Black protest; names of individual organizations
Clanky (trumpeter), 82
Clark, Charles, 78n, 86n, 116
Clarke, Kenny, 142n, 143n
Cleage, Albert, 97
Clouds, 45
Cocteau, Jean, 125, 178
Coda, 117, 147, 246–47, 252
Cohran, Phil, 83, 85, 87n, 88n, 94
Cole, Nat, 63, 262
Coleman, Ornette, 52, 66, 68n, 153, 272; acceptance of, 149; antagonism toward harmony, 108; Braxton's initial interest in, 54, 114, 115n; critical representation of, 263; effect of critical coverage on career, 242; European tour, 143; harmolodic theory of, 109, 110n; impact of modernism on, 109; influence on Abrams, 78n.2; influence on Braxton, 74, 117, 132, 135, 196; with Living Theater, 154; and musical spiritualism, 70, 230; named in Braxton's press coverage, 247, 252, 254, 257–59; in New York, 154–55; and New York Jazz Artists' Guild, 85n; opposition to critical categories, 103–4; in Paris, 145; reference to in Braxton's improvising, 117
Collective Black Artists, 156
Coltrane, John: 58, 66, 82n, 128, 269; acceptance of, 149; antagonism toward harmony, 108; critical representations of, 263; effect of critical coverage on career, 242; influence on Abrams, 81; influence on Braxton, 54, 56, 114, 135; influence on the Chicago jazz community, 79; motivating Braxton's performance proce-

Coltrane, John (*continued*)
dure, 117; and musical spiritualism, 71–72, 235; named in Braxton's press coverage, 1, 2, 247, 254, 257, 259, 263
Columbia Records, 53n, 161n.73, 249
Committee for Independent Political Action, 92
Como, Perry, 42
Composition Notes, 192n, 213n, 219n, 275
Concert music, 10. *See also* names of individuals and groups
Condroyer, Philippe, 183
Congress on Racial Equality (CORE), 57, 62, 91
Connick, Harry, 274
Cooke, Jack, 147–48
Cool jazz, 242
Cooper, Jerome, 248
Coordinating Council of Community Organizations (CCCO), 92, 140
Corea, Chick, 163–79, 230, 240, 244
Cottage Grove Avenue, 37, 78, 82
Coursil, Jacques, 143, 145
Cowell, Henry, 22, 228, 233
Cranshaw, Bob, 79n
Crawford, Richard, 210n
Creative Construction Company, 158
Creative music, 74, 99–100, 115, 229, 234, 245. *See also* Association for the Advancement of Creative Musicians
Criticism, jazz. *See* Jazz criticism
Crosby, Bing, 42
Crouch, Stanley, 270
Crown Propellor Lounge, 37
Crump, Paul, 93
Cruse, Harold, 63
Curran, Alvin, 160n
Cuscuna, Michael, 251
Cyrille, Andrew, 103, 150n

Dahlhaus, Carl, 13n.27
Daley, Mayor Richard J., 31, 92
Dance, Stanley: as creator of mainstream construct, 14
Danto, Arthur C., 272
Davis, Anthony, 273n, 275
Davis, Clive, 240, 249–50
Davis, Francis, 273n
Davis, Miles, 54, 163, 258; Braxton's initial interest in, 115n; challenging critical categories, 19n.43, 151, 157n.60, 238–39; in Chicago, 79; depicting black violence, 242n; depicting flux of postmodern, 238–39; influence on Braxton, 178; influence on jazz musicians, 240; in New York, 156n
Dawson, William, 34
Daylie, Holmes "Daddy-o," 38, 51
Debord, Guy, 257
DeJohnette, Jack, 54, 78, 82n, 156n; introduces Braxton to Corea, 163
De Lerma, Dominique-René, 97n.64, 235n
De Lio, Thomas, 225n
Dells, the, 117, 186
Delmark Records, 90, 178, 182
de Maria, Walter, 125
de Pillars, Murray N., 93n, 181n
Desmond, Paul, 51, 54, 74; influence on Braxton, 56, 115n, 135, 236; named as Braxton's hero, 59; named in Braxton's press coverage, 258–59
DeVeaux, Scott, 12n, 13n.27
Dewey, John, 23
DiMaggio, Paul, 10n
Dinwiddie, Gene, 78n, 82n
Dolphy, Eric: allusion to in Abrams's music, 106; anti-jazz experiments, 72; Braxton's initial interest in, 54, 74, 114, 115n; impact of modernism on, 110; named in Braxton's press coverage, 257–58; unaccompanied solo playing, 132
Domaine Musicale, 142
Donaldson, Jeff, 94
Donaldson, Lou, 153
Donovan, Gerald, 88n.36, 116
Doo-wop, 45–46
Dostoevsky, Feodor, 62
Double consciousness, 20
Douglass, Frederick, 63
Down Beat: on AACM, 88; Blindfold Test, 149, 169, 178, 243, 255; on Braxton, 117, 147–48, 178, 181–82, 225, 245–46, 252, 256n; coverage in 1969, 149–53; interviewing Corea, 169; in the 1980s, 269; "Racial Prejudice in Jazz," 65; readership profile, 151n.41

Drake, St. Clair, 29n
Du Bois, W. E. B., 20, 49n, 62
Du Bois, W. E. B., Freedom Center, 93
Duchamp, Marcel, 125
Duhamel, Antoine, 183
DuSable High School, 78–79
Dutilh, Alex, 184

Earth, Wind and Fire, 83n
Ebony, 33, 34
Echenoz, Jean, 181
Eighth Army Band, 112
El-Doradoes, 45
Electric Circus, 155
El Grotto Supper Club, 38
Ellington, Duke, 84, 190, 263, 270n, 274; and civil rights, 63–64; influence on Braxton, 178, 217; objections to critical labels, 103n
Ellis, Don, 110
Ellison, Ralph, 19, 62, 263n; blues impulse, 38; on Ellington, 190; expression of protest in *Invisible Man,* 201n; on jazz ethos, 170, 276; on Mahalia Jackson, 36; and signifying, 106; usage of mainstream label, 14n.30
Emmanuel, Gordan (Emanuel Cranshaw), 90n.45
Enchanters, 45
Erdman, Jean, 154
Erickson, Robert, 160n
Evans, Gil, 258
Evers, Medgar, 57
Ewart, Douglas, 216
Experimental Band. *See* Association for the Advancement of Creative Musicians
Experimentalism (musical): and Braxton, 4–5, 137; improvisation in, 126, 158–59; influence on Braxton's early music for improvising ensembles, 124–31; overview, 22–24; in relation to African-American music, 125–26, 160; in relation to free jazz, 23–24; spiritualism in, 158–59; vernacular ethos in, 159–62

Fabian, Johannes, 265n
Fair, Ronald, 93
Farmer, Art, 255
Faubus, Orval, 64
Favors, Malachi, 55, 78, 132; as Afrocentric theorist, 99, 114; church background, 103; early AACM performances, 82n; as member of Art Ensemble of Chicago, 87; in Paris, 142
Faye, Marty, 51
Feather, Leonard: and anti-jazz, 21n; civil rights and jazz, 63n, 64; and rock music, 151–52; State Department and jazz, 15n.33
Feldman, Morton, 122, 177, 217
Festival de Chatellerault, 182, 219
Fielder, Alvin, 82n, 103
Fifth Army Band, 56–57
Fifth Jack's, 80, 82–83
Finegan, Lee, 52n
Five Spot, 153
520 Club, 37
Flash Gordon, 39
Flavor Flav, 243
Forces in Motion, 274
Fort Knox, 56
Fort Sheridan, 56, 58
Foster, Hal, 243, 267
Fouché, Donald, 38
Fouché, Gregory, 38
Fouché, Lawrence, 38
France, jazz in. *See* Jazz: in Paris; Jazz criticism: French; Jazz, free: in Paris
Frankfurt School, 7n.9. *See also* Marxist criticism
Franklin, Aretha, 71, 200, 249
Frazier, E. Franklin, 35, 36n, 102
Free jazz. *See* Jazz, free
Freeman, Bud, 52n.67
Freeman, Howard, 39
Freud, Sigmund, 62
Fuller, Buckminster, 264
Fusion, 150–51, 177–78, 238, 249
Futura, 186

Gallery Row, 93
Garrett, Donald Rafael, 78–79, 82
Garvey, Marcus, 62
Gates, Henry Louis, Jr., 18n, 26, 106n; on indeterminacy, 126n, 136
Geertz, Clifford, 46
Gell, Jack, 51, 56
George, Nelson, 18, 249n.25

Getz, Stan, 52
GI Bill, 60
Giddins, Gary, 255, 257, 259, 270
Gillespie, Dizzy, 64
Gilmore, John (pianist), 90n.45
Gilmore, John (saxophonist), 79, 82
Gilmore, Mikal, 260
Gitler, Ira, 64n.95, 151
Giuffre, Jimmy, 154
Glass, Philip, 25, 160–61, 177, 218, 234
Goddet, Laurent, 146
Golson, Benny, 51
Gone Primitive, 261
Goodman, Benny, 154, 242
Gourgues, Maurice, 185
Graettinger, Robert, 52, 74
Granada Ballroom, 38
Grateful Dead, 249
Greenwich Village, 153–63
Griffin, Johnny, 79
Grofé, Ferde, 56
Gros-Claude, Paul, 184
Grossberg, Lawrence, 7n, 8
Grove Circle Lounge, 38

Haley, Bill, 45
Hall, Stuart, 260
Hamilton, David, 154
Hampel, Günter, 144–45, 150, 182
Hancock, Herbie, 78, 79n.7, 156n.58, 240
Harlem Music Center, 156
Harris, Eddie, 78–79, 87n
Harrison, Donald, 270
Harvey, David, 40, 243
Hawkins, Coleman, 132
Hawkins, "Screaming" Jay, 243
Haynes, Roy, 163n, 164
Hebdige, Dick, 7n, 17n, 260, 262, 266n
Hefti, Neal, 51
Heineman, Alan, 149–50
Heline, Corinne, 230
Henderson, Fletcher, 258
Hendrix, Jimi, 238, 243
Hennen, Burkhard, 219
Henry, Pierre, 129
Hentoff, Nat, 13n.27, 66, 68n, 70
Hepsters, 45
Herskovits, Melville, 36n
Hierarchy, cultural: and the arts, 2n; Braxton's response to, 60–61; divisions in, 8; and popular music, 9–10
Hi-Fi/Musical America, 154
Hindemith, Paul, 78n
Hines, Earl, 244
Hirsch, Arnold, 29, 30n.9, 62n
Hodges, Johnny, 190, 247
Holiday, Billie, 118, 262
Holland, Dave, 176, 182, 196, 248; with Circle, 163–65, 171–73
Holt, Scotty, 82n
Holt, Thomas C., 34
Hope, Lynn (al-Hajj Abdullah Rasheed Ahmed), 65
Hubbard, L. Ron, 168
Humphrey, Fred, 94
Hungry Eye, 88n.33
Hurston, Zora Neale, 19
Huyssen, Andreas, 6n, 11

Islam, 65
Ives, Charles, 204, 233

Jackson, Jessie, 93
Jackson, John Shenoy, 86, 90–91
Jackson, Mahalia, 33, 35–36, 46
Jamal, Ahmad (Fritz Jones), 38, 51, 54, 65, 79n.7
James, George G. M., 97, 100
Jameson, Frederic, 200
Jarman, Joseph, 55, 78, 86, 112; AACM concerts, 88n.34; in AACM study group, 114; arranging for Experimental Band, 79; duet with Braxton, 182, 208–10; indebtedness to Abrams and AACM, 81; involvement in performance art, 87; and little instruments, 99; in Paris, 142, 144, 182; trio with Braxton, 216; and unaccompanied performances, 131–32; writing poetry, 81
Jarrett, Keith, 240
Jazz: alternative groups, 85; and black protest, 19–21, 63–72, 85; Braxton as savior, 239–40, 245; business of, 85; in Chicago, 78–79; as classical construct, 12–21, 52–54, 269–74; and Coltrane, 239; and commercialization, 83–84; and Davis, Miles, 238–39; and erosion of cultural hier-

archy, 12–21; and evolutionary models, 12–14; fears of, 152n.47, 152–53, 239; forms of resistance in, 19–21; as motivation for formation of AACM, 83; multilinearity in, 129; musicians' limited historical knowledge of, 66; in the 1980s, 269–76; objections to term among musicians, 103–4, 153, 157n.60, 247; in Paris, 142–44; and postmodernism, 12–21, 238–40, 269–76; reports of decline of, 13n.26, 80n.8; rhythm as aesthetic center (Williams), 108; structural relationships to modernism, 111–12. *See also* Jazz, mainstream
Jazz, free: acceptance of, 149; Afrocentric/modernist linkages in, 63, 69; antagonism toward harmony, 108; as anti-jazz, 21, 72; appropriated into mainstream, 247, 252, 273n; appropriation of modernism, 24, 63, 74, 108–11; and black protest, 67–69; and Braxton's reputation, 1; and Circle, 163–79; as critique of mainstream, 4, 20–21; effect of criticism on reception of, 242; in Europe, 207–8; and experimentalism, 23–24; impact of modernism on, 109–12; interpreting modernism as spiritual music, 69–71; in New York, 155–57; in Paris, 143–46; oppositions to critical categories, 103–4; and postmodernism, 21, 269; revision of swing concept in, 165–66
Jazz, mainstream (critical category), 1; black appropriation of, 66; Braxton's appropriation of, 73–74; Braxton as savior of, 239–40, 242–43, 247–49, 252–54, 258–61; Braxton's entry into, 179; collapse of construct, 149–53; opposition to, 19–21; as pastiche, 272; as revisionist history, 14–21, 272; and white hipster, 68
Jazz and Blues, 147
Jazz and People's Movement, 150, 157
Jazz and Pop, 147, 154, 178
Jazz Composers' Guild, 85
Jazz Composers' Orchestra Association, 182
Jazz criticism: aversion to politics in, 64; difficulties in interpreting Braxton's music, 1–4, 148; early postwar writers, 13; and free jazz, 67–69; French, 13, 143–46, 180–86; and mass media, 240–43; as new criticism, 13n.27; primitivist images, 12–13, 242, 242n, 261–67; and production of signs, 240–43; radical, 67–69; representations of popular musicians, 242. *See also* Primitivism
Jazz Hot, 143, 145, 180–81, 184, 186
Jazz Monthly (UK), 147
Jazz-rock. *See* Fusion
Jenkins, Leroy, 90n, 103, 116n; AACM concerts, 88n; with Braxton's trio, 126–31, 148; in Paris, 142, 144
Jet, 33
Johnson, Bill, 126
Johnson, John H., 33
Johnson, Robert, 238
Joiner, Allan, 88n.35
Jones, Isham, 166
Jones, Leonard, 86n
Jones, LeRoi. *See* Baraka, Imamu Amiri
Jones, Philly Joe, 146
Joplin, Janis, 249
Joplin, Scott, 251
Jost, Ekkehard, 129n
Judson Hall (Peace Church), 158, 163

Kabbala, 230n
Kagel, Mauricio, 154
Kaleidoscope, 88
Kandinsky, Vladimir, 107n
Karenga, Maulana (Ronald Everett), 97
Kart, Lawrence, 147, 150
Keil, Charles, 19n, 102
Kelvin, Lord, 176–77, 228
Kendall, Ian, 239
Kenton, Stan, 52–54, 74
King, Reverend Martin Luther, Jr., 81, 91, 140, 263; affirming black religious protest, 36; Birmingham march, 57, 72; headquarters in Chicago, 92, 93
King (record co.), 46
Kinks, 249
Kirk, Rahsaan Roland, 79n, 154, 156
Koester, Robert, 90, 106n
Kofsky, Frank, 21n, 67–69

Konitz, Lee, 1n, 52, 59, 143n, 257, 178
Korea. *See* Seoul
Kramer, Jonathan, 129

La Coupe à Dix Francs, 183
Land, Harold, 181n.4
Lang, Eddie, 258
Lange, Art, 258
Lashley, Lester, 78n, 86n
Lashley, Sandra, 86n, 89
Lee, Jeanne, 145n, 212
Lefebvre, Henri, 257
Leonard, Neil, 102
Lequime, Michel, 185
Less, David, 259
Levin, Robert, 178
Levine, Lawrence, 18n, 69, 102
Lewis, George, 210, 275
Lewis, Jerry, 68
Lewis, John, 17, 74, 131, 263
Liebman, David, 157n.61, 163n
Ligeti, Gyorgy, 111
Lincoln, Abbey, 65
Lincoln Center (New York), 270
Lipman, Samuel, 11n.21
Lipsitz, George, 10n, 41
Little instruments, 99, 130
Little Richard (Penniman), 44, 45, 71, 243
Little Rock (Ark.), 31, 48
Litweiler, John, 90n; on Coltrane's influence on Braxton, 117; critical writing, 146–47, 257; on early AACM style, 79; interviewing Abrams, 100–101; interviewing Braxton, 115n; on precursors of the Experimental Band, 78n
Lock, Graham, 274
Loupias, Bernard, 180, 184
Lucier, Alvin, 126, 159–60
Lymon, Frankie, 45, 46, 74
Lynch, Kevin, 245n
Lytton, David, 93

McCall, Steve, 78, 83; with Braxton's trio, 126; in Paris, 142, 144, 145n.18
McCartney, Paul, 154
McCoy, Corky, 239n
McCoy, Sid, 51
McDonough, John, 151
McIntyre, Maurice (Kalaparusha Ahrah Difda), 78n, 86n, 90n.45, 116, 141n
McKie's Disc Jockey Lounge, 38, 79n.7
McKissick, Floyd, 91
McLean, Jackie, 58, 115n
McLuhan, Marshall, 11
MacMillan, Wallace, 78n
McRae, Barry, 244
Mailer, Norman, 68
Mainstream jazz. *See* Jazz, mainstream
Malcolm X, 62, 63, 72, 88n.34, 91, 97, 263
Manchester, Melissa, 249
Mancini, Henry, 51
Manilow, Barry, 249
Mann, Herbie, 63
March on Washington, 57
Marcus, Greil, 41
Marks, Morton, 209
Marsalis, Wynton, 269–70, 273n, 274
Marsh, Warne, 52, 59, 74–75, 257
Martin, Terry, 90
Martirano, Salvatore, 155
Marx, Karl, 62
Marxist criticism, 151
Mason, Lowell, 61
Media, mass: and contemporary cultural change, 7–12; effect on free jazz and experimentalism, 24; semiotics of, 240, 243, 256–61
Melody Makers, 50
Messiaen, Olivier, 106, 255
Met Records (Maury Alpert's), 51n.62
Meyer, Leonard, 5–6, 269
Meyrowitz, Joshua, 40
Midorikawa, Keiki, 183
Milhaud, Darius, 53n
Miller, Jim, 9n
Mills College, 53n, 274n
Mingus, Charles, 64, 85, 217, 263
Mr. Wizard, 39, 262
Mitchell, Blue, 153
Mitchell, Doug, 87n
Mitchell, Roscoe, 78, 112, 257; AACM performances, 82, 116; on aesthetic spiritualism, 101, 104–7; arranging for Experimental Band, 79; aversion to harmony, 104–5, 128; as Braxton's early role model, 55–56; concert music interests of AACM, 81,

114; critical comparison with Braxton, 147; criticism of jazz clubs, 90; on decline of clubs in Chicago, 80n.9; as influence on Braxton's music, 124, 132; in Paris, 142, 144; procedures paralleling Cage's, 128; recalling initial AACM meetings, 86; sponsors Braxton's AACM membership, 113; trio with Braxton, 216
Mitchell, Roscoe, Art Ensemble, 128, 147
MJT + 3, 79n.3
Modernism: and avant-garde, 2n; definition of, 2n; impact on free jazz, 109–12; linkages with Afrocentricity in jazz, 63, 69; and primitivism, 261–62; structural relationships to black music, 111–12
Moers Jazz Festival, 183
Moment form, 129–30
Monk, Thelonious, 262
Monterey Pop Festival, 151
Montgomery (Ala.), 48
Moonglows, 45
Moore, David (Amus Mor), 88n.34, 94, 106
Morgenstern, Dan, 150–51, 269
Morton, Jelly Roll, 59
Moye, Famadou Don, 99n, 144n
Muhammad, Elijah, 33, 38, 91, 97
Muhammad Speaks, 33, 65n.98
Murphy, Spud, 17
Murray, Albert, 19, 47, 66–67, 102, 238
Murray, David, 270
Murray, Sunny, 110
Musée d'Art Moderne de la Ville de Paris, 182
Museum of African-American History, 88n.33, 93, 96
Musica Elettronica Viva (MEV), 126–27, 145–46, 157–63
Mwanga, Kunle (George Conley), 183–84, 219n
Myers, Amina Claudine, 89
Myrick, Donald, 83n
Mysticism. *See* Spirituality

National Association for the Advancement of Colored People (NAACP), 31, 57; jazz musicians' support of, 63
National Endowment for the Arts, 90n
Nation of Islam, 65. *See also* Malcolm X; Muhammad, Elijah
Neal, Larry, 68n
Negro Digest, 93, 96
Negro History Bulletin, 33
Neidlinger, Buell, 154
Nelson, Oliver, 151
Nelson, Stanley, 265n
Nessa, Chuck, 90, 132
Nestico, Sammy, 51
Neuhaus, Max, 159–60
New England Conservatory, 110
New Negro, 262
Newport Jazz Festival, 54. *See also* Rump Festival
Newsweek, 265
New York, 153–63
New York Contemporary Five, 72. *See also* same heading in Music Index
New York Jazz Artists' Guild, 85
New York Times Sunday Magazine, 269
Nicholas, Albert, 149
Nkosi, Lewis, 98
NOMMO, 94–95
Nutty Professor, 68

Occhiogrosso, Peter, 258
Occult. *See* Spirituality
October Revolution, 85
Oliveros, Pauline, 27, 126, 160, 274
Omarlama, 209n
Onli, Turtel, 209n
Operation Push, 93
Organization of Black American Culture (OBAC), 94–95
Ori, Shosana, 62
Otherness, 261–67; African Americans as, 29; and experimentalism, 160; and jazz, 242, 262–63; popular images of (homologous figuration), 261–67. *See also* Primitivism
Outlaws, 249

Pad, 80
Palace, 182
Palace of Fine Arts, 191
Palmer, Robert, 252–55, 259
Paris: AACM in, 142; American jazz musicians in, 142–44; Braxton in,

Paris: AACM in (*continued*) 142–46; French musicians performing in, 143; performance venues in, 143
Paris Concert (Circle), 169
Paris Streets (sound track), 182n.8
Parker, Charlie, 20, 196, 235–36; allusions to, in Abrams's music, 106; as canonical figure, 13; named in Braxton's press coverage, 2, 247, 252, 254, 257, 259–60; popular representations of, 242, 263
Parker, Graham, 249
Parker, Little Junior, 44
Parrot (record co.), 46
Partch, Harry, 27, 110, 160, 228, 233
Patrick, Pat, 82
Peace Church. *See* Judson Hall
Pee Wee's, 156
Penderecki, Krzysztof, 111, 238
Pepper, Art, 52
Pershing Ballroom, 38
Peterson, Richard A., 9n, 249n
Phamous Lounge, 88n.33, 116
Picture titles. *See* Braxton, Anthony (compositions and compositional procedures)
Platters, 45
Pleasants, Henry, 11n
Plugged Nickel, 88n.33
Pluralism, 6–7
Pollack, Jackson, 176
Popular Music, 9–10, 240–42. *See also* Rock 'n' roll
Portal, Michel, 143
Postmodernism: and critics' confusion, 1–4; and free jazz, 21; instability of, 7–12, 200; and jazz, 240, 256–61, 269–76; and mass media, 240–43; and popular culture, 240, 256–57
Powell, Adam Clayton, 34
Powell, John, 54
Presley, Elvis, 44, 45, 242
Previn, André, 17n
Price, Sally, 265n
Primitivism, 261–67; in describing Braxton, 180, 245, 263–67; in describing jazz, 12–13, 242, 242n, 262–63, 265n, 274; and experimentalism, 160; and reporting of black music, 118n, 274. *See also* Jazz criticism; Otherness
Public Enemy, 243, 275
Pumphrey, Virgil (Absholom Ben-Shlomo), 88n.35

Racial and ethnic tensions: in the armed forces, 56–59; in Chicago, 29–32; in jazz, 65–69; in New York jazz, 156–57; press reports of, 29, 50. *See also* Braxton, Anthony (biographical)
Radio Free Jazz, 252
Radio programs. *See* Chicago
Reagon, Bernice Johnson, 18
Record companies (Chicago), 46
Record Row, 46
Record stores. *See* Met Records
Reed, Lou, 249
Reich, Steve, 126, 160–61, 218
Relph, Edward, 40, 41n.36
Restructuralism. *See* Braxton, Anthony (aesthetics)
Reynolds, H. Robert, 210
Reynolds Club, 88n.33
Rich, Buddy, 242n
Richarda Music, 90
Riley, Terry, 160, 177, 218
Ring Records, 182
Roach, Max, 65, 85, 143n, 255
Roberts, John Storm, 255
Roberts, Marcus, 270
Robert Schumann Quintet, 274
Robert Taylor homes, 37
Robinson, Troy, 78n, 79, 82n, 88n
Rock 'n' roll: and Braxton, 45–47; and cultural hierarchy, 9–10; overview, 41–45; and postmodernism, 43–45. *See also* Doo-wop
Rodgers, Richard, 42, 56
Rodney, Red, 53
Rogers, Joel A., 97, 100
Rollins, Sonny, 51, 54, 58, 71, 263; influence on Chicago musicians, 79; unaccompanied solo performances, 132
Roosevelt University, 51, 60, 114
Rosaldo, Renato, 18
Rosenboom David, 155
Rout, Leslie, 86n, 99
Rump Festival, 85. *See also* Newport Jazz Festival

Russell, George, 52n
Russell, Pee Wee, 258
Rzewski, Frederick, 25, 230; influence on Braxton, 127n, 145n, 178; and Musica Elettronica Viva, 157–63

Sachs, Curt, 226
Salle de la Mutualité, 145
Sam and Dave, 117, 186
Sanders, Pharoah, 156
Satie, Erik, 110–11, 178
Sato, Masahiko, 183
Saturday Review, 13
Sauter, Eddie, 52n
Saxophone music. *See* Braxton, Anthony (improvisations and improvisational methods)
Schematics, 47. *See also* Braxton, Anthony (compositions and compositional procedures): picture titles
Schillinger, Joseph, 78n
Schlippenbach, Alexander, 207
Schoenberg, Arnold, 60, 110–11, 226; influence on Braxton, 73–74, 114, 132, 178, 230, 275; named in Braxton's press coverage, 3, 259
Schuller, Gunther, 17, 74, 109, 131, 263; challenging Cage's significance, 125n; on Coleman's harmolodic theory, 110n
Science and technology. *See* Braxton, Anthony (aesthetics)
Scientology, Church of, 163n, 168–71, 177, 182, 186, 230
Scott, Sherri, 89, 94
Second Festival of Free Jazz de Colombes, 182
Segal, Joe, 51n, 79n.7
Seoul, 58, 72–73, 112
Serialism, 11, 22
Serkin, Peter, 154
Shaw, Artie, 84n, 242
Shearing, George, 17n
Shepp, Archie, 70n, 150, 179, 258, 272; as free-jazz spokesman, 67–69; in New York, 157; in Paris, 146. *See also* New York Contemporary Five in Music Index
Shihab, Sahib (Eddie Gregory), 65
Shorter, Wayne, 240
Silvert, Conrad, 259
Sims, Zoot, 149
Sinatra, Frank, 242
620 Club, 37
Skryabin, Alexandre, 111
Slugs, 156
Smith, Bill, 179n, 246–47, 252, 254
Smith, Leo, 103–5, 266n.82; in AACM study group, 114; with Braxton's trio, 126–31, 148; in Paris, 142; soloing with creative orchestra, 203
Smith, Leonard, 116n
Smith, Patti, 249
Smith, Will, 147–48, 247
Smithsonian Institution, 270
Sonic Arts Union, 129, 159
Soul jazz, 66–67, 242
Souls of Black Folk (Du Bois), 49
Source: The Magazine of the Avant-Garde, 161
Sousa, John Philip, 56
Southern Christian Leadership Conference (SCLC), 57, 91, 95; in Chicago, 92, 93
South Side (Chicago): black arts organizations, 93–95; black churches in, 35–36; as Bronzeville, 29; clubs in, 37–38, 155; community of artists in, 62; cultural richness of, 32–36; decline of grassroots organizations, 140–41; doo-wop in, 45–46; effect on Braxton, 25; expansion of, in 1950s, 30; hidden violence in, 29; overcrowding in, 29; racial conflict in, 31, 48–49; street gangs, 49; tenacity of vernacular in, 34–35. *See also* Chicago
Southside Bulletin, 93
South Side Community Center, 93
Spaniels, 45
Spirituality: and the AACM, 100–108; and Braxton's aesthetics, 3; and Circle, 168–71; and experimentalism, 158–59; and free jazz, 69–72, 163–79
Springsteen, Bruce, 242, 249
Sproles, Victor, 78
Stage Door, 37
State Department: and jazz as propaganda, 15–16, 64n.94

Stearns, Marshall, 43n
Stern, Chip, 257
Stitt, Sonny, 56
Stockhausen, Karlheinz, 110, 145; Braxton's musical references to, 26, 122, 236; influence on Braxton, 114, 115n, 137, 230n, 275; named in Braxton's press coverage, 3, 154n; named in Miles Davis's coverage, 238
Stone, Sly, 249
Stravinsky, Igor, 110–11, 260
Street gangs (Chicago), 49
Struggle, 92
Stuckey, Sterling, 26n, 43n, 69n, 102
Student Non-violent Coordinating Committee (SNCC), 57, 91
Studio We, 156
Sullivan, Ira, 79n
Sun Ra, 82–83, 156
Sun Ra Solar Arkestra, 79, 82–84, 156
Suzuki, Daisetz, 114, 230n
Szwed, John F., 20n, 36n, 69n, 98, 102

Tanaka, Hozumi, 183
Taylor, Billy, 53
Taylor, Cecil, 52, 68n, 153, 250; antagonism toward harmony, 108; Braxton's initial interest in, 54; distinguished from Braxton, 181; impact of modernism on, 109–10; in New York, 156; in Paris, 143n; physicality in music, 70n.114
Taylor, Penelope, 105
Teitelbaum, Richard, 161–62, 251
Tepperman, Barry, 244, 257
Territory bands, 84
Texas Chamber Orchestra, 274
Théâtre de la Cité Internationale, 182, 222
Thirdstream, 17, 20, 74, 109, 131
Thompson, Robert Farris, 108n, 209n
Thomson, Virgil, 11n
Threadgill, Henry, 55, 78, 112, 216, 270
Till, Emmett, 32
Time Magazine, 53, 269
Tomlinson, Gary, 238
Torch, 93
Torgovnick, Marianna, 261
Tormé, Mel, 152
Toscanini, Arturo, 10
Touré, Askia Muhammad (Rolland Snellings), 100
Town Hall, 182–83, 211, 244
Townley, Ray, 245–47
Trianon Ballroom, 38
Tri-Axium Writings, The, 26–27, 61n, 183, 229–37, 274. *See also* Braxton, Anthony (aesthetics)
Tristano, Lennie, 52, 149, 257
Trumbull Park (Illinois), 31, 50
Tucker, Bruce, 10n, 44
Tudor, David, 146
Tusques, François, 143, 145
Tynan, John, 21n
Tyner, McCoy, 156

Ullman, Michael, 250, 254
Uncle Willie (Braxton family), 39
United (record co.), 46
University of Chicago, 38, 88n, 90n.45, 116. *See also* Reynolds Club; South Side
U.S. Commission on Civil Rights, 48

Vallekilde Jazz Clinic, 183
Van Allen, William, 78, 86n
Vance, Joel, 239
Varèse, Edgard, 110–11; influence on Braxton, 114, 117, 128, 228, 230
Vaughan, Sarah, 63, 118, 200
Vee-Jay (record co.), 46, 79n
Velvet Underground, 154
Venuti, Joe, 258
Vig, Tommy, 149
Village Gate, 156
Village Vanguard, 156
Vitet, Bernard, 145
Vitous, Miroslav, 164
von Braun, Wernher, 39

Wachtmeister, Hans, 116n
Wagner, Richard, 56, 274
Waldron, Mal, 79n
Wallaschek, Richard, 118n
Warhol, Andy, 154
Warwick, Dionne, 249
Washington, Tom, 83n
Washington Park (Chicago), 30, 37–38, 51
Waterman, Richard, 112n

Waters, Muddy, 151
Watts, Alan, 114
Webern, Anton von, 234; Braxton's musical references to, 26; influence on Braxton, 74, 114, 178, 230; named in Braxton's press coverage, 3, 266
Weisbrot, Robert, 141
Welding, Pete, 151
Wells, Ida B., Houses, 30
Wesleyan University, 274n
West, Cornel, 35n, 42, 42n, 200n
Weston, Randy, 263
Westside Torch, 88
Wheeler, Kenny, 173–74, 176, 248
White, Hayden, 8n
White, Maurice, 83n
White City Roller Rink (Chicago), 31
White Elephant, 116
Whiteman, Paul, 242
Wigmore Hall, 183, 208
Williams, Martin: interviewing Coleman, 70; on mainstream construct, 14n.30; on neoclassicism in jazz, 270n; as new critic, 13n.27; on rhythm as aesthetic center, 108; on thirdstream, 17n; 19
Wilmer, Valerie, 87n, 90n
Wilson, John S., 13n, 26, 244, 259
Wilson, Olly, 43n, 107n, 108n
Wilson, Teddy, 149
Wilson Junior College (Chicago), 54–55, 78, 163
Wolfe, Tom, 16n, 39
Wolff, Christian, 159
Wolpe, Stefan, 52n
Wonder Inn, 79n.7, 82
Woodard, Rafiki, 62, 113
Woods, Phil, 142n, 143n, 181
World Saxophone Quartet, 275
Wright, Richard, 62

X Clan, 273
Xenakis, Iannis, 114

Yates, Peter, 125
Young, Lester, 118, 247

Zappa, Frank, 154
Zipkin, Michael, 255
Zorn, John, 275